Public information should be made **public.**

Public *information refers to everything that explains our citizenship.* **Public** *means everything that we agree should be available to the body politic.*

Making information **public** *is somewhat less generic. This* **public** *means presenting, designing & structuring this information so that it is accessible, available, understandable & free.*

Public *means that the simple basic questions in the minds of the American people are easily, readily & clearly answerable. It is our right to question & get answers.*

This book is a celebration & a visual demonstration of questions & answers leading to understanding.

This book demonstrates the power inherent in understanding & the notion that understanding is power.

In 1975 I began preparing for a gathering of five thousand architects in Philadelphia the following year to coincide with the 200th anniversary of the founding of the United States in that same city.

As national chairman of the AIA convocation, I entitled it the **Architecture of Information** & began to call myself an **Information Architect**.

This field is a three-way marriage among the information technology corporations, the talent of great American graphic designers & the abilities of researchers & librarians to focus on making the complex clear.

Now in the year 2000, the focus of this book is on the power of understanding. I hope readers will develop their own intricate road maps of follow-up questions to address our leaders, would-be leaders, each other, parents, friends & children.

The word **public** shares the same root as publication. So it is fitting to publish this book for the public. The idea has been part of my recurring vocabulary every four years over the past twelve years. Circumstances happily conspired to put off its birth until now—the millennium year.

Why is this moment a good one besides the symbolic three zeros?

For the first time, this is a moment in history when messages, content & dynamic images can be sent to hundreds of millions of people with seemingly less effort than scribing a page in a 13th Century

book of hours. Information technology has gained muscles & maturity. It has gone from **look at me, look at me** & the show off of **boys with their toys** to **why are we doing all this?**

The next great American business is the learning business. This business is the child of entertainment & information technology using information architecture as its guidebook.

UNDERSTANDING is a concept that addresses a special moment in history. The advent of the millennium has resulted in considerable & excellent media analysis focused on historical milestones & prognostications.

This book however looks at **now**—the beginning of what is a new year, a new president, a new decade, a new century, a new millennium & a new field of human endeavor. So by definition it is already out of date. However, it clearly presents the big picture that makes the complex clear & reveals a number of issues about the ownership of information. Certain segments of valuable up-to-date statistics were proprietary & therefore not available to us. It also reveals the crying need for standardization of selected modes of display. This would enable us to understand information comparatively.

We are at an amazing moment of a Gutenberg-level event, with electronic wings able to fly through understandable information of our own choosing. With Velcro claws we collect all the data that warm & answer our inherent curiosity & questions.

I dream of asking a question, a simple childlike question & receiving an answer. What a dream!

The dream is here.

*We are at the cusp of the marriage of information technology & information architecture. Our extraordinary ability to store & transmit data will make this dream **a waking dream.***

*Louis Kahn said **beginnings, beginnings, beginnings, beginnings—I love beginnings.***

This is such a beginning—the primitive formation of a new era.

This is the Romanesque before the Gothic.

This is the temples at Paestum before the Parthenon.

This is Cimabué & Giotto before Piero della Francesca.

*As the child of the 20th Century's information technology industry, the **Information Architect** shall become a mature, even robust, player in the 21st Century.*

Conversation is the most natural, effective, yet most complex mode of human connection. The goal of conversation is understanding between the participants.

Successful visual communication design can be defined as frozen conversation much as wonderful architecture is referred to as frozen music.

***Understanding** information is power.*

A frog found himself on a lily pad surrounded by alligators. If only I could hop far enough to clear the alligators and land on the next lily pad, *he cried.*

Why don't you just take off and fly? *said a voice. The frog looked up and saw a wise old owl sitting on a branch overhead. Just fly to the next lily pad, advised the owl.*

The frog got a running start, flapped his legs and came down right in the middle of the alligators. Stupid owl, he shouted, trying frantically to escape the hungry alligators, frogs can't fly!

That's an implementation issue, *said the owl.* I just deal in concepts.

As we go through life simply trying to clear the alligators and land on the next lily pad, we are forced to confront our share of issues every day. We don't have the owl's luxury of dealing only in concepts. Concepts are abstract. Issues are concrete. They have consequences, as the frog quickly discovered. While both concepts and issues require thought and imagination, issues also demand involvement, action, and resolution. Concepts are born of ideas. Issues are born of exigencies. Concepts live in an environment of wonderment and what ifs while issues exist in an atmosphere of urgency. Concepts are pondered; issues are decided. Concepts are like Sunday drives in the country. Issues are like rush hour traffic in a big city.

Issues can be personal or public. They can involve making decisions that affect only one person or multitudes. And, while some can be decided quickly, others take years to resolve. But regardless of their scope, issues inherently involve elements of conflict, choice, and consequence. Let me offer two extreme examples.

Deciding on an anniversary gift for my wife is an issue for me (though forgetting it would be an even bigger one) because

I've thought of several possibilities. This is a very personal issue. Its resolution will affect only my wife and me, and I can decide quickly without a great deal of consternation or consultation with other people.

*Deciding on the best way to ensure the long-term solvency of **Social Security** is a much more complex and public issue. We will be able to pay only 75 percent of full benefits after 2032, so there is a driving need to figure out how to make up the other 25 percent. Conflict emerges because a number of alternatives are being proposed, ranging from modest adjustments, to alternative forms of investing **Social Security** surpluses, to scrapping the current system. Each alternative has consequences. **Congress** and the **President** will need to choose among the various options (or some combination of them), and that choice will have consequences, both for the people who need and benefit from **Social Security** and for the elected representatives who have to make the decision.*

While these two examples are at opposite ends of the issue spectrum, they both get resolved through a process of persuasion and perception.

With so much information available to people today, the challenge of how to build and understand persuasive arguments that help people understand issues and become involved in resolving them, will determine whether we land on the next lily pad or in the stomach of the alligators.

Horace Deets *has been **Executive Director** of the **American Association of Retired Persons** (AARP) since 1988.*

HORACE DEETS

An ant makes its way across the lawn. It has no idea what lies beyond the blades of grass in front of it.

We are like ants when we look at numbers. We might understand what we can see, but the rest of our garden is a mysterious jungle. Yet America defines itself with numbers: from the #1 superpower, past the million men marching and the billions of burgers sold, to the trillions of our national debt. The mysterious jungle starts somewhere between a million and a billion. Million, billion, trillion; such little changes in the words hide huge differences in the quantities. If we define ourselves with numbers, shouldn't we try to understand them a little better?

How much bigger than a billion is a trillion? One thousand times. Three zeros bigger. It's a number so big, it needs to be seen in a human context before we can really grasp its size.

So, we might say: It's the year 1, the beginning of the first millennium, and you have a trillion dollars to spend, at the rate of a million dollars a day. At just before three years, you've reached a billion. You keep spending, and now you are in the year 2000. You still have 737 years to go, spending a million every day, before you reach the end of your trillion dollar pile.

We can see that in our minds because we know the length of a day, we can imagine spending a million dollars and we know all about millenniums at the moment. The elements of this word picture are ones we recognize.

The charts in **UNDERSTA**NDING *are pictures of numbers. Pictures help us to see numbers and to begin to understand what they mean. In these pages information architects have made pictures of time, money, distance, storage capacity, bandwidth by examining the numbers, and making them visible.*

Not only are some of these numbers big, but sometimes one set of statistics about a certain subject will disagree with a second set about the same subject. Round numbers are always false wrote Samuel Johnson. Today, round numbers are often more believable, even though we may have the computing power to state any number right down to the last insignificant digit. Right now (exactly 12:24 PM EDT on 28 July 1999) the U.S. Census home page tells me that the population of the U.S. is 273,103,725. The precision of those last three numbers is astonishing! How do they know that? They guess—they call it making a projection—based on a formula of how many people are being born and how many are dying in a given time period.

A mouse click away at the U.N. Population website, that too-precise guess of America's population by the Census Bureau has risen to 274,028,000. (At least they admit the guess by rounding off the last three numbers.) The U.N. number is a difference of enough people to populate a city the size of Detroit, currently the 10th largest in the country.

To understand numbers we must ask questions: What's the source? Is it impartial? What would Planned Parenthood's population number be?

Some scientists say that ants do not sleep. If they don't sleep, they don't dream. And if they don't dream, they have no imagination.

Understanding numbers is part imagination, part skepticism, part wonder. Read on, you'll understand.

Nigel Holmes *has designed maps, charts and diagrams for most major American publications including* **Time** *where he was* **Graphics Director***.*

NIGEL HOLMES

Public opinion polls play an increasingly influential role in American society.

This year Presidential candidates will spend millions on polling and virtually every congressional and gubernatorial candidate in a competitive race will hire a pollster. The news media conducts its own polls, as do foundations, university research centers, special interest groups and just about any organization with a stake in public opinion and the wherewithal to fund surveys.

Opinion surveys have proliferated because they are effective tools for their various constituencies. To successfully run an expensive media race, a candidate for high office must use polling to help guide the huge sums spent on these campaigns. Surveys are used to identify voter concerns, assess candidate images and test the effectiveness of advertising decisions. For editorial purposes news media surveys provide a systematic and independent overview of public opinion which is far more reliable than pundit judgements of **what Americans think** or **man on the street** interviews. The credibility of these polls is based upon a generally good record of predicting elections. (The published national polls had an average error of 1.9 percentage points for their final estimate of the Presidential vote in 1996.)

Special interest groups use polls to draw attention to issues or as lobbying tools and academics take readings of public opinion for scholarly purposes. In all of these realms, polling renders relatively crude and often unidimensional portrayals of public opinion, but these are far superior to the alternative of depending on pundits or other subjective descriptions of public opinion.

More often than not polling provides a corrective to the characterizations of public opinion by the media and political elites which was certainly true during the **Lewinsky** scandal and **President Clinton's** impeachment. National surveys that found consistent support for the President and little indications of expected big **Democratic** losses in the midterm election frustrated, and ultimately upended the assertions of the pundits and the chattering class.

Nonetheless, the criticism that surveys convert leaders into followers is a continuing one.

Bill Clinton in particular has been charged as offering poll-driven policies. Perhaps the best defense of the **President** and of the role of polling came from historian **Gary Wills** who pointed out in a **New York Times Magazine** article that complaints about lack of leadership are common in every period of history, and that accusing leaders of being followers because they watch polls is an oversimplification.

He describes leadership as a balancing act, with polls **showing good leaders how to juggle conflicting demands, and how to walk through the mine fields... It seems obscurantist to say so. The great leader uses every kind of knowledge that can be had.**

As a pollster, the public's will often appears inchoate and inconsistent on specific questions about national policy that the people prefer to delegate to elected leaders. But on the big questions about the leadership and direction of the country, the public is usually quite clear and polls, when conducted in a non-partisan objective manner, are generally right.

Preeminent pollster **Andrew Kohut** has been the **Director** of the **Pew Research Center** since 1993.

ANDREW KOHUT

Remarkable people create remarkable work.

The pages of this book are filled with the gifts of talented individuals who share a common passion. Their passion is to make the complex clear, to design understanding and to freeze visually the conversations that go between questions & answers.

This book could only be conceived with the knowledge that these remarkable contributors existed & that naturally attached to the theme of this project are the pheromones necessary to attract the deep financial support that was forthcoming from the best corporations and institutions in the USA.

America Online Inc.
www.aol.com

General Motors Corporation
www.gm.com

Hearst Communications Inc.
www.hearstcorp.com

Intel Corporation
www.intel.com

The Markle Foundation
www.markle.org

Mattel Inc.
www.mattel.com

Olympus America Inc.
www.olympusamerica.com

Ovations / United HealthCare
www.myovation.com

SmartPlanet
www.smartplanet.com

Steelcase Inc.
www.steelcase.com

USWeb / CKS
www.uswebcks.com

Xerox Corporation
www.xerox.com

The following are people and institutions who have contributed.

AARP *The Research Group*

Annie E. Casey Foundation

Aspen Institute *Charles Firestone*

Barnes & Noble *Steve Riggio whose early faith in this project was seminal to its realization*

DARPA *Shaun Jones*

The Foundation for World Change *Dr. Chris Stout*

GeoLytics

The Institute for the Future *Paul Saffo*

Intel *Ciaran Doyle & Lakshmi Pratury*

International Institute for Management Development *Christine Travers*

Kennedy School of Government

The Markle Foundation *Zoë Baird, Julia Moffett & John Glassie*

The Myers Report *Jack Myers*

Public Agenda *Deborah Wadsworth*

Public Policy Forecasting *Graham Molitor*

RR Donnelley & Sons Company *Robert Pyzdrowski, Ron Heyman, Gary Ryman & Marcus Williamson*

Web Strategies *Ron Pernick*

Worldwatch Institute *Mary Caron*

Xerox Office Printing Business *whose printer allowed this book to see the light of day in a quality and timely fashion*

Yonder *David Hill*

ACKNOWLEDGEMENTS

Thanks to my staff for their research efforts & technical coordination.

Gregory Peterson *gathered and edited the statistics that formed the beginning point of a number of the chapters in this volume.*

Loren Barnett Appel *receives my deep appreciation for her creativity and invaluable skills in production and design. Appel has a BFA in Graphic Design from Ohio University. Early work for magazines sparked an interest in the business of publishing and led her to the University of Baltimore's MBA program. Over the years, she has been involved with every phase of publishing through positions with various magazines and associations. Appel is currently the Director of TOP a company engaged in the research, writing, design and publishing of a library of books focused on finance, health and well-being. E-mail: lappel@edgenet.net.*

David Sume, *my right hand at TED, has lent his talents with arduous proofreading. E-mail: sumed@aol.com.*

Jonathan Kiefer *for much of the marginalia and proofreading.*

Michele Corbeil, Gary Jennings *and* **Kimberly Gough** *whose dedication keeps the wheels turning smoothly at TED.*

Thanks for access to the Herculean poll results of the Pew Research Center that were used in Tom Wood's chapter.

Andrew Kohut *is Director of the Pew Research Center for The People & The Press (formerly the Times Mirror Center for the People & the Press) in Washington, DC.*

Kohut *is a frequent press commentator on the meaning and interpretation of opinion poll results. In recent national elections he has served as a public opinion consultant and analyst for National Public Radio. He is a regular contributor to the NewsHour with Jim Lehrer and is the co-author of The People, The Press and Politics and Estranged Friends? The Transatlantic Consequences of Societal Change. Kohut received an A.B. degree from Seton Hall University in 1964 and studied graduate sociology at Rutgers, the State University, from 1964 to 1966.*

For their help researching most of the web sites that appear here & the extensive bibliographical information that will appear in our future web site www.understandingusa.com.

John Shuler *is an Associate Professor and Department Head/Documents Librarian at the University of Illinois of Chicago. Since receiving his MLS from the University of California, Los Angeles in 1983, Prof. Shuler has been a faculty member and documents librarian at universities in Oregon and New York. He has written, taught, and lectured on information policy issues, political analyses of the U.S. Government Printing Office, and its system of depository libraries.*

Cynthia Etkin *is currently with the Government Printing Office's Library Programs Service as a depository library inspector. She came to the GPO in September 1997 with nearly twenty years of government documents and law library experience. Cynthia has authored book chapters including Fulfilling the GPO Access Mandate: The Federal Bulletin Board Service and the GPO Locator in Government Information on the Internet (John Maxymuk, ed. 1995).*

Eliot Christian *has pursued issues of data and information management primarily from the perspective of environment and earth science at the interagency and international levels. He joined the United States Geological Survey in 1986, as a manager of data and information systems with a focus on strategic planning, standards, and new technologies.*

Bert Chapman *is Government Publications Coordinator/Assistant Professor of Library Science at Purdue University. He received his B.A. in history and political science from Taylor University, an M.A. in history from the University of Toledo, and an M.S.L.S. from the University of Kentucky. He has had articles published in Reference Services Review, Serials Review, Government Information Quarterly, and Journal of Government Information.*

Sarah Maximiek *is the Government Documents/ Reference Librarian at Elmira College in Elmira, NY. Her education includes a BA in History from SUNY College at Fredonia and an MLS from the University at Albany (NY).*

Ruth T. Kinnersley *is Coordinator, Access Services at Western Kentucky University Libraries. She has an M.A.Ed. from Olivet Nazarene University and an M.S.L.I.S. from the University of Illinois at Urbana Champaign. She has had articles published on the topics of management and Internet resources for teachers related to reading and children's literature.*

Jerry Stephens *is Branch Library Manager and Research Coordinator, U.S. Court of Appeals, Oklahoma City, Oklahoma. He has a B.A. (Political Science & History), University of Oklahoma, 1967; M.L.Sc. (Library Science & Political Science), University of Oklahoma, 1968; J.D., University of Kansas School of Law, 1976.*

Geoffrey Swindells *is Government Documents Coordinator at the University of Missouri Columbia. He received his A.B. in the History of Political and Social Thought from the University of California at Berkeley, and his M.S. in Library Service from Columbia University.*

Victoria Packard Texas *is Reference/ Government Documents/Map Librarian at A&M University-Kingsville's James C. Jernigan Library. Her particular research interests are in education and geographic information systems.*

Special thanks for her major collaboration on the first chapter.

Meredith Bagby *is the author of The Annual Report of the United States of America, a yearly financial, political, and social account of the state of the nation modeled after a corporation's annual report. She is also the author of Rational Exuberance, How Generation X is creating a New American Economy; was the "Generation X" reporter for CNN in New York; and has testified before Congress several times on issues affecting young adults. She was a financial analyst for Morgan Stanley, Dean Witter & Company and her education includes Harvard College and Columbia Law School.*

◉ *Throughout the book this symbol designates web sites and their descriptions provided by the team of federal librarians put together by* **John Shuler** *which will be hotlinked from our new web site www.understanding usa.com.*

Reed Agnew and *Don Moyer*, with *Grant Smith*, founded *Agnew Moyer Smith Inc.* in 1980 after working together at the *Westinghouse Corporate Design Center*. The firm, now with nearly 70 people, has six areas of design practice—*information architecture, branding and identity, interaction design, packaging, environmental graphics, and marketing support*. Clients include corporations, governments, agencies, and institutions both in the U.S. and abroad. *Steelcase, McDonald's, Westinghouse, Rockwell Automation,* and *Fisher Scientific* are a few notable clients.

Reed received a *B.S.* in engineering from *Lehigh University* along with honor awards in both writing and painting. Headed toward a career in architecture, he detoured to the *Westinghouse Design Center* where he was deeply influenced by consultants *Eliot Noyes, Paul Rand* and *Charles Eames,* and introduced to the broader possibilities that other design disciplines presented.

Don Moyer received a *B.F.A.* in Graphic Design from the *Philadelphia College of Art* (now the *University of the Arts*) and later an *M.F.A.* from *Yale University*. He worked as a designer in Philadelphia and Toronto before joining the *Westinghouse Corporate Design Center* in 1976.

Acknowledgments: Molly Bigelow, Margaret Bryant, Don Charlton, Erica De Angelis, Brenda George, Rick Henkel, Kurt Hess, Jonathan Hill, Melissa Kelley, Rita Lee, Todd Loizes, Faith Milazzo, Amy Oriss, John Reynolds, John Sotirakis, Zuleika Spencer, Sharon Wiskeman, Michael Yolch, Rand Ziegler.

E-mail: reed@amsite.com / don@amsite.com.

Michael Bierut studied graphic design at the University of Cincinnati's College of Design, Architecture, Art and Planning. Prior to joining the New York office of the international design consultancy Pentagram as a partner in 1990, he was vice president of graphic design at Vignelli Associates. His clients at Pentagram have included Mohawk Paper Mills, The Rock and Roll Hall of Fame and Museum, The Brooklyn Academy of Music, The Walt Disney Company, Princeton University, and the Minnesota Children's Museum.

He has won many design awards and his work is represented in the permanent collections of museums in New York, Washington D.C. and Montreal. He has served as president of the New York Chapter of the AIGA, and is currently the AIGA's national president. He is a vice president of the Architectural League of New York and a member of the AGI. He writes frequently about design and is a contributing editor to I.D. magazine; he is a coeditor of the Looking Closer anthologies of design criticism and designed and coedited the recent monograph Tibor Kalman: Perverse Optimist. He is also a visiting critic in Graphic Design at the Yale School of Art.

Acknowledgments: Brett Traylor, design and illustration; Sera Kil, research assistance.

E-mail: bierut@pentagram.com.
Web site: www.pentagram.com.

Hani Rashid and *Lise Anne Couture* are the principals of *Asymptote Architecture*, an award-winning New York-based design firm.

Hani Rashid received a *Master of Architecture* from the *Cranbrook Academy of Art* in 1985. Since 1989 he has been a professor at the *Columbia University Graduate School of Architecture*. He has been leading architectural research and experimentation with respect to digital technologies since the inception of the School's *Advanced Digital Design* program. A book dedicated to his research will be published in late 1999.

Lise Anne Couture received her *Master of Architecture* degree from *Yale University* in 1986. She currently teaches at the *Columbia University Graduate School of Architecture* as well as at *Parsons School of Design* where she has been a professor in the *Department of Architecture* since 1990.

Asymptote's work is at the forefront of the design of interactive three dimensional architectural environments intended for the space of the computer. Their commissions include the *Guggenheim Virtual Museum* and their design of a virtual environment for the *New York Stock Exchange*. *Asymptote* has also been commissioned for a new *Advanced Command Center* on the *NYSE* trading floor. This space will not only display their virtual project on a large scale for Operations' purposes but will also become a new backdrop for media reporting from the Exchange floor.

Acknowledgements: Phillippe Barman, John Cleater, Lelaine Lau, Florian Pfeifer, David Serero.

E-mail: info@asymptote.net.
Web site: www.asymptote.net.

Nancye Green and *Michael Donovan* are founding partners of *Donovan and Green*, now part of *USWeb / CKS*.

Ms. Green began her career with a degree in Political Science from *Newcomb College of Tulane University*, and then from *Parsons School of Design*. Her recent work includes the design of places where people come to be informed and entertained.

Ms. Green serves on the *Board of Hallmark Cards* and is Past President of both the *AIGA* and the *International Design Conference* in Aspen. She received an *Honorary Doctor of Fine Arts* from the *Corcoran School of Art* in 1998 and is currently an *Executive Partner* at *USWeb / CKS*.

Michael Donovan is a *Designer* and *Information Architect* with a passion for making the complex understandable. He holds degrees from *Iowa State University* and *Parsons School of Design*.

Mr. Donovan has taught *Environmental Design* at *Parsons School of Design* and *Exhibition Design* at *Pratt Institute*. He serves on several boards including those of *AIGA, Society of Environmental Graphic Designers, College of Design at Iowa State* and *Parson's School of Design*.

Acknowledgements: Susan Baggs, Dave Bellando, Mary Caputi, Alan Chun, Beatriz Cifuentes, Michael Collins, Mei Gee, Jason Goth, Denise Guerra, Michael Horowitz, Betsy Heistand, Auston Hughes, Lori Isbell, Jamie Kennard, Michael Large, Sarah LeSure, Diane La Verdi, Gail Leija, Marge Levin, Happy Li, Jim Maben, Thomas Maulick, Eric Mueller, Susan Myers, Frank Nichols, Tammy Pate, Ryan Paul, Ian Small, Brian Stanlake, Carol Sun, Cindy Yip.

E-mail: ngreen@uswebcks.com / mdonovan@uswebcks.com. Web site: www.uswebcks.com

***Robert M. Greenberg** is **Chairman** and **CEO** of **R/GA Digital Studios**, a design and production company well known for pioneering new media and the creative integration of film, video and computer-imaging techniques. **Bob** has forged a unique interdisciplinary approach to media, and along the way has won almost every industry award for creativity, including the **Academy Award**, **Clios** and **Cannes Lions**.*

*Bob has been presented with numerous awards and honors, including honorary **Doctor of Fine Arts** degrees from **The University of the Arts/Philadelphia College of Art** and **Otis College of Art and Design**, the prestigious **Fuji Medal**, conferred by unanimous vote of the **Society of Motion Picture & Television Engineers' Board of Governors**, the **New York City Mayor's Crystal Apple Award** and the **DaimlerChrysler Design Award**, which was accompanied by a show of **R/GA's** work at **San Francisco MoMA**.*

*He is an active member of many professional groups including the **AGI**; the **Academy of Motion Picture Arts & Sciences**; the **Technology Board** of the **National Academy of Television Arts & Sciences**; **Brooklyn Academy of Music Board of Trustees**; the **Board of Advisors** for **TED9**; the **Board of Governors** of the **Association of Independent Commercial Producers**; the **Board** of the **Ross Institute**; the **Advisory Board** for the **Newark Museum**; the **New York City Mayor's Subcommittee for Film, Theatre & Broadcasting**; the **Board of Trustees** of the **Studio School of Art** and the **Dean's Council Advisory Board** of **Tisch School of the Arts**.*

E-mail: bobg@rga.com. Web site: www.rga.com.

***Kit Hinrichs** studied at the **Art Center College of Design** in Los Angeles, California and began his career doing both illustration and design in several New York design offices. Later, he formed an independent design consultancy with **Anthony Russell**. In 1976, Kit and his wife Linda moved to San Francisco and formed a national partnership called **Jonson, Pedersen, Hinrichs & Shakery**. In 1986, the San Francisco office merged with **Pentagram**.*

*Kit's accumulated design experience incorporates a wide range of projects. At **Pentagram** he leads a graphic design team with expertise in corporate communications and promotion, packaging, editorial and exhibition design.*

*He has been an instructor at the **School of Visual Arts** in New York, the **California College of Arts and Crafts** in San Francisco and at the **Academy of Art** in San Francisco. He has been a guest lecturer at the **Stanford Design Conference**, **AIGA National Conferences**, and numerous other design associations and universities. Kit's work has been honored and published widely, and several of his pieces are part of the permanent collection of the **Museum of Modern Art**. He is co-author of three books, **Vegetables, Stars & Stripes**, and **Typewise**. Kit is an **AIGA Fellow** and past executive board member and a member of the **AGI**. Currently, he is a trustee of **Art Center College of Design**, a board member of the **San Jose Museum of Art**, and serves on the **Accessions Design and Architecture Committee** at the **San Francisco Museum of Modern Art**.*

*Acknowledgements: Thank you to **Susan Balthazor, Belle How, Amy Chan, Catherine Mesina, John Schleuning** and **Digital Pond** for their research and assistance in creating these images.*

E-mail: hinrichs@sf.pentagram.com.
Web site: www.sf.pentagram.com.

***Nigel Holmes** does explanation graphics. In 1966, he graduated from **The Royal College of Art** in London, and ran his own graphic design studio in England until 1978 when **Walter Bernard** hired him to work at **Time Magazine** in New York.*

*As **Graphics Director** of **Time**, his pictorial explanations of complex subjects gained him notoriety, many imitators and a few academic enemies.*

*After 16 years, **Time** gave him a sabbatical, and he never went back. Now he has his own company, which tries to explain things to and for a wide variety of clients, including **Apple, Encyclopaedia Britannica, GE, Kodak, The Natural Resources Defense Council, Sony** and **Visa**, and he continues to do explanatory diagrams for publications such as **Attaché, Discover, Esquire, Golf Digest, Modern Maturity, Navigator, Sports Illustrated, The New Yorker, The New York Times, Wired** and various divisions of **Time**.*

*He has written four books on aspects of information design, and a book you can put in your pocket that explains the Internet to busy people. It is based on lectures he gave to **Fortune 500** executives (really busy people), and is now in its 4th U.S. edition and has been translated into Danish.*

He has lectured in India, Japan, Brazil and all over Europe and the United States, at times attempting live performances of statistics, and at other singing about them (not very well) during the lecture.

E-mail: nigel@netaxis.com.

***Joel Katz** is **President** of **Joel Katz design associates**, an information design, wayfinding, and interpretation design firm whose work spans the corporate, institutional, and public sectors. The firm has a special expertise in diagrammatic cartography and the visualization of complex process and statistics.*

*Katz holds a **BA Scholar of the House with Exceptional Distinction** and **BFA** and **MFA** degrees in graphic design from **Yale**. He has taught at **Yale, Rhode Island School of Design**, and the **University of the Arts**, and is the co-author of two books. He was made an honorary life member of the **International Paediatric Nephrology Association** for his work on developing a graphic notation for visualizing infants' kidney function.*

*Projects include: illustrative diagrams of monoclonal antibody function using a Star Wars metaphor; **Walk!Philadelphia**, a pedestrian wayfinding system featuring heads-up diskmaps; and interpretive graphics for **Independence Mall**.*

*Katz writes and lectures widely; his diagrammatic and cartographic work has been featured in numerous publications, including **Information Architects** by **Richard Saul Wurman** and **The Best in Diagrammatic Graphics** by **Nigel Holmes**. Katz was the first president of **AIGA/Philadelphia**, and a director and vice president for chapters of **AIGA National**.*

*Collaborators: **David E. Schpok**, designer, is an **Associate** of **JKda**; **Monique Boujean Williams**, researcher, is a third-year **Ph.D.** candidate in **Demography** at the **University of Pennsylvania**; **Jennifer Long** and **Mary Torrieri** are designers at **JKda**.*

E-mail: jkatz@mapfarm.com.
Web site: www.joelkatzdesign.com.

INFORMATION ARCHITECTS

Krzysztof Lenk holds an MFA degree from the Academy of Fine Arts in Cracow (Poland) and was an IBM fellow at the IDCA Conference in 1983. Since 1982 he has been a professor at Rhode Island School of Design.

Paul Kahn has an English Literature degree from Kenyon College. He began working with text processing systems at Harvard University in 1977 as an analyst and production editor. He was an application specialist for communication software for Atex, Inc. In 1985 he moved into hypertext research at Brown University's Institute for Research in Information and Scholarship (IRIS) serving as Director from 1990-94. He teaches at Rhode Island School of Design.

Krzysztof Lenk is Director of Design and Paul Kahn is President of Dynamic Diagrams, an information design firm specializing in the mapping of knowledge and the presentation of information on the computer screen. Since its founding in 1991, d/D has worked with major companies in the fields of hardware (IBM, Silicon Graphics Inc., Sun Microsystems) and software (Microsoft, Netscape Communications), publishing (Encyclopaedia Britannica, Nature, McGraw-Hill, Verlagsgruppe Georg von Holtzbrinck), and financial services (Merrill Lynch), creating visualizations of information collections, and web site architecture and design. Dynamic Diagrams became part of Cadmus Communications in 1999.

Acknowledgement: Ryutaro Sakai. Born and educated as a designer in Japan, Ryutaro is now a Graduate Program student at Rhode Island School of Design.

E-mail: lenk@dynamicdiagrams.com / kahn@dynamicdiagrams.com. Web site: www.dynamicdiagrams.com.

Clement Mok joined Sapient in August 1998 with the acquisition of Studio Archetype. Since 1988 Clement has been helping establish clients' digital presence using interactive media and, more recently, the Internet. As Chief Creative Officer at Sapient, Clement plays a crucial role in helping to make Sapient synonymous with interactive design. Both an advocate and thought leader for the design industry, he has received hundreds of awards from numerous professional organizations and publications. Clement is uniquely qualified to oversee the multi-disciplined creative community at Sapient.

Clement began his design career in New York, where he developed print, broadcast graphics and exhibition projects for clients such as Rockefeller Center, Republic National Bank, and CBS. Prior to forming his own agency, Studio Archetype, he spent five years as a creative director at Apple Computer.

Mok is also founder of two other successful software companies. CMCD's Visual Symbol Library was the industry's first CD-ROM title company that provided royalty-free silhouetted images for digital manipulation. NetObjects, one of Fortune's 1996 Top 25 Coolest Technology Companies, develops Web site authoring software. Clement also holds patents to the company's award-winning software NetObjects Fusion.

Clement is the author of Designing Business: Multiple Media, Multiple Disciplines from Adobe Press and sits on the Board of Trustees at The Art Center College of Design and the Board of Directors of AIGA. He is on the advisory boards of numerous technology companies and colleges.

E-mail: cmok@sapient.com. Web site: www.sapient.com.

Ramana Rao, a founder of Inxight Software, Inc., leads its charge to build next-generation interface and information software products for the ever growing community of Internet users.

Throughout his career, Ramana has pursued the goal of building interactive systems that enable people to perform much better on various knowledge tasks. Ramana is the designer and co-inventor of Hyperbolic Tree and Table Lens, two innovative techniques for effectively interacting with large amounts of information.

In a ten year stint at Xerox's Palo Alto Research Center [PARC], Ramana was a key member of the team that pioneered the field of information visualization. His work includes 25 patent filings and numerous research papers.

Ramana has been a noted speaker at many conferences and is frequently quoted by the media on topics ranging from interactive design to corporate innovation.

Ramana received BS and MS degrees from Massachusetts Institute of Technology in computer science and engineering. He resides in California with his wife and two quickly growing daughters.

Acknowledgements: Ramana's "architecture" would have been left to stock molding and white paint, except for collaborations with several talented people. Jean Orlebeke generously contributed her talent on all aspects of the chapter's design and execution. Karen Theisen designed most data graphics and many spread elements. Erik Adigard and M.A.D. provided design advise throughout. Steve Kearsley contributed illustrations and Gabriella Rossi provided production assistance.

*E-mail: rao@inxight.com.
Web site: www.inxight.com.*

Tom Wood develops comprehensive, long-term communications programs for a select group of clients, specializing in information design for print and interactive media, corporate identity and literature systems.

Tom's primary concern is making information clear, effective and intriguing. He believes that skillful design is essential to business, and information design should be intuitive, poetic and experimental as well as an organizational and intellectual framework for understanding.

His designs for architecture, technology, publishing, medicine, energy and arts organizations encompass many disciplines including print, web sites, signage, and exhibition design. For ten years, he has directed the communications program for Louis Dreyfus, an international group of diversified businesses that is one of the largest privately held companies in the world. Tom began his career working with such diverse talents as Richard Saul Wurman, Massimo Vignelli and Tibor Kalman.

He has worked for SOM Architects and with Nicholson NY, where he developed one of the first interactive CD-ROM yellow page products.

His projects have appeared in numerous publications and exhibitions, including the American Center for Design, AIGA, Communication Arts, Graphic Design NY and Graphis. He served as treasurer for AIGA/NY and co-chaired Hands-On Business, an educational program on practical issues of design management. He graduated from the University of Cincinnati's School of Design, Architecture and Art.

Acknowledgements: Clint Bottoni and Mary Anne Costello for your hard work and dedication.

E-mail: wood@interport.net.

Reven Wurman

With the publication of his first book in 1962 at the age of 26, **Richard Saul Wurman** began the singular passion of his life: that of making information understandable. In his best-selling book, **Information Anxiety**, in 1990, he developed an overview of the motivating principles found in his previous works. **Follow the Yellow Brick Road** is the second of this series. Each of his books focuses on some subject or idea that he personally had difficulty understanding. They all stem from his desire to know rather than from already knowing, from his ignorance rather than his knowledge, from his inability rather than his ability.

Along the way, **Richard Saul Wurman** has received both **M. Arch.** & **B. Arch.** degrees from the **University of Pennsylvania**. In 1959 he was graduated with the highest honors and awarded the **Arthur Spayd Brookes Gold Medal**. He established a deep personal & professional relationship with the architect **Louis I. Kahn**. He is a fellow of the **American Institute of Architects (FAIA)**, and a former member of **AGI** (**Alliance Graphique Internationale**).

He has been awarded several grants from the **National Endowment for the Arts**, a **Guggenheim Fellowship**, two **Graham Fellowships** & two **Chandler Fellowships**. In 1991, **Richard Saul Wurman** received the **Kevin Lynch Award** from **MIT** for his creation of the **ACCESS** travel guides & was honored by a retrospective exhibition of his work at the **AXIS Design Gallery** in Tokyo, Japan on the occasion of their 10th Anniversary. In 1996, the **Pacific Design Center** awarded him their **Stars of Design** lifetime achievement award. The same year, he received the **DaimlerChrysler Design Award**. In 1993/1997 he was appointed a **Visiting Scholar** at **MIT** in the **Department of Architecture & Planning**. In 1994, he was named a **Fellow of the World Economic Forum** in Davos, Switzerland & awarded a **Doctorate of Fine Arts** by the **University of the Arts** in Philadelphia, PA. In 1995, he received an **Honorary Doctor of Letters** from **Art Center College of Design** & was **Chairman of Graphic Design & Product/Industrial Design** of the 1995 **Presidential Design Awards**. He created an annual design competition for the **AIGA** in 1995, **The Design of Understanding** & chaired the first jury. In 1997 and 1999, he was named to **Upside Magazine's** Elite 100 Most Influential People in the Digital World and in 1999 he received an **Honorary Doctorate of Fine Arts** from the **Art Institute of Boston**.

His career has spanned from a 13-year architectural partnership in Philadelphia, a **Director of GEE!** – **Group for Environmental Education**, to teaching at **Cambridge University**, England; **CCNY**; **UCLA**; **USC**; **Washington University, St. Louis** & **Princeton University**. In 1958 he was a member of the initial year of exploration at Tikal, Guatemala. He is also the **CEO** of **TOP Publishing Group** and is on the **Editorial Board of Novartis Magazine**.

Richard Saul Wurman continues to be a regular consultant to major corporations in matters relating to the design & understanding of information. He is married to novelist **Gloria Nagy**, has four children (Tony, Vanessa, Reven and Josh) and lives in Newport, Rhode Island.

E-mail: wurman@ted.com. Web site: www.ted.com.

Conferences Chaired:
International Design Conference in Aspen
    The Invisible City '72
First Federal Design Assembly (Co-Chairman) '73
AIA National Convention, Architecture of Information '76
TED (10) '84-'00
TEDMED (2) '95 & '98
TEDSELL '96
TEDNYC '97
TEDCITY Toronto '00

A selection of RSW titles:
1960's
Cities: A Comparison of Form and Scale
The Notebook and Drawings of Louis I. Kahn
Urban Atlas: 20 American Cities
    (with Joseph Passonneau)
Various Dwellings Described in a Comparative Manner

1970's
Aspen Visible
Guidebook to Guidebooks
Making the City Observable
Man Made Philadelphia (with J.A. Gallery)
The Nature of Recreation (with Alan Levy & Joel Katz)
Our Man Made Environment Book 7 (with Alan Levy)
What-If, Could-Be: An Historic Fable of the Future
Yellow Pages Career Library (12 volumes)
Yellow Pages of Learning Resources

1980's
Baseball Access	**Olympic Access**
Dog Access	**Paris Access**
Football Access	**Polaroid Access**
Hawaii Access	**Rome Access**
Las Vegas Access	**SF Access**
London Access	**Summer Games Access**
LA Access	**Tokyo Access**
Medical Access	**Winter Games Access**
New Orleans Access	
NYC Access	
Hats	

Information Anxiety
Wall Street Journal **Guide to Understanding Money & Markets**
Wash DC Access
What Will Be Has Always Been, The Words of Louis I. Kahn

1990's
Barcelona Access
Boston Access
C, The Charleston Guide
California Wine Country Access
Chicago Access
Danny Goodman's Macintosh Handbook (Danny Goodman)
Florence/Venice/Milan Access
Follow the Yellow Brick Road (with Loring Leifer)
Fortune **Guide to Investing in the 90's**
Information Architects (with Peter Bradford)
N, The Newport Guide
On Time, Airline Guide to North America
Office Access
San Diego Access
Twin Peaks Access (with David Lynch)
USAtlas

Nigel Holmes with **Meredith Bagby**

Federal Income
Where does the government's money come from?

Federal Expenses
Where does the money go?

Federal Debt
How big is our debt?

Social Security
Will the baby boom bankrupt Social Security?

Medicare
Is Medicare in critical condition?

The Economy
Boom or bust?

State Budgets
How do the states spend their money?

Welfare
Who are the poor?

Education
How educated are we?

Crime
How much does crime cost?

Report Card
How do we measure up?

Individual income tax
$899.7 billion

The tax levied on your salary and any other income you have, such as profits made on investments or interest earned on savings. It's a "progressive" tax, which means that the higher your income the greater percentage of it you'll pay to the government. Tax rates range from 15% to 39.6%.

47.8%

Corporate income tax
$189.4 billion

A tax on corporate income. Rates range from 15% to 38%.

10.1%

Social insurance tax (FICA)
$636.5 billion

The Social Security and Medicare tax, which is withheld from your salary. The rate is 15%: half is paid by you and half by your employer. The self-employed pay the full 15% of their income themselves.

33.8%

Excise tax
$69.9 billion

A tax on goods such as tobacco and alcohol.

3.7%

Estate and gift tax
$27.0 billion

Estate tax is levied on property at the time of death. Gift tax is due on large gifts.

Customs duty
$18.4 billion

A tax on certain imports coming into the U.S.

Miscellaneous receipts
$42.1 billion

Money that may be received from holding accounts, or rent from government-owned property. In 2000, this also includes money from tobacco legislation.

Source: 1999 Budget of the United States Government (Office of Management and Budget—OMB)

The weight of the U.S. Budget for fiscal year 2000: 40 pounds

Are U.S. Government statistics accurate? According to the **Economist**, we are **pretty accurate.** The magazine has consistently ranked the U.S. sixth or lower in statistical quality, compared to other industrialized nations.

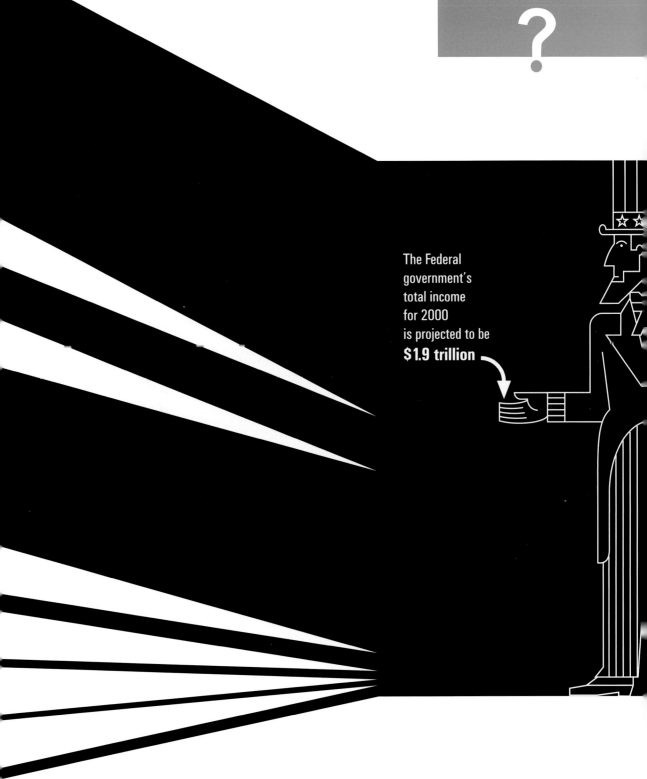

Federal
Income

*Where does the
government's money
come from?*

?

The Federal
government's
total income
for 2000
is projected to be
$1.9 trillion

I would like to electrocute everyone who uses the word **fair** in connection with income tax policies.   WILLIAM F. BUCKLEY

Nearly $4 trillion passes through electronic banking networks every day.

In 1997, the total number of people employed by the U.S. Federal government was 4,261,000.

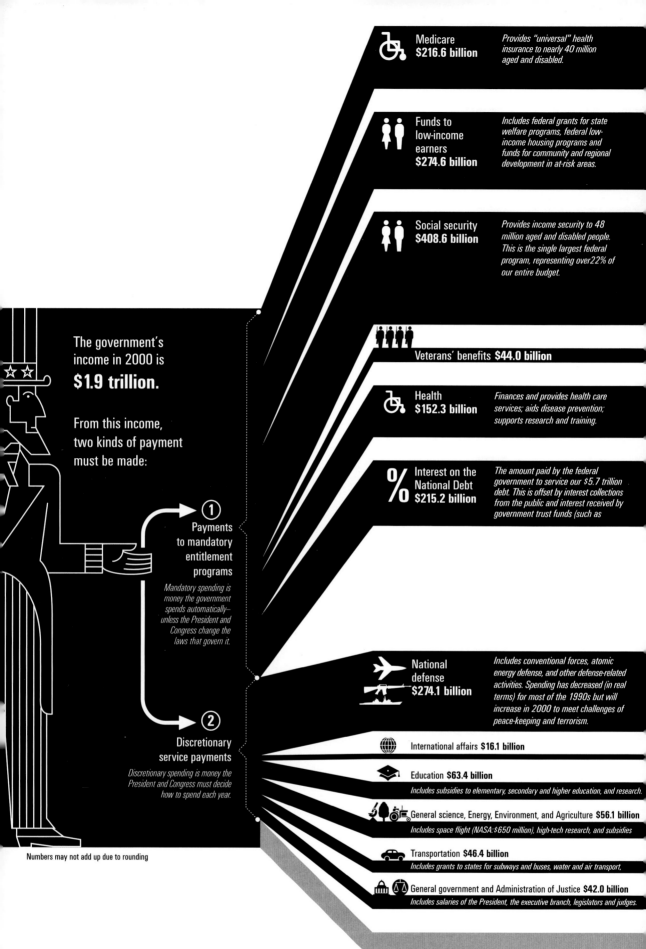

Medicare $216.6 billion

Provides "universal" health insurance to nearly 40 million aged and disabled.

Funds to low-income earners $274.6 billion

Includes federal grants for state welfare programs, federal low-income housing programs and funds for community and regional development in at-risk areas.

Social security $408.6 billion

Provides income security to 48 million aged and disabled people. This is the single largest federal program, representing over 22% of our entire budget.

Veterans' benefits $44.0 billion

Health $152.3 billion

Finances and provides health care services; aids disease prevention; supports research and training.

Interest on the National Debt $215.2 billion

The amount paid by the federal government to service our $5.7 trillion debt. This is offset by interest collections from the public and interest received by government trust funds (such as

The government's income in 2000 is **$1.9 trillion.**

From this income, two kinds of payment must be made:

① Payments to mandatory entitlement programs

Mandatory spending is money the government spends automatically–unless the President and Congress change the laws that govern it.

② Discretionary service payments

Discretionary spending is money the President and Congress must decide how to spend each year.

National defense $274.1 billion

Includes conventional forces, atomic energy defense, and other defense-related activities. Spending has decreased (in real terms) for most of the 1990s but will increase in 2000 to meet challenges of peace-keeping and terrorism.

International affairs $16.1 billion

Education $63.4 billion

Includes subsidies to elementary, secondary and higher education, and research.

General science, Energy, Environment, and Agriculture $56.1 billion

Includes space flight (NASA: $650 million), high-tech research, and subsidies

Transportation $46.4 billion

Includes grants to states for subways and buses, water and air transport,

General government and Administration of Justice $42.0 billion

Includes salaries of the President, the executive branch, legislators and judges.

Numbers may not add up due to rounding

Source: 1999 Budget of the United States
Government (OMB)

From time to time you'll hear the phrases **on-budget** and **off-budget**. The law requires that revenues and expenses of two federal programs, **Social Security** and the **Postal Service**, be excluded from budget totals—in other words they are categorized as off-budget.

In order to to satisfy this legal requirement, the budget displays on-budget, off-budget, and unified totals. The unified budget is the most useful indicator of how much the government must borrow. Usually the deficit is reported from the unified budget. The off-budget deficit looks larger than the on-budget deficit because **Social Security** is running a surplus.

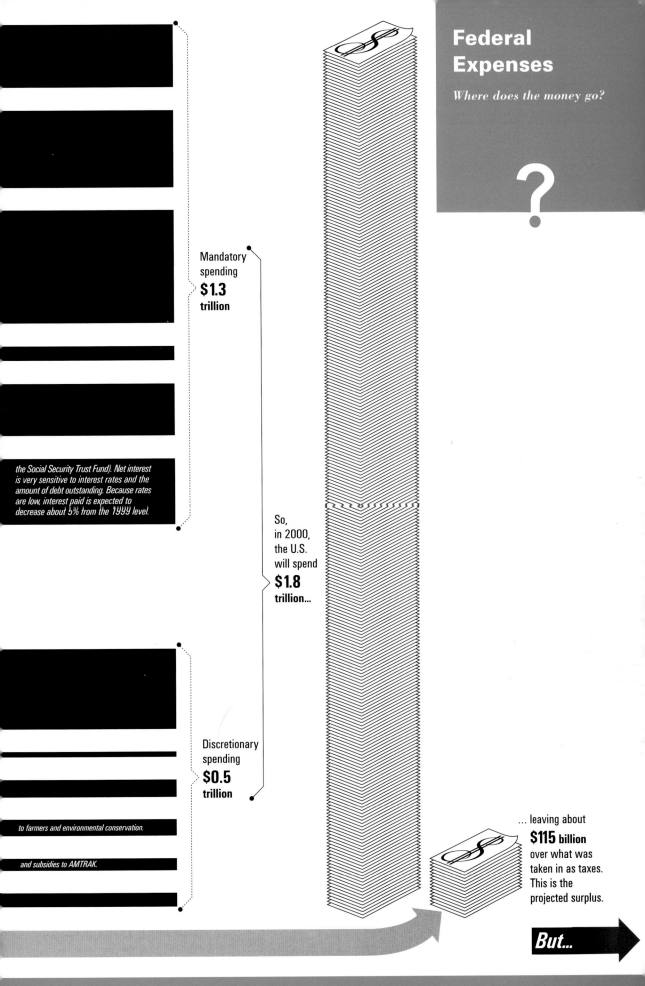

Federal Expenses

Where does the money go?

?

Mandatory spending
$1.3 trillion

the Social Security Trust Fund). Net interest is very sensitive to interest rates and the amount of debt outstanding. Because rates are low, interest paid is expected to decrease about 5% from the 1999 level.

So, in 2000, the U.S. will spend
$1.8 trillion...

Discretionary spending
$0.5 trillion

to farmers and environmental conservation.

and subsidies to AMTRAK.

... leaving about
$115 billion
over what was taken in as taxes. This is the projected surplus.

But...

The law sets the first Monday in February as the **President's** deadline for submitting his proposed budget to **Congress** for the next fiscal year.

The U.S. government's fiscal year begins on 1 October.

○ Center on Budget and Policy Priorities. www.cbpp.org
The Center is a nonpartisan research group that analyzes government policies and programs that primarily affect those in the low to moderate income range. Their site contains many timely reports.

Each unit on these pages represents $10 billion

The **National Debt** is the amount of money the United States has borrowed to finance its annual deficits.

The money is borrowed from two sources:

1 U.S. and foreign citizens and institutions, including foreign governments, that invest in Treasury bills and other securities. *This is called The Debt Held by the Public.*

2 The U.S. government's own accounts, such as trust funds for the Social Security and Medicare programs, civil service and military retirement plans, unemployment insurance and transportation funds.

Is the debt dangerous?
Economists argue about whether the debt is bad or good for our economy.

Those who say it's good argue that just like a corporation or a family, America uses debt to grow. Further, we owe most of the debt to ourselves—our own banks, funds and individual investors.

Those who say it's bad argue that there is a real cost of the debt. For instance, each year we pay over $200 billion just to finance the debt. In 2000, it's our fourth largest federal expense, costing roughly the same amount as the whole Medicare program. In addition, we owe a significant amount of money to foreigners, not to ourselves.

...let's compare the size of the **$115 billion** surplus...

Estimates of continued annual surpluses suggest it would be possible to pay off the National Debt by 2015. But no past deficit or surplus estimates have been accurate.

...to the **$5.7 trillion NATIONAL DEBT**

Sources: 1999 Budget of the United States Government (OMB); Economic Report of the President, February 1999 (Council of Economic Advisors)

What caused the debt in the first place? The U.S. first got into debt in 1790 when it assumed the **Revolutionary War** debts of the **Continental Congress**. At the end of 1790, the gross public debt was approximately $75 million.

Why don't we just print all the money we need to pay off the debt? The immediate effect of printing new money may be lower interest rates. As time goes on, however, the excess money introduced into the economy would lead to higher inflation, and invariably to higher interest rates.

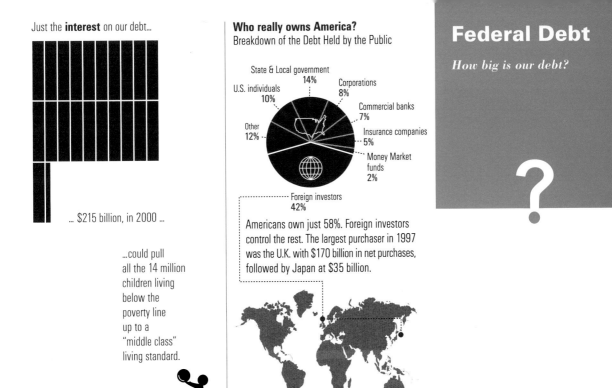

Just the **interest** on our debt...

... $215 billion, in 2000 ...

...could pull all the 14 million children living below the poverty line up to a "middle class" living standard.

Who really owns America?
Breakdown of the Debt Held by the Public

- State & Local government 14%
- U.S. individuals 10%
- Corporations 8%
- Commercial banks 7%
- Other 12%
- Insurance companies 5%
- Money Market funds 2%
- Foreign investors 42%

Americans own just 58%. Foreign investors control the rest. The largest purchaser in 1997 was the U.K. with $170 billion in net purchases, followed by Japan at $35 billion.

Federal Debt

How big is our debt?

?

If the debt was paid down at the rate of a dollar a second, it would take 130,000 years (the time that has passed since Neanderthals lived here.)

Or, look at it this way: each of these units is $10 billion.

So ▪▪▪ represents $1 billion. There are one thousand million dollars in this little red rectangle.

Want to help the country pay off the debt? There is a Treasury account called **Gifts for the Reduction of the Public Debt** for voluntary donations. Send your money to **Bureau of the Public Debt**, Department G., Washington D.C. 20239-0601. Donations are deductible from taxable income for the year of the donation, subject to any limitations on charitable contributions.

○ Congressional Budget Office. Congress. U.S.
www.cbo.gov
This office supplies Congress with nonpartisan economic analysis of programs and budgets necessary for decision-making. Find reports, budget projections, testimony, and more at their official site.

○ Financial Reports and the Financial Condition of the Federal Government. Financial Management Service. Dept. of the Treasury. U.S.
www.fms.treas.gov/conditn.html
Find daily and monthly treasury statements, the federal budget, the annual report of the government and various reports on the financial status of the United States government including receipts, expenditures, budget deficits, and the gold report.

The big problem with Social Security is the aging of our society.

The program operates as a pay-as-you-go system, where the earnings of **current workers** pay for the benefits of **current retirees**. By the time the 77 million baby boomers (those born between WWII and 1964) reach retirement, there will be just over two workers to pay for retired persons. The ratio was fifteen to one when the program started 60+ years ago.

When Social Security started

When the boomers retire

The Social Security Trust Fund

In 1983, Congress chose to hike SS payroll taxes long before extra cash was needed to pay for the boomers' benefits. Thus boomers were "prefunding" a portion of their own future retirement benefits. However, Congress soon found ways to borrow from these surplus funds to pay for deficits in other programs—including other senior programs such as Medicare.

How fast is America aging?

In 40 years, the elderly will outnumber college-age youth by nearly four to one.

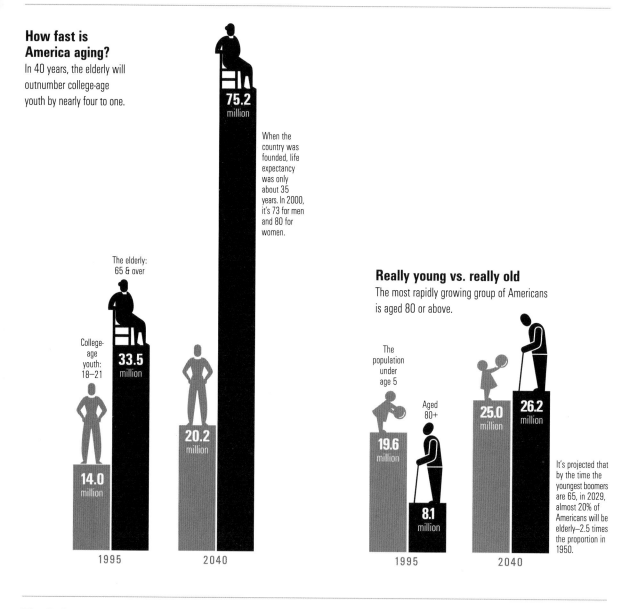

When the country was founded, life expectancy was only about 35 years. In 2000, it's 73 for men and 80 for women.

75.2 million

The elderly: 65 & over

33.5 million

College-age youth: 18–21

14.0 million

20.2 million

1995

2040

Really young vs. really old

The most rapidly growing group of Americans is aged 80 or above.

The population under age 5

19.6 million

Aged 80+

8.1 million

25.0 million

26.2 million

It's projected that by the time the youngest boomers are 65, in 2029, almost 20% of Americans will be elderly–2.5 times the proportion in 1950.

1995

2040

The "minority" share of America's population is rising.

Some suggest we may be inflaming ethnic tension as a more ethnic workforce is asked to pay for the retirement of an older, whiter population.

Hispanics and non-whites, as a % of the total population

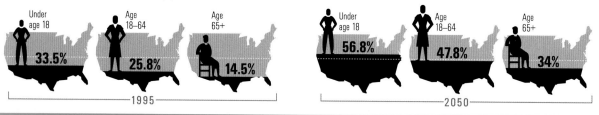

Under age 18 — **33.5%**
Age 18–64 — **25.8%**
Age 65+ — **14.5%**
— 1995 —

Under age 18 — **56.8%**
Age 18–64 — **47.8%**
Age 65+ — **34%**
— 2050 —

Sources: U.S. Bureau of the Census; Congressional Budget Office; OMB; Current Population survey; Social Security Administration; Peter G. Peterson, Gray Dawn (How the Coming Age Wave Will Transform America—and the World)

In an Americans Discuss Social Security survey, 72% said their opinions about changing social security are very strong or somewhat strong. 63% said their understanding of the Social Security debate is only fair or poor.

Race options on the Census Bureau's form for the 2000 census: White; Black African American or Negro; Asian Indian; Chinese; Filipino; Japanese; Korean; Vietnamese; other Asian; Native Hawaiian; Guamanian or Chamorro; Samoan; other Pacific Islander; some other race. You are allowed to check more than one option. A separate question deals with Spanish/Hispanic/Latino origins.

How much do we spend on the elderly?

The federal budget dispenses nearly ten times as much in benefits to each senior citizen as it does to each child.

Per capita annual federal spending on children and the elderly

Age 65 & over
$15,636

Health benefits
$5,514

Federal pensions
$1,157

Social Security
$8,136

Under age 18
$1,693

Other
$829

Public spending on pensions and health benefits rises as the nation goes gray ...

Spending as a % of GDP

1995: **10.5%** of GDP

2030: **17%** of GDP

... and the number of those aged 85+ could far exceed the official projection

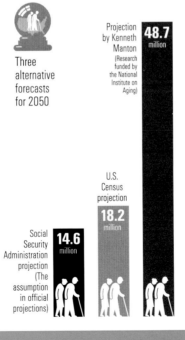

Three alternative forecasts for 2050

Social Security Administration projection (The assumption in official projections)
14.6 million

U.S. Census projection
18.2 million

Projection by Kenneth Manton (Research funded by the National Institute on Aging)
48.7 million

Social Security provides monthly benefits to 48 million retired and disabled workers, and to their eligible spouses, children and dependents.

Often called our most popular social program, Social Security is the major source of income (providing at least 50% of total income) for 66% of beneficiaries, and is the only source of income for 18%. Overall, more than two-fifths of the aged are kept out of poverty by Social Security.

The economic status of the elderly as a group has improved remarkably during the past three decades.

The poverty rate of the elderly has fallen to less than half of what it was in the 1970s. At the time, the elderly were twice as likely to live in poverty than others. Today the situation is exactly reversed: at 11%, the elderly poverty rate is just half of the 22% poverty rate for children under 18.

○ Social Security Online. Social Security Administration. U.S.
www.ssa.gov
The official web site of the Social Security Administration provides a plethora of information about social security, benefits, statistics, policy and research data, as well as the chance to conduct some business with the agency online.

○ Policy.com Issue of the Week, 6/1/98: Social Security.
www.policy.com/issuewk/98/0601/index.html
Policy.com's Issue of the Week examines the Social Security system and reform issues facing this program.

In addition to facing the same demographic problems of Social Security, Medicare must contend with the burden of rising health care costs. In 1956, the average family spent 3.8% of its income on health care. Today that family spends twice that—7.8% of their total income.

What Medicare costs

Without reform, annual Medicare expenditures will climb from $217 billion in 2000 to between $2.2 trillion and $3 trillion by the year 2030. As a result, Medicare could become the most expensive federal program. The Balanced Budget Act of 1997 insured the solvency of the Medicare Part A Trust Fund until 2015.

Medicare
costs
in 2000:
**$217
billion**

Sources: National Bipartisan Commission on the future of Medicare; U.S. Healthcare Financing Administration; U.S. Bureau of the Census

The government has mailed handbooks explaining healthcare to 39 million beneficiaries of **Medicare**. It has also set up a toll-free telephone number, 800-633-4227, and an Internet site, www.medicare.gov. The **Healthcare Financing Administration** calls their effort the biggest peacetime education program the Federal government has ever undertaken.

○ Health Care Financing Administration. Dept. of Health and Human Services. U.S. www.hcfa.gov
Find reports, data, laws and regulations about Medicare, Medicaid, and child health insurance programs from the web site of the federal agency that administers these programs.

Medicare
costs in 2030:

$2.2 to $3 trillion

$3 trillion

$2.75 trillion

$2.5 trillion

$2.25 trillion

$2 trillion

$1.75 trillion

$1.5 trillion

$1.25 trillion

$1 trillion

$750 billion

$500 billion

$250 billion

The two parts of Medicare

Since July of 1966, the federal Medicare program has provided two coordinated healthcare plans for the elderly.

Part A is a hospital insurance plan which covers hospital and related services. When politicians talk about Medicare going bankrupt they are referring to Part A of Medicare. It has been running deficits since 1996, and is expected to go bankrupt in 2015.

Part B is a voluntary, supplementary medical insurance program, partially financed by monthly premiums paid by participants. This covers the cost of physicians and related medical services.

As the Medicare system faces financial crisis, the cost borne by beneficiaries rises. Today, beneficiaries pay nearly 30% of their healthcare costs from their own pockets— averaging almost $3,000 per person—to pay for premiums, services, and products not covered by Medicare.

Medicare

Is Medicare in critical condition?

?

Healthcare costs in general have risen faster than inflation over the past two decades, and the consumers' share, shown here, has more than quadrupled.

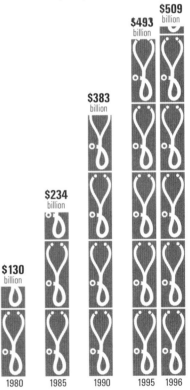

$130 billion — 1980
$234 billion — 1985
$383 billion — 1990
$493 billion — 1995
$509 billion — 1996

Reasons for the rise include:
- Increased lifespan
- Availability of complex, expensive procedures
- Lack of information for consumers
- Inefficient incentives for patients and doctors

Medicare: The Official Government Site for Medicare Information. Health Care Financing Administration. Dept. of Health and Human Services. U.S.
www.medicare.gov
Medicare, administered by HCFA, provides health insurance to Americans over 65 with certain disabilities and is the largest health insurance program in the United States. The HCFA web site contains reports, current and proposed health plans, contacts, and tips on how to avoid fraud.

✓ Is the economy strong?

The economic expansion that began as the Persian Gulf War ended has become the longest peacetime expansion in the 20th century. Clinton boasted: "America's economy is the healthiest in a generation and the strongest in the world." America seemed unshaken by the financial tremors felt throughout Asia, Latin America, and much of Europe throughout the late 1990s.

Low inflation

One of the most welcome aspects of the country's economic expansion has been low inflation. Despite tight labor markets for much of the late 1990s, the Consumer Price Index (CPI), the most widely used measure of inflation, has remained below 4%.

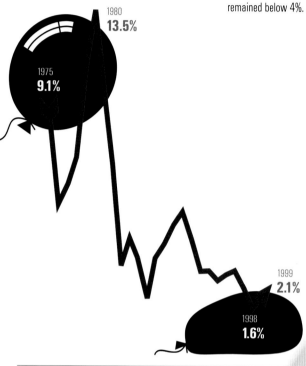

1980
13.5%

1975
9.1%

1999
2.1%

1998
1.6%

Low unemployment

The unemployment rate has sunk far below the level that most economists thought possible without giving rise to inflation.

1982
9.7%

1975
8.5%

The biggest problem for companies now is to find skilled labor to fill new jobs. As a result, many companies are looking abroad for labor. A special provision in our immigration policy allows for high-skilled workers such as computer programmers to get green cards ("resident alien" status).

1999
4.2%

A soaring stock market

Nowhere can one see the "good times roll" better than in the stock market of the 1990s. The value of the Dow Jones Industrial Average has more than quadrupled since 1990.

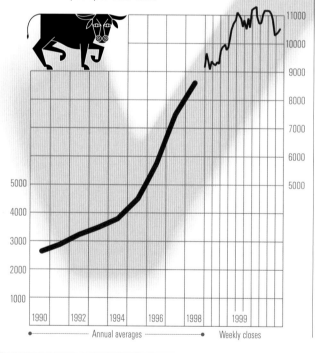

11000
10000
9000
8000
7000
6000
5000 — 5000
4000
3000
2000
1000

1990 | 1992 | 1994 | 1996 | 1998 | 1999

•———— Annual averages ————• Weekly closes

Income growth

The booming economy of the 1990s has meant real income gains for many Americans. Median household income has risen 13% over the last 25 years.

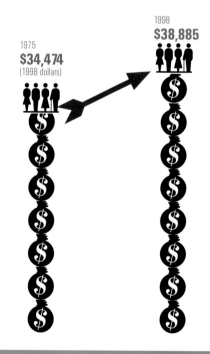

1998
$38,885

1975
$34,474
(1998 dollars)

Sources: The Council of Economic Advisors; Bureau of Labor Statistics; U.S. Bureau of the Census; U.S. Bureau of Economic Analysis

Foreign assets held in the U.S. currently total $5.5 trillion. U.S. assets held abroad total $4.3 trillion, leaving the U.S. in a negative investment position of $1.2 trillion.

While inflation in the U.S. seems to stay low, other countries' rates are sky high. Russia had 88% inflation in 1999, though it was expected to fall to 23% in 2000. Turkey's rate was 60% in 1999, with a forecast of 38% for 2000. At the other end of the scale, Japan, Argentina, China and Hong Kong had slight deflation in 1999. Except for Japan, consumer prices in those nations were expected to rise in 2000.

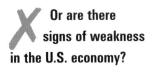 **Or are there signs of weakness in the U.S. economy?**

?

Income inequality

There is no doubt that the 1990s have seen significant income growth. But not everyone has seen their income grow at the same rate. Top-earning households claim a huge portion of U.S. household income. In 2000, the country is experiencing the widest gap between the rich and the poor since the Census Bureau began keeping track of those statistics in 1947.

... compared to the top one-fifth of families, which brings home **48.4%** of the total income of the country.

While the gap between the rich and the poor is glaring, inequalities are less severe between the sexes, and narrowing among racial groups. Women have made progress, with earnings reaching 75% of men's, up from 69% in 1986. Blacks earn 63% and Hispanics earn 68% of whites' earnings based on median household incomes.

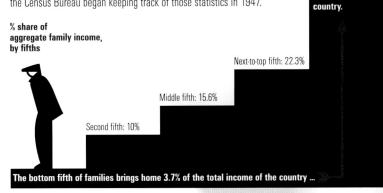

% share of aggregate family income, by fifths

Next-to-top fifth: 22.3%

Middle fifth: 15.6%

Second fifth: 10%

The bottom fifth of families brings home 3.7% of the total income of the country ...

Low savings rates

Economists have long been telling us that our savings rate, both public and private, is significantly lower than that of other industrialized countries. The overall American savings rate is just 4.8%, less than one fourth of Korea's rate, and well below the industrial average.

Savings as a % of GDP

Korea **23.7%**

Japan **15.1%**

Switzerland **13.2%**

Italy **8.2%**

Germany **7.7%**

France **7.3%**

U.S. **4.8%**

It's no surprise that Americans have huge amounts of personal debt. According to the Nilson Report, the average amount individuals spend using credit cards is $9,000 per year. The average amount of debt outstanding at any time is $4,300 per person.

Trade imbalance

Throughout the 1980s and 1990s, America had a negative trade balance with the rest of the world. That means that what we have bought from abroad has far exceeded what we have sold.

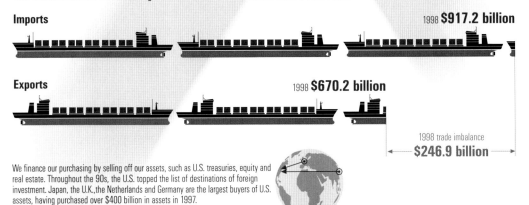

Imports

1998 **$917.2 billion**

Exports

1998 **$670.2 billion**

1998 trade imbalance
$246.9 billion

We finance our purchasing by selling off our assets, such as U.S. treasuries, equity and real estate. Throughout the 90s, the U.S. topped the list of destinations of foreign investment. Japan, the U.K., the Netherlands and Germany are the largest buyers of U.S. assets, having purchased over $400 billion in assets in 1997.

○ Economic Indicators. Council of Economic Advisors. Congress. U.S. www.access.gpo.gov/congress/cong002.html Browse individual issues from 1998 to the present or search the 1995 database for data on employment and wages, income and spending, federal finance, consumer and producer price indexes, business activity, and money and banking.

Total spending in billions

$97.0

Colors show the proportion of the total budget that goes to individual categories

States' budgets: what they spend

In 1997, states spent about $800 billion dollars—that's 40% as much as the Federal government spent. The majority of the money went to two main areas: Education (K–12, and higher education) 32%, and Medicaid, 20%. Welfare accounted for a relatively small portion of states' budgets, at 3.1%.

Where the money comes from

States collect taxes from a variety of sources: corporate tax, sales tax, and in most states, personal income tax. Altogether states take in over $500 billion in taxes each year. The rest of the money that states receive comes from federal grants.

Municipalities and counties take in another $500 billion—mostly in property and sales tax.

■ Elementary and secondary education

■ Higher education

Welfare

Medicaid

Corrections

Transportation

Other
depending on the state, this includes:
- state police
- juvenile institutions
- parks & recreation
- general aid to local governments
- spending for hospitals
- general health programs

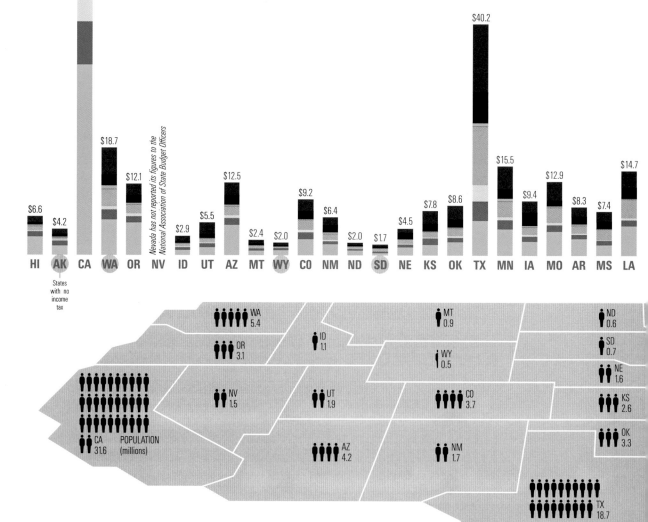

$6.6 HI

$4.2 AK
States with no income tax

$97.0 CA

$18.7 WA

$12.1 OR

Nevada has not reported its figures to the National Association of State Budget Officers NV

$2.9 ID

$5.5 UT

$12.5 AZ

$2.4 MT

$2.0 WY

$9.2 CO

$6.4 NM

$2.0 ND

$1.7 SD

$4.5 NE

$7.8 KS

$8.6 OK

$40.2 TX

$15.5 MN

$9.4 IA

$12.9 MO

$8.3 AR

$7.4 MS

$14.7 LA

WA 5.4 | MT 0.9 | ND 0.6
OR 3.1 | ID 1.1 | WY 0.5 | SD 0.7
NE 1.6
CA 31.6 POPULATION (millions) | NV 1.5 | UT 1.9 | CO 3.7 | KS 2.6
OK 3.3
AZ 4.2 | NM 1.7
TX 18.7

Sources: National Association of State Budget Officers; National Governors Association; U.S. Bureau of the Census

Top seven Governor's salaries (1998-99): New York $130,000; Illinois $126,590; Michigan $124,195; Washington $121,000; Maryland $120,000; California $114,286.

The top Mayors get more: best-paid is Richard M. Daley of Chicago ($170,000), second is Rudy Giuliani of New York ($165,000) (1997 figures).

Do states have debt?

Because many states have a balanced budget requirement written into their constitution, they have less debt collectively than the Federal government. Total state debt is approximately $500 billion. Local governments have another $700 billion in debt. That puts the grand total of total nonfederal public debt at $1.2 trillion, compared to $5.7 trillion of national debt.

The good news is that almost all states reported a surplus for fiscal year 1998. And about half of those states used the money to pay back their debt or to set up "rainy day" funds.

State Budgets

How do the states spend their money?

?

Bar chart values:
$17.8 WI, $28.1 IL, $14.2 IN, $11.8 KY, $14.4 TN, $12.1 AL, $29.2 MI, $33.0 OH, $5.3 WV, $18.1 VA, $20.7 NC, $11.3 SC, $20.6 GA, $39.1 FL, $67.0 NY, $32.7 PA, $15.2 MD, $4.0 DE, $24.1 NJ, $16.7 VT, $22.4 MA, $14.4 CT, $3.6 RI, $2.3 NH, $3.9 ME

Map figures:
MN 4.6, WI 5.1, IA 2.8, IL 11.8, MO 5.3, AR 2.5, MI 9.5, IN 5.8, OH 11.1, KY 3.9, TN 5.2, MS 2.7, AL 4.2, LA 4.3, WV 1.8, VA 6.6, NC 7.2, SC 3.7, GA 7.2, FL 14.2, NY 18.1, PA 12.1, DE 0.7, MD 5.0, NJ 7.9, VT 0.6, NH 1.1, ME 1.2, MA 6.1, CT 3.3, RI 1.0

There are a total of 87,453 local governments in the U.S. These include: County, Municipal, Township, School District, and Special District governments.

National Conference of State Legislatures, Budgets—State. www.ncsl.org/programs/fiscal/budissus.htm NCSL is a network to foster communication and cooperation among state legislatures by sharing information on state issues. The budget page from their web site provides the capital budgets and budget conditions for all the states, describes the budget process, and more.

Where did welfare go?

The Personal Responsibility and Work Opportunity Reconciliation Act of 1996 replaced the 60-year old federally-run welfare program. Under the new system, states have broad authority to implement their own welfare programs, following strict federal guidelines. They emphasize work as a condition for receiving benefits and limit the amount of time that recipients can stay on welfare.

Welfare case loads have decreased in nearly every state, dropping on aggregate 27% since 1996. In eight states, case loads have declined by more than 40% in the past year. This decline is due in large part to a strong economy and record low unemployment.

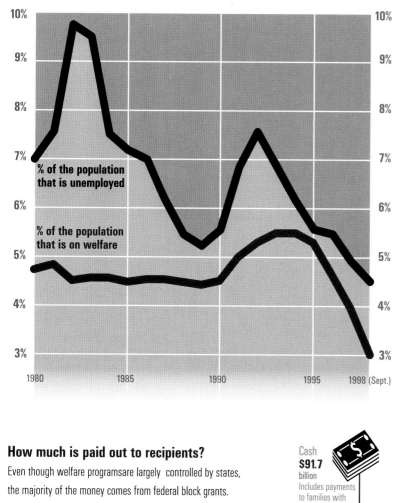

% of the population that is unemployed

% of the population that is on welfare

1980   1985   1990   1995   1998 (Sept.)

How much is spent on Medicaid?

Medicaid is medical care for the poor. Medicaid is mandated by the Federal government and administered by the states. It represents 20% of state budgets, and its cost has more than quadrupled since 1985. The reasons for this cost growth include: an increase in eligibility and a high rate of inflation for medical goods and services.

$26 billion
$41 billion
$73 billion
$156 billion
$202 billion

Projection

Includes state and federal spending. The projection assumes a federal share of 57%.

1980 1985 1990 1995 2000

How much is paid out to recipients?

Even though welfare programs are largely controlled by states, the majority of the money comes from federal block grants.

Total federal, state, and local welfare spending on items other than Medicaid (see opposite)
(1996)

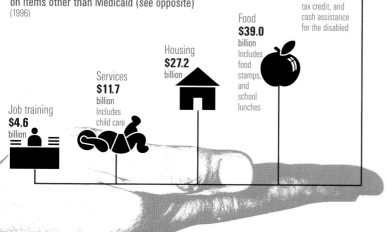

Cash
$91.7 billion
Includes payments to families with dependent children, the earned income tax credit, and cash assistance for the disabled

Food
$39.0 billion
Includes food stamps, and school lunches

Housing
$27.2 billion

Services
$11.7 billion
Includes child care

Job training
$4.6 billion

Sources: Library of Congress, Congressional Research Service; U.S. Bureau of the Census; Bureau of Labor Statistics

In 1980, the CEO of a large U.S. company could expect an income 40 times that of the workers in the factory. By 1990, that had risen to 85 times the amount.

In 1930, Babe Ruth made $80,000. When asked why he made more than President Hoover, Ruth said, I had a better year than he did.

Defining poverty

The Census Bureau divides us into three broad income groups: **the rich** (households with an income of more than $100,000), **the middle class** ($25,000 to $100,000), and **the poor** and **near poor** (less than $25,000).

What's the median income ?

half the households in the U.S. earn more ...

Median income: $38,885

... half the households in the U.S. earn less

Household income is used rather than family income, because it is more comprehensive. It includes singles living alone and nonfamily members living together.

The median *family* income was $46,737 in 1998.

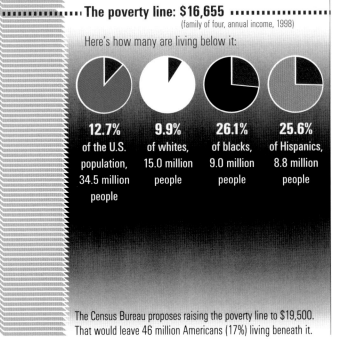

The poverty line: $16,655
(family of four, annual income, 1998)

Here's how many are living below it:

12.7%
of the U.S. population, 34.5 million people

9.9%
of whites, 15.0 million people

26.1%
of blacks, 9.0 million people

25.6%
of Hispanics, 8.8 million people

The Census Bureau proposes raising the poverty line to $19,500. That would leave 46 million Americans (17%) living beneath it.

But more than 30% of poor households get no help

Despite the variety of federal and state programs available, many low-income households do not actually receive any form of public assistance.

Why? The reasons include: lack of information, language barriers, and the stigma attached to welfare.

Of the 13 million poor households in the U.S., only 4.4 million receive any cash benefits

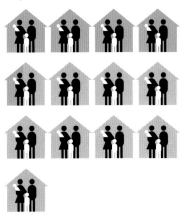

President Clinton gets $200,000, plus an expense allowance of $50,000 and a travel allowance of $100,000

1988's highest-paid executive was **Disney Chairman Michael Eisner**, who made $40.1 million—2,395 times as much as an average worker. 1998's highest-paid executive was **Disney Chairman Michael Eisner**, who made $575.6 million—25,052 times as much as an average worker.

○ Policy.com Issues Library: Welfare and Housing, Welfare to Work. www.policy.com/issues/issue304.html Policy.com is a nonpartisan policy news and information service that highlights research, opinions, and events relating to public policy issues. In the **Welfare to Work** Issues Library, summaries of and links to the works of various organizations, research institutes, government agencies, and think tanks are provided for this reform initiative.

Federal, state and local governments spend nearly $400 billion every year to run our primary and secondary education system.

This accounts for nearly 8% of the GDP, and equals $6,000 per public school student per year–the most any country spends on education, any way you measure it.

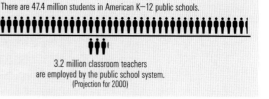

There are 47.4 million students in American K–12 public schools.

3.2 million classroom teachers are employed by the public school system.
(Projection for 2000)

But we don't get the best results.

Despite the fact that the U.S. spends more on education (on a gross and per capita basis) than any other country, the most recent report from the National Assessment of Educational Progress shows that we rank 28th (out of 41 countries) for student achievement in math, and 17th in science.

Scoring was on a scale of 200 to 800 points

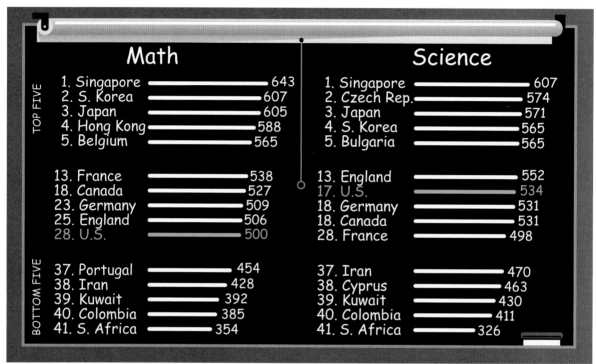

Math

TOP FIVE
1. Singapore — 643
2. S. Korea — 607
3. Japan — 605
4. Hong Kong — 588
5. Belgium — 565

13. France — 538
18. Canada — 527
23. Germany — 509
25. England — 506
28. U.S. — 500

BOTTOM FIVE
37. Portugal — 454
38. Iran — 428
39. Kuwait — 392
40. Colombia — 385
41. S. Africa — 354

Science

1. Singapore — 607
2. Czech Rep. — 574
3. Japan — 571
4. S. Korea — 565
5. Bulgaria — 565

13. England — 552
17. U.S. — 534
18. Germany — 531
18. Canada — 531
28. France — 498

37. Iran — 470
38. Cyprus — 463
39. Kuwait — 430
40. Colombia — 411
41. S. Africa — 326

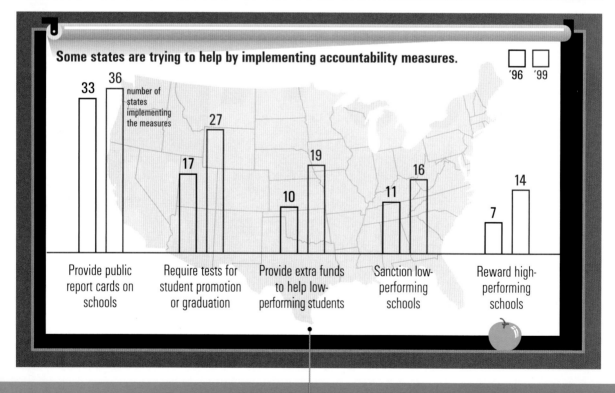

Some states are trying to help by implementing accountability measures.

'96 '99

| | 33 | 36 |
number of states implementing the measures

Provide public report cards on schools	Require tests for student promotion or graduation	Provide extra funds to help low-performing students	Sanction low-performing schools	Reward high-performing schools
33 / 36	17 / 27	10 / 19	11 / 16	7 / 14

Sources: U.S. Department of Education; The National Assessment of Educational Progress Tests

America spends $240 billion on colleges and universities. The College Board calculated the average cost of tuition and fees at private four-year colleges in the fall of 1999 to be $15,380, an increase of $$671 from the previous school year. The average public college cost is $3,356 ($109 more than the previous year.)

Accounting, tax, and consulting firm KPMG LLP conducted a 1999 on-line poll, asking college students what events they predicted would occur in their lifetime. According to the students, a visit from extraterrestrials is twice as likely as another Great Depression.

Education is the most important determinant of economic status.

Young adults with college degrees earn over 70% more than those without, and those with high school diplomas earn 30% more than those without. Between 1980 and 1997, the earnings of those with at least undergraduate degrees rose significantly faster than the earnings of those who had completed only high school.

The educational attainment of adults 25 and over

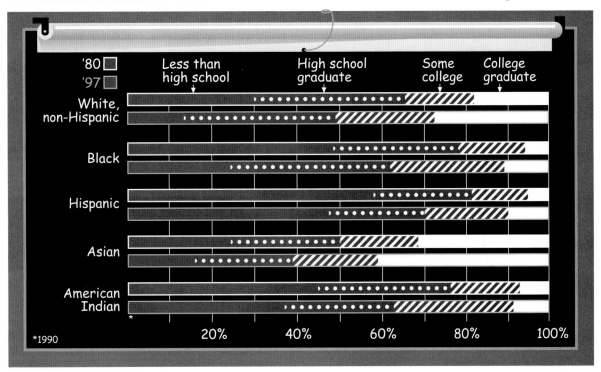

'80 ☐
'97 ☐

| | Less than high school | High school graduate | Some college | College graduate |

White, non-Hispanic
Black
Hispanic
Asian
American Indian

*1990

20%   40%   60%   80%   100%

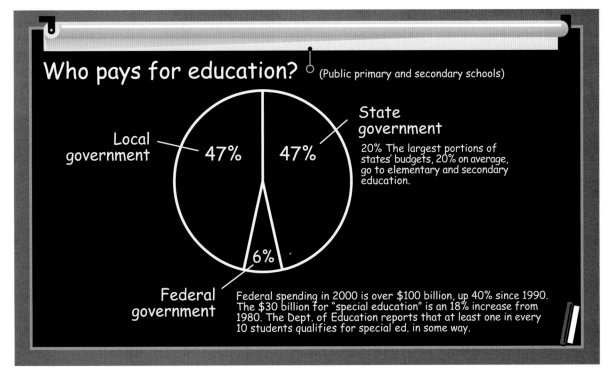

Who pays for education? ○ (Public primary and secondary schools)

Local government — 47%   47% — **State government**

20% The largest portions of states' budgets, 20% on average, go to elementary and secondary education.

Federal government — 6%

Federal spending in 2000 is over $100 billion, up 40% since 1990. The $30 billion for "special education" is an 18% increase from 1980. The Dept. of Education reports that at least one in every 10 students qualifies for special ed. in some way.

What are your chances of going to jail?
There are over 1.3 million prisoners in America today, representing an annual average growth rate of 6% since 1990.

If recent incarceration rates continue,
an estimated **5% of all Americans** will
spend time in prison during their lifetime.

For **black males,** the chance
of going to jail is ████

██████████████████████ 🏃🏃🏃🏃🏃🏃🏃🏃🏃🏃🏃🏃
🏃🏃🏃🏃🏃🏃🏃🏃🏃🏃🏃🏃🏃🏃🏃🏃🏃🏃🏃🏃🏃🏃🏃🏃🏃🏃🏃🏃🏃🏃🏃🏃

Meanwhile, the prison system is overflowing …

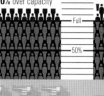

State prisons:
20% over capacity

Federal prisons:
27% over capacity

Full

50%

$60,000

is what it costs to keep one prisoner in jail for a year

(that's ten times the cost of
educating a child for a year)

Capital punishment

34 states
and the
federal
prison
system
currently
hold over
3,000
prisoners
on death
row.

According
to trends,
about 2%
of these
can expect
to be
executed
within the
next year.

Sources: U.S. Federal Bureau of
Investigation; National Association of
State Budget Officers

Consumer goods worth $15.5 billion are
stolen each year. That's $155 per
household.

Of the U.S.'s 15,848 murders in 1996,
10,744 (68%) were by gun.

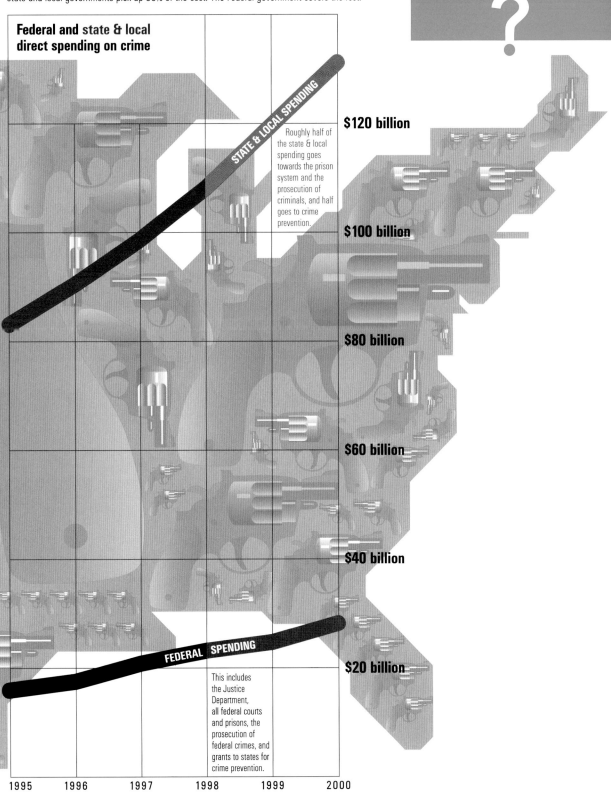

The Good News

Violent crime (which includes murder and rape) has declined for the past five years.

The Bad News

Juvenile crime is still very high—60% above the 1980 level. Juveniles account for about 20% of all arrests and 20% of violent crime arrests.

Federal, state, and local governments together spend more than $150 billion on fighting and preventing crime. That represents an increase of over 100% from 1985, and is the equivalent of spending $550 on crime annually for every resident. Generally, state and local governments pick up 85% of the cost. The Federal government covers the rest.

Federal and state & local direct spending on crime

STATE & LOCAL SPENDING

$120 billion

Roughly half of the state & local spending goes towards the prison system and the prosecution of criminals, and half goes to crime prevention.

$100 billion

$80 billion

$60 billion

$40 billion

FEDERAL SPENDING

$20 billion

This includes the Justice Department, all federal courts and prisons, the prosecution of federal crimes, and grants to states for crime prevention.

| 1995 | 1996 | 1997 | 1998 | 1999 | 2000 |

There is no death penalty in: Alaska, D.C., Hawaii, Iowa, Maine, Massachusetts, Michigan, Minnesota, North Dakota, Rhode Island, Vermont, West Virginia, Wisconsin. Hanging is one of the methods of execution in New Hampshire, Montana and Washington, and the firing squad one of the methods in Utah.

America's Report card

As a kid, receiving your report card could be a harrowing experience. It was tough to get measured against other kids.

How does the U.S. compare to other countries and what kind of grades should we get as an economy and as a society?

For a benchmark we chose a series of variables—some measure the robustness of our economy and others measure our quality of life. We compared ourselves to other industrialized countries, as represented by the Organization for Economic Cooperation and Development (OECD).

Then we gave the U.S. a "grade" in each category. If the U.S. was in the top 20% we got an "A." If we fell in the lowest 20%, we got an "F". If we were average, a "C." Yes, this is a normal grade distribution (you remember those from college) with no grade inflation!

% Change in GDP (1990-1998)
Economic growth is usually measured by the average annual change in gross domestic product

Per Capita GDP
A general measure of wealth: the gross domestic product per person

Unemployment Rate
The percentage of people unemployed and looking for work

Ratio of Economic Inequality
Measured by the *Gini Coefficient*, which is a way of showing the distribution of wealth. Higher gini coefficient numbers indicate a higher level of inequality between the rich and the poor

Federal debt as % GDP
A way of measuring our fiscal health: how much we produce each year compared with how much debt the government has racked up.

Trade Balance as % GDP
The difference between exports and imports as a percentage of the gross domestic product

Net National Savings as % GDP
The total savings, public and private, compared to the GDP

Average Life Expectancy
The average life expectancy (both men and women) is an indicator of overall health

Healthcare Resources
Number of doctors per 1,000 of the population. A good indicator of the health resources available

R&D
A measure of how much of the GDP is devoted to research and development—both in the private and public sectors

Graduation Rates
The percentage of the population that has graduated from high school and higher

Education: Test Scores
The average percentage of correct answers in the National Assessment of Educational Progress Tests

High Tech Market Share
A measure of how much market share a country controls in high tech industries. Here the US is at the top of the list

Air Quality
Emissions of sulphur oxides, nitrogen oxides and carbon dioxide

Municipal Waste
The annual amount of waste

Source: Organization for Economic Cooperation and Development

O Budget Documents. Office of Management and Budget. Executive Office of the President. U.S. www.access.gpo.gov/usbudget Contains the U.S. budgets from fiscal year 1996 to present as well as a searchable database of supporting and related documents such as historical tables, mid-session reviews and analytical perspectives.

O Office of Management and Budget. Executive Office of the President. U.S. www.whitehouse.gov/OMB Find financial management policies, government-wide performance plans, Y2K reports, and the information and regulatory policies for the government.

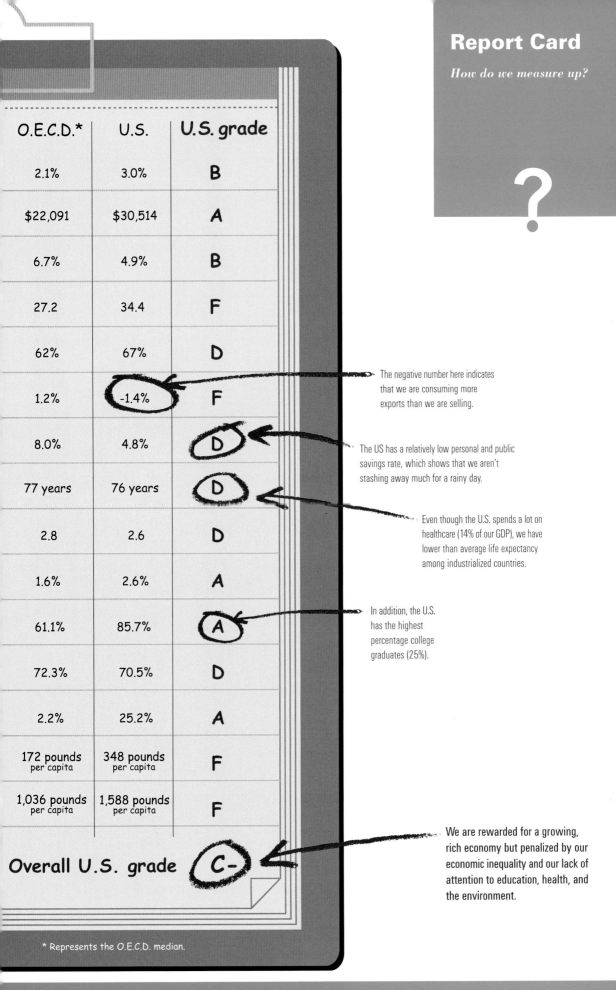

O.E.C.D.*	U.S.	U.S. grade
2.1%	3.0%	B
$22,091	$30,514	A
6.7%	4.9%	B
27.2	34.4	F
62%	67%	D
1.2%	-1.4%	F
8.0%	4.8%	D
77 years	76 years	D
2.8	2.6	D
1.6%	2.6%	A
61.1%	85.7%	A
72.3%	70.5%	D
2.2%	25.2%	A
172 pounds per capita	348 pounds per capita	F
1,036 pounds per capita	1,588 pounds per capita	F

Overall U.S. grade (C-)

The negative number here indicates that we are consuming more exports than we are selling.

The US has a relatively low personal and public savings rate, which shows that we aren't stashing away much for a rainy day.

Even though the U.S. spends a lot on healthcare (14% of our GDP), we have lower than average life expectancy among industrialized countries.

In addition, the U.S. has the highest percentage college graduates (25%).

We are rewarded for a growing, rich economy but penalized by our economic inequality and our lack of attention to education, health, and the environment.

* Represents the O.E.C.D. median.

○ State Government Finance Data by State. Census Bureau. Dept. of Commerce. U.S.
www.census.gov/govs/www/state.html
Annual revenue, expenditure, indebtedness, and cash/securities data for state governments collected by the Census Bureau.

○ Governments Division: Federal, State and Local Governments. Census Bureau. Dept. of Commerce. U.S.
www.census.gov/govs/www/index.html
The annual financial data of various levels of government, from county to federal, may be found at this site. Most data is available from 1992 and may vary between types/levels of government.

○ The Public Debt Online. Bureau of the Public Debt. Dept. of the Treasury. U.S.
www.publicdebt.treas.gov/opd/opd.htm
The Bureau of Public Debt is responsible for borrowing the money needed to operate the Federal Government and account for its debt. Their web site, The Public Debt Online provides a daily tabulation of the federal debt to the penny. Monthly statements, interest rates, and gift contribution

Reed Agnew / Don Moyer

Age & Race
Who lives here?

Demographic Snapshots
Who are we?

Population Distribution
Where do we live? Where don't we live?

Patterns of Race
Where are densities above and below average?

Age, Sex & Marriage
Where are densities above and below average?

Income, Origin & Education
Where are densities above and below average?

Population Growth Rate
How do births, deaths and migration affect growth?

Distribution of Wealth
How much money do we make?

Becoming President
How do you get to the White House?

The Electoral College
Does your vote count?

Lobbying
What does a lobbyist do? What is a special interest group?
What is a political action committee?

One thousand equals 270 million.

Suppose that the entire population of the United States is represented by just 1,000 people. If those 1,000 people were divided in proportion to the entire population, how would the major demographic categories compare?

This diagram shows 1,000 people representing the U.S. population divided into three major age groups and arranged by race.

Source: U.S. Census Bureau

Key

White
827 per 1,000

Black
126 per 1,000

Asian or Pacific Islander
38 per 1,000

Native American
9 per 1,000

How many is 270 million people?
There are nearly 270 million people in the U.S. If you listed all of their names in a phone book, you'd need 614,000 pages—a stack of phone books almost 75 feet high.

Number of children in the population
is at a record high at 70 million. But as a percentage of the population, children have dropped from 32 percent in 1980 to 29 percent in 1997. Meanwhile, the population over age 65 has steadily increased both in numbers and as a percent of the population, now representing 13 percent of U.S. citizens.

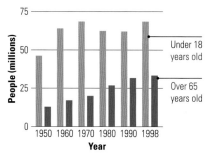

Under 18 years old

Over 65 years old

People (millions)

75

50

25

0

1950 1960 1970 1980 1990 1998

Year

New arrivals.
Less than eight percent of Americans were born outside the U.S.

Deck the halls.
Of the over 192 million households celebrating Christmas, less than 49 percent celebrate with real trees and more than 51 percent celebrate with artificial trees.

Music makers.
More than 20 million Americans play the piano, but only a little more than one million play the saxophone.

United States
Population

World population is over six
billion. The population of the
United States is about four and
a half percent of the total world
population.

Over 65 years old

18 to 65 years old

Under 18 years old

Are you Hispanic?
Out of 1,000 U.S. citizens, 110 say
they are of Hispanic origin. That
means they can be any race and
they or their ancestors are from a
Spanish-speaking country—Cuba,
Mexico, Puerto Rico, Spain, etc.
Hispanics are included in the big
diagram at left. If they were pulled
out, they would form the multiracial
group below.

100 White Hispanic

1 Native American
Hispanic

**Hispanic
(all ages)**

3 Asian
Hispanic

6 Black Hispanic

⊙ Income. Current Population Survey.
Census Bureau. U.S.
www.census.gov/hhes/www/income.html
Census Bureau, on a periodic basis, issues
detailed reports that examine all aspects
and income in the United States.

⊙ Estimates of Population. Census Bureau.
U.S.
www.census.gov/population/www/estimates/
popest.html
The Population Estimates Program produces monthly national population
estimates by age, sex, race, and Hispanic
origin for the United States.

In focus.

Using 1000 people to represent the whole population of the U.S., here are some significant demographic facts.

Source: U.S. Census Bureau

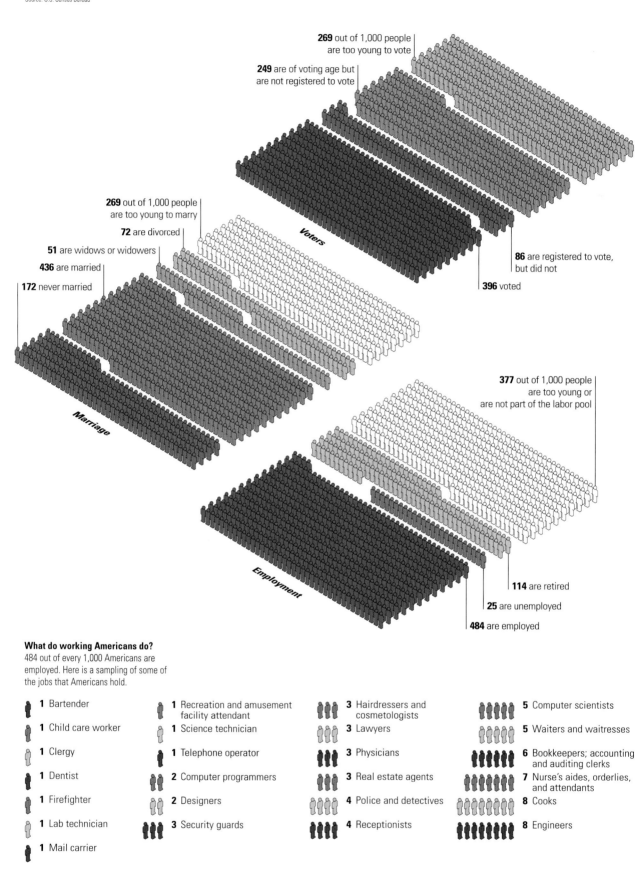

269 out of 1,000 people are too young to vote

249 are of voting age but are not registered to vote

Voters

86 are registered to vote, but did not

396 voted

269 out of 1,000 people are too young to marry

72 are divorced

51 are widows or widowers

436 are married

172 never married

Marriage

377 out of 1,000 people are too young or are not part of the labor pool

114 are retired

25 are unemployed

484 are employed

Employment

What do working Americans do?
484 out of every 1,000 Americans are employed. Here is a sampling of some of the jobs that Americans hold.

- **1** Bartender
- **1** Child care worker
- **1** Clergy
- **1** Dentist
- **1** Firefighter
- **1** Lab technician
- **1** Mail carrier

- **1** Recreation and amusement facility attendant
- **1** Science technician
- **1** Telephone operator
- **2** Computer programmers
- **2** Designers
- **3** Security guards

- **3** Hairdressers and cosmetologists
- **3** Lawyers
- **3** Physicians
- **3** Real estate agents
- **4** Police and detectives
- **4** Receptionists

- **5** Computer scientists
- **5** Waiters and waitresses
- **6** Bookkeepers; accounting and auditing clerks
- **7** Nurse's aides, orderlies, and attendants
- **8** Cooks
- **8** Engineers

Home work.
More than 300,000 American kids are being educated at home instead of in public schools.

Locked up.
Less than one percent of Americans are in prison or jail. There are almost 15 times as many men in prison or jail as there are women.

At your service.
More than seven percent of Americans work for the government at some level. This figure does not include military personnel, who account for only one half of one percent of the total U.S. population.

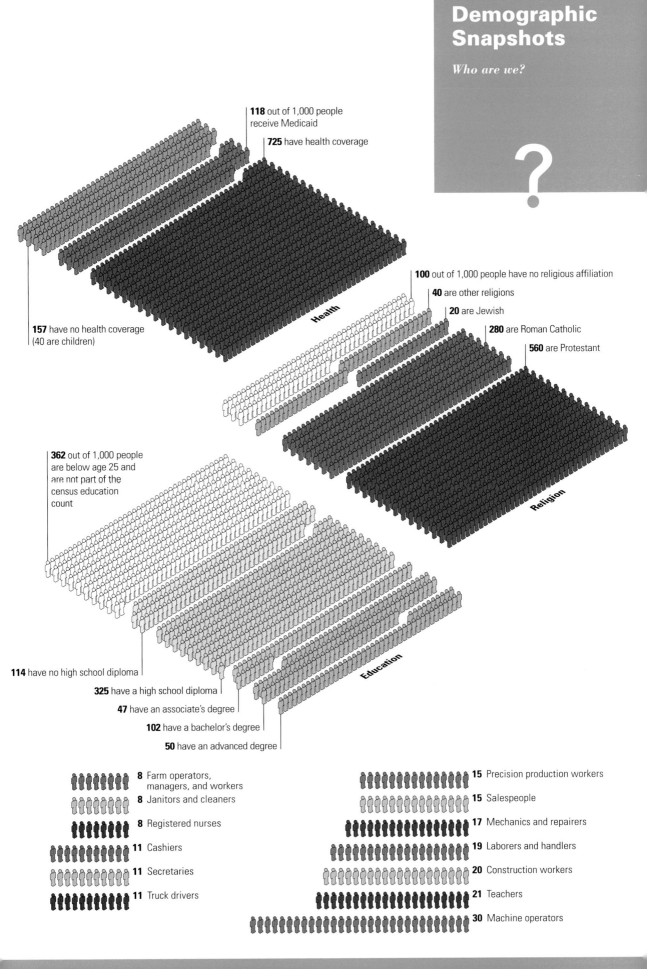

Demographic Snapshots

Who are we?

?

118 out of 1,000 people receive Medicaid

725 have health coverage

157 have no health coverage (40 are children)

Health

100 out of 1,000 people have no religious affiliation

40 are other religions

20 are Jewish

280 are Roman Catholic

560 are Protestant

Religion

362 out of 1,000 people are below age 25 and are not part of the census education count

114 have no high school diploma

325 have a high school diploma

47 have an associate's degree

102 have a bachelor's degree

50 have an advanced degree

Education

8 Farm operators, managers, and workers

8 Janitors and cleaners

8 Registered nurses

11 Cashiers

11 Secretaries

11 Truck drivers

15 Precision production workers

15 Salespeople

17 Mechanics and repairers

19 Laborers and handlers

20 Construction workers

21 Teachers

30 Machine operators

On the road.
Almost 140 million Americans own cars. Nearly 21 million Americans say that they never use seat belts.

Staring at the screen.
More than 35 percent of all American households own a computer. More than 98 percent of all households own a color TV. Almost 30 percent own three or more TVs.

Heavy petting.
More than 27 percent of U.S. households own cats. Most own more than two. More than 31 percent of U.S. households own dogs. Most own more than one.

The population of the United States
is not distributed evenly. Instead, we tend to bunch up in communities, leaving the spaces in between more sparsely inhabited. Most Americans live in or near cities; today 53 percent live in the 20 largest cities. 75 percent of all Americans live in metropolitan areas.

This map shows population density. The relative height of each major city reflects its population in 1990.

Source: U.S. Census Bureau

Go West. Nevada is the fastest growing state, followed by Arizona, Idaho, Colorado, and Utah.

Wyoming has the lowest population density of all states in the lower 48 with an average of five people per square mile.

What happens in the empty spaces? Some of it is farming country. More than one quarter of America's crop land is used to grow corn. One third of what is produced is exported to other countries.

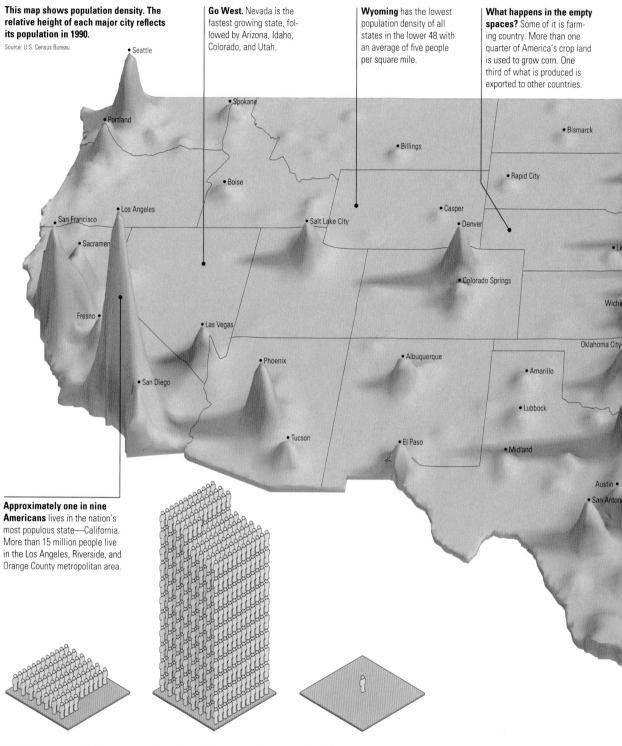

Seattle • Spokane • Portland • Bismarck • Billings • Boise • Rapid City • Los Angeles • San Francisco • Casper • Salt Lake City • Sacramen[to] • Denver • L[?] • Fresno • Colorado Springs • Wichi[ta] • Las Vegas • San Diego • Oklahoma City • Phoenix • Albuquerque • Amarillo • Lubbock • Tucson • El Paso • Midland • Austin • San Anton[io]

Approximately one in nine Americans lives in the nation's most populous state—California. More than 15 million people live in the Los Angeles, Riverside, and Orange County metropolitan area.

Distributing our population evenly would put an average of 76 people per square mile.

New Jersey is the most densely populated state with an average of more than 1,000 people per square mile.

Alaska is a sparsely populated state with an average of one person per square mile.

On the move.
Americans are among the most mobile populations in the industrialized world. In a typical year, one in six Americans moves.

Smaller neighbors.
The population of the United States is about nine times greater than that of Canada and about two and a half times greater than Mexico.

⭕ Construction Statistics. Census Bureau. U.S.
blue.census.gov/const/www/index.html
Census Bureau, on a monthly basis, tracks the numbers of housing units authorized by permits, started, sold or completed.

Fourth place.
The area of the United States is 3,536,341 square miles, making it the fourth largest country in the world. Canada and China are both slightly larger. Russia is almost twice as large.

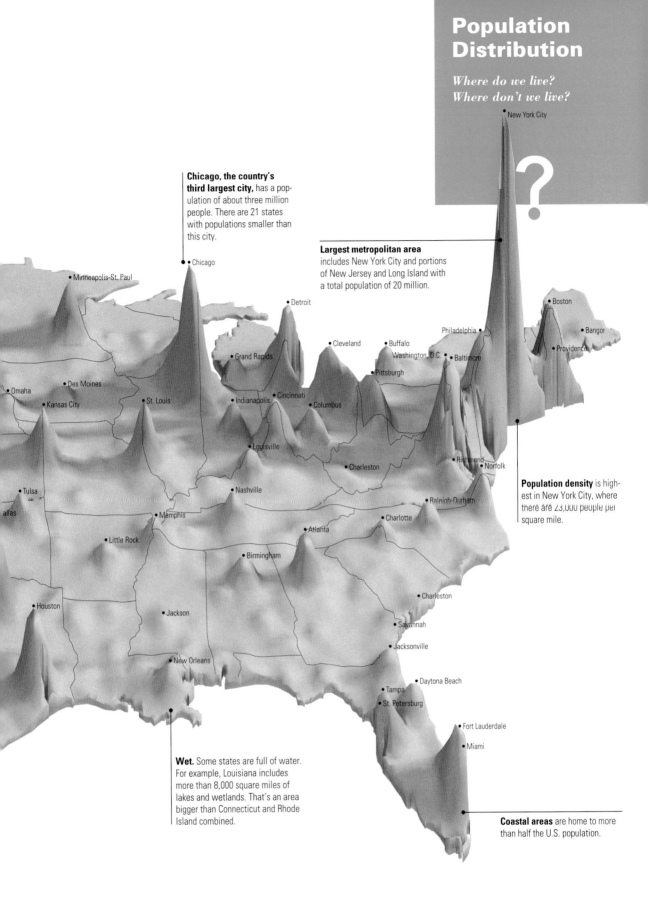

Population Distribution

Where do we live?
Where don't we live?

Chicago, the country's third largest city, has a population of about three million people. There are 21 states with populations smaller than this city.

Largest metropolitan area includes New York City and portions of New Jersey and Long Island with a total population of 20 million.

Population density is highest in New York City, where there are 23,000 people per square mile.

Wet. Some states are full of water. For example, Louisiana includes more than 8,000 square miles of lakes and wetlands. That's an area bigger than Connecticut and Rhode Island combined.

Coastal areas are home to more than half the U.S. population.

City labels on map:
New York City, Minneapolis-St. Paul, Chicago, Detroit, Boston, Bangor, Cleveland, Buffalo, Philadelphia, Providence, Grand Rapids, Washington, D.C., Baltimore, Omaha, Des Moines, Pittsburgh, Kansas City, St. Louis, Cincinnati, Indianapolis, Columbus, Louisville, Richmond, Norfolk, Tulsa, Charleston, Nashville, Raleigh-Durham, Dallas, Memphis, Charlotte, Little Rock, Atlanta, Birmingham, Houston, Jackson, Charleston, Savannah, Jacksonville, New Orleans, Daytona Beach, Tampa, St. Petersburg, Fort Lauderdale, Miami

Shrinking population.
Several states lost population between the 1980 and 1990 censuses—Iowa, North Dakota, West Virginia, and Wyoming.

Small countries.
Most nations are small and have small populations. More than half of the world's countries have fewer people than the state of Virginia.

Big countries.
The world's 10 most populous countries have two thirds of the world's population.

How was this map created? We couldn't have done it without several computer applications. Using 1990 U.S. Census figures loaded into MapInfo GIS (geographic information system) software, we produced a grayscale image of the U.S. Light tones represented high populations and dark values sparse populations. We then converted this grayscale image into a 3D model inside FormZ. Finally, we cleaned up rough spots in Adobe Photoshop® and overlaid the state boundaries and city labels in Adobe Illustrator®.

Mix is changing.

The racial composition of the population becomes more diverse every year. Immigration and higher birth rates among Blacks, Asians, and Native Americans means that minority groups will increase as a percentage of total population in the coming years.

The largest numbers of Whites can be found in California and the New York City metropolitan area. Of the states, Vermont has the highest percentage of Whites—98.5 percent. Salt Lake City, Utah, is the metropolitan area with the highest percentage—95 percent.

More than half of the Black population resides in the south. The largest numbers of Blacks can be found in New York state and the New York City metropolitan area. Mississippi is the state with the largest percentage of Blacks—51 percent. Memphis, Tennessee, is the metropolitan area with the highest percentage—42 percent.

White Americans as a percentage of the population

Key

Above average, 86.8–100%
■ High-density population
▦ Low-density population

Average, 66.8–86.7%
■ High-density population
▦ Low-density population

Below average, 0–66.7%
■ High-density population
▦ Low-density population

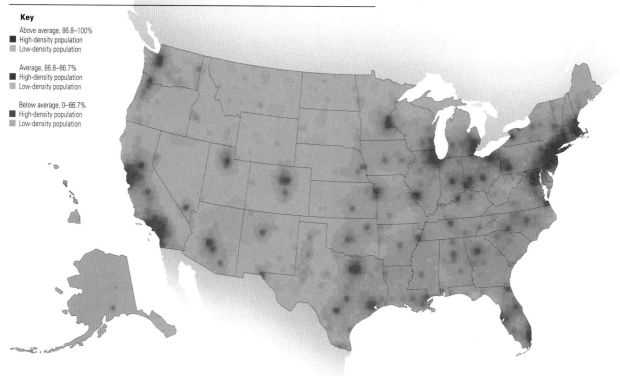

Black Americans as a percentage of the population

Key

Above average, 19.3–64%
■ High-density population
▦ Low-density population

Average, 5.3–19.2%
■ High-density population
▦ Low-density population

Below average, 0–5.2%
■ High-density population
▦ Low-density population

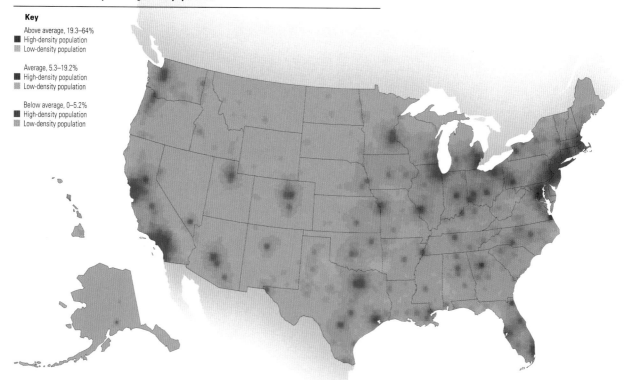

Source: U.S. Census Bureau

More minority households have kids.
Over 40 percent of minority households in 1995 had at least one child under age 18, compared with 32 percent of non-Hispanic White households. This difference arises primarily because a greater share of minorities are in the prime childbearing years, and minorities tend to have higher fertility rates.

Fast track.
Asian Americans are the most rapidly growing race in America due to high birth rates, high life expectancy, and high immigration numbers—33 percent of current immigrants come from Asian countries. According to the U.S. Census Bureau this racial category includes people from countries such as China, India, Iran, Korea, Philippines, Taiwan, Turkey, and Vietnam.

Go East.
Over the last decade, Asian Americans have become less geographically concentrated. In 1860 nearly 100 percent of Asian Americans lived in the western U.S. In 1940 nearly 90 percent lived in the west, compared to 46 percent in 1990.

Asians and Pacific Islanders can be found in the largest numbers in California and the Los Angeles metropolitan area. Hawaii is the state with the largest percentage of Asians—62 percent. Honolulu is the metropolitan area with the highest percentage—64 percent.

Native Americans can be found in the largest numbers in California and the Los Angeles metropolitan area. Alaska is the state with the largest percentage of this group—16 percent. Tulsa, Oklahoma, is the metropolitan area with the highest percentage—six and a half percent.

Asian or Pacific Islander Americans as a percentage of the population

Key

Above average, 5.5–86%
■ High-density population
▒ Low-density population

Average, 0.5–5.49%
▨ High-density population
▨ Low-density population

Below average, 0–0.49%
■ High-density population
▒ Low-density population

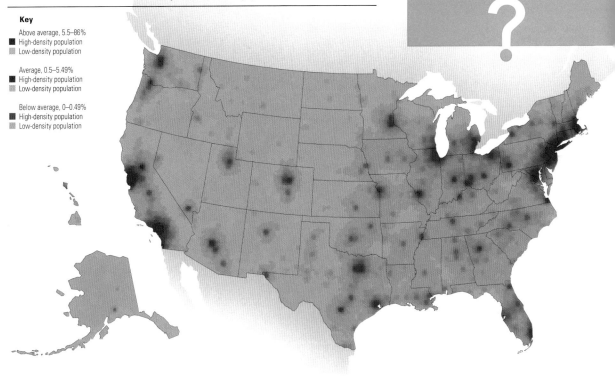

Native Americans as a percentage of the population

Key

Above average, 25.1–92%
■ High-density population
▒ Low-density population

Average, 1–25%
■ High-density population
▒ Low-density population

Below average, 0–0.9%
■ High-density population
▒ Low-density population

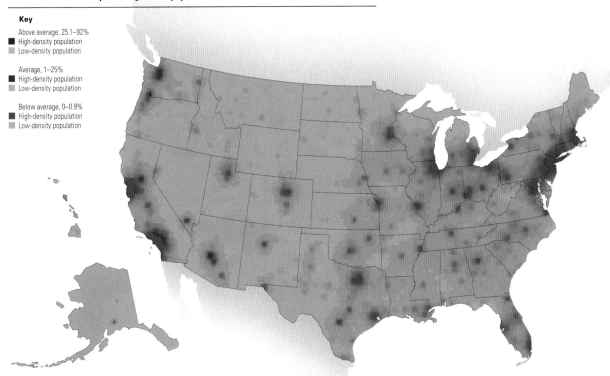

Alaska natives.
Alaska's Native American population densities are smaller in urban areas. While the total Native American, Eskimo, and Aleut population is almost 16 percent, Anchorage, Alaska, has only six percent.

Different states.
Although there are only 1,937,391 Native Americans in the U.S., ten states had more Native Americans than Black Americans (Alaska, Arizona, Idaho, Montana, New Mexico, North Dakota, Oklahoma, South Dakota, Utah, and Wyoming).

Reservations large and small.
There are 275 Indian reservations in the United States. The largest is the Navajo reservation with some 16 million acres of land in Arizona, New Mexico, and Utah. Many of the smaller reservations are less than 1,000 acres with the smallest less than 100 acres.

Graying of America.

The average age of Americans is now 35 and rising. The fastest growing age group is made up of those 85 years and older.

Not as young as you were.

One in four Americans is 18 or younger. But the percentage of Americans under 18 is decreasing.

Over 65.

The average number of people in the population that are over 65 is about 13 percent and increasing. According to U.S. Census figures for 1990, the 10 counties with the greatest percentage of residents over 65 are all in Florida. All have over 25 percent.

Americans under the age of 18 as a percentage of the population

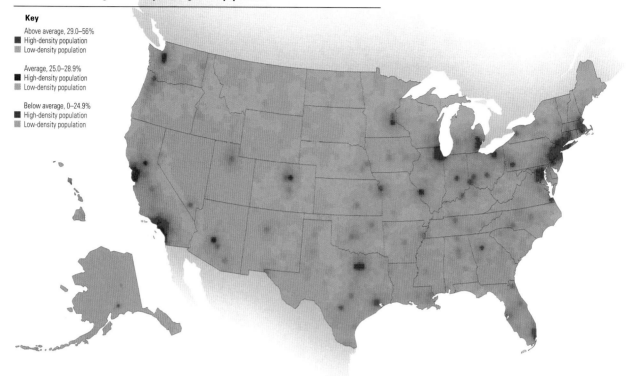

Key

Above average, 29.0–56%
■ High-density population
▨ Low-density population

Average, 25.0–28.9%
■ High-density population
▨ Low-density population

Below average, 0–24.9%
■ High-density population
▨ Low-density population

Americans over the age of 65 as a percentage of the population

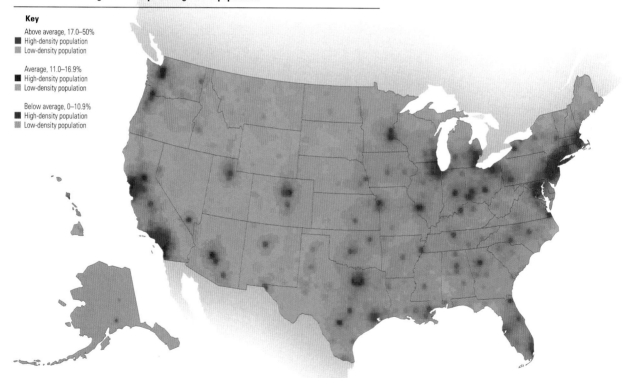

Key

Above average, 17.0–50%
■ High-density population
▨ Low-density population

Average, 11.0–16.9%
■ High-density population
▨ Low-density population

Below average, 0–10.9%
■ High-density population
▨ Low-density population

Growing youngsters.
The number of Americans age 17 and younger rose by six percent between 1990 and 1994, from 64 million to 68 million. The child population increased in all but three states and the District of Columbia during the first half of the decade, but growth rates varied widely. Nevada showed the largest gain (a 26 percent increase), while West Virginia had the largest drop (a loss of four percent).

On the move.
Young adults are the most mobile people in our society. About one in three people age 20 to 29 changes his or her address in a given year.

Bible Belt Break Ups.
Behind Nevada, the Bible Belt (Tennessee, Arkansas, Alabama and Oklahoma) is the region with the second highest frequency of divorce—roughly 50 percent above the national average.

Where's Dad?
The percentage of children living with two parents has been declining among all major racial and ethnic groups. In 1996, 68 percent of American children lived with two parents, down from 85 percent in 1970. Twenty-five percent of children live with only their mother; four percent live with only their father; and four percent live with neither of their parents.

Where are the guys?

The U.S. average is 96 males for every 100 females. Western states tend to have more men then women. Alaska's north slope tops the range with more than 180 men per 100 women.

Married life.

Married Americans make up about half the population. The states with the highest concentrations of married people are Iowa and West Virginia.

Patterns of Age, Sex & Marriage

Where are densities above and below average?

?

Male to female ratio (number of males per every hundred females)

Key

Above average,
98.0–186 males per 100 females
■ High-density population
▓ Low-density population

Average,
88.0–97.9 males per 100 females
■ High-density population
▓ Low-density population

Below average,
0–87.9 males per 100 females
■ High-density population
▓ Low-density population

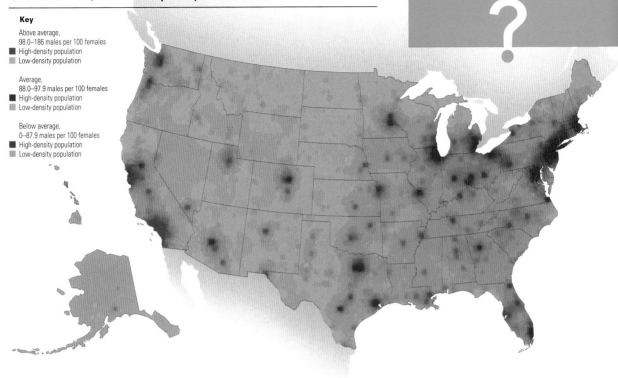

Married Americans as a percentage of the population

Key

Above average, 63.0–93%
■ High-density population
▓ Low-density population

Average, 60.0–62.9%
■ High-density population
▓ Low-density population

Below average, 0–59.9%
■ High-density population
▓ Low-density population

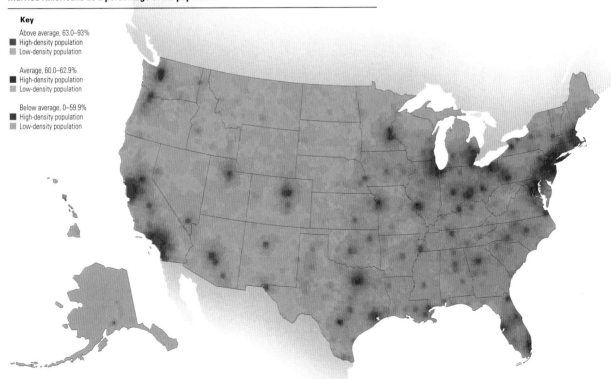

Marrying and remarrying.

Marriage has not gone out of style. The United States has the highest marriage rate in the industrialized world. But divorce in the United States is also common. The U.S. divorce rate is nearly twice as high as those in other industrialized countries. Most Americans who divorce eventually remarry, however. Nearly half of all marriages in 1990 were remarriages for one or both partners.

Divorce is up.

The currently divorced population is the fastest growing marital status category. The number of divorced people has more than quadrupled, from four million in 1970 to 18.3 million in 1996. They represented 10 percent of adults age 18 and over in 1996, up from three percent in 1970. The chance of a marriage ending in divorce is about 50 percent.

Waiting to marry.

The median age for first marriages in the United States is at an all-time high. For men, it was 26.7 years of age in 1994; for women, 24.5.

Hispanic growth.

The Hispanic population is growing quickly, although not as fast as the Asian American population. Six percent of the population was of Hispanic origin in 1980. In 1997 almost 11 percent of the population was Hispanic.

Hispanic boom.

By 2015, Hispanics are expected to surpass non-Hispanic African Americans as the country's largest minority group. In California and New Mexico, Hispanics are projected to surpass non-Hispanic whites as the largest racial or ethnic group by 2015.

New arrivals.

The U.S. has a higher proportion of immigrants today than at any time since before World War II. In 1990, about 20 million, or eight percent, of us were not born in the United States. The government estimates that there are about five million illegal immigrants in the country.

Americans of Hispanic origin as a percentage of the population

Key

Above average, 17.0–94%
■ High-density population
▢ Low-density population

Average, 5.0–16.9%
■ High-density population
▢ Low-density population

Below average, 0–4.9%
■ High-density population
▢ Low-density population

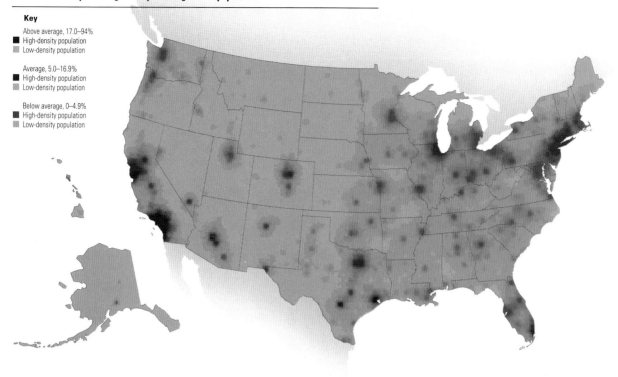

Foreign-born Americans as a percentage of the population

Key

Above average, 12.0–46%
■ High-density population
▢ Low-density population

Average, 4.0–11.9%
■ High-density population
▢ Low-density population

Below average, 0–3.9%
■ High-density population
▢ Low-density population

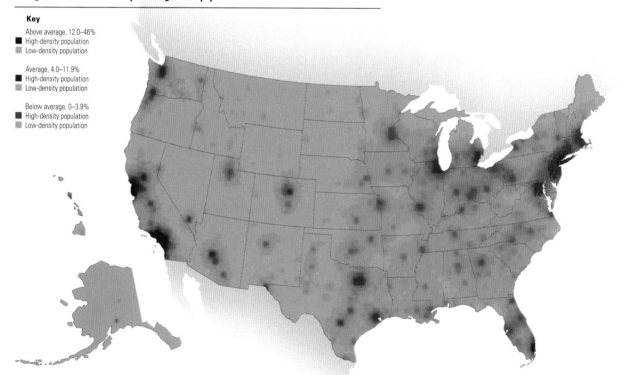

Source: U.S. Census Bureau

Who is Hispanic?

Anyone who retains a cultural connection to his or her Spanish-speaking roots is considered Hispanic. This population includes diverse cultures, ethnicities, and nationalities, with links to Spanish settlers, Blacks from the islands, indigenous Indian populations, and mixed races. Spanish-speaking countries in the Caribbean, Central America, and South America all contribute people to the U.S. Hispanic population, but approximately two out of three Hispanics in the U.S. are from Mexico.

Women graduates.

Since 1981, graduating college classes have had more women than men. Typically, almost six out of 10 graduating college students are women.

Working more and making less.

Nearly 60 percent of women 16 years or older were members of the work force in 1996, up from 52 percent in 1980 and up from 36 percent in the mid 1950s. The gap between men's and women's earnings remains broad; on average, women earn about 75 percent of what men earn.

Median income.

The 1997 U.S. median income was $37,005. The states with the highest median income were Alaska and New Jersey. The states with the lowest percentage of people below the poverty level were Indiana, New Hampshire, and Utah.

Higher education.

Almost 15 percent of Americans have an advanced degree. In Connecticut and Massachusetts this proportion is nearly 20 percent. Arkansas, Kentucky, Mississippi, and West Virginia are states in which less than 10 percent of the population has an advanced degree.

Patterns of Income, Origin & Education

Where are densities above and below average?

?

Income per household

Key

Above average, $41,001–$120,000
- High-density population
- Low-density population

Average, $31,001–$41,000
- High-density population
- Low-density population

Below average, $0–$31,000
- High-density population
- Low-density population

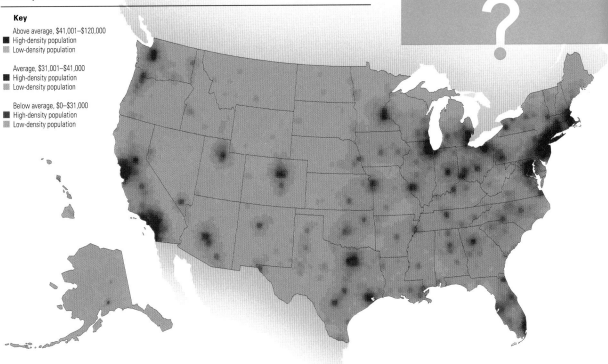

Americans with college, graduate, or doctoral degrees as a percentage of the population

Key

Above average, 12.0–31%
- High-density population
- Low-density population

Average, 8.0–11.9%
- High-density population
- Low-density population

Below average, 0–7.9%
- High-density population
- Low-density population

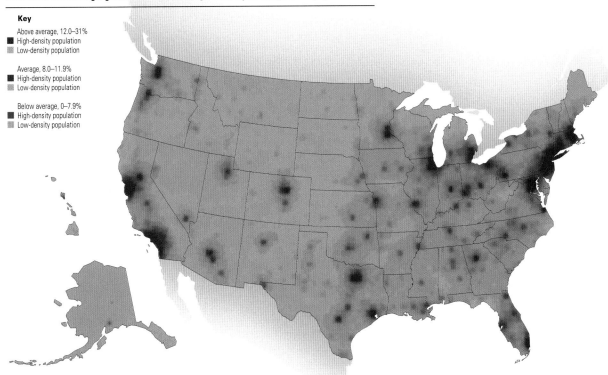

College dropouts.

The number of students seeking a college education is at an all-time high with 15 million enrolling in a typical year. But the number of students who receive degrees has not increased much in the last 15 years. Typically, only two out of three freshmen return for their sophomore year.

Special thanks to Matt Graham of Landbase Systems (412.563.9120) for his coaching on GIS mapping issues and assistance de-gooing the U.S. Census data.

Faster some years, slower others.
The U.S. population has increased every year this century, but not grown at a steady or predictable rate.

Who lives, dies, comes, and goes.
Four factors—births, deaths, immigration, and emigration—determine how fast the population grows. For the population to grow, the number of births combined with the number of immigrants must exceed the number of deaths combined with the number of emigrants. The difference between these two amounts in a single year produces the net population growth.

What next?
Nobody knows for sure. U.S. population growth is uncertain, but the Census Bureau makes elaborate estimates that vary based on future scenarios. By changing the rates of the big factors in population growth—fertility rates, migration numbers, and changes in life expectancy, some theories as to how fast the U.S. might grow emerge.

The red line in this diagram shows the net population growth from 1910 through 1998. The growth rate results from subtracting the number of deaths and emigrants from the number of births and immigrants each year.
Source: U.S. Census Bureau

Key

The Great Depression, from 1929 to 1941, caused the most significant drop in birth and immigration rates this century.

The Baby Boom began in 1946, one year after the end of World War II, and ended in 1964. During this time, record numbers of babies were born, adding 77 million people, or roughly 30 percent of the 1998 U.S. population. In 1957, at the height of the Baby Boom, there were 25.3 births per every 1,000 people—the highest birth rate this century.

Births and deaths don't affect the net growth equally. The number of deaths tends to grow at a steady pace, but births fluctuate so rapidly that they directly impact the net growth. As a result, the pattern of net growth seems to roughly mimic the pattern of the number of births.

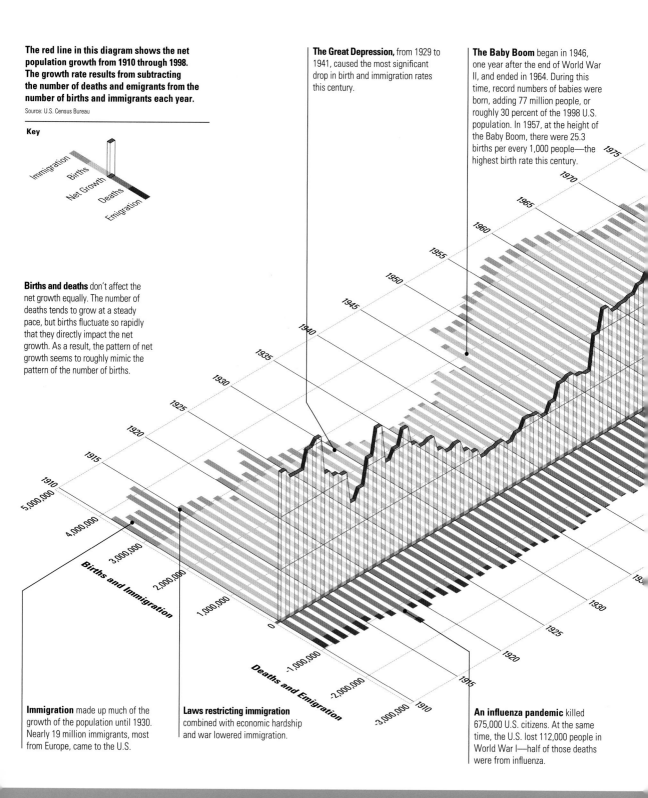

Immigration made up much of the growth of the population until 1930. Nearly 19 million immigrants, most from Europe, came to the U.S.

Laws restricting immigration combined with economic hardship and war lowered immigration.

An influenza pandemic killed 675,000 U.S. citizens. At the same time, the U.S. lost 112,000 people in World War I—half of those deaths were from influenza.

Old Boomers.
The aging of the Baby Boomers will be one of the most significant demographic forces shaping U.S. society for the next 40 years. Politics will become more focused on saving Social Security and how to deal with the pools of people entering elderly years. Experts say the number of births will reach over four million again by 2005 as the Baby Boomer grandchildren are born.

What is the future of immigration?
Net immigration is projected to be a predominant factor in future population growth. The Census' medium estimate predicts for every 10 immigrants:

○ 4 will be Hispanic
○ 3 will be Asian
○ 2 will be White
● 1 will be Black

Is the population replacing itself?
The U.S. population must produce 2,100 babies for every 1,000 women to maintain the population at its current level. Since 1980, we have averaged 1,900 per 1,000 women, which is slightly below the replacement rate. Experts say unless our birth rate increases or we admit more immigrants, the U.S., along with many other industrialized nations, could gradually start to depopulate.

Baby Boom echo started in 1977 when Boomers began having children of their own. These children—called Millennials—added 72 million people to the population, or 28 percent of the total population in 1998. The peak of the Echo Boom was 1990, with four million recorded births. Since then, the number has declined, as Boomers pass childbearing age.

A steady stream.
In 1998 immigration reached its highest point since the beginning of the century. These immigrants came mostly from Latin America and Asia and as a result, the Hispanic and Asian populations are the country's fastest growing.

In 1998 the birth rate of the United States was 14.4 births per every 1,000 people.

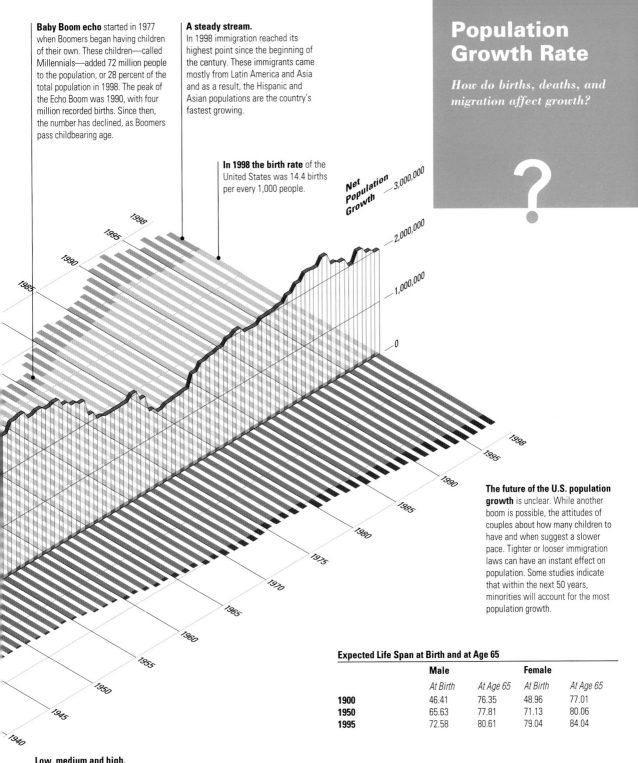

Net Population Growth

The future of the U.S. population growth is unclear. While another boom is possible, the attitudes of couples about how many children to have and when suggest a slower pace. Tighter or looser immigration laws can have an instant effect on population. Some studies indicate that within the next 50 years, minorities will account for the most population growth.

Expected Life Span at Birth and at Age 65

	Male		Female	
	At Birth	*At Age 65*	*At Birth*	*At Age 65*
1900	46.41	76.35	48.96	77.01
1950	65.63	77.81	71.13	80.06
1995	72.58	80.61	79.04	84.04

Low, medium and high.
The Census uses existing data to predict future population growth. These estimates require assumptions about future immigration rates, fertility, and life expectancy. This diagram shows the increase in total U.S. population since 1950 and three Census Bureau estimates as to how fast the population might grow in the future.

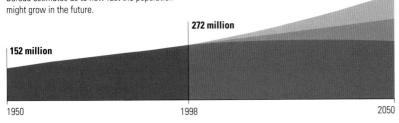

152 million

272 million

1950   1998   2050

High estimate	**519 million**
Fertility rate	2,580 births/1,000 women
Yearly immigration	1.37 million people
Life expectancy	89.4 years

Medium estimate	**394 million**
Fertility rate	2,245 births/1,000 women
Yearly immigration	820,000 people
Life expectancy	82.0 years

Low estimate	**283 million**
Fertility rate	1,910 births/1,000 women
Yearly immigration	300,000 people
Life expectancy	74.8 years

Every day.
According to the U.S. Census Bureau, on a typical day in the U.S., one baby is born every eight seconds. There is one death every 14 seconds.

What are the leading causes of death?
Of the 2,314,245 people who died in 1997, over half died from either heart disease or cancer.

What is the life expectancy of U.S. citizens?
In 1998, the life expectancy of all U.S. citizens was 76.7 years. In 1900, it was 47.3. When broken down by race and sex, life expectancy varies:

	Both	**Men**	**Women**
Total	76.7	73.9	79.4
White	77.3	74.6	79.9
Black	71.5	67.8	75.0

⚪ Mortality Data. National Center for Health Statistics. Dept. of Health and Human Services. U.S.
www.cdc.gov/nchswww/about/major/dvs/mortdata.htm
Latest statistics and clinical information on the leading causes of death.

A few people have most of the money.

Twenty percent of the people have 85 percent of the nation's total wealth. The remaining 80 percent share only 15 percent of the total wealth.

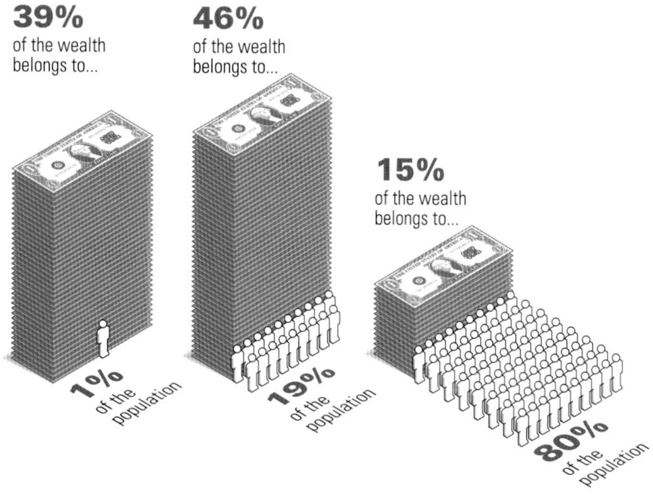

39%
of the wealth belongs to...

46%
of the wealth belongs to...

15%
of the wealth belongs to...

1%
of the population

19%
of the population

80%
of the population

The composition of wealth.

The wealth of middle income families is tied up in their homes and savings accounts, while the super rich can have more assets available to invest and leverage their investments to create even greater wealth.

	Middle income — Two thirds of the wealth is invested in homes and 17% resides in savings.	Super rich — Over 80% of the wealth resides in investments, stocks, and financial securities.
Real Estate & Businesses	7%	45%
Stocks	7%	37%
Deposits	17%	11%
Homes	69%	7%

This diagram shows the 1997 distribution of income for Americans in households earning under $100,000 per year, divided by race and gender. Each figure represents 250,000 people.

Source: U.S. Census Bureau

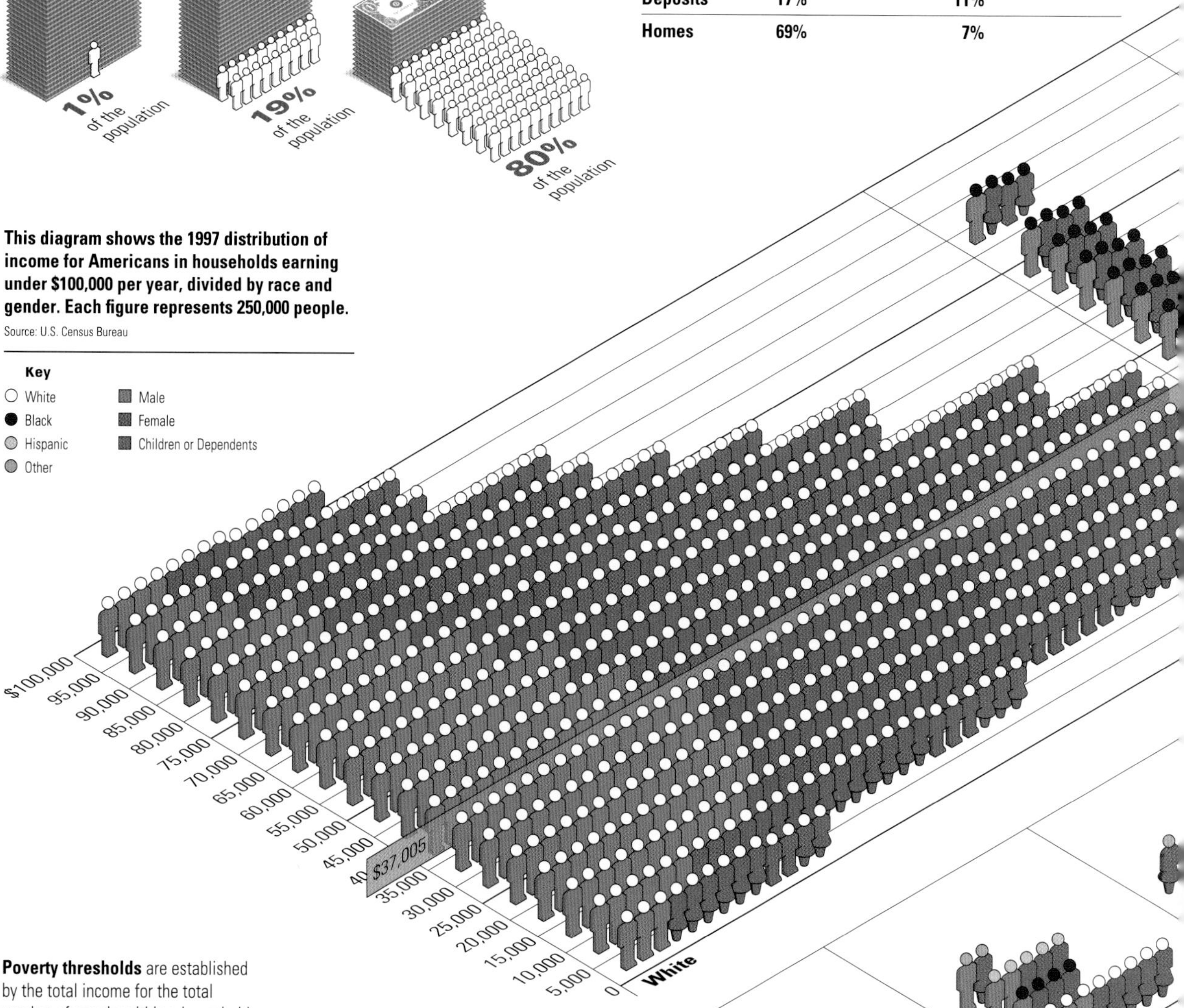

Key
- ○ White
- ● Black
- ◐ Hispanic
- ◑ Other
- ▨ Male
- ▨ Female
- ▨ Children or Dependents

$100,000
95,000
90,000
85,000
80,000
75,000
70,000
65,000
60,000
55,000
50,000
45,000
40,000
$37,005
35,000
30,000
25,000
20,000
15,000
10,000
5,000
0

White

Poverty thresholds are established by the total income for the total number of people within a household. For example, $16,400 is the poverty threshold for a household of four.

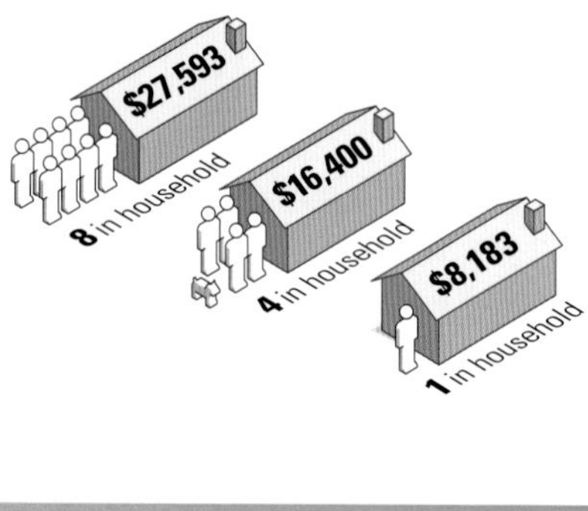

$27,593
8 in household

$16,400
4 in household

$8,183
1 in household

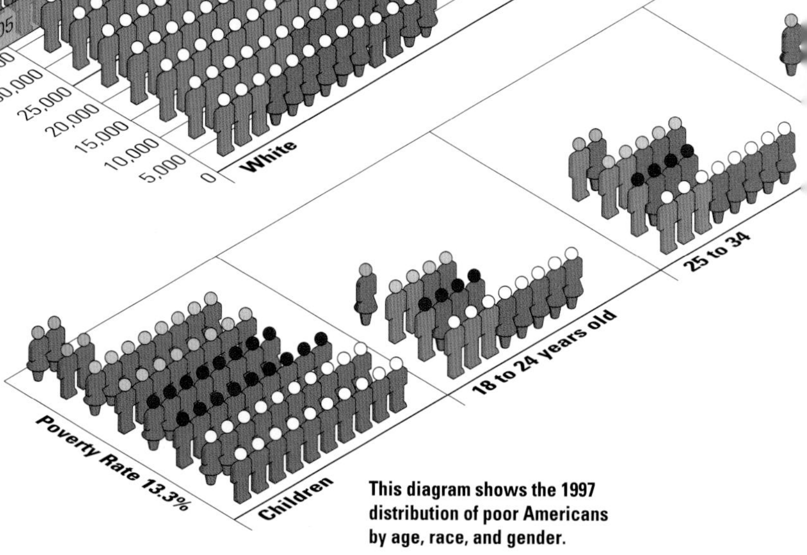

Poverty Rate 13.3%

Children

18 to 24 years old

25 to 34

This diagram shows the 1997 distribution of poor Americans by age, race, and gender.

Where does poverty start?

Poverty thresholds are set by the U.S. Census Bureau and vary by household size and composition. If a household's total income is less than the threshold, the household—everyone in it—is considered poor. How poverty is defined and calculated is an ongoing social and political debate. The current poverty thresholds include money income (before taxes) and exclude capital gains and non-cash benefits, such as public housing, Medicaid, and food stamps.

Children are poor.

Even though children represent only 26 percent of the total population, they make up 40 percent of the poor—and over half of those children are under age six.

Families matter.

The poverty rate for children under age six living in households with a single female parent is 59.1 percent, more than five times the rate for children in households of married couples (10.6 percent).

Median income.
America's median income is $37,005. Half of all Americans make more than the median, half make less.

Median income by race:

White	$40,577
Black	$25,050
Hispanic	$26,628
Asian, Pacific Islander	$45,249

Other

Hispanic

Black

65 and over

55 to 64

45 to 54

35 to 44

The super rich.
According to 1997 tax returns, only one tenth of one percent of American households earned more than $1 million.

more than $1,000,000

900,000

800,000

700,000

600,000

500,000

400,000

300,000

200,000

100,000

The poorest Americans.
More than 13 percent of all Americans (35.6 million) live in households that fall below their poverty thresholds. Forty-one percent of those considered poor (14.6 million) are severely poor —their total income is less than half their poverty threshold.

Numbers versus percentages.
It's important to consider both the total number of poor Americans and their relative percentages.

There are twice as many poor White Americans as there are poor Hispanic Americans. However, a Hispanic American is almost three times more likely to be poor than a White American.

White	**16.5 million** Whites are poor	**8.6%** of White population is poor
Black	**9.1 million** Blacks are poor	**26.5%** of Black population is poor
Hispanic	**8.3 million** Hispanics are poor	**27.1%** of Hispanic population is poor

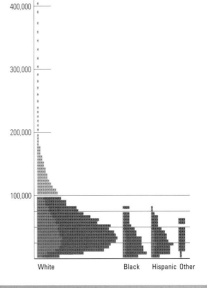

White   Black   Hispanic Other

What is median income?
Median income is the amount which divides income distribution into two equal groups. Half have income above the median; half have income below the median. The diagram above includes a yellow line to indicate the 1997 median income: $37,005.

What is mean income?
Mean income is the amount obtained by dividing the total aggregate income of the population by the number of people in the population. The 1997 mean income for households was $49,692.

The richest American.
Bill Gates, chairman of Microsoft Corporation, is America's richest person—with a 1999 net worth estimated at $85 billion. To chart Gates's net worth on the diagram above, the diagram would have to grow 46,041 feet tall—almost nine miles high!

One step at a time.
Reaching the White House is a long trip. It may take years. Basically, you've got to convince millions of voters that you know how to run a big, rambunctious country like the United States.

Source: Larry Elowitz, *Introduction to Government*, 1992

This list highlights some of the key steps along the path to the presidency.

1 Raise a few million. To demonstrate that you have broad national appeal, you've got to raise at least $5,000 from small contributors (contributions of $250 or less) in at least 20 different states—that's $100,000 and it's the bare minimum to get started as a candidate. You'll need every penny.

2 Take a stand that will appeal to both the public and people who are active in your political party.

3 Hire some help. Get a handler to make you look good. Professionals are available to help you package yourself so that you'll have maximum appeal. Hire a spin-doctor to package you for the media and help you put the most positive spin on everything that happens. It's vital that you seem credible and attractive to the print and broadcast media. Special consultants can help.

4 Declare your candidacy early enough to become a household name before the first primary. Some candidates now become visible more than 15 months before Election Day.

5 Buy opinion polls to find out what the public thinks of you, your issues, and your opponents. Make changes to increase your appeal.

6 Keep good records. You've got to be able to show where all your campaign contributions came from if you expect to receive matching federal campaign funds. Each candidate must turn in periodic reports to the Federal Election Commission to detail both income and expenditures.

7 Win in a straw poll. Straw polls are trial elections that state parties use for fund-raising and publicity. The results of these elections don't count, but if you make a good showing, you'll get lots of positive publicity. The Iowa caucus is typically the first and most visible straw poll.

8 Eat rubber chicken. Fund-raising dinners will nourish your campaign. Get out and meet people. Impress them with your wit and wisdom. Listen to their concerns.

9 Distinguish yourself from your same-party opponents. Until you emerge as your party's chosen candidate, you've got to flaunt your issues. Separate yourself from the herd. Later you can move to the middle of the road.

10 Win some state primaries to show your voter appeal. A good showing is vital to financial support. The New Hampshire primary is the first and the most visible. It's tiny, but the press loves to cover it. In recent years, it is rare for a candidate to become president without first winning in New Hampshire. In fact, in the last 40 years only Bill Clinton did not carry the New Hampshire primary.

11 Cash Uncle Sam's check. Candidates who receive many small contributions from many people qualify for matching federal funds. The money keeps coming until you gain less than 10 percent of the popular vote in two consecutive primaries and fail to win 20 percent in a subsequent primary.

Presidential Trivia
Of the 42 presidents…

19 were born in New York, Ohio, or Virginia
21 had fathers who were farmers or planters
1 had a father who was president
1 had a grandfather who was president
18 had 6 or more brothers and sisters
13 were the first-born in their families
41 were married
1 was divorced
6 were childless
1 had 15 children

Becoming President

How do you get to the White House?

?

18 Debate. Demonstrate your ability to think on your feet and show voters that you are fit to be a president.

19 Get out the vote any way you can. Stimulate volunteer efforts. Mailings, phone calls, and ads are expensive. And priceless. Meet the voters face to face. Do it while the cameras are rolling.

20 Return favors. Support your party's local candidates loyally if you expect party support to keep you afloat. Visit the cities and states where local elections are close to give your party's candidates a boost. Help them and they'll help you.

21 Sling mud but wear Teflon. Disparage your opponent's record and values carefully. Negative campaigning can backfire. Be prepared to counter low blows directed your way.

22 Target swing states. Don't waste time in states where you're likely to lose or where you have a strong lead. Go to the undecided states where electoral votes are plentiful and hit hard.

23 Don't stop running until the last vote is cast. Your official presidential campaign ends on Election Day—the Tuesday after the first Monday in November. Don't plan any time off until the race is over.

24 Get to work. The race was the easy part. Now it's time to make good on your promises so that four years from now, you can win the race all over again.

12 Make news. Stage events. Get yourself on TV nightly. With millions of voters watching TV, exposure is great for your campaign.

13 Secure your party's endorsement. Win enough primaries and demonstrate public support in opinion polls, and you'll have the endorsement locked up before you get to the national convention.

14 Unify the party. You'll need the support of your former opponents to finish the race. Make peace and pull the party together.

15 Craft a viable party platform. Choose issues that everyone loves and no one hates. It's harder than it sounds. Be prepared to make some compromises. Move to the middle of the road. Politically, Americans are largely similar. No extreme candidate can win. If you supported extreme positions to win attention early in the campaign, it's time to shift to a more moderate position. Make exciting promises.

16 Choose a running mate who can pull in extra votes, level out platform imbalances, and keep feet out of mouth.

17 Escape mainstream media. Find ways to talk directly to the voters. Appear on MTV or a talk show to avoid distortion of your ideas by news commentators or editors.

6 were in their 40s when they took office
26 were in their 50s when they took office
9 were in their 60s when they took office
1 was in his 70s when he took office

8 died in office
4 were assassinated
30 were college graduates
27 had military service
26 were lawyers
15 served as vice president
15 served as senators
19 served as representatives
16 served as state governors

13 were Democrats
17 were Republicans
1 was elected for a fourth term
1 was elected for a third term
14 were elected for a second term
9 who succeeded to the presidency were subsequently elected in their own right
2 were impeached
1 resigned

○ Code of Federal Regulations. Government Printing Office. U.S. www.access.gpo.gov/nara/cfr/ The Code of Federal Regulations (CFR) is a codification of the general and permanent rules published in the Federal Register by the Executive departments and agencies of the Federal Government.

Your vote counts—indirectly.

The president and vice president are elected by the states, not directly by your popular vote. When you vote for a presidential candidate, you are really voting for an elector in your home state, who in turn pledges to vote for a presidential and vice-presidential candidate. On election day, there are 51 separate elections (50 states plus the District of Columbia) to determine each state's electors.

This diagram shows how many electors each state has and how they voted in each election since 1960.

Source: Encyclopædia Britannica

Key
- Democrat
- Republican
- George C. Wallace
- Harry F. Byrd
- Outside party's endorsement

The number of electors is fixed at 538.

It will increase only if we add more states to the Union. The number of electors for each state is the same as the number of senators and representatives that state has—a reflection of the state's population. But the electors are not the same people as the members of Congress. Electors are selected for each election year by their respective political parties, usually as a reward for years of faithful service to the party.

Capture a majority.

To become president, a candidate needs 270 electoral votes—a simple majority of the 538 electors.

Winner takes all.

State contests are winner-take-all. The candidate with a majority of the popular vote gets all the electoral votes in the state. Winning the popular vote by even the slightest margin gives a candidate all the electoral votes for that state.

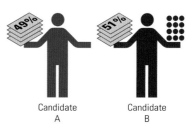

Candidate A   Candidate B

	CA	NY	TX	FL	PA	IL	OH	MI	NJ	NC	GA	V
1996 379 ● Clinton / 159 ● Dole												
1992 370 ● Clinton / 168 ● Bush												
1988 111 ● Dukakis / 426 ● **Bush** / 1 ● Bentsen												
1984 13 ● Mondale / 525 ● **Reagan**												
1980 49 ● Carter / 489 ● Reagan												
1976 297 ● **Carter** / 240 ● Ford / 1 ● Reagan												
1972 17 ● McGovern / 520 ● **Nixon** / 1 ● Hospers												
1968 191 ● Humphrey / 301 ● **Nixon** / 46 ● Wallace												
1964 486 ● **Johnson** / 52 ● Goldwater												
1960 303 ● **Kennedy** / 219 ● Nixon / 15 ● Byrd												

Win where it counts most.
Winning the 11 most populated states gives a candidate the 270 electoral votes needed to become president, so most candidates work hard to win these states.

The number of electors changes as states gain or lose population. For example, California, Florida, and Texas have grown over the past 40 years, while Illinois, New York, and Pennsylvania have lost electors.

All votes are not equal.
Another vote in a state that a candidate has already won isn't worth much. And neither is a vote in a state where a candidate trails and cannot possibly win. The most valuable votes are in states where the race is close and a small gain could tip the balance and give the candidate a majority. This is the reason that candidates invest their time and money in states where the race is close—especially if the state has a lot of electors.

Swing states can go either way in a presidential election. Swing states with many electoral votes attract the most attention from presidential candidates. In recent elections, Illinois, Michigan, Missouri, New Jersey, New York, Ohio, and Pennsylvania have been significant swing states.

Can the outcome of the electoral vote differ from the popular vote?
Yes. It's happened twice in our history. But it can't be off by much. Rutherford B. Hayes (1876) and Benjamin Harrison (1888) won enough electoral votes to become president even though their opponents had slightly more popular votes. The electoral system was developed to allow the states to select national leaders. It was not intended to match the popular vote exactly, every time.

Can a rogue elector vote for a candidate other than the one that carried his state?
Yes. It has occurred from time to time (look for the purple dots above), but it's never made any difference in an election. Typically, the party appoints an elector who is inclined to honor a pledge.

What happens if no candidate wins the 270 electoral votes needed to become president?
With three or more candidates, it is possible that none will have the 270 votes needed to win. In that case, the House of Representatives chooses the president and the Senate chooses the vice president.

Power to the states.

The founding fathers adopted the electoral system to give states an important say in national government and to make sure that not all the power went to the most populated states. The electoral system ensures that voters in states with small populations still have a significant voice. For example, Delaware, a state with a small population, has one elector for every 250,000 residents, but California, the most populous state, has one elector for every 600,000 residents.

Playing the game.

Presidential candidates recognize the nature of the electoral system when they plan their campaigns. They focus on states where the contest is close and pay special attention to states with lots of electoral votes.

The Electoral College

Does your vote count?

?

| MA | MO | TN | WA | WI | MD | MN | AL | LA | AZ | CO | CT | KY | OK | SC | IA | MS | OR | AR | KS | NE | NM | UT | WV | HI | ID | ME | NH | NV | RI | AK | DE | MT | ND | SD | VT | WY | DC |

In a rut.

Some states tend to support one party or the other in every presidential race. A candidate who thinks an opponent controls a given state will shift resources elsewhere.

Third parties

have a hard time breaking into the system. If a party forms around a faction that has split from one of the traditional parties, it tends to divide the vote and hand the election to the opposition. But, third parties can bring innovative ideas to the national agenda. Traditional parties are quick to co-opt popular ideas, neutralizing the threat of an independent party. For example, the initial plan for Social Security was proposed by the Socialist Party but was later adopted by the Democrats in an effort to win the 1932 election.

Independent candidates

can make strong showings but seldom have the resources to oppose major parties. The closest anyone has come recently was in 1968, when George Wallace split from the Democratic Party and won 46 electoral votes with his American Independent Party's platform (law and order, opposition to desegregation). In 1992, H. Ross Perot got nearly 20 percent of the popular vote, but because he failed to capture the majority in any state he didn't win a single electoral vote.

Are all states winner-take-all?

Not every state. Maine and Nebraska have their own versions of the electoral system, where the electors can split their votes. Occasionally, other states will split their electoral votes, but these splits have never altered the outcome of any election.

Why not change to a system based on popular votes?

Changes like this have been proposed, but they've gone nowhere. A purely popular vote would require even more widespread campaigning by candidates and might favor third parties at the expense of the traditional parties. Changes to the electoral system would require a constitutional amendment.

○ Federal Elections Commission. U.S.
www.fec.gov/
In 1975, Congress created the Federal Election Commission (FEC) to administer and enforce the Federal Election Campaign Act (FECA)—the statute that governs the financing of federal elections.

Lobbyists pull a lot of strings.
Lobbyists work for special interest groups. Their goals are to defeat legislation that is undesirable to their clients and to promote legislation that is favorable. They know everything about how the legislative process works and use every trick in the book. Lobbyists make sure legislators at the federal and state levels understand how the special interest group feels about specific laws and highlight the voting power and campaign contributions that the group can offer. They supply information, schmooze, threaten, and funnel campaign contributions.

Twenty to one.
Many lobbyists are part of big Washington firms that work for many different special interest groups at the same time. Estimates in 1998 put the number of active lobbyists at more than 11,000—more than 20 for every member of Congress. Many high-powered lobbyists are former members of Congress who have established contacts and understand how the system works.

What is a special interest group?
Any group of people with a shared interest is a special interest group (SIG). These groups organize and work energetically to influence lawmaking. SIGs can be organized into six types:
• Economic special interest groups are concerned about legislation that affects their business, trade, or union.
• Civic special interest groups focus on issues they think are right for the country. Consumer advocacy groups and environmental organizations are good examples.
• Governmental special interest groups look out for the interests of states and municipalities.

This diagram shows the activities of a lobbyist.
Sources: Federal Election Commission, Center for Responsive Politics

Key
Action ▮▮▮▶   Money ●●●▶

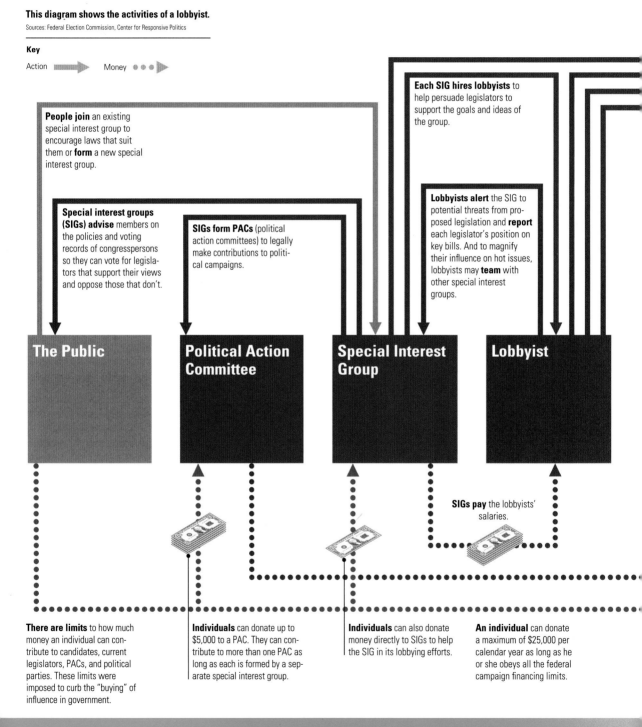

Each SIG hires lobbyists to help persuade legislators to support the goals and ideas of the group.

People join an existing special interest group to encourage laws that suit them or **form** a new special interest group.

Special interest groups (SIGs) advise members on the policies and voting records of congresspersons so they can vote for legislators that support their views and oppose those that don't.

SIGs form PACs (political action committees) to legally make contributions to political campaigns.

Lobbyists alert the SIG to potential threats from proposed legislation and **report** each legislator's position on key bills. And to magnify their influence on hot issues, lobbyists may **team** with other special interest groups.

The Public

Political Action Committee

Special Interest Group

Lobbyist

SIGs pay the lobbyists' salaries.

There are limits to how much money an individual can contribute to candidates, current legislators, PACs, and political parties. These limits were imposed to curb the "buying" of influence in government.

Individuals can donate up to $5,000 to a PAC. They can contribute to more than one PAC as long as each is formed by a separate special interest group.

Individuals can also donate money directly to SIGs to help the SIG in its lobbying efforts.

An individual can donate a maximum of $25,000 per calendar year as long as he or she obeys all the federal campaign financing limits.

The term "lobbyist" comes from the 19th century, when representatives of special interest groups gathered in the lobby of the Willard Hotel in Washington, D.C., to talk to members of Congress.

What makes a person a lobbyist?
A registered lobbyist must spend at least 20 percent of his or her time lobbying, work for a client paying more than $5,000, have multiple contacts with legislative staff, members of Congress, or high-level executive branch officials, and spend at least $20,500 over a semiannual period. Though unregistered, many other people also use lobbyist tactics and their own personal clout to influence government.

***Fortune*'s ranking of SIGs with the most clout:**
1 American Association of Retired Persons
2 American Israel Public Affairs Committee
3 National Federation of Independent Business
4 National Rifle Association of America
5 AFL-CIO of America
6 Association of Trial Lawyers of America
7 Christian Coalition
8 Credit Union National Association
9 National Right to Life Committee
10 American Medical Association

- Ideological special interest groups exist solely to promote the particular views of their members. The Christian Coalition and Americans for Democratic Action are examples.
- Civil rights special interest groups have been formed by groups that have historically faced legal discrimination or unfair opportunities. Examples include the National Association for the Advancement of Colored People (NAACP) and the National Organization of Women (NOW).
- Single-issue interest groups focus on one concern, for example Mothers Against Drunk Driving (MADD).

What is a political action committee?
A political action committee (PAC) is created by a SIG to legally raise and distribute money to candidates. A PAC is nothing more than a big bank account. PACs became a major element of political life after 1971, when campaign finance legislation limited the amount of money that an individual can contribute. Each PAC could contribute up to $5,000 to each candidate for each campaign (an individual can only give $1,000). To gain influence in government no matter who wins, some PACs contribute to both sides in a close race.

Lobbying

What does a lobbyist do? What is a special interest group? What is a political action committee?

?

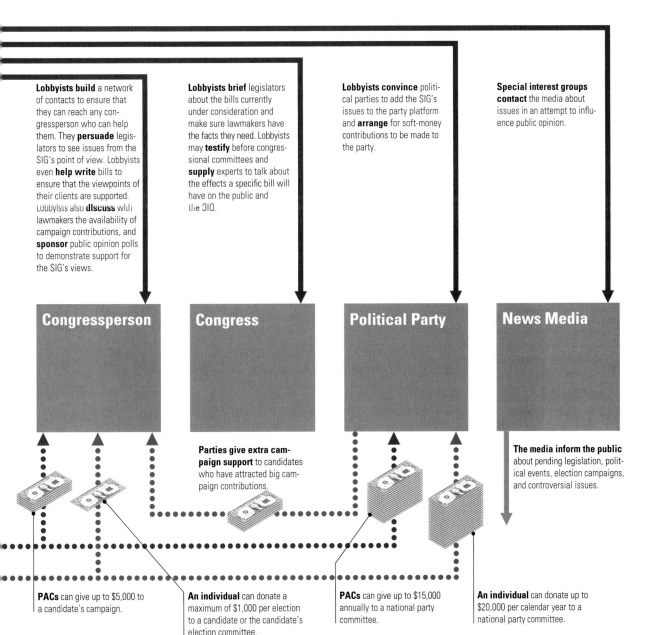

Lobbyists build a network of contacts to ensure that they can reach any congressperson who can help them. They **persuade** legislators to see issues from the SIG's point of view. Lobbyists even **help write** bills to ensure that the viewpoints of their clients are supported. Lobbyists also **discuss** with lawmakers the availability of campaign contributions, and **sponsor** public opinion polls to demonstrate support for the SIG's views.

Lobbyists brief legislators about the bills currently under consideration and make sure lawmakers have the facts they need. Lobbyists may **testify** before congressional committees and **supply** experts to talk about the effects a specific bill will have on the public and the SIG.

Lobbyists convince political parties to add the SIG's issues to the party platform and **arrange** for soft-money contributions to be made to the party.

Special interest groups contact the media about issues in an attempt to influence public opinion.

Congressperson

Congress

Political Party

News Media

Parties give extra campaign support to candidates who have attracted big campaign contributions.

The media inform the public about pending legislation, political events, election campaigns, and controversial issues.

PACs can give up to $5,000 to a candidate's campaign.

An individual can donate a maximum of $1,000 per election to a candidate or the candidate's election committee.

PACs can give up to $15,000 annually to a national party committee.

An individual can donate up to $20,000 per calendar year to a national party committee.

What is the difference between hard money and soft money?
The amount of money that can be given to a candidate legally by an individual or a PAC is limited. That's hard money. It must be declared and reported. But there is a way to throw more money behind a candidate. Soft money gets around the limits imposed on hard money by allowing individuals, corporations, and unions to help a candidate by contributing to the candidate's party.

Do campaign contributions end up in the candidate's pocket?
Not very often. There are too many people watching, inside and outside the party, to get away with it easily. And for most candidates, it is much more important to win than it is to put away a few dollars. Some candidates go deeply in debt to keep their campaign rolling.

Do foreign countries lobby our government?
Yes. In 1998, there were more than 500 active agents. Foreign agents are lobbyists working on behalf of a foreign country, corporation, or industry. Foreign interests can hire a U.S. lobbyist or send one from their country. These lobbyists may be seeking economic or political support, promoting business expansion into their country, or marketing their goods and services to the U.S.

Navaho weaving, circa 1975 from the collection of Kit Hinrichs

Clement Mok

Economics of Raising a Child
What are the costs involved in raising a child?

Children at Risk
What factors influence a child's well-being? Who is at risk?
And where are they?

Domestic Violence & Child Abuse
How common are these problems?

Baby Boom Echo
What characterizes this generation of teens?

K-12 Schools
Who attends school? Who completes high school?
And what are the costs associated with it?

Literacy
What is literacy? And what is its impact?

Affirmative Action
Has affirmative action worked?

Technology in the Classroom
Who has access? How is it being used? Is it effective?

The Cost of Higher Education
Who's educated? And at what cost?

Higher Education
What are people studying?

Suicide
What causes suicide? How frequently does it occur? Who's at risk?

The cost of raising a child born in 1997

What is the cost of educating a child to age 21?

What is the average amount of income a person forgoes while raising a child from birth to age 21?

Estimated Cumulative Expenditures

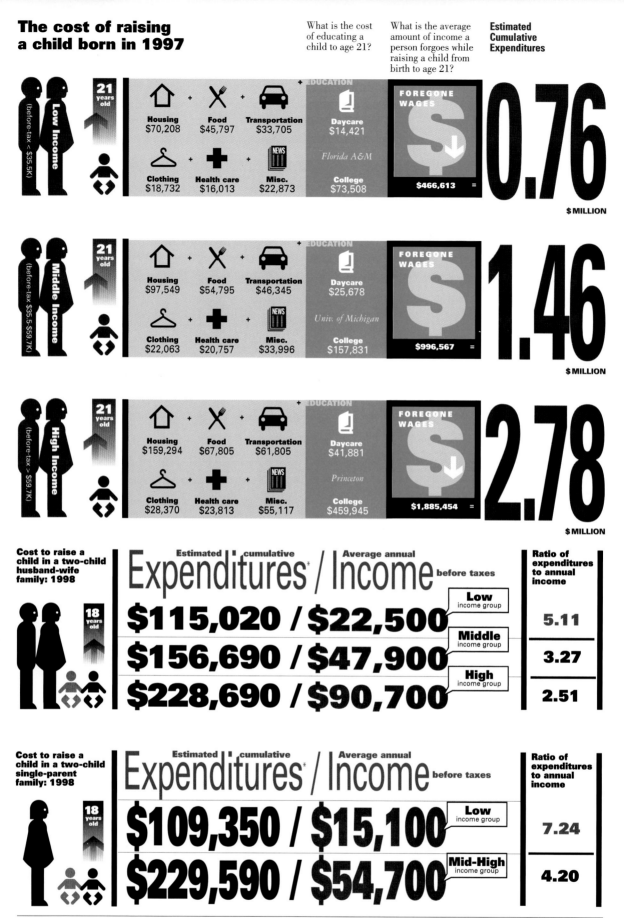

Low Income (before-tax < $35.5K) — 21 years old

Housing $70,208	Food $45,797	Transportation $33,705
Clothing $18,732	Health care $16,013	Misc. $22,873

EDUCATION
Daycare $14,421
Florida A&M College $73,508

FOREGONE WAGES $466,613 =

$0.76 $MILLION

Middle Income (before-tax $35.5-$59.7K) — 21 years old

Housing $97,549	Food $54,795	Transportation $46,345
Clothing $22,063	Health care $20,757	Misc. $33,996

EDUCATION
Daycare $25,678
Univ. of Michigan College $157,831

FOREGONE WAGES $996,567 =

$1.46 $MILLION

High Income (before-tax > $59.7K) — 21 years old

Housing $159,294	Food $67,805	Transportation $61,805
Clothing $28,370	Health care $23,813	Misc. $55,117

EDUCATION
Daycare $41,881
Princeton College $459,945

FOREGONE WAGES $1,885,454 =

$2.78 $MILLION

Cost to raise a child in a two-child husband-wife family: 1998 — 18 years old

Estimated ▪ cumulative **Expenditures*** / **Income** Average annual — before taxes

Expenditures* / Income	Income group	Ratio of expenditures to annual income
$115,020 / $22,500	Low income group	5.11
$156,690 / $47,900	Middle income group	3.27
$228,690 / $90,700	High income group	2.51

Cost to raise a child in a two-child single-parent family: 1998 — 18 years old

Estimated ▪ cumulative **Expenditures*** / **Income** Average annual — before taxes

Expenditures* / Income	Income group	Ratio of expenditures to annual income
$109,350 / $15,100	Low income group	7.24
$229,590 / $54,700	Mid-High income group	4.20

*Estimates are based on 1990-92 Consumer Expenditure Survey data updated to 1998 dollars using the Consumer Price Index. The figures represent estimated expenditures on the younger child in a two-child family. Estimates are about the same for the older child. To estimate expenditures for an only child, multiply the total expenditures by 1.24. To estimate expenditures for each child in a family with three or more children, multiply the total expense for each by approximately 0.77.

❑ According to one government calculation, the direct cost of raising a child to age 18 has risen by 20% since 1960 (adjusted for inflation and changes in family size).

❑ Only 19% of all fertility treatments actually produced a take-home baby—averaging $8,000 a try. It's not uncommon for infertile couples to spend $50,000 or more in pursuit of pregnancy.

Economics of Raising a Child

What are the costs involved in raising a child?

?

Though statistics indicate that higher income earners can afford children more easily, their level of forgone wages is quite steep. In fact, statistics show that middle-aged women with graduate degrees are over three times more likely to be childless than those who dropped out of high school. Similarly, two-income married couples earning over $75,000 are 70% more likely to be childless than those earning under $20,000.

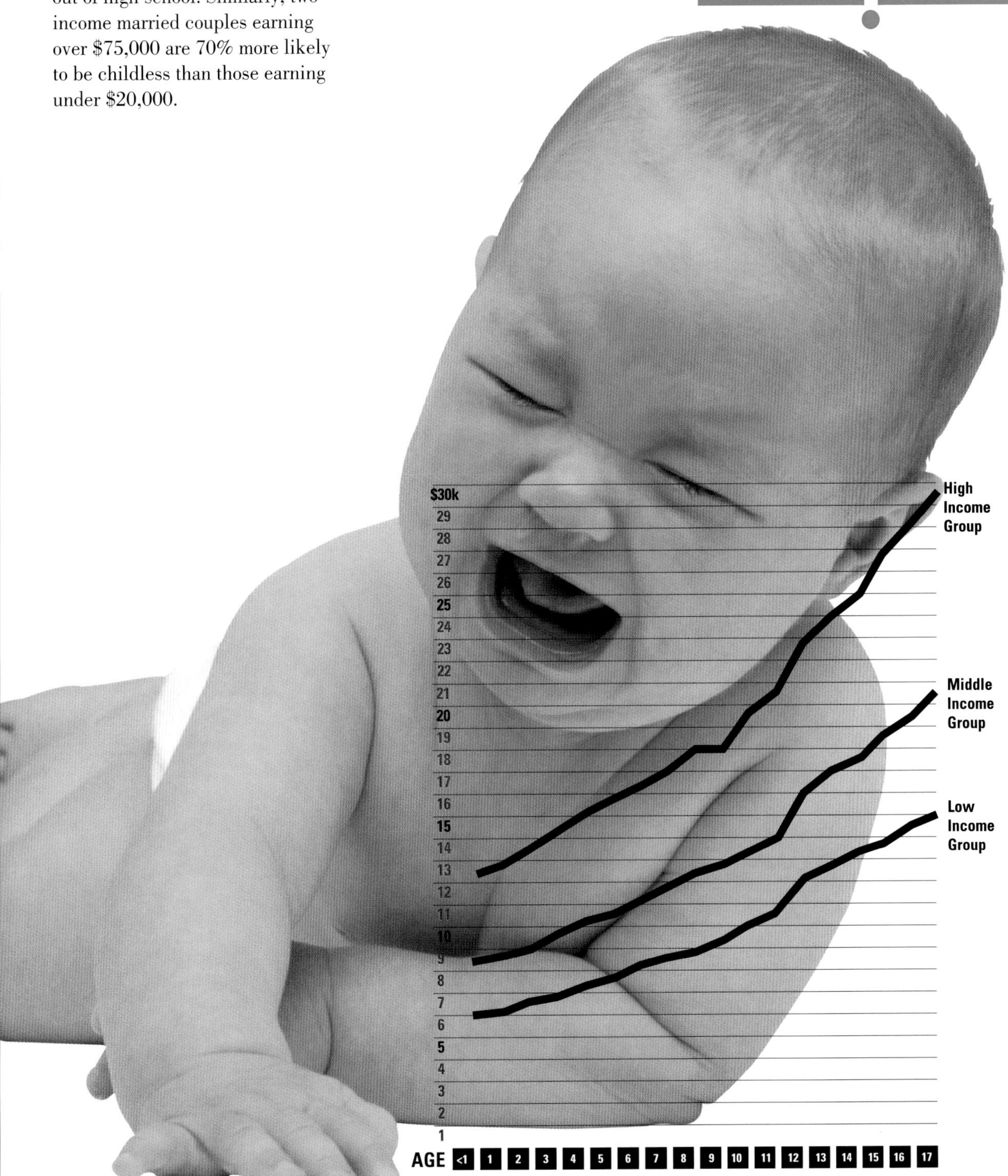

High Income Group

Middle Income Group

Low Income Group

| $30k |
| 29 |
| 28 |
| 27 |
| 26 |
| 25 |
| 24 |
| 23 |
| 22 |
| 21 |
| 20 |
| 19 |
| 18 |
| 17 |
| 16 |
| 15 |
| 14 |
| 13 |
| 12 |
| 11 |
| 10 |
| 9 |
| 8 |
| 7 |
| 6 |
| 5 |
| 4 |
| 3 |
| 2 |
| 1 |

AGE <1 1 2 3 4 5 6 7 8 9 10 11 12 13 14 15 16 17

Estimated annual expenditures*on children born in 1998

❑ According to the March of Dimes, the lifetime health costs of a child born with cerebral palsy, average **$503,000**; with Down's syndrome, **$451,000**; and with spina bifida, **$294,000**.

Compared to the average cost of keeping a middle-class child born in 1997 healthy to age 18, the health costs of a disabled child are 10 to 20 times higher.

32%

of children are being raised by a single parent.

One of the attributes of strong families, time together, is likely to be diminished since the time that a single parent has to nurture, monitor, care for, and guide children is inevitably limited.

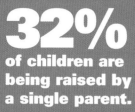

19%

of children are growing up with a head of household who has not graduated from high school.

Studies broadly indicate that the less education a mother has, the less likely that her young child will be read-to at home or be fully ready for school. Children born to a mother who has less than a high school diploma are now twice as likely to drop out of school as the children of a mother who is a high school graduate.

21%

of children are growing up in poverty.

Children who grow up poor are more likely to become teen-age parents, drop out of high school, and be unemployed as young adults. Families with more financial resources are able to give their children a far broader range of experiences, which increases their access to opportunities.

Teenage childbearing is problematic because it often diminishes the opportunities of both the child and young mother. Births to teenage mothers under age 18 are particularly troublesome because most of the these mothers are unmarried and have not completed high school. Their children are ten times more likely to live in poverty.

12%

of children are growing up in households that rely on public assistance.

Chronic dependence on public assistance has been shown to undermine parental self-esteem and efficacy. Over time, many parents who rely on welfare reveal a diminished sense of control over their own lives and the lives of their children. In some instances, parents begin to feel that there is no alternative to public support, thus accommodating themselves and their children to an expectation of dependence.

28%

of children are living with parents who do not have full-time, year-round employment.

Working parents serve as influential role models and impart the value of work and earning to their children. Beyond the dignity-enhancing value of work, when a parent has secure employment, children learn earlier and more broadly about the world of work and career and enlarge their own sense of adult possibilities.

20+% under the national average	
0-20% under the national average	
0-20% over the national average	
20+% over the national average	
Key	
Rank 40-51	
Rank 30-39	
Rank 14-30	
Rank 1-14	

Children who are living in families with four or more risk factors are considered "High Risk."

They represent

13%

of the population of children.

The 1999 National Composite Rank is each state's standing on the condition of children from best(1) to worst (51). The rankings are based on low-birth-weight babies; infant mortality; child deaths; teen deaths by accdent; homicide, and suicide; teen birthrate; high school dropout rate; teen unemployment; parental unemployment; children in poverty; and single parent households.

"1999 Kids Count Data Book," The Annie F. Casey Foundation

America's Children at Risk. Census Brief. Dept. of Commerce. Census Bureau. U.S. www.census.gov/prod/3/97pubs/cb-9702.pgf Brief Census report on the variety of risks facing children in the United States. Includes social, education and economic factors.

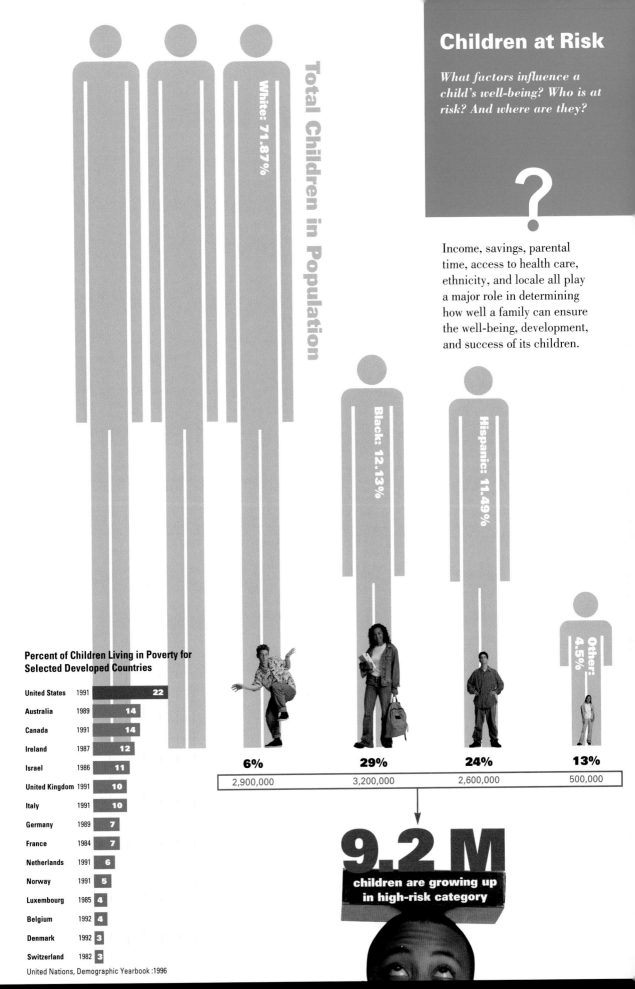

Children at Risk

What factors influence a child's well-being? Who is at risk? And where are they?

?

Income, savings, parental time, access to health care, ethnicity, and locale all play a major role in determining how well a family can ensure the well-being, development, and success of its children.

Total Children in Population

White: 71.87%

Black: 12.13%

Hispanic: 11.49%

Other: 4.5%

6%	**29%**	**24%**	**13%**
2,900,000	3,200,000	2,600,000	500,000

9.2 M
children are growing up in high-risk category

Percent of Children Living in Poverty for Selected Developed Countries

United States	1991	22
Australia	1989	14
Canada	1991	14
Ireland	1987	12
Israel	1986	11
United Kingdom	1991	10
Italy	1991	10
Germany	1989	7
France	1984	7
Netherlands	1991	6
Norway	1991	5
Luxembourg	1985	4
Belgium	1992	4
Denmark	1992	3
Switzerland	1982	3

United Nations, Demographic Yearbook :1996

❏ Only **17%** or 1.5 million of California's children are vulnerable, while **39%** of children living in the District of Columbia are in the high-

❏ The percentage of children in poverty is perhaps the most global and widely used indicator of child well-being. Despite the enormous wealth

rate is the highest among 17 developed countries. Our poverty rate is 50% higher than the next highest rate.

Researchers have long been aware of the link between domestic violence and child abuse. Even if children are witnesses to acts of violence rather than the intended targets, they can be affected in the same way as children who are physically and/or sexually abused. Since domestic violence is a pattern of behavior, not a single event, episodes may become more severe and more frequent over time, resulting in an increased likelihood that the children will eventually become victims.

Domestic violence often includes child abuse. Children may be victimized and threatened as a way of punishing and controlling the victim of domestic violence.

● The Violence Against Women Act: Breaking the Cycle of Violence. Executive Summary. Violence Against Women Office. Dept. of Justice. U.S. www.usdoj.gov/vawo/cycle.htm The Violence Against Women Act is landmark legislation—combining tough law enforcement strategies with important safeguards for victims of domestic violence and sexual assault.

❏ **Domestic Violence**
Recent surveys indicate that increased public awareness about domestic violence has encouraged women to come forward. Surveys indicate that approximately 30% of women have faced some form of abuse. Reported perpetrators of child abuse are equally divided among men and women, but the majority of perpetrators of domestic violence are men.

3,000,000⁺ reported cases

or 47 out of every 1,000 U.S. children were reported as victims of child maltreatment in 1997.

Reports of child abuse have increased 41% between 1988 and 1997. Experts attribute much of the increase in reporting to greater public awareness of and willingness to report child maltreatment, as well as changes in how states collect reports of maltreatment.

1,054,000 confirmed cases

or 15 out of every 1,000 U.S. children were abused in 1997.

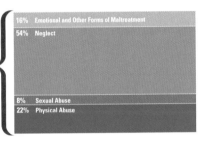

16%	Emotional and Other Forms of Maltreatment
54%	Neglect
8%	Sexual Abuse
22%	Physical Abuse

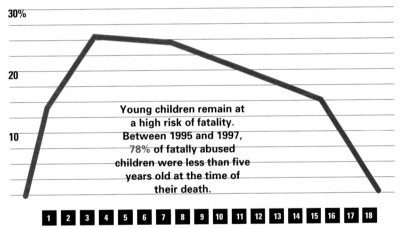

30%

20

10

Young children remain at a high risk of fatality. Between 1995 and 1997, 78% of fatally abused children were less than five years old at the time of their death.

| 1 | 2 | 3 | 4 | 5 | 6 | 7 | 8 | 9 | 10 | 11 | 12 | 13 | 14 | 15 | 16 | 17 | 18 |

Age of Victims

Based on information from 18 states, reports of abuse in day care, foster care, or other institutional care settings represented about 3% of all confirmed cases of child maltreatment in 1997.

Children from families with annual an income below $15,000 were 22 times more likely to experience maltreatment compared to children from families with an annual income above $30,000.

❑ Child Fatalities

Using 1996 statistics provided by children protective service (CPS) agencies, it is estimated that more than three children die each day as a result of child abuse or

41%

of these deaths are children known to CPS agencies as current or prior cases.

Extreme Child Poverty Rises Sharply in 1997. Children's Defense Fund. www.childrensdefense.org/publications/extremepoverty.html
An examination of recent welfare reforms and their impact on children in poverty.

Ethnically Diverse

Teens are more ethnically diverse than the overall U.S. population. The percent of Hispanic teens, African American teens and Asian American teens are all above the national average.

% U.S. Population

% Teenage Population

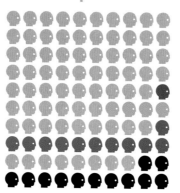

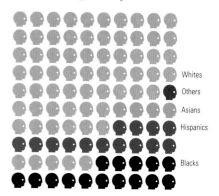

Whites
Others
Asians
Hispanics
Blacks

Number of Births

4.0M

Where does the money teens spend come from?

Part-time job	26%
Asking parents	25%
Allowance	22%
Household chores	11%
Baby sitting	10%
Gifts	6%

3.0

2.0

$141,000,0

Richest Generation Ever

According to a Rand Youth Poll, spending by teens has increased every year since 1953 despite eight recessions and a fluctuating teen population. Teenage Research Unlimited (TRU) reports that teens collectively spent $93 billion of their own funds (allowances, gifts, employment, etc.) and $47 billion of family money.

1.0

'44

'54   **Baby Boom**   '64

❑ During the school year 39% of all teens between 15 and 17 work an average of 18 hours each week. During summertime, 59% of teens work either full-time or part-time.

❑ By the time they graduate from high school 80% of all teens will have had at least one job (usually part-time).

❑ Today teens spend average of 51 minutes a day doing homework, down from 70 minutes a decade ago.

Teens have the highest percentage of Internet users, with 89.2% having already been online. According to *Newsweek*, 77% of all teens would rather look something up on the Internet than in a book. At present, more male teens use the Internet than female teens. On average, teens surf the Internet 5.1 hours per week primarily at home, at school, and at their friends' homes.

Baby Boom Echo

What characterizes this generation of teens?

?

TEENAGERS

Despite much recent attention, the population of teens (ages 12–17) as of July 1, 1999 is only

8.6%

of the American population.

000,000 spent in '98

❏ By the time they enter college, 40% of teens will have their own vehicle.

❏ Over 10% of all high school students have a credit card (co-signed by a parent), and 55% of all teens have a telephone calling card.

Average spending per pupil in public elementary and secondary school, 1997 ($ Thousands)

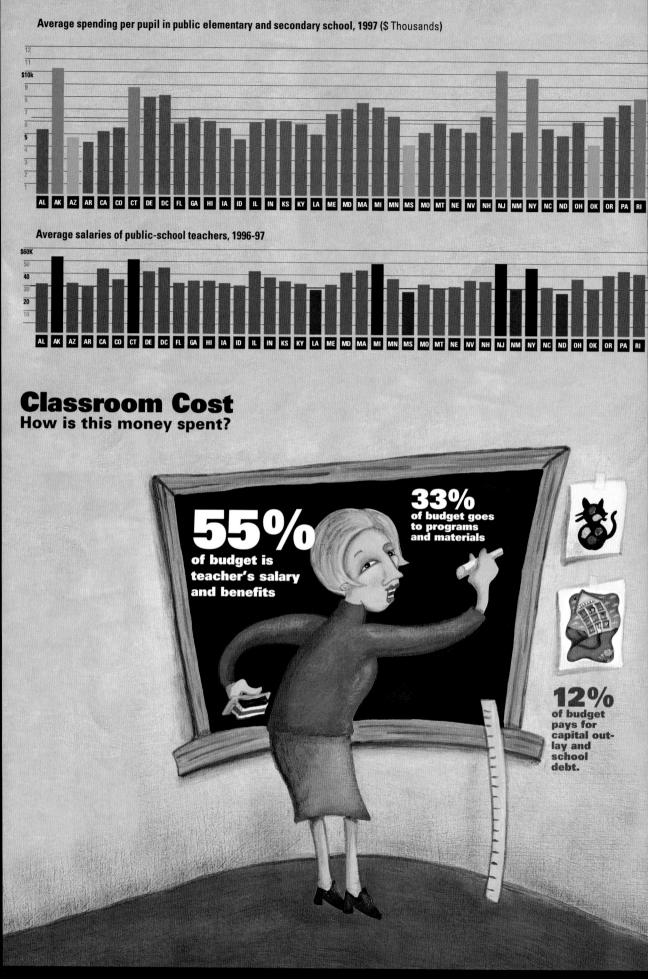

States (x-axis): AL AK AZ AR CA CO CT DE DC FL GA HI IA ID IL IN KS KY LA ME MD MA MI MN MS MO MT NE NV NH NJ NM NY NC ND OH OK OR PA RI

Average salaries of public-school teachers, 1996-97

States (x-axis): AL AK AZ AR CA CO CT DE DC FL GA HI IA ID IL IN KS KY LA ME MD MA MI MN MS MO MT NE NV NH NJ NM NY NC ND OH OK OR PA RI

Classroom Cost
How is this money spent?

55% of budget is teacher's salary and benefits

33% of budget goes to programs and materials

12% of budget pays for capital outlay and school debt.

⬤ Dept. of Education. U.S.
www.ed.gov
The lead agency in the U.S. federal government dealing with education policies and programs.

❏ Teachers' salaries rose 19% from 1980 to 1997. Virtually all of this increase occurred during the mid-80s. Since 1991, the average teacher's salary actually fell slightly, after adjusting for inflation.

❏ The number of minority students increased 5% between 1986 and 1996. Hispanics account for 3.5% of the increase, while Blacks account for less than one half of 1%.

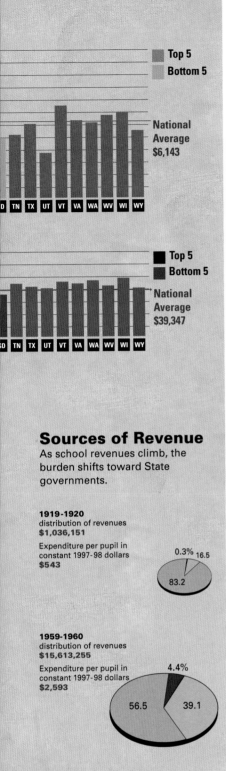

National Average $6,143

D TN TX UT VT VA WA WV WI WY

- Top 5
- Bottom 5

National Average $39,347

D TN TX UT VT VA WA WV WI WY

- Top 5
- Bottom 5

Sources of Revenue

As school revenues climb, the burden shifts toward State governments.

1919-1920
distribution of revenues
$1,036,151

Expenditure per pupil in constant 1997-98 dollars
$543

0.3% 16.5
83.2

1959-1960
distribution of revenues
$15,613,255

Expenditure per pupil in constant 1997-98 dollars
$2,593

4.4%
56.5 39.1

1995-1996
distribution of revenues
$293,610,849

Expenditure per pupil in constant 1997-98 dollars
$7,287

Federal
6.6%

Local
45.9

State
47.5

One out of 50 children is educated at home

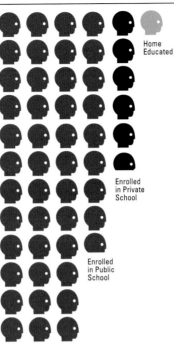

Home Educated

Enrolled in Private School

Enrolled in Public School

Private schools saw largest gain in pupil-teacher ratio

1960

1 : 25.8 — Public School
1 : 30.7 — Private School

1990

1 : 17.2 — Public School
1 : 14.7 — Private School

K-12 Schools

Who attends school? Who completes high school? And what are the costs associated with it?

?

Just 50 years ago, the number of high school graduates among 17-year-olds was only 59%. In recent decades, graduation increased dramatically. For the 1989-90 school year, 74.2% graduated – a total of 2,587,000 students. Vermont ranks the highest with 89%, and South Carolina ranks the lowest with 54.4%.

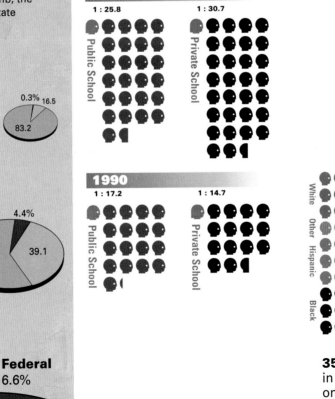

White · Other · Hispanic · Black

35.1% of the population in elementary and secondary school is made up of minorities–blacks, hispanics, and others.

7%

percentage of **white** high school dropouts among 16- to 24-year-olds. (1996)

13%

percentage of **black** high school dropouts among 16- to 24-year-olds. (1996)

29.4%

percentage **hispanic** high school dropouts among 16- to 24-year-olds. (1996)

20%

of adults read at or below 5th grade level.

Quantitative Literacy

The knowledge and skills required to apply arithmetic operations, either alone or sequentially, to numbers embedded in printed materials such as balancing a checkbook, figuring out a tip, or determining the interest on a loan from an advertisement.

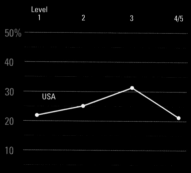

Percentage of adult population... *...at each quantitative literacy level,*

❑ Dropouts experience the most unemployment, with a 10% average, compared to an average unemployment rate of 2.5% for those with college degrees.

Mean monthly income

$452

without a high school diploma

Mean monthly income

$1,829

with a bachelor's degree

$790M

was spent in 1999 by the federal government on adult education and family literacy — a substantial increase over the previous year when it spent $484 million. This is in addition to the $958 million spent by state and local governments.

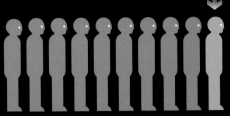

1.5M **Adult Basic Education**
(below 8th grade skill level)

0.9M **Adult Secondary Education**
(8th -12th grade skill level)

1.6M **English as a Second Language**

One out of every ten people of the 40+ million adults with literacy needs is enrolled in a program that assists them in improving their skills.

Literacy

What is literacy? And what is its impact?

In the past, literacy was considered the ability to read at a very basic level. Today, the world is changing in ways that demand and reward greater knowledge and skills. The global economy, the Internet, NAFTA, and other developments have changed what it means to be literate.

Document Literacy

The knowledge and skills required to locate and use information in different formats, such as job applications, payroll forms, transportation schedules, maps, tables, and charts.

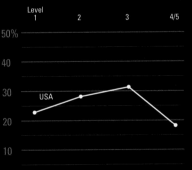

...at each document literacy level,

Prose Literacy

The knowledge and skills needed to understand and use information from printed texts, including editorials, news stories, poems, and fiction.

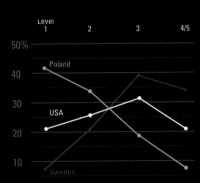

...and at each prose literacy level,

Literacy is defined more broadly to include applying reading, writing, and math skills to obtain and use information and solve problems. Literacy is not something people have or don't have. Rather, it is a range or continuum of skills that help people function in daily life, with individuals falling at different places on that continuum.

	1	2	3	Level 4/5
Sweden	7.5	20.3	39.7	34.2
Netherlands	10.5	30.1	44.1	15.3
Germany	14.4	34.2	38.0	13.4
Canada	16.6	25.6	35.1	22.7
Australia	17.0	27.1	36.9	18.9
Switzerland (French)	17.6	33.7	38.6	10.0
Belgium (Flanders)	18.4	28.2	39.0	14.3
New Zealand	18.4	27.3	35.0	19.2
Switzerland (German)	19.3	35.7	36.0	8.9
USA	20.7	25.9	32.4	21.1
United Kingdom	21.8	30.3	31.3	16.6
Ireland	22.6	29.8	34.1	13.5
Poland	42.6	34.5	19.8	3.1

● National Center for Education Statistics. Dept. of Education. U.S.
nces.ed.gov/
NCES is the primary federal entity for collecting and analyzing data that are related to education in the United States and other nations.

43%

of people with the lowest literacy skills live in poverty. 17% receive food stamps, and 70% have no job or a part-time job.

● Educational Resources Information Center. National Library of Education. Dept. of Education. U.S.
www.accesseric.org/
A national information system designed to provide users with ready access to an extensive body of education-related literature.

Myth: The only way to create a color-blind society is to adopt color-blind policies. **Fact:** Although this assertion sounds intuitively plausible, the reality is that color-blind policies often put racial minorities at a disadvantage. For instance, all else being equal, color-blind seniority systems tend to protect white workers against job layoffs, because senior employees are usually white. Likewise, color-blind college admissions favor white students because of their earlier educational advantages. Unless pre-existing inequities are corrected or otherwise taken into account, color-blind policies do not eliminate racial injustice – they reinforce it.

Myth: Affirmative action may have been necessary 30 years ago, but the playing field is fairly level today. **Fact:** Despite the progress that has been made, the playing field is far from level. Women still earn 74 cents for every male dollar. Black people have twice the unemployment rate of white people, half the median family income, and half the proportion of those who attend four years or more of college. In fact, without affirmative action the percentage of black students on many campuses would drop below 2%. This would effectively choke off black people's access to higher education and severely restrict progress toward racial equality.

Myth: Affirmative action is nothing more than an attempt at social engineering by liberal Democrats. **Fact:** In truth, affirmative action programs have spanned seven different presidential administrations – four Republican and three Democratic. Although the originating document of affirmative action was President Johnson's Executive Order 11246, the policy was significantly expanded in 1969 by President Nixon and then Secretary of Labor George Shultz. President Bush also enthusiastically signed the Civil Rights Act of 1991, which formally endorsed the principle of affirmative action. Thus, despite the current split along party lines, affirmative action has traditionally enjoyed the support of Republicans as well as Democrats.

Myth: The public doesn't support affirmative action anymore. **Fact:** This myth is based largely on opinion polls that offer an all-or-none choice between affirmative action as it currently exists and no affirmative action at all. When intermediate choices are added, surveys show that most people want to maintain some form of affirmative action. A recent Time/CNN poll found that 80% of the public felt "affirmative action programs for minorities and women should be continued at some level." What the public opposes are quotas, set asides, and "reverse discrimination." For example, when the same poll asked people whether they favored programs "requiring businesses to hire a specific number or quota of minorities and women," 63% opposed such a plan As these results suggest, most members of the public oppose extreme forms of affirmative action that violate notions of procedural justice – they do not oppose affirmative action itself.

Myth: Support for affirmative action means support for preferential selection procedures that favor unqualified candidates over qualified candidates. **Fact:** Although affirmative action is sometimes mistakenly equated with this form of preferential treatment, federal regulations explicitly prohibit affirmative action programs in which unqualified or unneeded employees are hired. In fact, most supporters of affirmative action actually oppose this form of preferential selection and instead support a selection process in which a female or minority candidate is chosen from a pool of equally qualified applicants (e.g., students with identical college entrance scores).

Myth: A large percentage of white workers will lose out if affirmative action is continued. **Fact:** Government statistics don't support this myth. According to the Commerce Department, there are fewer than two million unemployed black civilians and more than 100 million employed white civilians. Even if every unemployed black worker were to displace a white worker, less than two percent of whites would be affected. Furthermore, affirmative action pertains only to job-qualified applicants, so the actual percentage of affected whites would be a fraction of a percent. The main sources of job loss among white workers have to do with factory relocations and labor contracting outside the U.S., computerization and automation, and corporate downsizing.

Myth: Affirmative action tends to undermine the self-esteem of women and racial minorities. **Fact:** Although affirmative action may have this effect in some cases, interview studies and public opinion surveys suggest that such reactions are rare. For instance, a recent Gallup Poll asked employed blacks and employed white women whether they had ever felt that others questioned their abilities because of affirmative action. Nearly 90% of respondents said no (which is understandable – after all, white men, who have traditionally benefited from preferential hiring, do not feel hampered by self-doubt or a loss of self-esteem). Indeed, in many cases affirmative action may actually raise the self-esteem of women and minorities by providing them with employment and opportunities for advancement. There is also evidence that affirmative action policies increase job satisfaction and organizational commitment among beneficiaries.

Excerpted from S. Plous. "Ten Myths About Affirmative Action," *Journal of Social Issues*, Winter 1996, Vol.52, Issue 4, pp. 25-31, www.socialpsychology.org/affirm.htm

❏ For every dollar earned by men, women as a whole earn 74 cents, African American women earn 63 cents, and Latina women earn 57 cents.

● Policy.com. Issue of the Week, 2/22/99: Affirmative Action in Focus. www.policy.com/issuewk/1999/0222_58/index.html
Issues and debate about affirmative action.

❏ Women and minorities make up two-thirds of the population and 57% of the workforce, yet they account for only 3% of senior management positions at Fortune 1000 industrial corporations.

Myth: If Jewish people and Asian Americans can rapidly advance economically, African Americans should be able to do the same.
Fact: This comparison ignores the unique history of discrimination against black people in America. As historian Roger Wilkins has pointed out, blacks have a 375-year history on this continent: 245 of those involving slavery, 100 involving legalized discrimination, and only 30 involving anything else. Jews and Asians, on the other hand, have immigrated to North America – often as doctors, lawyers, professors, entrepreneurs, and so forth. Moreover, European Jews are able to function as part of the white majority. To expect blacks to show the same upward mobility as Jews and Asian Americans is to deny the historical and social reality that black people face.

Myth: You can't cure discrimination with discrimination. **Fact:** The problem with this myth is that it uses the same word – discrimination – to describe two very different things. Job discrimination is grounded in prejudice and exclusion, whereas affirmative action is an effort to overcome prejudicial treatment through inclusion. The most effective way to cure society of exclusionary practices is to make special efforts at inclusion, which is exactly what affirmative action does. The logic of affirmative action is no different from the logic of treating a nutritional deficiency with vitamin supplements. For a healthy person, high doses of vitamin supplements may be unnecessary or even harmful, but for a person whose system is out of balance, supplements are an efficient way to restore the body's balance.

Myth: Affirmative action has not succeeded in increasing female and minority representation. **Fact:** Several studies have documented important gains in racial and gender equality as a direct result of affirmative action. For example, according to a recent report from the Labor Department, affirmative action has helped five million minority members and six million white and minority women move up in the workforce. Likewise, a study sponsored by the Office of Federal Contract Compliance Programs showed that between 1974 and 1980 federal contractors, who were required to adopt affirmative action goals, added black and female officials and managers at twice the rate of noncontractors. There have also been a number of well-publicized cases in which large companies (e.g., AT&T, IBM, Sears Roebuck) increased minority employment as a result of adopting affirmative action policies.

● Affirmative Action Review: Report to the President. Executive Office of the President. U.S.
www.whitehouse.gov/WH/EOP/OP/html/aa/aa-index.html
On March 7, 1995, President Clinton directed that a review be conducted of the Federal government's affirmative action programs. This is the report based on that review.

❏ A Gallup Poll conducted in 1997 found that 67% of those polled, and 65% of whites, support reserving some college openings for black students when not doing so would mean that

blacks would be badly under-represented on campus. 74% agree that affirmative action means "making equal opportunities for everyone including women and minorities."

Internet Access
1997-98

CLASSROOM LOCAL AREA NETWORK * CLASSROOM

➤ Schools have begun to provide Internet access throughout their buildings, rather than just linking together the more centralized locations such as the library/media center or computer lab.

WHILE THE MAJORITY OF SCHOOLS HAVE INTERNET ACCESS IN THE LIBRARY

THE GREATEST GROWTH IN TERMS OF LOCATION OF INTERNET ACCESS OCCURRED IN CLASSROOMS AND ADMIN

Technology penetration in schools

% of Public Schools

	%
CD-ROM	97%
Internet	85%
LAN	78%
Cable	76%
Modem	66%
Videodisc	60%
WAN	44%
Satellite	29%

... in classrooms

% of Classrooms

	%
Computers	75%
LAN	54%
Internet	44%

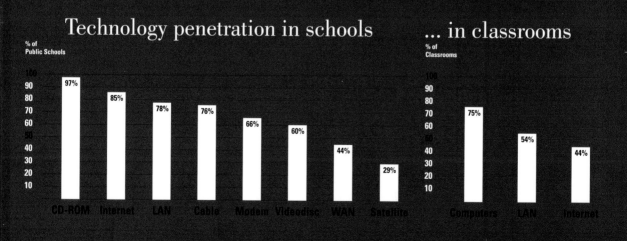

Educational Technology Office. Dept. of Education. U.S.
www.ed.gov/Technology/
Agency encourages and supports federal programs designed to improve technology services throughout the American education system.

58%
of schools have access to the Internet from at least one classroom.

70%
of schools have access to the Internet from a library/media center.

Technology in the Classroom

Who has access? How is it being used? Is it effective?

"How much do you think computers have helped improve student learning?"

31% said a great amount

54% said a great amount

Teachers

General Public

"I thought computers would be better than television. I had high hopes — and I came back with huge disillusionment. In fact, I was horrified with what I saw in schools and people's homes. We have jumped into [education technology] way too soon."

— **Jane Healy,**
Educational psychologist and author of
Failure to Connect: How Computers Affect Our Children's Minds — for Better and Worse

Computers and Internet connections are fast becoming standard features of the American public school, but many teachers do not make regular use of them for teaching. This problem is created by some school districts that put computers into classrooms without showing teachers how to use them.

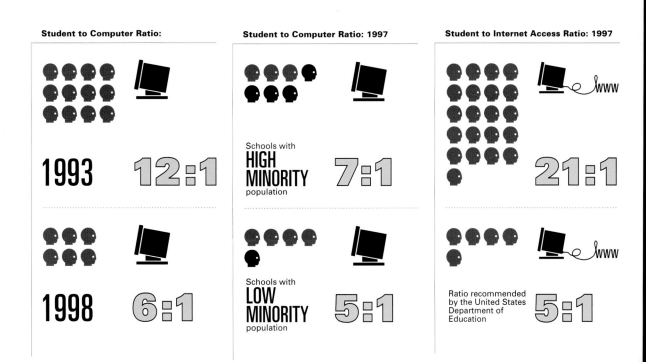

Student to Computer Ratio:

1993 — 12:1

1998 — 6:1

Student to Computer Ratio: 1997

Schools with **HIGH MINORITY** population — 7:1

Schools with **LOW MINORITY** population — 5:1

Student to Internet Access Ratio: 1997

21:1

Ratio recommended by the United States Department of Education — 5:1

81% of teachers surveyed were either beginners in using technology or at an intermediate level.

7% of teachers surveyed were advanced enough in their technology skills that they could integrate technology into their curriculum.

14% of teachers surveyed use the Internet for "instructional purposes."

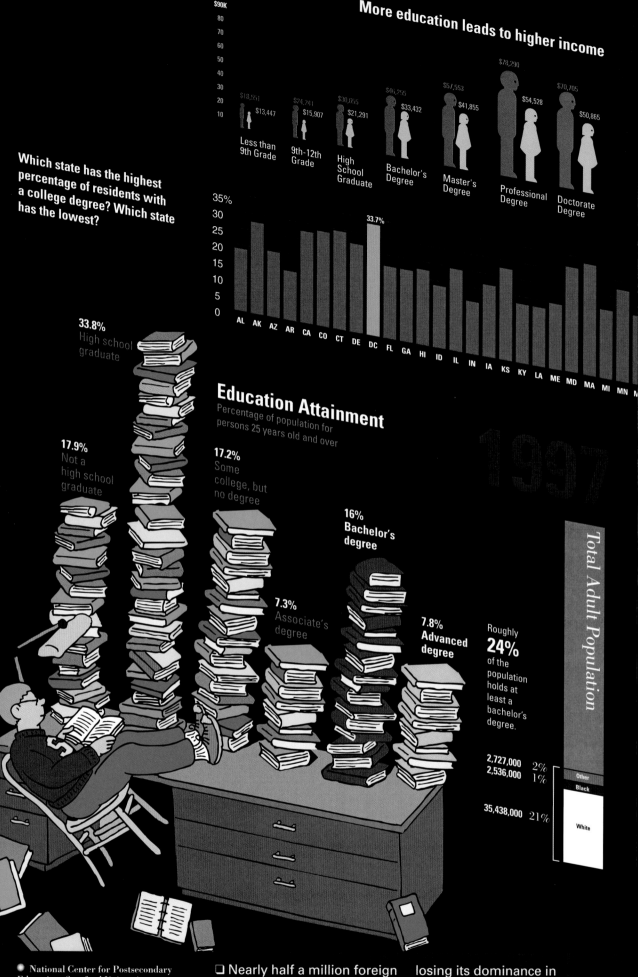

More education leads to higher income

	Less than 9th Grade	9th-12th Grade	High School Graduate	Bachelor's Degree	Master's Degree	Professional Degree	Doctorate Degree
Male	$18,591	$24,241	$30,665	$46,255	$57,563	$78,290	$70,705
Female	$13,447	$15,907	$21,291	$33,432	$41,855	$54,528	$50,865

Which state has the highest percentage of residents with a college degree? Which state has the lowest?

33.7% — DC

AL AK AZ AR CA CO CT DE DC FL GA HI ID IL IN IA KS KY LA ME MD MA MI MN M

Education Attainment
Percentage of population for persons 25 years old and over

1997

33.8% High school graduate

17.9% Not a high school graduate

17.2% Some college, but no degree

7.3% Associate's degree

16% Bachelor's degree

7.8% Advanced degree

Roughly **24%** of the population holds at least a bachelor's degree.

Total Adult Population

2,727,000	2%	Other
2,536,000	1%	Black
35,438,000	21%	White

● National Center for Postsecondary Education. Stanford University. www.stanford.edu/group/ncpi/index.html NCPI's mission is to provide leadership for the transformation and improvement of postsecondary education in its diverse forms--from research universities and comprehensive colleges to community colleges and vocational-technical schools.

❏ Nearly half a million foreign students attend U.S. colleges and universities each year. Although U.S. colleges and universities remain the world leaders in attracting foreign students, the United States is losing its dominance in international education. In the early 1990s, about 40% of all international students studied in the U.S., whereas in 1996–97 the figure dropped to **32%.**

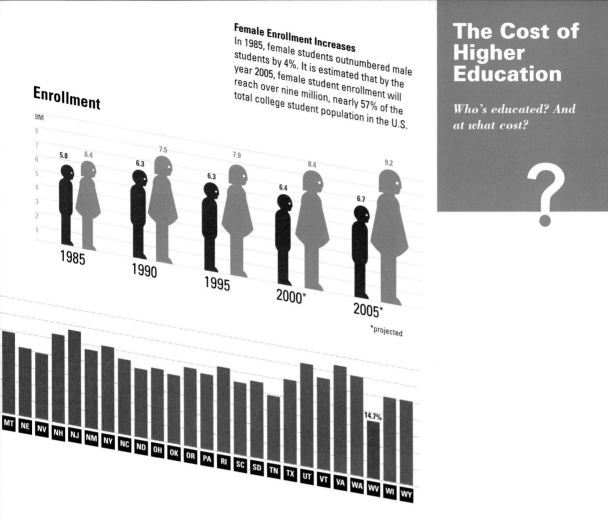

Enrollment

9M
8
7
6
5
4
3
2
1

5.8 6.4

6.3 7.5

6.3 7.9

6.4 8.4

6.7 9.2

1985

1990

1995

2000*

2005*

*projected

Female Enrollment Increases
In 1985, female students outnumbered male students by 4%. It is estimated that by the year 2005, female student enrollment will reach over nine million, nearly 57% of the total college student population in the U.S.

The Cost of Higher Education

Who's educated? And at what cost?

?

MT NE NV NH NJ NM NY NC ND OH OK OR PA RI SC SD TN TX UT VT VA WA WV WI WY

14.7%

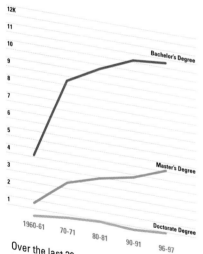

12K
11
10
9
8
7
6
5
4
3
2
1

Bachelor's Degree

Master's Degree

Doctorate Degree

1960-61 70-71 80-81 90-91 96-97

Over the last 30 years, the number of bachelor's and master's degrees conferred has increased along with the growth in women's enrollment in institutions of higher learning. In 1995–96, women earned the majority of bachelor's and master's degrees, and around two-fifths of doctorate degrees.

$19,000
18,000
17,000
16,000
15,000
14,000
13,000
12,000
11,000
10,000
9,000
8,000
7,000
6,000
5,000
4,000
3,000
2,000
1,000

$18,071

31%
Increase

Private Colleges

$6,534

20%
Increase

Public Colleges

1966-67 76-77 86-87 96-97

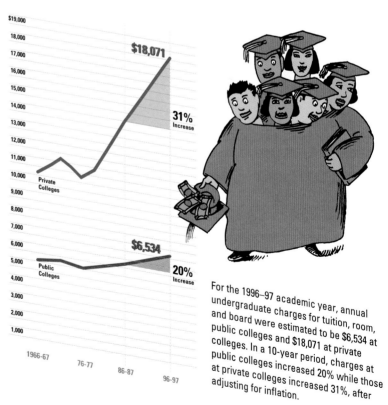

For the 1996–97 academic year, annual undergraduate charges for tuition, room, and board were estimated to be $6,534 at public colleges and $18,071 at private colleges. In a 10-year period, charges at public colleges increased 20% while those at private colleges increased 31%, after adjusting for inflation.

❑ After adjusting for inflation and for constant dollars, statistics show that per-student expenditures increased about **16%** throughout the 1980s, but only **7%** between 1988 and 1995.

❑ Spending for computer hardware and software by colleges was about $2.8 billion for the 1997–1998 school year. The average spent per student was **$149** for public colleges and **$283** for private colleges.

A research report developed by the NPD Group, a market research firm, measured the daily activities of 3,000 different people each year since 1992. This sampling of 24,000 men and women demonstrated a falloff in younger readers who said they spent at least 30 minutes of the day reading. The percentage is relatively stable for people 55 and older.

The older the age group, the more people are reading. People over 50 are reading an average of an hour a day, nearly double the time of people in their 20s and below.

Even though there are fewer people reading, the amount of time people actually spend reading has decreased only slightly, from 46 minutes a day to 44 minutes.

Young Males 18–34
percent who read at least 30 minutes of books, magazines, newspapers, or computer screens.

36%
1992

22%
1999

❑ An increasing number of college graduates now hold jobs traditionally held by workers without college degrees. But this is not an indication that students are making unwise investments in higher education. On the contrary, the number of people returning to college education has increased over time, even as more graduates take jobs in these other occupations.

 Comprehensive, searchable sources for information about standardized tests, applications, comparative school lists (from private high schools to graduate schools to study-abroad programs), financing, and special needs students.
www.petersons.com
www.collegeboard.org
www.collegeview.com

After declining for several years, the number of degrees conferred in the humanities and the social and behavioral sciences has grown since the mid-1980s. Combined with business management degrees, these three types of degrees constitute half or more of all degrees conferred since 1971.

Over the last two decades, health sciences degrees have doubled while education degrees have decreased by more than one-half during the same period.

Higher Education

What are people studying?

?

Changing opportunities within the job market affect the fields in which students choose to major. In turn, the majors that students choose affect the demand for courses and faculty, as well as the supply of new graduates in different fields.

Percentages of the categories of bachelor's degrees conferred

Legend:
- Other technical /professional
- Health sciences
- Business management
- Life sciences
- Physical sciences
- Computer and Information sciences
- Education
- Mathematics
- Engineering & Engineering Technologies
- Social/Behavioral sciences
- Humanities

Chart values by year:

Category	71	76	81	86	91	95
	6.2	11.2	12.8	11.8	12.0	13.3
	3.0	5.9	6.8	6.5	5.4	6.9
	13.7	15.3	21.3	24.0	22.8	20.2
	4.3					
	2.5	5.9	4.6	3.9	3.6	4.8
	0.3	2.3	2.6	2.2	1.5	1.7
	21.0	0.6	1.6	4.2	2.3	2.1
	3.0	16.7	11.6	8.8	10.1	9.5
	5.9	1.8	1.2	1.7	1.4	1.2
		5.0	8.1	9.7	7.2	6.8
	23.0	19.1	15.1	13.6	16.8	17.3
	17.1	16.3	14.3	13.4	15.7	16.6

❑ According to a study by the U.S. Department of Education, the number of degrees granted in six technology-related areas (engineering, engineering technology, computer sci- ence, business information systems, mathematics, and physics) fell from 218,820 in 1990 to 207,684 in 1996. In examining a slightly different combination of technology-related degrees, the study found a drop of between 5 and 8% over the same period. The decrease is a cause for concern since the technology industry's employment growth exceeds the supply of technically skilled workers

Among the nations with a population of more than one million people, 73% of children murdered lived in the U.S. And of those killed by guns, 86% were U.S. children. 54% of the suicides were our children.

No national data on attempted suicides are available; reliable scientific research, however, has found that:

More women than men report a history of attempted suicide, with a gender ratio of about 2:1.

A person commits suicide about every 17 minutes in the U.S., but it is estimated that an attempt is made about once every minute.

Over 32,000 peop

Suicide is a complex behavior. The risk factors for suicide frequently occur in combination. Preventive interventions must be complex and intensive if they are to have lasting effects.

Recognition and appropriate treatment of mental and substance abuse disorders for particular high-risk age, gender, and cultural groups is the most promising way to prevent suicide and suicidal behavior.

Most school-based, information-only suicide prevention programs have not been evaluated for their effectiveness. Research suggests that such programs may actually increase distress in the young people who are most vulnerable.

90% of all suicides were among whites; males account for 75% of all suicides and females 18%.

Suicide among black youths, once uncommon, has increased by two-thirds over the past 15 years.

❏ **Depression**
Over 60% of all people who commit suicide suffer from major depression. If one includes alcoholics who are depressed, this figure rises to over 75%.

❏ **Alcohol**
Alcoholism is a factor in about 30% of all completed suicides.

❏ **Firearms**
83% of gun-related deaths in homes are the result of a suicide. Death by firearm is the fastest growing method of suicide.

Suicide

What causes suicide? How frequently does it occur? Who's at risk?

?

In 1996 only 1.3% of total deaths in the U.S. were from sucide.In contrast, 32% were from heart diseases, 23% from cancers, and 7% from stroke.

le kill themselves
every year.

Suicide is the ninth leading cause of death in the U.S., but it is the third leading cause of death for young people aged 15-24 (after motor vehicle accidents and unintentional injury).

Suicide, like homicide, has come to play a proportionately large role in teenage deaths over the past several decades. Between 1970 and 1990, the suicide death rate for youth ages 15 through 19 nearly doubled. Since 1990, the overall death rate has stabilized. The strongest risk factors for attempted suicide are depression, alcohol or drug disorder, and aggressive or disruptive behaviors.

Nearly 60% of all suicides are committed with a firearm.

❏ Medical Illness

The highest suicide rates are found among those over 50. In over half of those deaths, medical illness plays an important role in the motivation. People with AIDS are 20 times more likely to commit suicide.

White men over 50 represent 10% of the population, but they are responsible for 33% of suicides.

The suicide rate for women peaks between the ages of 40 and 54, and again after 75.

Suicide Research Consortium. National Institute of Mental Health. Dept. of Health and Human Services. U.S. www.nimh.nih.gov/research/suicide.htm The Consortium coordinates program development in suicide research across the Institute, identifies gaps in the scientific knowledge base on suicide across the life span.

Flag postage stamp, circa 1960 from the collection of Kit Hinrichs

Krzysztof Lenk / Paul Kahn

Business
What is happening as we shift towards a service economy?

Top Companies
Has the computer business affected our world status?

Business Growth
Why do big businesses get bigger?

Mergers & Acquisitions
Why have mergers increased in size and number?

Wages & Earnings
Who earns more money?

Employee Compensation
Why are CEO's incomes increasing faster than average?

Immigration
Where are our immigrants from? Where are they living?

Foreign Trade
What are we gaining and loosing?

Global Trade
Why are we the biggest importer, exporter and deficit holder?

Global Economy
Why does the U.S. not have the highest GNP per capita?

The United Nations
How does it run on such a small budget?

What is BUSINESS?

◆ The activity of buying or selling goods or services. Goods are things that are produced in order to be sold. Services is a business that provides help or does jobs for people rather than produces things.

To provide something for money.

Sell →

Company or Store

A person or an organization that makes or sells goods and/or services.

← **Buy**
To acquire something for money.

Customer

Someone who buys goods or services.

◆ Top 3 franchises by number in 1997 are: 1) McDonald's, 15,394; 2) 7-Eleven Convenience Stores, 13,819; 3) Subway, 12,914; 4) Burger King Corp., 8,422; 5) Jani-King, 6,285. (Source: *Entrepreneur*, Jan. 1999)

Sales
The total number of products that a company sells during a particular time, measured in the amount of money brought to the company.

Money that you gain by selling things or doing business.

Cost
The amount of money you must pay in order to produce something.

Profit

Labor cost

Labor
All the people who work in an industry or country.

Others
Cost of materials, depreciation cost, rent, heating/lighting expenses, etc.

Tax
Profit after tax

Wages
The money you get each day, week, or month, that is usually paid according to the number of hours that you work.

Others
Social insurance costs for employees, etc.

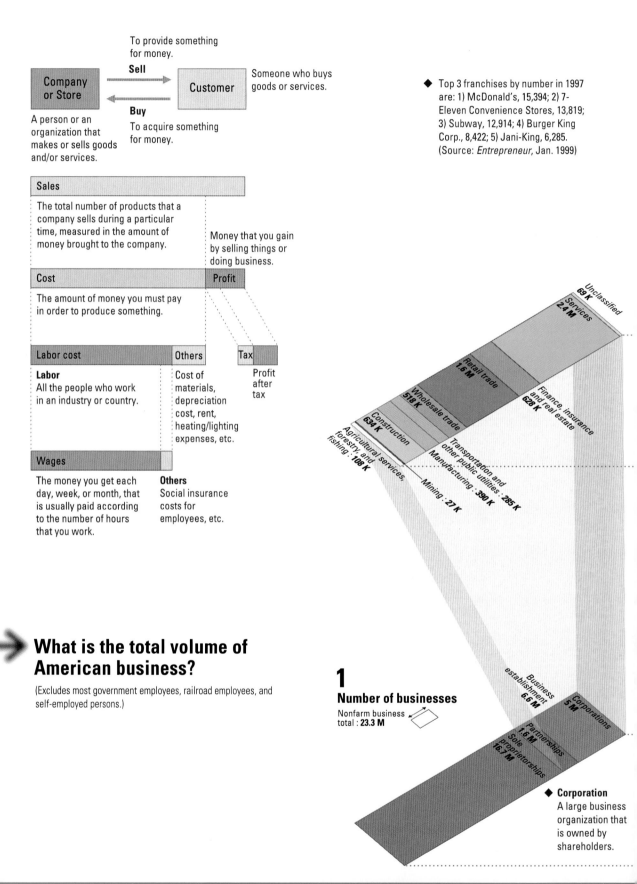

What is the total volume of American business?

(Excludes most government employees, railroad employees, and self-employed persons.)

1
Number of businesses
Nonfarm business total : **23.3 M**

Agricultural services, forestry, and fishing : **108 K**
Construction **634 K**
Wholesale trade **518 K**
Retail trade **1.6 M**
Services **2.4 M**
Unclassified **69 K**
Finance, insurance and real estate **628 K**
Transportation and other public utilities : **285 K**
Manufacturing : **390 K**
Mining : **27 K**

Business establishment **6.6 M**
Corporations **5 M**
Partnerships **1.6 M**
Sole proprietorships **16.7 M**

◆ **Corporation**
A large business organization that is owned by shareholders.

"Corporations have become the dominant institution of our time, occupying the position of the church in the Middle Ages, and the nation-state of the past two centuries," according to *Fast Company* magazine. Of the 100 largest economies in the world, 51 are corporations. General Motors, for example, is a larger economy than Denmark or Thailand, according to the Institute for Policy Studies.

The nine industrial divisions listed in the U.S. Office of Management and Budget's Standard Industry Classification: 1) agriculture, forestry and fishing; 2) mining; 3) construction; 4) manufacturing; 5) transportation and public utilities; 6) finance, insurance and real estate; 7) wholesale trade; 8) retail trade; 9) services.

The service sector, which includes government, health, computer and data processing, and child day care services, among others, is responsible for 3/4 of U.S. employment, and is expected to account for 4 of every 5 jobs by 2005.

U.S. national income, 1997 Total : 6,647 B

(dollars)

Compensation of employees 4,687 B		Corporate profits 741 B

Rental income 158 B

Proprietors' income 551 B

Net interest 432 B

Source : Bureau of Economic Analysis, U.S. Dept. of Commerce

◆ **National income** is the total of labor and property earnings from the production of goods and services. It measures the total factor costs of goods and services produced by the economy. Income is measured before deduction of taxes.

Business

What is happening as we shift towards a service economy?

?

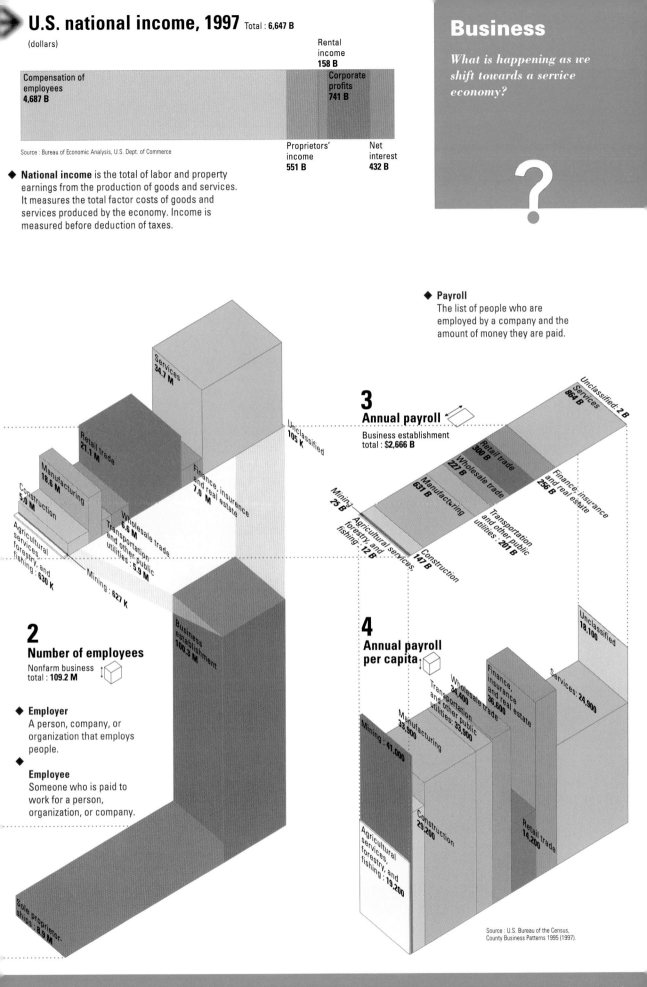

◆ **Payroll**
The list of people who are employed by a company and the amount of money they are paid.

3
Annual payroll
Business establishment total : $2,666 B

Unclassified: 2 B
Services: 864 B
Finance, insurance and real estate: 256 B
Retail trade 300 B
Wholesale trade 227 B
Manufacturing 631 B
Transportation and other public utilities : 201 B
Construction 147 B
Mining 25 B
Agricultural services, forestry, and fishing : 12 B

Services 34.7 M
Unclassified 105 K
Retail trade 21.1 M
Manufacturing 18.6 M
Construction 5.0 M
Finance, insurance and real estate 7.0 M
Wholesale trade 6.6 M
Transportation and other public utilities : 5.9 M
Agricultural services, forestry, and fishing : 630 K
Mining : 627 K
Business establishment 100.3 M

2
Number of employees
Nonfarm business total : 109.2 M

◆ **Employer**
A person, company, or organization that employs people.

◆ **Employee**
Someone who is paid to work for a person, organization, or company.

Sole proprietorships : 8.9 M

4
Annual payroll per capita

Mining : 41,000
Transportation and other public utilities: 33,900
Wholesale trade 34,400
Manufacturing 33,900
Finance, insurance and real estate 36,600
Unclassified 18,100
Services: 24,900
Construction 29,200
Retail trade 14,200
Agricultural services, forestry, and fishing : 19,200

Source : U.S. Bureau of the Census, County Business Patterns 1995 (1997).

Small businesses account for 99% of the 23.3 million nonfarm businesses in the United States today, according to the Small Business Administration.

Trade credit: the most often utilized form of short-term business financing, whereby a supplier provides a company with needed materials in exchange for a scheduled later payment, with added interest.

Franchised business represents nearly 40% of all U.S. retail sales. The Department of Commerce estimates that by 2000, franchising will account for more than half of all sales.

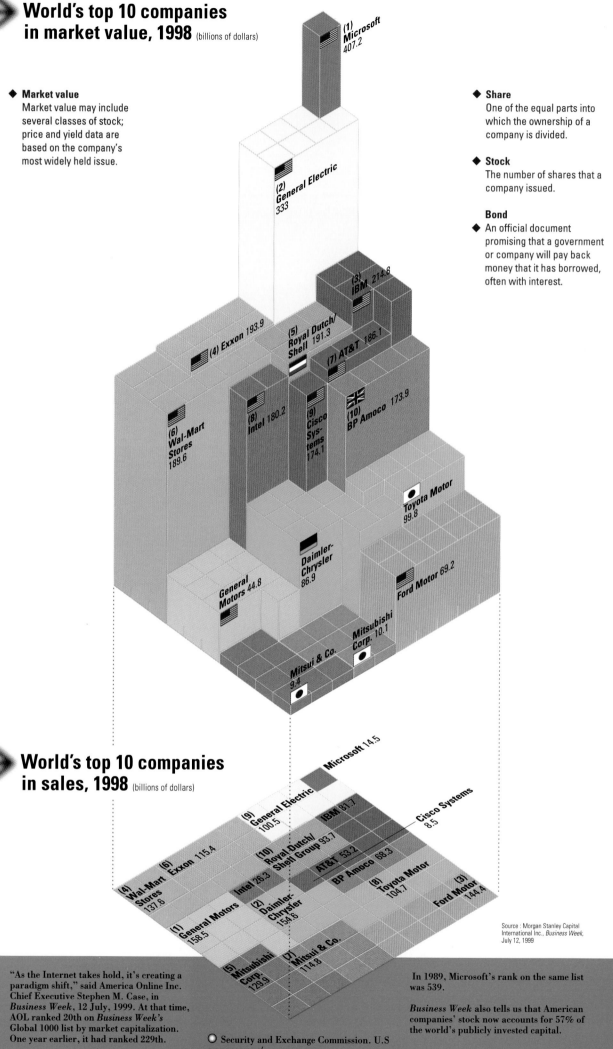

World's top 10 companies in market value, 1998 (billions of dollars)

(1) Microsoft 407.2

(2) General Electric 333

(3) iBM 214.8

(4) Exxon 193.9

(5) Royal Dutch/Shell 191.3

(7) AT&T 186.1

(6) Wal-Mart Stores 189.6

(8) Intel 180.2

(9) Cisco Systems 174.1

(10) BP Amoco 173.9

Toyota Motor 99.8

Daimler-Chrysler 86.9

Ford Motor 69.2

General Motors 44.8

Mitsubishi Corp. 10.1

Mitsui & Co. 9.4

◆ **Market value**
Market value may include several classes of stock; price and yield data are based on the company's most widely held issue.

◆ **Share**
One of the equal parts into which the ownership of a company is divided.

◆ **Stock**
The number of shares that a company issued.

Bond
◆ An official document promising that a government or company will pay back money that it has borrowed, often with interest.

World's top 10 companies in sales, 1998 (billions of dollars)

Microsoft 14.5

(9) General Electric 100.5

IBM 81.7

Cisco Systems 8.5

(6) Exxon 115.4

(10) Royal Dutch/Shell Group 93.7

AT&T 53.2

BP Amoco 68.3

(4) Wal-Mart Stores 137.6

Intel 26.3

(2) Daimler-Chrysler 154.6

Toyota Motor 104.7

(8)

(3) Ford Motor 144.4

(1) General Motors 158.5

(5) Mitsubishi Corp. 129.9

(7) Mitsui & Co. 114.8

Source : Morgan Stanley Capital International Inc., *Business Week*, July 12, 1999

"As the Internet takes hold, it's creating a paradigm shift," said America Online Inc. Chief Executive Stephen M. Case, in *Business Week*, 12 July, 1999. At that time, AOL ranked 20th on *Business Week's* Global 1000 list by market capitalization. One year earlier, it had ranked 229th.

○ Security and Exchange Commission. U.S www.sec.gov/
An independent, nonpartisan, quasijudicial regulatory agency with responsibility for administering the federal securities laws.

In 1989, Microsoft's rank on the same list was 539.

Business Week also tells us that American companies' stock now accounts for 57% of the world's publicly invested capital.

World's top 10 companies by profits, share-price gain, return on equity, 1998

Profits (billions of dollars)

1	9.3	General Electric, U.S.
2	6.37	Exxon, U.S.
3	6.33	IBM, U.S.
4	6.07	Intel, U.S.
5	5.94	Ford Motor Company, U.S.
6	5.81	Citigroup, U.S.
7	5.81	DaimlerChrysler, Germany
8	5.61	Bank of America, U.S.
9	5.37	Philip Morris, U.S.
10	5.25	Merck, U.S.

Share-price gain (% change from 1998 in U.S. dollars)

1	1,142	Ameritrade Holding, U.S.
2	834	CMGI, U.S.
3	723	E*Trade Group, U.S.
4	708	Amazon.com, U.S.
5	690	Metromedia Fiber Network, U.S.
6	513	Realnetworks, U.S.
7	473	America Online, U.S.
8	441	Yahoo!, U.S.
9	377	Charles Schwab, U.S.
10	351	Ecostar Communications, U.S.

Return on equity (%)

1	497.4	British American Tobacco, U.K.
2	311.7	Unisys, U.S.
3	270	General Mills, U.S.
4	262.9	Quaker Oats, U.S.
5	198.8	Vodafone Group, U.K.
6	185.2	Rentokil Initial, U.K.
7	148.2	Imperial Chemical Industries., U.K.
8	145.5	Avon Products, U.S.
9	130.6	Reuters Group, U.K.
10	126.6	Adidas-Salomon, Germany

Source : Morgan Stanley Capital International Inc., *Business Week*, July 12, 1999

Top Companies

Has the computer business affected our world status?

?

Top 10 countries by market value in the Global 1000 Companies, 1998
(billions of dollars)

Total market value and sales of each countries' Global 1000 companies.

Why is the market value of U.S. companies 5.9 times that of Japanese companies when U.S. sales are only 2.2 times as great?

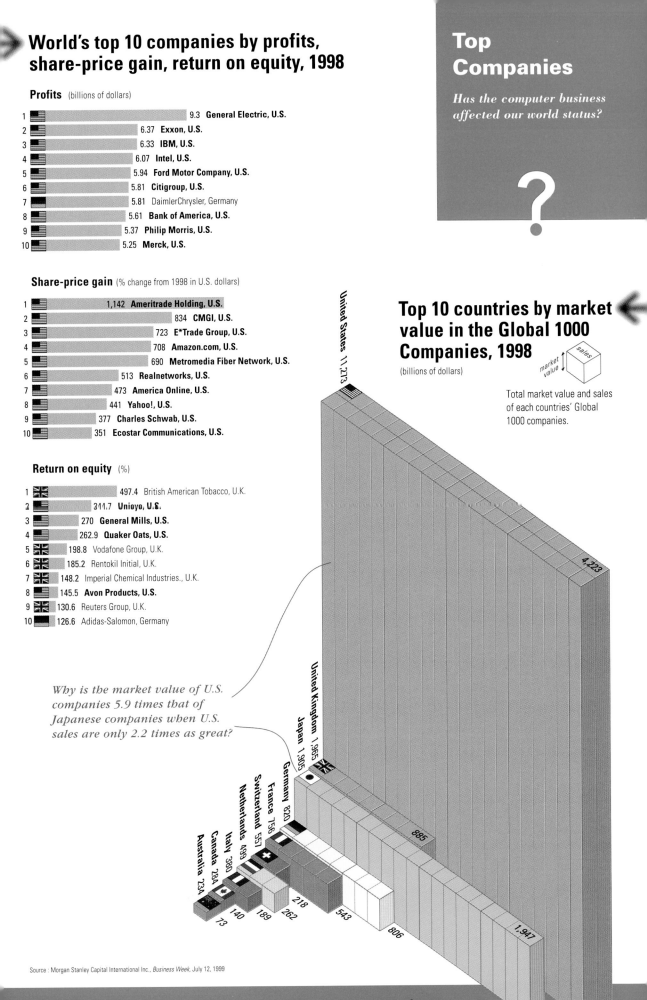

United States 11,273 / 4,223
United Kingdom 1,965 / 885
Japan 1,905 / 1,947
Germany 820 / 806
France 756 / 543
Switzerland 557 / 218
Netherlands 499 / 262
Italy 380 / 189
Canada 284 / 140
Australia 234 / 73

The National Center for Employee Ownership reports that 15 million U.S. workers now own about $500 billion in stock through employee stock ownership plans, 401(k)s, and broad-based stock options.

According to *Fast Company* magazine, the 5 largest American companies with more than 30% employee ownership are United Parcel Service, with 315,000 employees, Kroger Co. (200,000), Publix Supermarkets (95,000), Rockwell International (82,670), and United Airlines (77,900).

The Center for Responsive Politics, a nonprofit research group that collects data regarding money in politics, found that Microsoft's total political campaign contributions increased by 460% between 1991 and 1998.

Number of new business incorporations, number and liabilities of business failures by regions, 1997
Source: Dun & Bradstreet

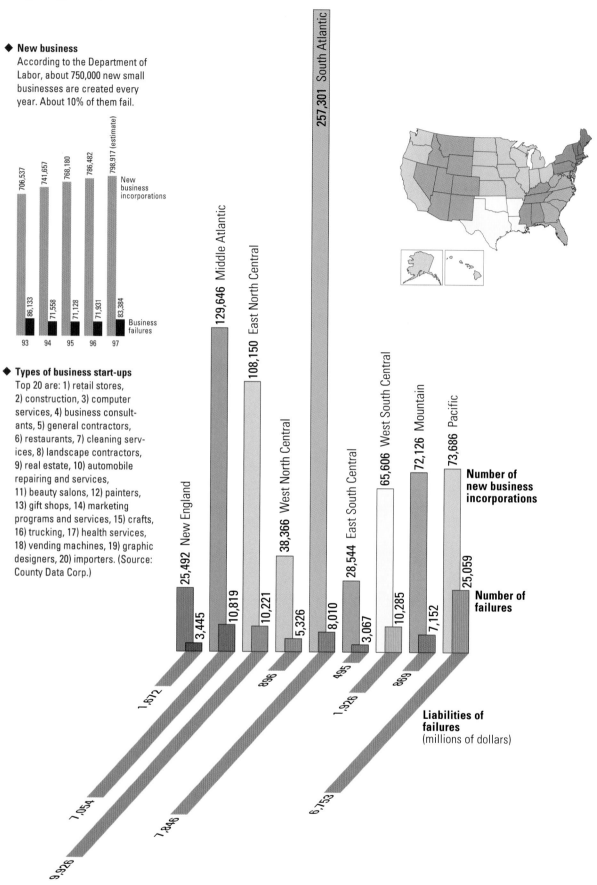

◆ **New business**
According to the Department of Labor, about 750,000 new small businesses are created every year. About 10% of them fail.

New business incorporations:
706,537 (93) | 741,657 (94) | 768,180 (95) | 786,482 (96) | 798,917 (estimate) (97)

Business failures:
86,133 (93) | 71,558 (94) | 71,128 (95) | 71,931 (96) | 83,384 (97)

◆ **Types of business start-ups**
Top 20 are: 1) retail stores, 2) construction, 3) computer services, 4) business consultants, 5) general contractors, 6) restaurants, 7) cleaning services, 8) landscape contractors, 9) real estate, 10) automobile repairing and services, 11) beauty salons, 12) painters, 13) gift shops, 14) marketing programs and services, 15) crafts, 16) trucking, 17) health services, 18) vending machines, 19) graphic designers, 20) importers. (Source: County Data Corp.)

Number of new business incorporations
- New England: 25,492
- Middle Atlantic: 129,646
- East North Central: 108,150
- West North Central: 38,366
- South Atlantic: 257,301
- East South Central: 28,544
- West South Central: 65,606
- Mountain: 72,126
- Pacific: 73,686

Number of failures
- New England: 3,445
- Middle Atlantic: 10,819
- East North Central: 10,221
- West North Central: 5,326
- South Atlantic: 8,010
- East South Central: 3,067
- West South Central: 10,285
- Mountain: 7,152
- Pacific: 25,059

Liabilities of failures (millions of dollars)
- New England: 1,672
- Middle Atlantic: 9,926
- East North Central: 7,846
- West North Central: 896
- South Atlantic: 7,054
- East South Central: 1,926
- West South Central: 495
- Mountain: 869
- Pacific: 6,753

The 5 most stressful American jobs are U.S. President, firefighter, senior corporate executive, Indy-class race car driver, and taxi driver; the 5 least stressful are medical records technician, janitor, forklift operator, musical instrument repairer, and florist, according to the *National Business Employment Weekly Jobs Rated Almanac*.

In 1994, The National Center on Education and the Economy tells us, 1 in 3 newly created jobs required a college degree.

A Census Bureau survey revealed that women owned more than 6.4 million businesses in 1992, generating $1.6 trillion in revenues.

○ AntiTrust. Dept. of Justice. U.S. www.usdoj.gov/atr/index.html
The Department promotes and protects the competitive process—and the American economy—through the enforcement of the antitrust laws.

What is a MERGER? An ACQUISITION?

◆ **Merger**

Company A → ← Company B = New company C [Company A / Company B]

◆ **Acquisition**

Company A → Company B (= target) = Company A = acquirer

Announced worldwide and U.S. mergers and acquisitions
Source : Securities Data Co.

- World total value (billions of dollars)
- U.S. total value (billions of dollars)
- World total number of deals
- U.S. total number of deals

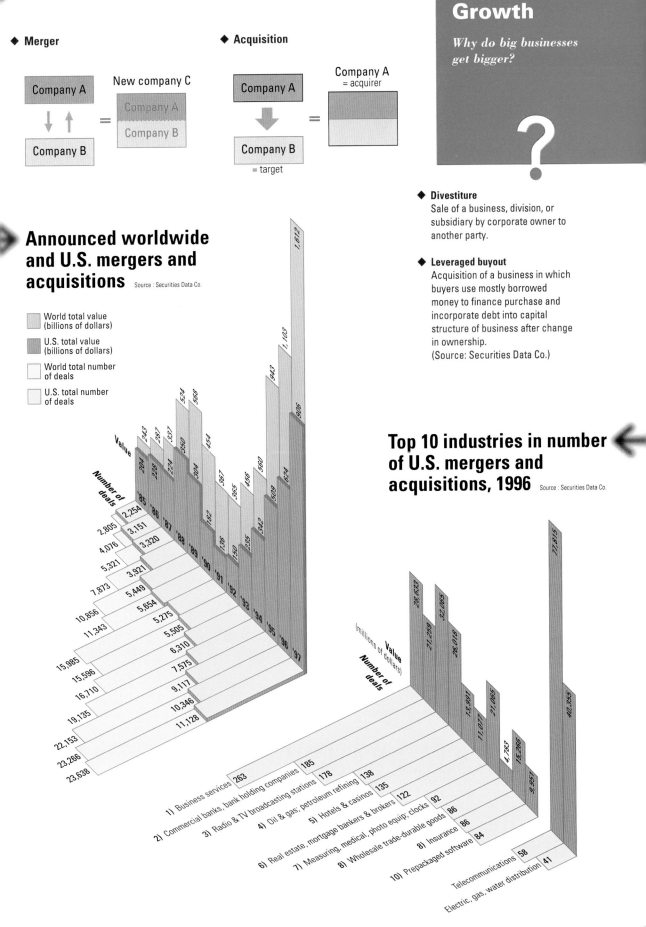

Value

'85	'86	'87	'88	'89	'90	'91	'92	'93	'94	'95	'96	'97
243	287	337	560	524	568	454	182	136	150	235	342	509	624 ...

World/US values: 204, 223, 224, 560, 304, 367, 385, 456, 560, 943, 1,103, 1,612, 905

Number of deals

Year	World	U.S.
'85	2,805	2,254
'86	4,076	3,151
'87	5,321	3,320
'88	7,873	3,921
'89	10,856	5,449
'90	11,343	5,654
'91	15,985	5,275
'92	15,596	5,505
'93	16,710	6,310
'94	19,135	7,575
'95	22,153	9,117
'96	23,266	10,346
'97	23,638	11,128

Top 10 industries in number of U.S. mergers and acquisitions, 1996
Source : Securities Data Co.

Value (millions of dollars) / **Number of deals**

Rank	Industry	Number of deals	Value
1)	Business services	263	28,633
2)	Commercial banks, bank holding companies	185	21,259
3)	Radio & TV broadcasting stations	178	32,085
4)	Oil & gas; petroleum refining	138	26,118
5)	Hotels & casinos	135	13,991
6)	Real estate, mortgage bankers & brokers	122	11,077
7)	Measuring, medical, photo equip., clocks	92	21,005
8)	Wholesale trade-durable goods	86	4,783
8)	Insurance	86	15,266
10)	Prepackaged software	84	9,435
	Telecommunications	58	77,815
	Electric, gas, water distribution	41	40,355

World's 25 largest mergers and acquisitions, 1989-1998

(billions of dollars) Source : Securities Data Company

- U.S. acquisition
- Foreign acquisition

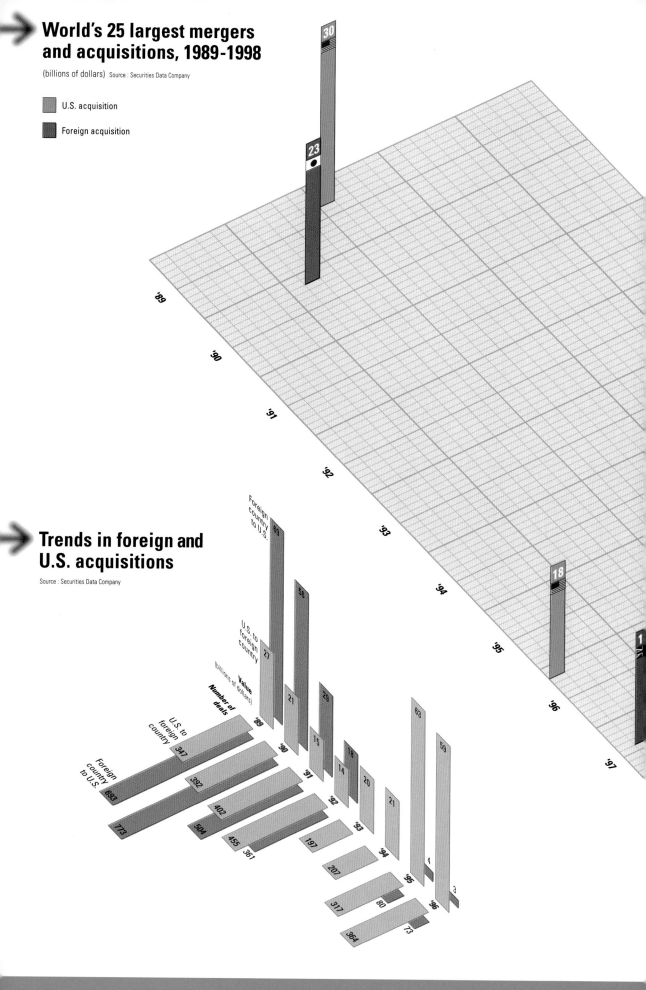

Trends in foreign and U.S. acquisitions

Source : Securities Data Company

Foreign country to U.S. 69

U.S. to foreign country 27

58

21 29

15 18 20 21

14

63 59

4 3

(billions of dollars) **Value**

Number of deals

U.S. to foreign country 347

Foreign country to U.S. 683

392

773

402

504

455 361

197

207

317 80

364 73

'89 '90 '91 '92 '93 '94 '95 '96

30

23

18

17

'89 '90 '91 '92 '93 '94 '95 '96 '97

One increasingly common way for companies to increase their power in the global marketplace is through purchasing or merging with their rivals. Eliminating the competition can keep prices from falling, and thereby protect profitability. What's more, the CEO's who broker such deals enjoy hefty financial bonuses for doing so.

From 1995-1997, more companies (over 27,600) merged than did during the entire decade of the 1980s, according to the *New York Times 1999 Almanac*.

The proposed 1998 combination of Lockheed Martin Corp. and Northrup Grumman Corp. was the only merger stopped by the U.S. government that year, due to Pentagon complaints that defense contractors were better left separate.

Mergers & Acquisitions

Why have mergers increased in size and number?

What would Karl Marx think of today's global concentration of capital?

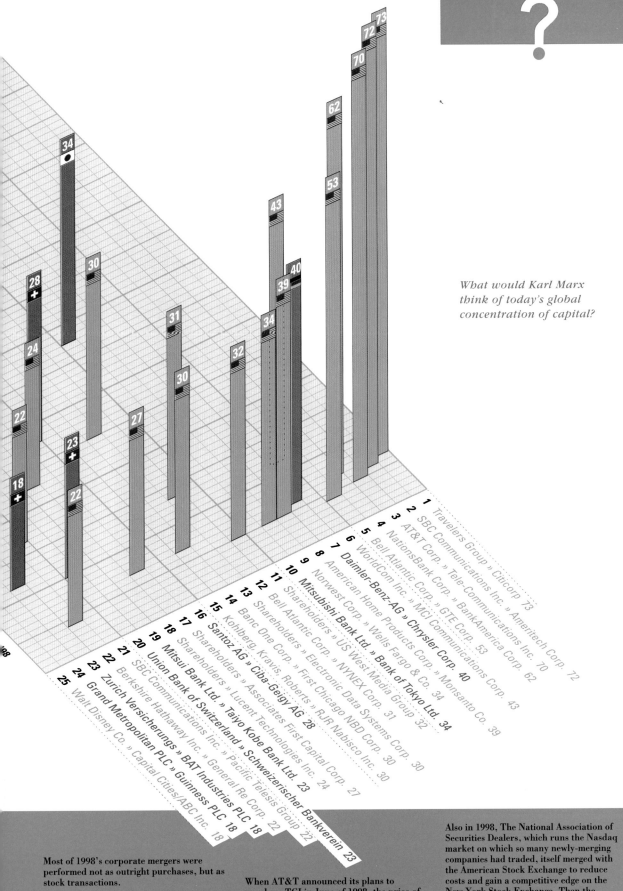

Most of 1998's corporate mergers were performed not as outright purchases, but as stock transactions.

When AT&T announced its plans to purchase TCI in June of 1998, the price of AT&T stock actually fell.

Also in 1998, The National Association of Securities Dealers, which runs the Nasdaq market on which so many newly-merging companies had traded, itself merged with the American Stock Exchange to reduce costs and gain a competitive edge on the New York Stock Exchange. Then the Chicago Board Options Exchange followed suit, buying the Pacific Exchange.

Average earnings of year-round full-time workers by age and educational attainment, 1996

(thousands of dollars)

Source: U.S. Bureau of the Census,
Current Population Reports

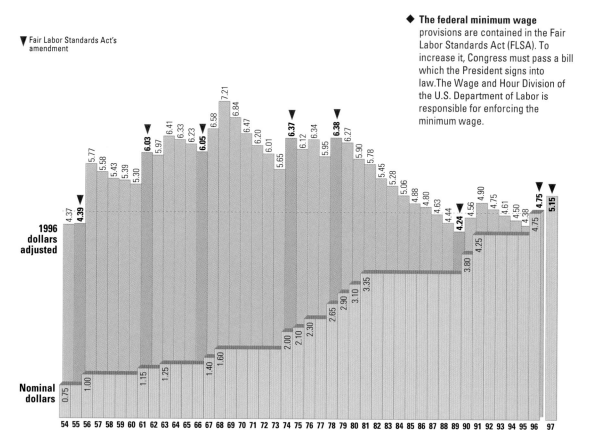

	All workers			Men	Women				Less than 9th grade
	45.8	33.1	18.9				13.3		
18 - 24	51.7					19.2			
	49.9				17.0	19.8			
25 - 34		42.0				21.6	14.2		
35 - 44					26.1	20.7	14.7		
45 - 54	42.1					26.6	15.7		
55 - 64					30.9				
65 -					31.2	20.2	17.7		
					27.6				
All ages					35.2	15.2			
					28.4				

◆ **Labor force**
The civilian labor force comprises all civilians in the noninstitutional population 16 years and over, classified as "employed" or "unemployed".
Among U.S. total population, 266.8 million, the civilian labor force comprises 136.3 million, or 67%.
Among the civilian labor force, there are 1.6 million (or 1.2%) minimum wage workers, and 2.8 million (or 2%) under minimum wage workers.

◆ **Unemployment rate**
is the percentage of unemployed or not seeking work in the civilian labor force.
In 1997, the rate was 4.9%, or 6.7 million.

Amount of the Federal Minimum Wage, 1954-1996

(hourly wage, dollars)   Source: U.S. Bureau of Labor Statistics

▼ Fair Labor Standards Act's amendment

◆ **The federal minimum wage**
provisions are contained in the Fair Labor Standards Act (FLSA). To increase it, Congress must pass a bill which the President signs into law. The Wage and Hour Division of the U.S. Department of Labor is responsible for enforcing the minimum wage.

1996 dollars adjusted

4.37, 4.39, 5.77, 5.58, 5.43, 5.39, 5.30, 6.03, 5.97, 6.41, 6.33, 6.23, 6.05, 6.58, 7.21, 6.84, 6.47, 6.20, 6.01, 5.65, 6.37, 6.12, 6.34, 5.95, 6.38, 6.27, 5.90, 5.78, 5.45, 5.28, 5.06, 4.88, 4.80, 4.63, 4.44, 4.24, 4.56, 4.90, 4.75, 4.61, 4.50, 4.38, 4.75, 5.15

Nominal dollars

0.75, 1.00, 1.15, 1.25, 1.40, 1.60, 2.00, 2.10, 2.30, 2.65, 2.90, 3.10, 3.35, 3.80, 4.25, 4.75, 5.15

54 55 56 57 58 59 60 61 62 63 64 65 66 67 68 69 70 71 72 73 74 75 76 77 78 79 80 81 82 83 84 85 86 87 88 89 90 91 92 93 94 95 96 97

The U.S. Bureau of Labor Statistics expects the American labor force to grow to 149 million in 2006. By that time, the median age of the labor force will approach 41, a level not seen in the United States since the 1960s.

The Urban Institute's 1998 "Does Work Pay? An Analysis of the Work Incentives Under TANF" study concluded that when a single parent, two-child family moves from no work and welfare to a part-time minimum wage job, family income "grows dramatically"—by an average of 51% for 20 hours of work per week at $5.15 per hour.

In 1997, a full-time worker (40 hours per week) earning the minimum wage would have monthly wages of $824.

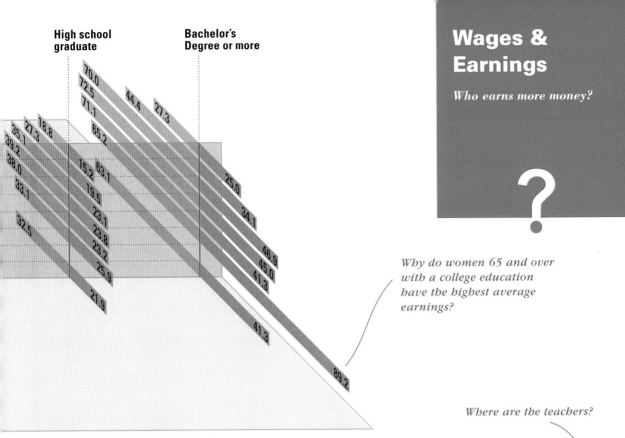

High school graduate

70.0
72.5
71.1
65.2

35.1
27.3
18.8

39.2
38.0
33.1

32.5

15.2
19.5
23.1
23.8
23.2
25.9
21.9

63.1

Bachelor's Degree or more

44.4   27.3

25.0

34.1

46.9
45.9
41.3

41.3

89.2

Wages & Earnings

Who earns more money?

?

Why do women 65 and over with a college education have the highest average earnings?

Where are the teachers?

Median weekly earnings of full-time workers by occupation, 1997

(dollars)   Source: U.S. Bureau of Labor Statistics

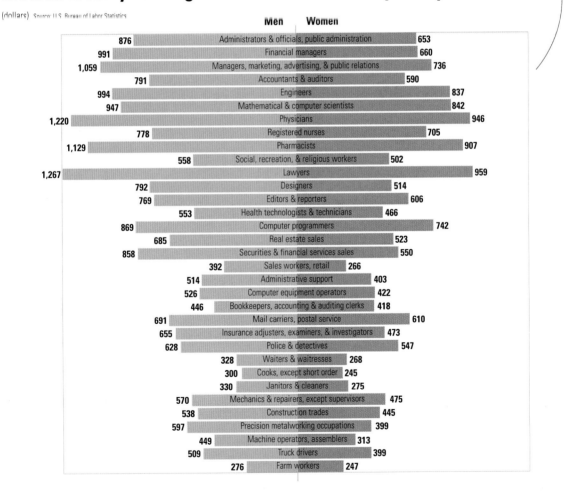

	Men	Women
Administrators & officials, public administration	876	653
Financial managers	991	660
Managers, marketing, advertising, & public relations	1,059	736
Accountants & auditors	791	590
Engineers	994	837
Mathematical & computer scientists	947	842
Physicians	1,220	946
Registered nurses	778	705
Pharmacists	1,129	907
Social, recreation, & religious workers	558	502
Lawyers	1,267	959
Designers	792	514
Editors & reporters	769	606
Health technologists & technicians	553	466
Computer programmers	869	742
Real estate sales	685	523
Securities & financial services sales	858	550
Sales workers, retail	392	266
Administrative support	514	403
Computer equipment operators	526	422
Bookkeepers, accounting & auditing clerks	446	418
Mail carriers, postal service	691	610
Insurance adjusters, examiners, & investigators	655	473
Police & detectives	628	547
Waiters & waitresses	328	268
Cooks, except short order	300	245
Janitors & cleaners	330	275
Mechanics & repairers, except supervisors	570	475
Construction trades	538	445
Precision metalworking occupations	597	399
Machine operators, assemblers	449	313
Truck drivers	509	399
Farm workers	276	247

In 1997, 79% of Americans spoken to by Washington's Peter Hart and Associates said they had "pretty much or most everything" they needed.

The number of children living in poverty (who have at least one working parent) has increased by 35% since 1989, according to Baltimore's Annie E. Casey Foundation.

From 1979 to 1995, says the U.S. Census Bureau, the median earnings of an American woman with a full-time job increased by $1,925, in constant dollars. In the same span, the median earnings of an American man with a full time job increased by $2,816.

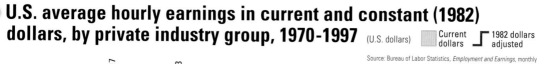

U.S. average hourly earnings in current and constant (1982) dollars, by private industry group, 1970-1997

(U.S. dollars)

Legend: Current dollars | 1982 dollars adjusted

Source: Bureau of Labor Statistics, *Employment and Earnings*, monthly

All industry average
- 70: 3.23
- 80: 6.66 / 8.03
- 90: 7.52 / 10.01
- 95: 7.39 / 11.43
- 97: 7.55 / 12.28

Mining
- 70: 3.85
- 80: 9.17 / 9.58
- 90: 9.90 / 10.71 / 10.28
- 95: 13.68
- 97: 15.30 / 16.17

Construction
- 70: 5.24
- 80: 9.94
- 90: 9.76 / 11.61 / 10.35 / 9.86 / 13.03
- 95: 13.77
- 97: 15.09 / 16.03

Manufacturing
- 70: 3.35
- 80: 7.27 / 8.33
- 90: 8.00 / 8.49 / 8.14 / 8.10
- 95: 10.83
- 97: 12.37 / 13.17

Transportation, public utilities
- 70: 3.85
- 80: 8.87 / 9.58
- 90: 9.14 / 10.36 / 9.71 / 9.18
- 95: 12.92
- 97: 14.13 / 14.93

Wholesale trade
- 70: 3.43
- 80: 6.95 / 8.53
- 90: 8.04 / 8.12 / 8.11 / 8.27
- 95: 10.79
- 97: 12.43 / 13.44

Retail trade
- 70: 2.44
- 80: 4.88 / 6.07 / 5.70
- 90: 4.97 / 5.07 / 5.13
- 95: 6.75
- 97: 7.69 / 8.34

Finance, insurance, real estate
- 70: 3.07
- 80: 5.7 / 7.64 / 6.6
- 90: 7.97 / 8.20 / 7.49
- 95: 9.97
- 97: 12.32 / 13.33

Services
- 70: 2.81
- 80: 5.8 / 6.99 / 6.83
- 90: 7.39 / 7.37 / 7.55
- 95: 9.83
- 97: 11.39 / 12.28

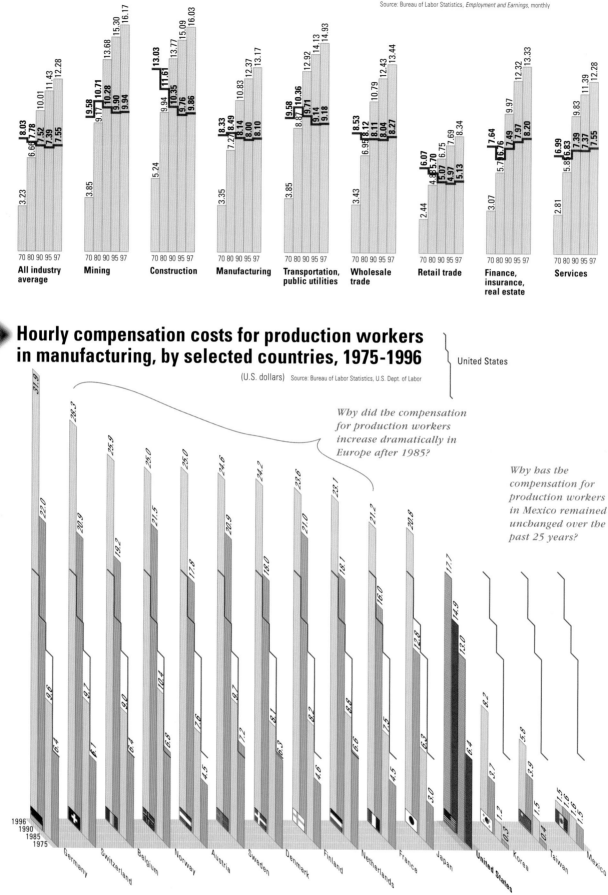

Hourly compensation costs for production workers in manufacturing, by selected countries, 1975-1996

(U.S. dollars) Source: Bureau of Labor Statistics, U.S. Dept. of Labor

United States

Why did the compensation for production workers increase dramatically in Europe after 1985?

Why has the compensation for production workers in Mexico remained unchanged over the past 25 years?

Years: 1996 / 1990 / 1985 / 1975

Germany: 31.9 / 22.0 / 9.6 / 6.4
Switzerland: 28.3 / 20.9 / 9.7 / 6.1
Belgium: 25.9 / 19.2 / 9.0 / 6.4
Norway: 25.0 / 21.5 / 10.4 / 6.8
Austria: 25.0 / 17.8 / 7.6 / 4.5
Sweden: 24.6 / 20.9 / 9.7 / 7.2
Denmark: 24.2 / 18.0 / 8.1 / 6.3
Finland: 23.6 / 21.0 / 8.2 / 4.6
Netherlands: 23.1 / 18.1 / 8.8 / 6.6
France: 21.2 / 16.0 / 7.5 / 4.5
Japan: 20.8 / 12.8 / 6.3 / 3.0
United States: 17.7 / 14.9 / 13.0 / 6.4
Korea: 8.2 / 3.7 / 1.2 / 0.3
Taiwan: 5.8 / 3.9 / 1.5 / 0.4
Mexico: 1.5 / 1.6 / 1.5

Real wages in 1998 were 13% below what they were in 1974, according to the July/August 1998 Compensations & Benefits Review. The average nonsupervisory employee still makes almost $41 per week less in real terms than he or she did in 1974.

From 1997 to 1998, real wages in the service-producing industries increased 3.9%. Wages in transportation and utilities increased 4%, and wages in finance, 5.4%. Wages in manufacturing, however, only increased by 1.9%.

Productivity in 1997 increased 1.7% in the nonfarm business sector. In manufacturing, productivity increased 4.4% (its largest hike in more than 10 years), especially in the making of durable goods, which saw a dramatic increase of 5.7%.

◆ **1999 highest paid CEO**
Charles B. Wang, CEO of Computer Associates International, got the largest public-company bonanza ever. He raked in stock worth $670 million when the shares met price targets set in 1995. Computer Associates took a $675 million after-tax charge for $1.1 billion in payouts to Wang and other top execs.

◆ **1998 highest paid CEO**
is Michael Eisner, CEO of Walt Disney, with $575.6 million. In comparison, an average worker's pay is $22,976. (*Business Week*)

10 highest-paid CEO's direct compensation 1997, and an average CEO's income

(dollars)

230,465,214 Sanford I. Weill / Travelers Group Inc.

4,300,000 average CEO in the U.S.

#	Amount	CEO / Company
1	50,006,865	Philip J. Purcell / Morgan Stanley, Dean Witter & Co.
2	49,256,475	Robert B. Shapiro / Monsanto Co.
3	39,825,020	John F. Welch Jr. / General Electric Co.
4	33,188,729	Harvey Golub / American Express Co.
5	29,211,298	Charles A. Heimbold / Bristol-Myers Squibb Co.
6	28,232,225	Lawrence A. Bossidy / AlliedSignal Inc.
7	28,102,284	William C. Steere Jr. / Pfizer Inc.
8	25,390,342	Reuben Mark / Colgate-Palmolive Co.
9	23,651,938	David H. Komansky / Merrill Lynch & Co.
10	4,300,000	average CEO in the U.S.

An average CEO's income and an average payroll per capita by major industry groups, 1997 (dollars)

◆ J. P. Morgan thought a CEO's wages should be no more than 20 times that of the average employee in that company.

19,200	Agricultural services, forestry, and fishing
41,000	Mining
29,200	Construction
33,900	Manufacturing
33,900	Transportation and other public utilities
34,400	Wholesale trade
14,200	Retail trade
36,600	Finance, insurance, and real estate
24,900	Services
18,100	Unclassified
26,600	All groups average

Source: Study conducted by William M. Mercer Inc. for *The Wall Street Journal*, U.S. Bureau of the Census, County Business Patterns 1995(1997), *Hightower*

In 1998, computer science graduates received starting salary offers averaging $40,843—a 9% increase from figures posted in 1997, according to the National Association of Colleges and Employers' April 1998 Salary Survey Report.

A recent study conducted for the Information Technology Association of America by Virginia Polytechnic Institute estimates that 346,000 computer programmer and systems analyst jobs are vacant in U.S. companies with more than 100 employees.

The July/August, 1998 Compensation and Benefits Review projected 1998 salary increases:
For executives: 4.2%
For middle managers: 4.1%
For technical and administrative workers: 4.0%

States with highest foreign-born population percentage

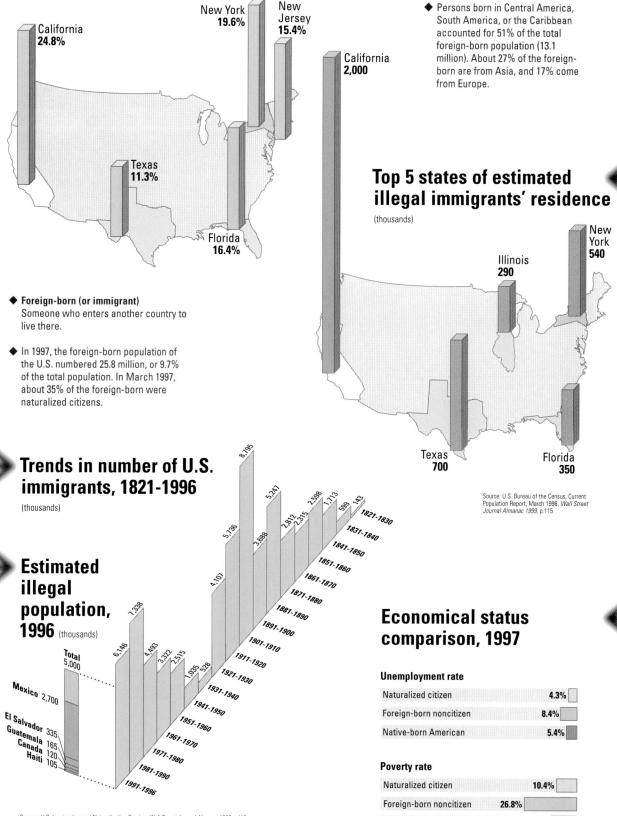

California 24.8%

New York 19.6%

New Jersey 15.4%

Texas 11.3%

Florida 16.4%

California 2,000

◆ Persons born in Central America, South America, or the Caribbean accounted for 51% of the total foreign-born population (13.1 million). About 27% of the foreign-born are from Asia, and 17% come from Europe.

◆ **Foreign-born (or immigrant)**
Someone who enters another country to live there.

◆ In 1997, the foreign-born population of the U.S. numbered 25.8 million, or 9.7% of the total population. In March 1997, about 35% of the foreign-born were naturalized citizens.

Top 5 states of estimated illegal immigrants' residence

(thousands)

New York 540

Illinois 290

Texas 700

Florida 350

Source: U.S. Bureau of the Census, Current Population Report, March 1998, *Wall Street Journal Almanac 1999*, p.115

Trends in number of U.S. immigrants, 1821-1996

(thousands)

8,795
5,247
5,736
3,688
2,812
2,315
2,598
1,713
599
143

1821-1830
1831-1840
1841-1850
1851-1860
1861-1870
1871-1880
1881-1890
1891-1900
1901-1910
1911-1920
1921-1930
1931-1940
1941-1950
1951-1960
1961-1970
1971-1980
1981-1990
1991-1996

4,107

Estimated illegal population, 1996 (thousands)

7,338
6,146
4,493
3,332
2,515
1,035
528

Total 5,000

Mexico 2,700

El Salvador 335
Guatemala 165
Canada 120
Haiti 105

Source : U.S. Immigration and Naturalization Service, *Wall Street Journal Almanac 1999*, p.115

Economical status comparison, 1997

Unemployment rate

Naturalized citizen	4.3%
Foreign-born noncitizen	8.4%
Native-born American	5.4%

Poverty rate

Naturalized citizen	10.4%
Foreign-born noncitizen	26.8%
Native-born American	12.9%

Source: U.S. Bureau of the Census, Current Population Report, March 1998, *Wall Street Journal Almanac 1999*, p.115

As the natural increase of the U.S. population slows, immigration has become an increasingly important factor in population and labor-force dynamics.

Although white non-Hispanics are expected to account for by far the largest share of the labor-force in 2006 (73%), their rate of population growth is actually slower than that of black, Asian, and Hispanic groups.

○ Immigration and Naturalization Service. Dept. of Justice. U.S. www.ins.usdoj.gov/graphics/index.html The Federal agency that administers the nation's immigration laws. You will see that INS mission involves a variety of inter-related functions.

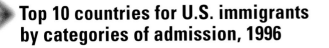

Top 10 countries for U.S. immigrants by categories of admission, 1996

Immigration

Where are our immigrants from? Where are they living?

?

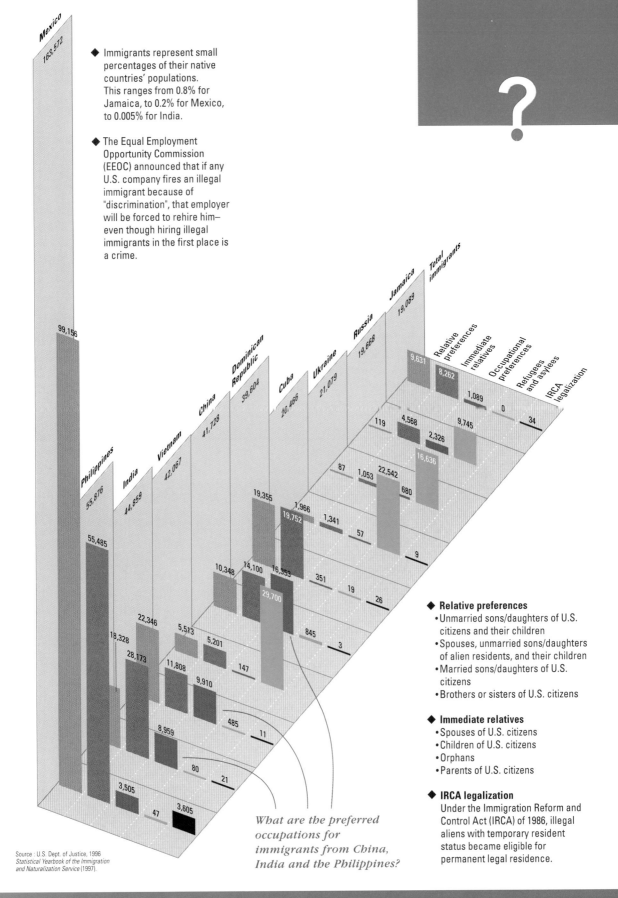

◆ Immigrants represent small percentages of their native countries' populations. This ranges from 0.8% for Jamaica, to 0.2% for Mexico, to 0.005% for India.

◆ The Equal Employment Opportunity Commission (EEOC) announced that if any U.S. company fires an illegal immigrant because of "discrimination", that employer will be forced to rehire him— even though hiring illegal immigrants in the first place is a crime.

What are the preferred occupations for immigrants from China, India and the Philippines?

Source : U.S. Dept. of Justice, 1996
Statistical Yearbook of the Immigration and Naturalization Service (1997).

◆ **Relative preferences**
• Unmarried sons/daughters of U.S. citizens and their children
• Spouses, unmarried sons/daughters of alien residents, and their children
• Married sons/daughters of U.S. citizens
• Brothers or sisters of U.S. citizens

◆ **Immediate relatives**
• Spouses of U.S. citizens
• Children of U.S. citizens
• Orphans
• Parents of U.S. citizens

◆ **IRCA legalization**
Under the Immigration Reform and Control Act (IRCA) of 1986, illegal aliens with temporary resident status became eligible for permanent legal residence.

The U.S. Census Bureau ranked Africa highest among continents of origin of the most highly educated immigrants to the U.S. in 1995.

"About 8 million foreigners emigrate to the U.S. legally every year. In addition, the Immigration and Naturalization Service (INS) estimates another 300,000 a year enter illegally or overstay their visas, adding to the 4 million illegal immigrants that already live in the country," according to the *Annual Report of the United States.*

March, 1998 Census Bureau reports indicate that about 25% of both foreign-born and native-born Americans aged 25 and over had completed four or more years of college. At the same age level, 34.7% of the foreign-born population, and 15.6% of the native-born population had not finished high school.

What is FOREIGN TRADE?

◆ The activity of buying, selling, or exchanging goods, between countries.

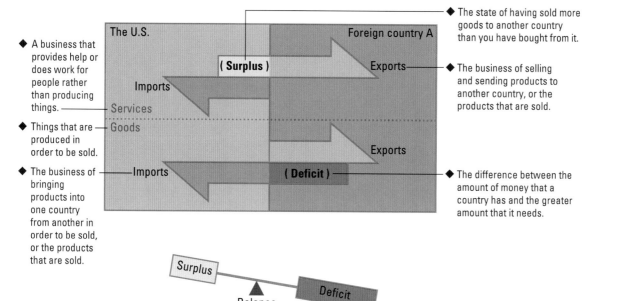

The U.S. — Foreign country A

◆ A business that provides help or does work for people rather than producing things. — Services

◆ Things that are produced in order to be sold. — Goods

◆ The business of bringing products into one country from another in order to be sold, or the products that are sold. — Imports

(Surplus)

Imports

Exports

Exports

(Deficit)

◆ The state of having sold more goods to another country than you have bought from it.

◆ The business of selling and sending products to another country, or the products that are sold.

◆ The difference between the amount of money that a country has and the greater amount that it needs.

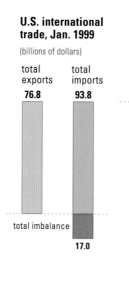

Surplus

Balance

Deficit

◆ **Exchange Rates**
Because countries have their own currencies, trade also involves exchanging or trading currencies . The exchange rate between currencies represents the ratio at which they can be exchanged or the price of one currency in terms of the other.
The exchange rate for almost all world currencies is now determined by the market. The exchange rate of a currency rises or appreciates when the demand for it rises and/or the supply falls. This may happen because foreign buyers want to buy more of a nation's goods or because consumers within the country decide to buy fewer imports. It may also happen because the country reduces its money supply. Countries' central banks can manipulate exchange rates slightly by buying and selling their own and other currencies. (Source: *New York Times Almanac 1999*, p.500)

◆ **The balance of trade** is an important issue because it indicates how a nation's economy changes and, ultimately, about its competitiveness vis-à-vis other countries. A rising balance of trade deficit indicates an economy is unable to sell its goods abroad, and that consumers favor imports over domestically produced goods.

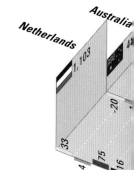

Netherlands   Australia

1,103   4

-20

33   75

-14   16

U.S. international trade, Jan. 1999
(billions of dollars)

total exports — 76.8
total imports — 93.8

total imbalance — 17.0

U.S. trade deficit, regional view Jan.1998 / Jan.1999
(year to date at an annual rate, billions of dollars)

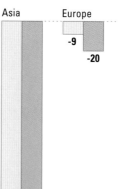

Asia   Europe

-9
-20

-160
-175

Top 5 countries with which the U.S. trades Feb. 1999
(billions of dollars)

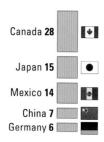

Canada **28**
Japan **15**
Mexico **14**
China **7**
Germany **6**

Source : U.S. trade in perspective, Department of Commerce, International Trade Administration, Trade development; U.S. Census Bureau.

○ Foreign Trade. Census Bureau. Dept. of Commerce. U.S.
www.census.gov/foreign-trade/www/pub/ftd/msftd.html
Census Bureau's latest information on imports, exports, shipping, and customs data.

The fastest growing U.S. export sectors are chemicals, pharmaceuticals, food, and electronic equipment.

Machinery and transport equipment together comprise the largest category within 10 U.S. goods classifications for both imports and exports. Among all the top 10 countries with which the U.S. has a trade surplus, and 7 of the top 10 countries with which it has a trade deficit, machinery and transport equipment are the most often traded goods.

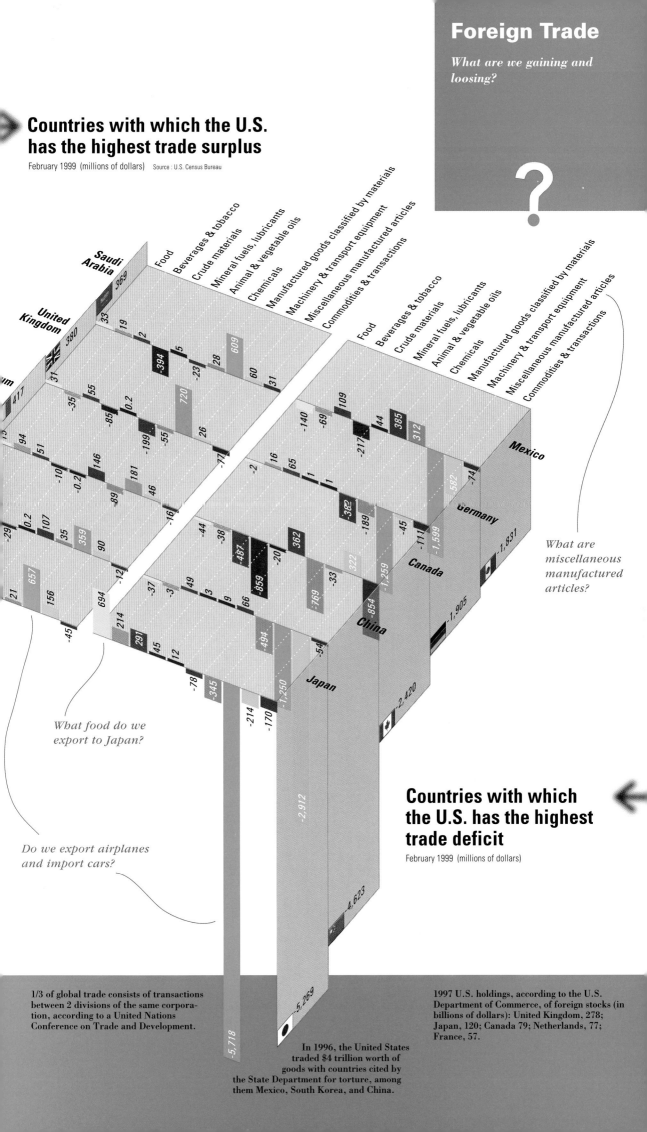

Foreign Trade

What are we gaining and loosing?

?

Countries with which the U.S. has the highest trade surplus

February 1999 (millions of dollars)   Source : U.S. Census Bureau

What are miscellaneous manufactured articles?

What food do we export to Japan?

Do we export airplanes and import cars?

Countries with which the U.S. has the highest trade deficit

February 1999 (millions of dollars)

1/3 of global trade consists of transactions between 2 divisions of the same corporation, according to a United Nations Conference on Trade and Development.

In 1996, the United States traded $4 trillion worth of goods with countries cited by the State Department for torture, among them Mexico, South Korea, and China.

1997 U.S. holdings, according to the U.S. Department of Commerce, of foreign stocks (in billions of dollars): United Kingdom, 278; Japan, 120; Canada 79; Netherlands, 77; France, 57.

Top 12 world traders' exports, imports, balance, and GNP, 1996/97 (billions of dollars)

Legend:
- GNP (1996)
- Exports in goods (1997)
- Imports in goods (1997)
- Trade balance, plus (1997)
- Trade balance, minus (1997)

◆ The U.S. is by far the world's leading importer and exporter, accounting for over 12% in each category.

◆ Over the last 5 years, as the economy has grown, the U.S. trade deficit has continued to widen, climbing from $38.6 billion in 1992 to $110 billion in 1997. The entire U.S. trade deficit is in the manufactured goods sector; the U.S. runs a small surplus in the services sector. U.S. exports of goods have not kept up with imports in part because the strength of the dollar makes American goods more expensive for foreign nations to buy, while the U.S. has more money to spend on cheaper imports.

◆ The balance of payments account is the list of transactions between a country and the rest of the world. This account has three parts: **1) the current account:** a record of exports and imports of goods (e.g. oil, clothing) and services (e.g. tourism); **2) the capital account:** a record of exports and imports of assets such as bank loans and corporate stock purchases; and **3) the official reserves account:** a record of a country's sales and purchases of official reserve assets at its central bank. (Source: *New York Times Almanac 1999* p.500-501)

Hong Kong's exports are greater than its GNP because it serves as a gateway for China.

United States 7,434

Exports, world total 5,455

Imports, world total 5,600

Japan 5,149

Germany 2,365

France 1,534

United Kingdom 1,152

Italy 1,140

Canada 570

Netherlands 403

Hong Kong 183

China 906

Belgium-Luxembourg 287

Korea 483

Values:
- -210 / 899 / 689
- 442 / 70
- 338 / 83 / 512
- 267 / 21 / 421
- 307 / -27 / 288
- 209 / 30 / 280
- 201 / 13 / 239
- 177 / 17 / 214
- 209 / -21 / 194
- 143 / 188
- 153
- 40
- 12
- 156 / 168
- 145 / -8 / 287
- 137 / 483

Source: World Trade Organization, The World Bank, *The 1998 World Bank Atlas*

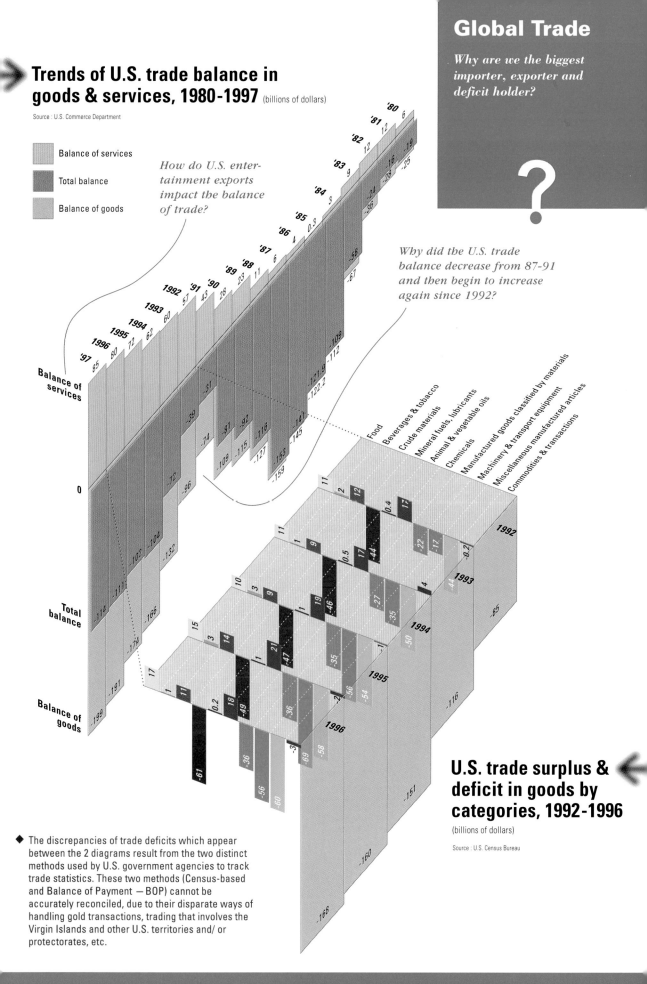

Trends of U.S. trade balance in goods & services, 1980-1997 (billions of dollars)

Source : U.S. Commerce Department

- Balance of services
- Total balance
- Balance of goods

How do U.S. enter-tainment exports impact the balance of trade?

Global Trade

Why are we the biggest importer, exporter and deficit holder?

?

Why did the U.S. trade balance decrease from 87-91 and then begin to increase again since 1992?

Balance of services

Total balance

Balance of goods

'97 '96 '95 '94 '93 1992 '91 '90 '89 '88 '87 '86 '85 '84 '83 '82 '81 '80

U.S. trade surplus & deficit in goods by categories, 1992-1996

(billions of dollars)

Source : U.S. Census Bureau

Food / Beverages & tobacco / Crude materials / Mineral fuels, lubricants / Animal & vegetable oils / Chemicals / Manufactured goods classified by materials / Machinery & transport equipment / Miscellaneous manufactured articles / Commodities & transactions

1992 / 1993 / 1994 / 1995 / 1996

◆ The discrepancies of trade deficits which appear between the 2 diagrams result from the two distinct methods used by U.S. government agencies to track trade statistics. These two methods (Census-based and Balance of Payment — BOP) cannot be accurately reconciled, due to their disparate ways of handling gold transactions, trading that involves the Virgin Islands and other U.S. territories and/ or protectorates, etc.

The total amount of private capital going from the U.S., Japan, and the European Union to developing countries rose from $44.4 billion in 1990 to $243.8 billion in 1996, according to the 1999 *New York Times Almanac*.

Foreign Direct Investment (FDI) is invest-ment by private companies, either through an existing enterprise or the building of new facilities, within the territory of another nation.

The United States accounts for more than 12% of the world's imports and exports, more than any other nation.

What is GNP?

◆ **GNP (Gross National Product)** is the total market value of **final goods and services** (i.e., income) of residents of a country, including income they receive from abroad, but not including payments to foreigners.

◆ **What is final goods and services?**
Intermediate goods such as plastic, glass, cotton, etc., are not counted since they are not in their final state. Including only final goods and services prevents double counting and thus avoids an overstatement of GDP (GNP). Final goods include household purchases, since they will not be used to produce other goods and services.

Countries with highest GNP, 1996

(billions of dollars)

GNP $228 billion

Luxembourg and Singapore (Less than GNP $100 billion)

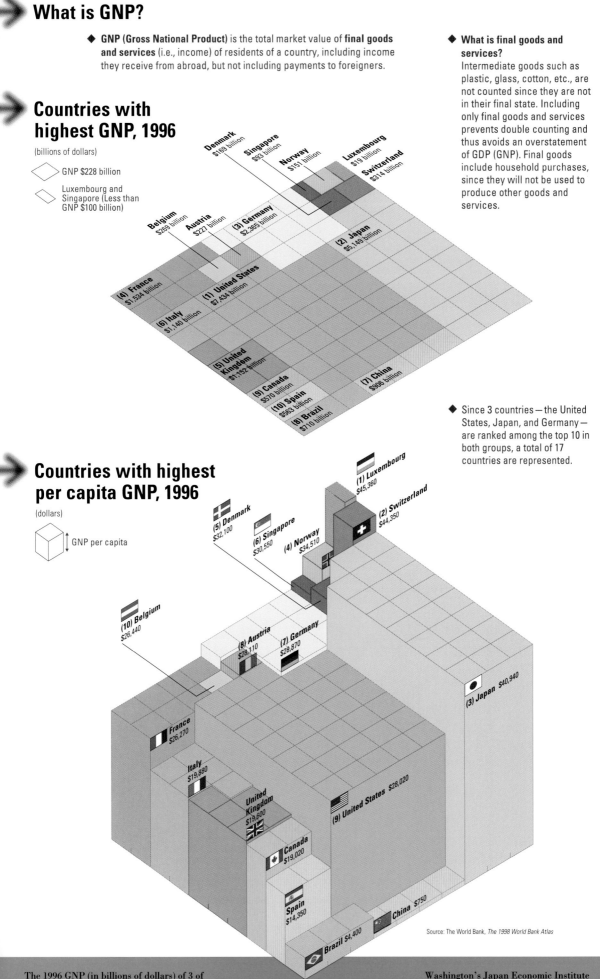

Denmark $169 billion
Singapore $93 billion
Norway $151 billion
Luxembourg $19 billion
Switzerland $314 billion
Belgium $269 billion
Austria $227 billion
(3) Germany $2,365 billion
(2) Japan $5,149 billion
(4) France $1,534 billion
(1) United States $7,434 billion
(6) Italy $1,140 billion
(5) United Kingdom $1,152 billion
(9) Canada $570 billion
(10) Spain $563 billion
(8) Brazil $710 billion
(7) China $906 billion

◆ Since 3 countries — the United States, Japan, and Germany — are ranked among the top 10 in both groups, a total of 17 countries are represented.

Countries with highest per capita GNP, 1996

(dollars)

GNP per capita

(1) Luxembourg $45,360
(2) Switzerland $44,350
(5) Denmark $32,100
(6) Singapore $30,550
(4) Norway $34,510
(10) Belgium $26,440
(8) Austria $28,110
(7) Germany $28,870
(3) Japan $40,940
France $26,270
Italy $19,880
United States $28,020
United Kingdom $19,600
Canada $19,020
Spain $14,350
China $750
Brazil $4,400
(9) United States $28,020

Source: The World Bank, *The 1998 World Bank Atlas*

The 1996 GNP (in billions of dollars) of 3 of the world's major economies: United States, 7,434; European Union, 8,469, and Japan, 5,149, according to the World Bank.

The 15 member states of the European Union: Austria, Belgium, Denmark, Finland, France, Germany, Greece, Ireland, Italy, Luxembourg, Netherlands, Portugal, Spain, Sweden, and the United Kingdom.

Washington's Japan Economic Institute reports that Japan estimates the bad debt held by its banks represents 17.5% of that nation's GDP. In 1988, the bad debt held by American S&Ls totaled 3.2% of the U.S. GDP.

◆ **GDP (Gross Domestic Product)** is the market value for all **final goods and services** produced within a nation in a given time period.

◆ **Economic classification by the World Bank** (based on average annual per capita income)

| High-income : $9,636~ |
| Middle-income : $786~$9,635 |
| Low-income : ~$785 |

Developing country

Unemployment rate trends, 1990-1998 (%)

Source : U.S. Bureau of Labor Statistics

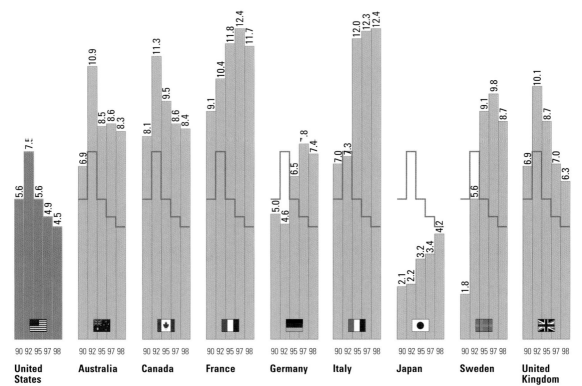

90 92 95 97 98	90 92 95 97 98	90 92 95 97 98	90 92 95 97 98	90 92 95 97 98	90 92 95 97 98	90 92 95 97 98	90 92 95 97 98	90 92 95 97 98
United States	**Australia**	**Canada**	**France**	**Germany**	**Italy**	**Japan**	**Sweden**	**United Kingdom**

United States: 5.6, 7.5, 5.6, 4.9, 4.5
Australia: 6.9, 10.9, 8.5, 8.6, 8.3
Canada: 8.1, 11.3, 9.5, 8.6, 8.4
France: 9.1, 10.4, 11.8, 12.4, 11.7
Germany: 5.0, 4.6, 6.5, 7.8, 7.4
Italy: 7.0, 7.3, 12.0, 12.3, 12.4
Japan: 2.1, 2.2, 3.2, 3.4, 4.2
Sweden: 1.8, 5.6, 9.1, 9.8, 8.7
United Kingdom: 6.9, 10.1, 8.7, 7.0, 6.3

◆ America's unemployment rate (which count only those people who are both "unemployed" and "currently looking for work") is at a historically low level. Yet each percentage point of unemployment represents more than 1.3 million Americans without paying jobs. What's more, these official unemployment statistics do not include: the "discouraged" job-seeker who has unsuccessfully sought work for so long that he is not currently looking; the worker who received compensation for doing freelance work or odd jobs, etc.; the workers who were "laid off"; or the workers who are too proud to admit being without work, and others. (Source: Hightower)

The Joint Committee on Taxation in Washington recently estimated that multi-national corporations legally avoided $10.1 billion in U.S. taxes by using foreign accounts in 1988.

The 1997 *Annual Report of the United States* specifies, "Currently the future liabilities of the federal government total $20.7 trillion. This translates to almost $80,000 owed for every man, woman, and child in the U.S.A."

○ Restoring Global Financial Stability. United States Information Agency. www.usia.gov/regional/ea/asiafin/globefin.htm USIA site designed to highlight American efforts to sustain a rational international financial system.

What is the United Nations?

◆ • Established in 1945. Members: 185 countries; Four purposes • to maintain international peace and security • to develop friendly relations among nations • to cooperate in solving international problems and in promoting respect for human rights • to be a center for harmonizing the actions of nations.

United Nations System   52,280 workers. Annual cost : $18.2 B

United Nations
8,700 workers, Annual budget : $1.26 B

- General Assembly
- Security Council
  - 5 permanent countries: China, France, Russia, United States, United Kingdom
  - 10 elected countries, 2 year terms
- Secretariat
  - Secretary-General
  - Emergency Relief Coordinator
- Economic and Social Council
- Trusteeship Council
- International Court of Justice

Special Agencies

- World Bank Group
  - IBRD IDA The World Bank
  - IFC MIGA ICSID
- ILO (International Labor Org.)
- FAO (Food and Agriculture Org. of the UN)
- UNESCO (UN Educational, Scientific and Cultural Org.)
- WHO (World Health Org.)
- IMF (International Monetary Fund)
- ICAO (International Civil Aviation Org.)
- UPU (Universal Postal Union)
- ITU (International Telecommunication Union)
- WMO (World Meteorological Org.)
- IMO (International Maritime Org.)
- WIPO (World Intellectual Property Org.)
- IFAD (International Fund for Agricultural Development)
- UNIDO (UN Industrial Development Org.)
- IAEA (International Atomic Energy Agency)

UN Programs and Funds

- UNDP (UN Development Program)
- UNICEF (UN Children's Fund)
- WFP (World Food Program)
- UNFPA (UN Population Fund)
- UNEP (UN Environment Program)
- Habitat (UN Centre for Human Settlements)
- UNCTAD (UN Conference on Trade and Development)
- WTO (World Trade Org.)
- UNHCR (UN High Commisioner for Refugees)

Legend:
- Peace
- Justice, human rights and international law
- Humanitarian assistance
- Development

◆ **General Assembly**
All UN member states are represented in the General Assembly, a kind of parliament of nations which meets to consider the world's most pressing problems.

◆ **Security Council**
The UN Charter gives the Security Council primary responsibility for maintaining international peace and security. The Council may convene at any time, day or night, whenever peace is threatened.

◆ **Economic and Social Council**
The Council plays a key role in fostering international cooperation for development. It also consults with non-governmental organizations (NGOs), thereby maintaining a vital link between the United Nations and civil society.

◆ **International Court of Justice**
Consisting of 15 judges elected by the General Assembly and the Security Council, the Court decides disputes between countries.

Source : The UN in brief, Facts about the United Nations, www.un.org.

Budget comparison, the UN and other organizations

(billions of dollars)   Source : www.un.org, www.worldbank.org

- 1.26 UN regular budget (1999)
- 1.3 UN peacekeeping cost (1997)
- 1.8 WHO total budget (1998-99)
- 2 Vermont's annual budget
- 4.8 UN economic & social development cost
- 4.8 EU administrative cost (1998)
- 4.95 New York State University system annual budget
- 18.2 UN system total cost
- The World Bank's total lending 28.6
- New York City's annual budget 31.3

The UN system is a major purchaser of goods and services, totalling nearly $3 billion a year. UNICEF buys half of the vaccines produced in the world, while the UN Population Fund is the world's largest purchaser of contraceptives.

U.S. companies are consistently the largest sellers of goods and services to the UN. In 1997, U.S. companies secured 59% of procurement done by the UN Headquarters in New York ($192 million out of $327.5 million).

The World Health Organization has concluded an agreement with the British pharmaceutical company SmithKline Beecham for a $1.5 billion, 20-year campaign to eradicate elephantiasis globally.

Information technology companies are providing technical assistance to an automated customs system developed by the UN Conference on Trade and Development.

Top 10 contributors to the UN regular budget, 1998/1999

UN regular budget, 1999
(millions of dollars)

Total arrears
(millions of dollars)

UN regular budget per capita, 1998
(U.S. dollars)

United States

United States 742
208
102
68
56
53
29
27
17
15

(3) Japan
(8) Germany
(10) France
Italy
United Kingdom
Canada
Spain
Netherlands
Russia
Liechtenstein

1.11
1.52
1.26
1.19

(1) Liechtenstein
(2) Luxembourg
(4) Norway
(5) Denmark
(6) Sweden
(7) Iceland
(9) Austria

1.77
1.76
1.48
1.39
1.33
1.28
1.25

United States -218
Ukraine -133
Russia -98
Japan -55
Belarus -47
Brazil -15
Yugoslavia -13
Iraq -11
Iran -11
Argentina -10

-1,294

Source : www.un.org, Questions and
answers about the United Nations

Top 10 countries in total arrears to the UN, December 1998

◆ The figures include arrears to the UN regular budget, to UN peacekeeping operations and to the UN International Tribunals for the former Yugoslavia and Rwanda. Of the 185 member states, 68 (or 36%) had not paid their regular budget dues in full.

◆ **The World Bank** is a lending institution whose aim is to help integrate countries into the wider world economy and promote long-term economic growth that reduces poverty in developing countries.

◆ **The International Monetary Fund** acts as a monitor of the world's currencies by helping to maintain an orderly system of payments between all countries, and lends money to members who face serious balance of payments deficits.

◆ **The World Health Organization** coordinates, programs aimed at the attainment by all people of the highest possible level of health. It works to solve health problems in areas such as immunization, health education and the provision of essential drugs.

In 1997, Time-Warner co-chairman Ted Turner announced a $1 billion donation to UN development and assistance programs. The world's Rotary Clubs have given more than $400 million to WHO's efforts to eradicate polio, and the world's Lions Clubs support many UNICEF programs.

UN appeals raise over $1 billion a year for emergency assistance to people affected by war and natural disaster.

The U.S. is both the highest-assessed UN member ($304 million) and the UN member with the greatest debt ($1.6 billion).

Joel Katz

Cost of Living

How much do things really cost and how have costs changed?
Where is it most expensive to live?

Spending & Saving

How much more or less are we spending, and on what?
What percentage of our income do we spend, and on what?
How much are we saving and paying in taxes?

Income & Debt

What is our income, by race? What kind of debt do we incur,
by age? How is Americans' debt distributed? Who lends us money?

Investing

How many mutual funds are there and how do we invest in them?
Who buys stock? Where do we keep our IRA accounts?

Aging & Retirement

How long is our retirement becoming? How much are the elderly
increasing? How is the racial makeup of the elderly changing?

Social Security

How solvent is the Social Security program? How much
does it cost? What is the ratio of workers to beneficiaries?
Who gets benefits and how much? How have entitlement
programs increased compared to other programs?
How important is Social Security to the elderly?

Poverty by Age

How old are the poor? How does the age of the poor compare
with the age of the country? What percentage of each age is
poor? How does education affect income?

Poverty by Characteristic

What are our chances of being poor? Where do the poor live?
Of what race and family composition are the poor?

Housing

Who owns and who rents? How much does housing cost?
What housing types do we occupy and how many rooms
do we live in?

Homelessness

Who are the homeless?
How many of them are there and how are they counted?
How old, what gender, family composition, and race are they?

The purchasing power of a 1950 dollar shrank to just under 15¢ by 1997.

By the numbers

Percentage change in goods and services between 1990 and 1998 relative to the consumer price index of 29.4%. For example, college tuition and fees have increased 83.6% in current dollars but only (!) 54.2% in real, constant dollars.

+54.2%: college tuition and fees

+42%: butter

+40%: cable television

+34.2%: cigarettes and tobacco products

+25.4%: airfare

+20.7%: physicians' services

+18.6%: legal services

+14.4%: bread

+6.9%: public transportation within cities

+2.9%: motor vehicle maintenance and repair

-0.2%: rent

-4.4%: over-the-counter drugs

-4.8%: poultry

-5.4%: milk

-10.9%: furniture and bedding

-12.8%: new cars

-21.1%: electricity

-28.1%: carbonated drinks

-41.6%: women's dresses

-52.2%: televisions

-89.8%: personal computers and information processing equipment

Time Well Spent

In *Time Well Spent: The Declining Real Cost of Living in America*, published in the 1997 annual report of the Federal Reserve Bank of Dallas and updated since, authors W. Michael Cox and Richard Alm exhaustively document the cost of the goods and services that make up our lives in terms of hours (or minutes) of work. These graphs are based on those data, which reveal that—with the notable exception of higher education—the real cost of the products and services we buy is now significantly less than when they were introduced. Cost decreases are, expectedly, greatest in products affected by the rapid pace of technological innovation. (New home costs, which have increased since 1970, can be explained by the wonderful features with they are equipped.)

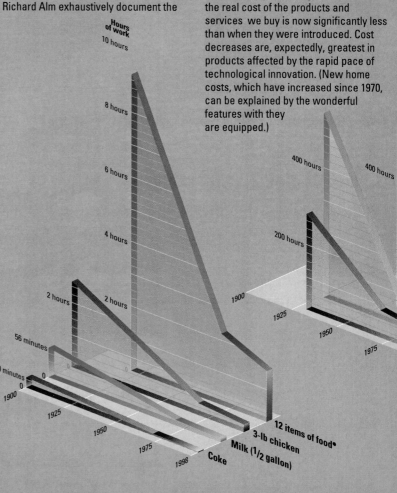

The inflation bite

Since 1950, inflation has taken 85¢ from the value of every dollar.

In 1944, IBM's Mark I mainframe computer cost $200,000 (1944 dollars; almost $2,000,000 1997 dollars). It performed 3 calculations a second, which equaled, in work time, 732,681 lifetimes of work per MIPS (millions of instructions per second).[3]

In 1997, a personal computer cost $1,000, performed 166 MIPS, and cost 27 minutes of work per MIPS to operate.[3]

⊙ Consumer Price Indexes. Home Page. Labor Statistics Bureau. Dept. of Labor. U.S. stats.bls.gov/cpihome.htm
The CPI represents changes in prices of all goods and services purchased for consumption by urban households. User fees (such as water and sewer service) and sales and excise taxes paid by the consumer are also included.

Notes

● The 12-item food basket cited by Cox and Alm includes 3 lbs. of tomatoes, 5 lbs. of sugar, 1 dozen eggs, 1 dozen oranges, ½ gallon of milk, and 1 lb. each of bacon, coffee, ground beef, lettuce, beans, bread, and onions.

1 Based on a family of four with $60,000 annual income, residing in a 2,200 sq. ft., 8-room, 4-bedroom, 2.5-bath home, and owning two vehicles. Source: Runzheimer International.

The cost of a three-pound chicken has risen from $1.23 in 1919 to $3.15 in 1997 in current dollars. In constant dollars it has declined to 39¢ (a decrease of 68%). In work time it has declined from 2 hours 37 minutes to just 14 minutes (a decrease of 91%).[3]

Cost of Living

How much do things really cost and how have costs changed? Where is it most expensive to live?

?

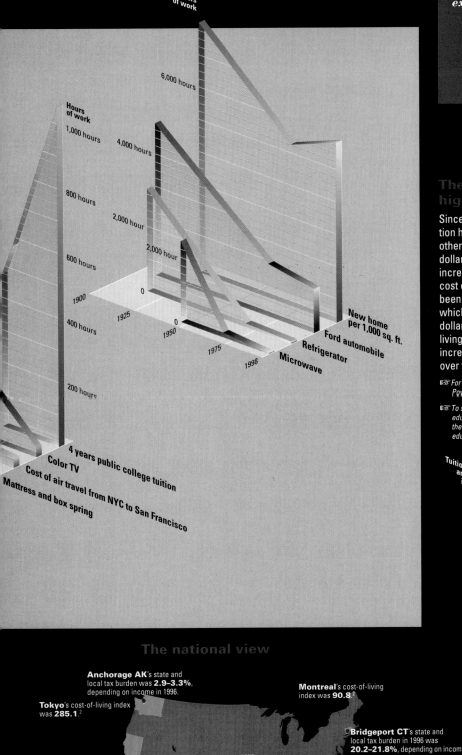

The national view

The higher cost of higher education

Since 1980, the costs for higher education have increased faster than for all other goods and services. In current dollars, higher education costs have increased 328%, or 68% more than the cost of living. The greatest increase has been in the costs of private institutions, which have increased 367% in current dollars, or 88% more than the cost of living. These costs are recovered by the increased earnings of college graduates over those without a college degree.

☞ *For annual salaries by educational attainment, see* Poverty by Age.

☞ *To see how much more we are spending on higher education and other goods and services, and to see the percentage of our income that we spend on education, see the following spread.*

Anchorage AK's state and local tax burden was **2.9–3.3%**, depending on income in 1996.

Tokyo's cost-of-living index was **285.1**.[2]

Montreal's cost-of-living index was **90.8**.[2]

Bridgeport CT's state and local tax burden in 1996 was **20.2–21.8%**, depending on incom

San Francisco's of-living index was **134.8**.[1]

s 1998 cost-

Dallas's 1998 cost-of-living index was **94.6**.[1]

2 Based on a U.S. expatriate family of two with a base salary of $75,000, factoring a combination of housing, transportation, and goods and services.

3 W. Michael Cox and Richard Alm. *Time Well Spent: The Declining Real Cost of Living in America.* 1997 annual report of the Federal Reserve Bank of Dallas. Cox and Alm's calculations use the average hourly wage for production and nonsupervisory workers in manufacturing. In 1897, this wage was less than 15¢ an hour; by 1997 it had climbed to $13.18.

Sources

W. Michael Cox and Richard Alm. *Time Well Spent: The Declining Real Cost of Living in America.* 1997 annual report of the Federal Reserve Bank of Dallas.

U.S. Department of Commerce, Economics and Statistics Administration, Bureau of the Census. *Statistical Abstract of the United States,* 118th Edition, 1998. Washington DC.

Wall Street Journal. *The Wall Street Journal Almanac,* 1999. New York.

U.S. Department of Commerce, Economics and Statistics Administration, Bureau of the Census; U.S. Department of

Housing and Urban Development, Office of Policy Development and Research. *American Housing Survey for the United States in 1995.* Current Housing Reports H150/95RV. Washington DC.

American Chamber of Commerce Researchers Association. *Cost of Living Index: Comparative Data for 329 Urban Areas,* 1998.

American Institute for Economic Research. *Economic Education Bulletin,* Volume XXXVIII, No. 12, 1998.

The growth rate of health costs has been significantly higher than the growth rate of wages for the last 30 years.

The elderly spend almost as much on health care (13%) as they do on food (15%); under-25s spend more than six times on food (19%) as on health care (3%).

Since 1986, our percentage of saving, after taxes, has declined by more than two-thirds. In that same period, the percentage of our total income allocated to taxes has increased almost 16%.

How our spending patterns have changed, and the budget bite

Between 1984 and 1997, the percentage of our income after taxes we spend on many products and services has changed significantly. These changes do not consider the actual cost of these products and services, but only the change in the percentage of our income that we spend on them. The light grey bars show the percentage of our budget that goes to each of these necessities and non-necessities.

☞ To see how the cost of these goods and services has changed, see the preceding spread.

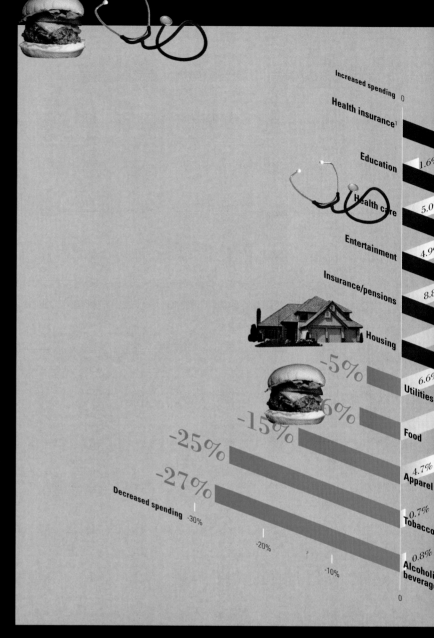

Increased spending 0

Health insurance[1]

Education 1.6%

Health care 5.0

Entertainment 4.9%

Insurance/pensions 8.8

Housing 6.6%

-5%

-6%

-15%

-25%

-27%

Utilities

Food

4.7% Apparel

0.7% Tobacco

0.8% Alcoholic beverages

Decreased spending -30%   -20%   -10%   0

The national view

The residents of **Seattle** spent **89.3%** of their income in 1996–97, highest in the country.

The residents of **Boston** spent **71.8%** of their income in 1996–97.

The residents of the **West** spent **98%** of their after-tax income in 1997, **more** than any other region.

The residents of the **Northeast** spent **89.8%** of their after-tax income in 1997, **less** than any other region.

Saving, spending, taxes

As taxes and spending go up, savings go down. Saving as a percentage of disposable personal income after taxes.

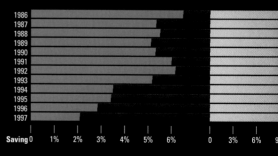

1986
1987
1988
1989
1990
1991
1992
1993
1994
1995
1996
1997

Saving 0   1%   2%   3%   4%   5%   6%   0   3%   6%   9

The Coca-Cola Company has a 44% share of the non-alcoholic beverage market. Private label companies have a 2% share.

The most complaints to the Better Business Bureaus in 1997 were lodged against franchised auto dealers, followed by auto repair shops and home remodeling contractors.

In the fourth quarter of 1998, personal savings as a percentage of income fell to 0.

The young spend seven times more than the elderly on education; the elderly spend almost five times more than the young on health care.

The young, the old, and Hispanics spend more than they earn. We assume that the young are subsidized by their parents and credit card debt and the old by their savings.

Spending & Saving

How much more or less are we spending, and on what? What percentage of our income do we spend, and on what? How much are we saving and paying in taxes?

?

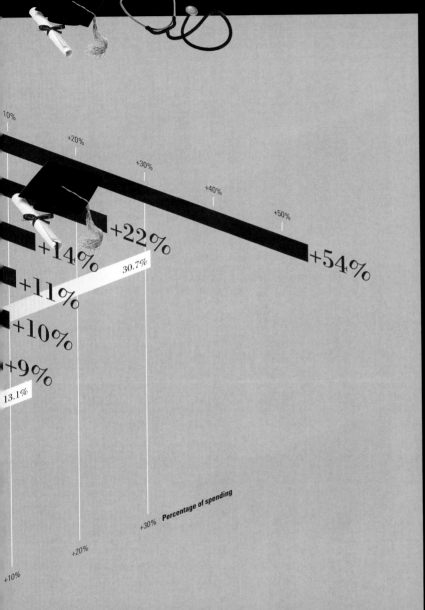

10%
+20%
+30%
+40%
+50%

+22%
+14%
30.7%
+54%

+11%
+10%
+9%
13.1%

+30% Percentage of spending
+20%
+10%

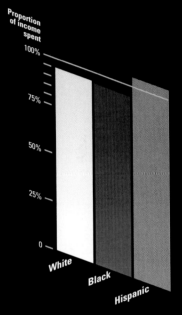

Spending by race

Proportion of income spent

100%
75%
50%
25%
0

White
Black
Hispanic

☞ *Hispanics may be of any race. For a discussion of racial and ethnic classifications and how data from persons of Hispanic origin influence the data reported for whites, see Poverty by Characteristic. It is assumed that the proportion of income spent by Hispanics is inflating the proportion of income spent by whites.*

Spending by age

Proportion of income spent, overall and for housing, education, and health care.

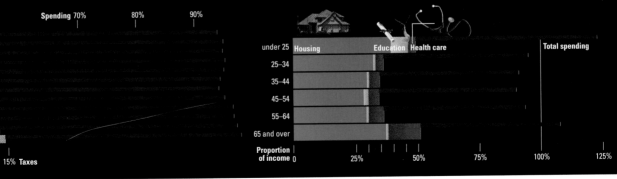

Spending 70%   80%   90%

under 25 Housing   Education Health care   Total spending
25–34
35–44
45–54
55–64
65 and over
Proportion of income 0   25%   50%   75%   100%   125%

2%   15% **Taxes**

Notes

1 Health insurance is included in health care and so is not shown as percentage of spending.

Sources

U.S. Department of Commerce, Economics and Statistics Administration, Bureau of the Census. *Statistical Abstract of the United States*, 118th Edition, 1998. Washington DC.

Wall Street Journal. *The Wall Street Journal Almanac*, 1999. New York.

U.S. Department of Commerce, Economics and Statistics Administration, Bureau of the Census; U.S. Department of Housing and Urban Development, Office of Policy Development and Research. *American Housing Survey for the United States in 1995*. Current Housing Reports H150/95RV. Washington DC.

American Chamber of Commerce Researchers Association. *Cost of Living Index: Comparative Data for 329 Urban Areas*, 1998.

U.S. Department of Commerce, Bureau of Economic Analysis. *Consumer Expenditure Survey*, 1997.

smallest median debt as
a percentage of their income,
16%, compared to all families
earning between $10,000 and
$100,000.

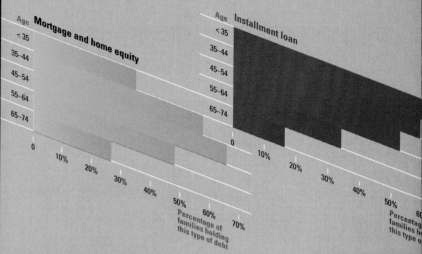

Debt by age: percentage

Percentage of Americans holding one or
more of four types of debt in 1997.

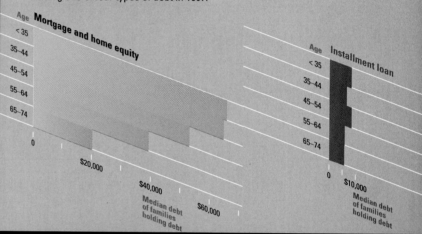

Debt by age: dollars

Median amount of debt for families
holding one of four types of debt in 1997.

The national view

Income in 1997 dollars

North Dakota's average
cost for auto insurance was
$402 per vehicle in 1996.

The **Northeast**'s 1997
median household income
was **$38,929**, up **1.7%**
from 1996.

The **West**'s 1997
median household
income was **$39,162**,
up **3.1%** from 1996.

The **Midwest**'s 1997 median
household income was
$38,316, up **2.4%** from
1996.

New Jersey's average cost
for auto insurance was
$1,103 per vehicle in 1996.

The **South**'s 1997 median
household income was
$34,345, up **3.6%** from
1996.

Type of
debt

Investment
real estate
mortgage

Credit card

Installment

Home mortgage/
home equity

The number of ATM transactions increased
from 3.6 billion in 1985 to 11.0 billion in
1997.

The number of POS (point-of-sale) transactions increased from 14 million in 1985 to
1.4 billion in 1997.

The number of commercial banks decreased
by 37% between 1985 and 1997, from
14,417 to 9,143; the number of branches
increased 39%, from 43,293 to 60,320.

The number of savings institutions
decreased by 51% between 1985 and 1997,
from 3,626 to 1,779; the number of
branches decreased 40%, from 20,980 to
12,672.

⊙ Social Security Administration. U.S.
www.ssa.gov
Official web site of the agency. Contains
information, data, reports and other
sources of information about SSA programs
and services.

The largest percentage of American heads-of-families with debt greater than 40% of their annual income are between the ages of 55 and 64.

What is our income, by race? What kind of debt do we incur, by age? How is Americans' debt distributed? Who lends us money?

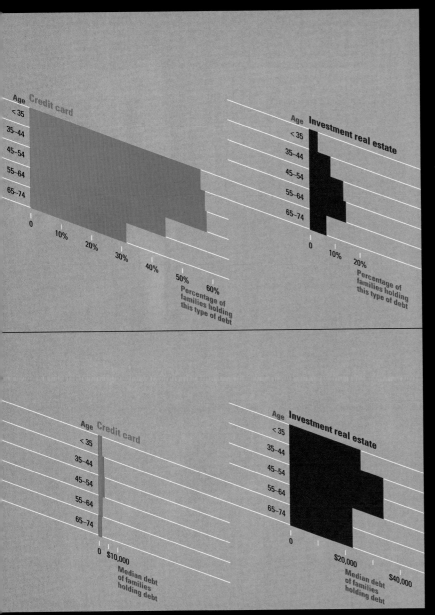

Income by race

Only Blacks have attained and surpassed the high-income year for other races of 1989. Median household income in 1997 dollars.

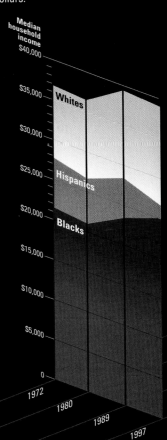

How we use our debt and where we borrow

In 1997, most debt was incurred for home and other real estate purchase and improvement. The largest source for our debt was commercial banks.

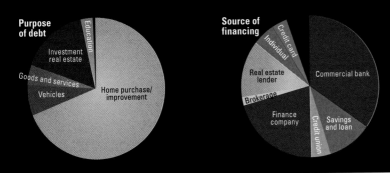

Purpose of debt
- Education
- Investment real estate
- Goods and services
- Vehicles
- Home purchase/improvement

Source of financing
- Credit card
- Individual
- Real estate lender
- Brokerage
- Finance company
- Credit union
- Savings and loan
- Commercial bank

⚪ Isaac Shapiro and Robert Greenstein. The Widening Income Gulf. Center on Budget and Policy Priorities. www.cbpp.org/9-4-99tax-rep.htm Report that examines Congressional Budget Office data indicating a growing income gap among segments of American society.

Notes

1 Based on a family of four with $60,000 annual income, residing in a 2,200 sq. ft., 8-room, 4-bedroom, 2.5-bath home, and owning two vehicles. Source: Runzheimer International.

2 Based on a U.S. expatriate family of two with a base salary of $75,000, factoring a combination of housing, transportation, and goods and services.

Sources

U.S. Department of Commerce, Economics and Statistics Administration, Bureau of the Census. *Statistical Abstract of the United States*, 118th Edition, 1998. Washington DC.

Wall Street Journal. *The Wall Street Journal Almanac*, 1999. New York.

American Chamber of Commerce Researchers Association. *Cost of Living Index: Comparative Data for 329 Urban Areas*, 1998.

Federal Reserve Board of Governors.

By the numbers

54.5% of 1997's mutual funds investments were by individuals ($2.5 trillion).

94%: increase in the number of companies listed on the New York Stock Exchange between 1980 and 1997, from 1,570 to 3,047.

49%: decrease in the number of bond issuers listed on the New York Stock Exchange in the same period, from 1,045 to 533.

757%: increase in the market value of securities listed on the New York Stock Exchange between 1980 and 1997, in **current** dollars, from $1,243 billion to $9,413 billion.

389%: increase in the market value of securities listed on the New York Stock Exchange between 1980 and 1997, in **constant** dollars.

28%: increase in the percentage of families with stock holdings between 1989 and 1995, from 31.6% to 40.3%.

45%: increase in the percentage of stock holdings among these families' financial assets between 1989 and 1995, from 28.6% to 41.5%.

88%: increase in the percentage of families with income less than $10,000 owning stock, 3.3% to 6.2%, between 1989 and 1995.

0.7%: decrease in the percentage of families with income greater than $100,000 owning stock, 81.8% to 81.1%, between 1989 and 1995.

The growth of mutual funds

The personal finance story of the last quarter century has been America's love affair with mutual funds. The number of mutual funds increased by almost 4½ times between 1985 and 1997; their assets have increased more than 6 times in constant (1997) dollars.

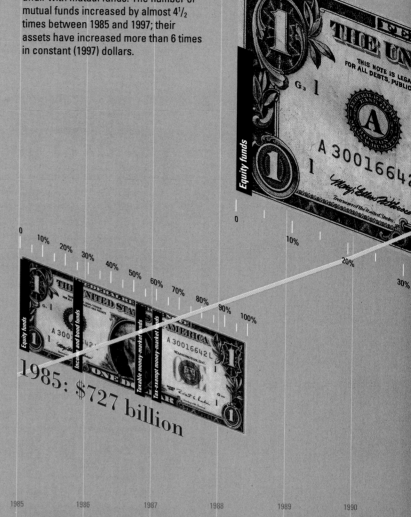

The rich get richer

The rich's share of America's wealth keeps getting larger. The richest 20% of Americans is the only group whose percentage of wealth is increasing.

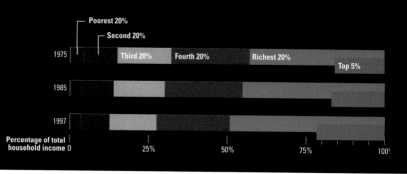

Percentage of total household income

In 1995, the wealthiest ½ of 1% of America's households owned 65% of publicly traded stock.

The next wealthiest ½ of 1% owned 12% of publicly traded stock.

The next wealthiest 4% owned 18% of publicly traded stock.

The next wealthiest 5% owned 3% of publicly traded stock.

The next wealthiest 10% owned ½ of 1% of publicly traded stock.

The remaining 80% of Americans owned 0% of publicly traded stock.

The upper limit of income of the poorest quintile of households in 1997 was $15,400; for the second quintile $29,200; for the third quintile, $46,000; for the fourth quintile, $71,500.

The lower limit of income of the top 5% was $126,550.

In 1997, 65.5 million Americans, in 37.4% of households, owned mutual funds.

Investing

How many mutual funds are there and how do we invest in them? Who buys stock? Where do we keep our IRA accounts?

?

Number of mututal funds — 7,000

Growth in the number of mutual funds, 1985–1997

6,000

5,000

Income and bond funds

Tax-exempt money-market funds

Taxable money-market funds

4,000

3,000

1997: $4,490 billion

40%
50%
60%
70%
80%
90%
100%

2,000

1,000

1992   1993   1994   1995   1996   1997

Who owns stock

The racial and ethnic composition of stock-owning Americans was much whiter than that of the U.S. population as a whole in 1997. The upper pie shows stock ownership by race; the lower pie shows the racial composition of the country as a whole.

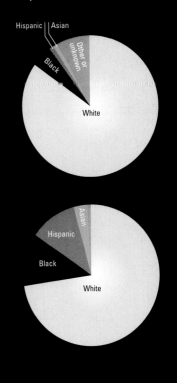

Hispanic | Asian

Other or unknown

Black

White

Asian

Hispanic

Black

White

Who holds the IRA money

Between 1985 and 1996 IRA holders moved their accounts away from savings institutions and commercial banks in favor of mutual funds companies and self-directed plans.

1985

Credit unions
Life insurance companies
Savings institutions
Self-directed
Mutual funds
Commercial banks

Credit unions | Savings institutions

Life insurance companies

Commercial banks

Self-directed

Mutual funds

1996

In 1995, the wealthiest ½ of 1% of America's households owned 28% of Americans' net worth.

The next wealthiest ½ of 1% owned 7% of Americans' net worth.

The next wealthiest 4% owned 21% of Americans' net worth.

The next wealthiest 5% owned 12% of Americans' net worth.

The next wealthiest 10% owned 12% of Americans' net worth.

The remaining 80% of Americans owned 19% of Americans' net worth.

Sources

U.S. Department of Commerce, Economics and Statistics Administration, Bureau of the Census. *Statistical Abstract of the United States,* 118th Edition, 1998. Washington DC.

Wall Street Journal. *The Wall Street Journal Almanac,* 1999. New York.

American Chamber of Commerce Researchers Association. *Cost of Living Index: Comparative Data for 329 Urban Areas,* 1998.

Survey of Consumer Finances.

Federal Reserve Board of Governors.

Median household income increases up to the age of 54 and then declines.

The cost of health care rises dramatically after age 45.

59% of the over-65 population in 1998 were women, but

71% of the over-85 population in 1998 were women.

59% of Americans over 65 are women, but

73% of Americans over 65 living in poverty are women.

40%: mean income of Americans over 65 as percentage of the mean income of those aged 45–54.

24.7%: poverty rate of the elderly in 1970;

10.8%: poverty rate of the elderly in 1996.

46.4% of men over 65 have pension income, but only

26.4% of women do.

3%: full-time private wage and salary workers with 401(k) plans in 1983;

27%: full-time private wage and salary workers with 401(k) plans in 1993.

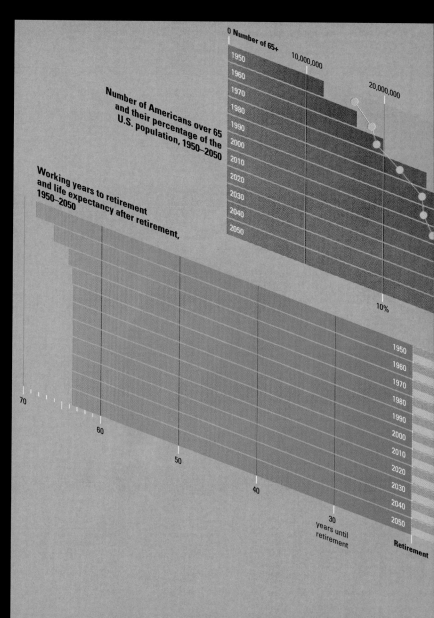

Number of Americans over 65 and their percentage of the U.S. population, 1950–2050

Number of 65+
0 10,000,000 20,000,000

1950
1960
1970
1980
1990
2000
2010
2020
2030
2040
2050

10%

Working years to retirement and life expectancy after retirement, 1950–2050

70
60
50
40
30
Years until retirement

Retirement

1950
1960
1970
1980
1990
2000
2010
2020
2030
2040
2050

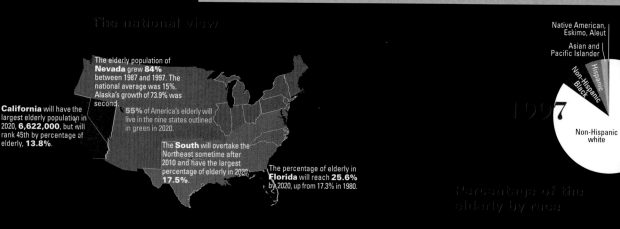

The national view

The elderly population of **Nevada** grew **84%** between 1987 and 1997. The national average was 15%. Alaska's growth of 73.9% was second.

California will have the largest elderly population in 2020, **6,622,000**, but will rank 45th by percentage of elderly, **13.8%**.

55% of America's elderly will live in the nine states outlined in green in 2020.

The **South** will overtake the Northeast sometime after 2010 and have the largest percentage of elderly in 2020, **17.5%**.

The percentage of elderly in **Florida** will reach **25.6%** by 2020, up from 17.3% in 1980.

Percentage of the elderly by race

Native American, Eskimo, Aleut

Asian and Pacific Islander

Non-Hispanic Black

Hispanic

1997

Non-Hispanic white

The percentage of workers 65 and over who worked for less than 12 months increased from 10% in 1987 to 16.1% in 1998.

Of the 80% of Baby Boomer retirees who plan to work during retirement, almost 35% expect to work mainly for interest or enjoyment; almost 23% plan to work mainly for income.

16% plan not to work at all.

39% of Boomers have given a great deal of thought to their retirement years; 15% have not given the subject much thought at all.

84% of Boomers feel that they need more money to live comfortably than their parents' generations; 42% believe that they will have more money when they retire; 31% expect Social Security to meet their needs as well as it met the needs of their parents' generation.

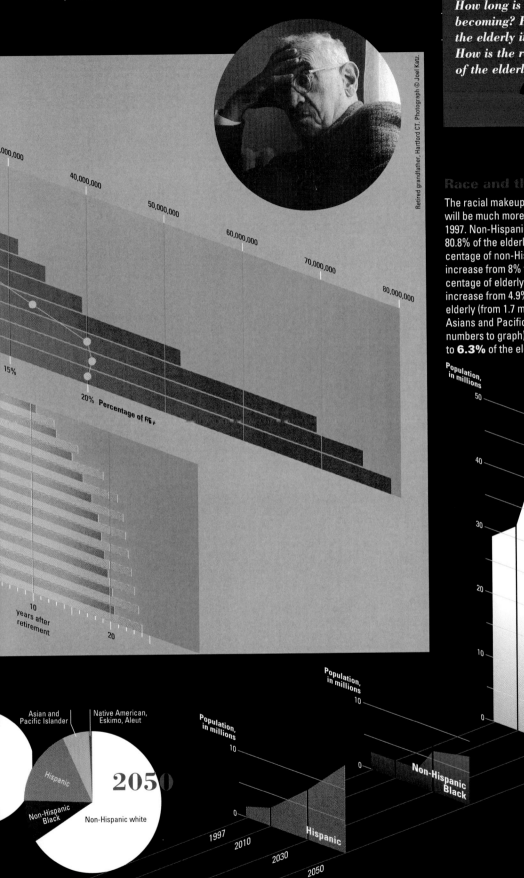

For every hundred persons aged 50–64, the number of persons 85 and older will increase by 50%, from 10 to 15.

Aging & Retirement

How long is our retirement becoming? How much are the elderly increasing? How is the racial makeup of the elderly changing?

?

Retired grandfather, Hartford CT. Photograph © Joel Katz.

Race and the Elderly

The racial makeup of America's over-65s will be much more diverse in 2050 than in 1997. Non-Hispanic whites will drop from 80.8% of the elderly to **66%**. The percentage of non-Hispanic Blacks will increase from 8% to **9.6%**. The percentage of elderly Hispanics will increase from 4.9% to **17.5%** of the elderly (from 1.7 million to 13.7 million). Asians and Pacific Islanders (too few in numbers to graph) will increase from 2% to **6.3%** of the elderly.

Population, in millions

50 — 40 — 30 — 20 — 10 — 0

Non-Hispanic white

Population, in millions

40,000,000 50,000,000 60,000,000 70,000,000 80,000,000

15%

20% Percentage of 65+

10 years after retirement

20

Population, in millions

10 — 0

Non-Hispanic Black

Population, in millions

10 — 0

Hispanic

1997 2010 2030 2050

Asian and Pacific Islander | Native American, Eskimo, Aleut

Hispanic

2050

Non-Hispanic Black

Non-Hispanic white

70% of Baby Boomers don't want to depend on their children during retirement; 9% believe that people ought to be able to depend on their family financially during retirement.

Sources

U.S. Department of Commerce, Economics and Statistics Administration, Bureau of the Census. *Statistical Abstract of the United States*, 1998.

U.S. Department of Commerce, Economics and Statistics Administration, Bureau of the Census; U.S. Department of Health and Human Services, National Institutes of Health, National Institute on Aging. *65+ in the United States*. Current Population Reports, Special Studies, P23-190, 1996.

U.S. Department of Commerce, Economics and Statistics Administration, Bureau of the Census. *Current Populations Reports: Population Projections of the United States by Age, Sex, Race, and Hispanic Origin, 1995–2050*. P25-1130.

Bureau of Labor Statistics, *Employee Tenure in 1998*, USDL 98-387; *Job Tenure*, January 1987.

AARP/Roper Starch. *Baby Boomers Envision their Retirement: An AARP Segmentation Analysis*, 1999.

U.S. Department of Commerce. *Money Income in the United States*, 1996.

The poorest 20% of the elderly get 90% of their income from Social Security; the wealthiest 20% get only 20%.

Without Social Security, the poverty rate would more than quadruple, from 10.8% to 48%.

Running out of time

Although the number of workers paying into the Social Security program continues to increase, the aging of America's population and the increasingly lower age of retirees and disabled workers is relentlessly raising the annual cost of benefits faster than the program's annual income. The Social Security Trust Fund is projected to rise until the year 2020, at which point it will begin to fall precipitously. Without significant changes to the program, the Trust Fund is expected to be exhausted in **2032**.

☞ *To see the increasing numbers of the elderly and retired, see the preceding spread.*

☞ *To see the need for Social Security by the elderly and retired, see the following spread.*

Increased percentage of Americans receiving Social Security benefits

The percentage of Americans receiving Social Security benefits has increased from 2.3% in 1950 to **16.4%** in 1997, and in numbers from 3,477,243 in 1950 to **43,971,086** in 1997.

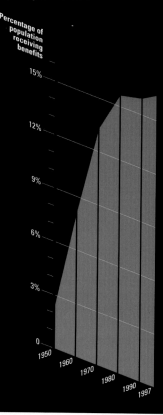

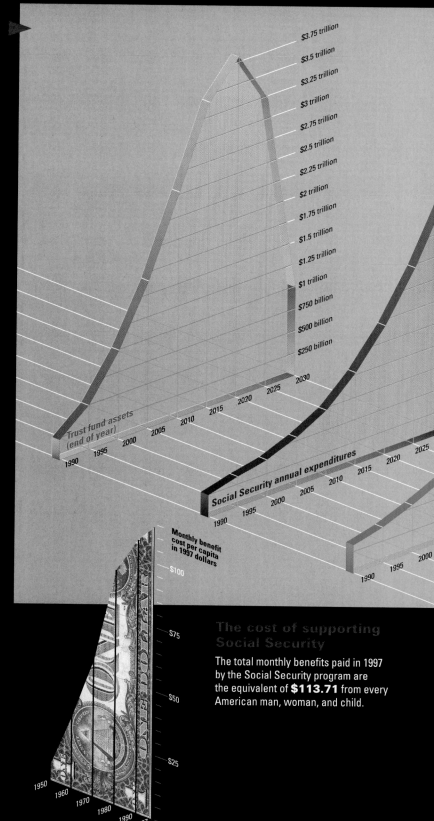

The cost of supporting Social Security

The total monthly benefits paid in 1997 by the Social Security program are the equivalent of **$113.71** from every American man, woman, and child.

73% of the aged poor in 1996 were women.

Only 26% of women had pension income in 1994.

The median income from pensions for Americans 66–84 years old in 2030 will be 5% more than in 1990 (in constant 1990 dollars).

"Between half and two-thirds of [the Baby Boomer] generation is going to need a floor of protection to keep them out of financial hardship—the traditional role of Social Security."

Peter G. Peterson
President, Concord Coalition
21 March 1998

Two-thirds of Americans over 65
depend on Social Security for at
least half of their income.

*How solvent is the Social
Security program? How
much does it cost? What is
the ratio of workers to
beneficiaries?*

?

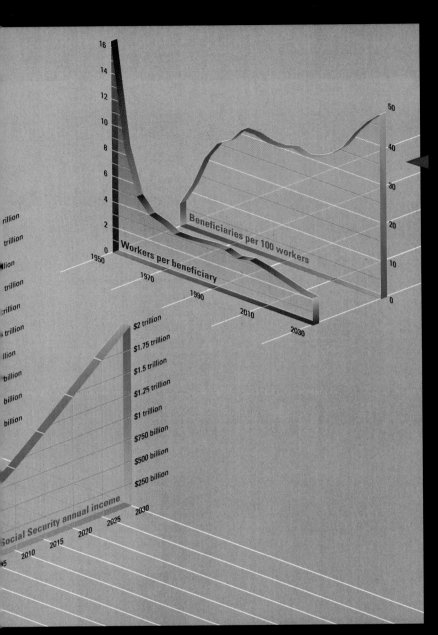

Contributors and beneficiaries

The perpetuation of the Social Security
system is predicated on a number of
workers to support every beneficiary. As
the percentage of workers in the population decreases, and as the number of
beneficiaries increases, the necessary
ratio of workers to beneficiaries is lost.
The number of workers to beneficiaries
is projected to decrease from **16.5** in
1950 to **2.1** in 2030, or **87%**. Similarly,
the number of beneficiaries per 100
workers is projected to increase from **6**
in 1950 to **48** in 2030, an **800%**
increase.

By the numbers

28% of Baby Boomers earning
less than $30,000 annually and

7% earning more than $70,000
annually expect to rely on Social Security
for most or all of their retirement income.

36% of Baby Boomers earning
more than $70,000 annually but only

18% earning less than $30,000
annually feel very optimistic about their
retirement years.

12% of Baby Boomers earning
more than $70,000 annually and

44% earning less than $30,000
annually feel that they won't be able to
retire.

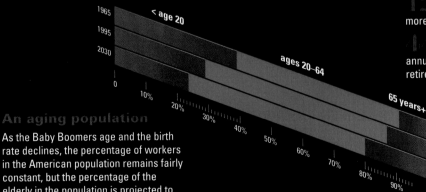

An aging population

As the Baby Boomers age and the birth
rate declines, the percentage of workers
in the American population remains fairly
constant, but the percentage of the
elderly in the population is projected to
almost double between 1965 and 2030.

Sources

U.S. Department of Commerce, Economics and Statistics
Administration, Bureau of the Census. *Statistical Abstract of
the United States*, 1998.

Social Security Administration. *Annual Statistical Supplement
to the Social Security Bulletin*, 1998.

Social Security Administration, Office of Research, Evaluation
and Statistics. *Fast Facts and Figures about Social Security*,
1998.

Wall Street Journal. *The Wall Street Journal Almanac*, 1999.
New York.

Social Security Administration. *1997 Annual Report of the
Board of Trustees of the Federal OASDI Trust Funds*.

U.S. Census Bureau. *Current Population Survey*, March 1997.

U.S. Bureau of the Census, Current Population Reports,
P60-198. *Poverty in the United States*. 1996.

ERBI Datebook on Employee Benefits, 4th edition.

Lewin-VHI. *Baby Boomer Pension Benefits: Will They Be
Adequate for the Future?* Research Division, AARP, 1994.

AARP/Roper Starch. *Baby Boomers Envision their Retirement:
An AARP Segmentation Analysis*, 1999.

By 2030, Baby Boomers will be the largest aged population in American history. 55% of them expect to get their money back from the Social Security system. 48% expect to count on Social Security during retirement. 15% expect to rely on Social Security for most or all of their retirement income.

By the numbers

43,971,086: number of Americans receiving Social Security benefits in 1997, equivalent to the total population of California and Illinois.

$30.5 billion: total monthly benefits paid by the Social Security program in 1997.

7 times: the **percentage** of Americans who received Social Security benefits in 1997 compared to 1950.

13.7 times: the increase in Social Security benefits between 1950 and 1997, in **current** dollars.

20.5 times: the increase in Social Security benefits between 1950 and 1997, in **constant** (1997) dollars.

Bread or guns

Social Security and Medicare payments have both increased at a significantly faster pace than defense expenditures between 1980 and 1997. (This graph is in billions of current dollars; in constant dollars, defense spending has actually declined).

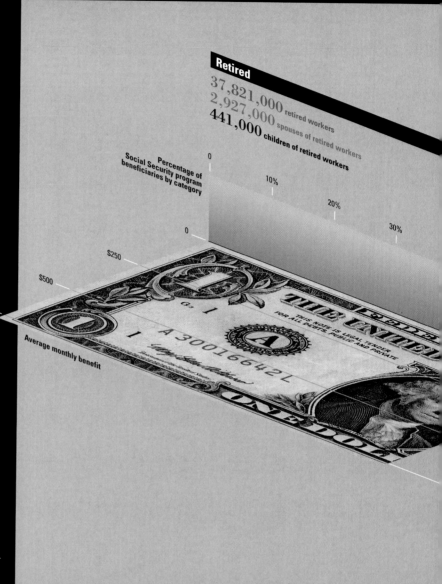

Retired
37,821,000 retired workers
2,927,000 spouses of retired workers
441,000 children of retired workers

Percentage of Social Security program beneficiaries by category

0   10%   20%   30%

0

$250

$500

$750

Average monthly benefit

$234.3 $264.8

$63.4

Medicare $190.20, +200%

National defense $272.40, +2.9%

Social security $376.10, +60.5%

1980

1997

Wyoming received the least Social Security money in 1996, **$183 million**.

Arizona had the country's lowest average benefit per capita in 1996, **$399**.

Only **West Virginia**, **Kentucky**, and **Louisiana** have less than a **60%** Social Security direct deposit participation rate.

New York received the most Social Security money in 1996, more than **$22 billion**; it also had the country's highest average benefit per capita, **$6,811**.

Florida, the fourth most populous state with the equivalent of **45%** of California's population, has the second largest number of Social Security beneficiaries, **76%** of California's.

☞ To see the increasing numbers of the elderly and retired, see Aging and Retirement.

☞ To see the anticipated collapse of the Social Security system, see the preceding spread.

68% of Baby Boomers expect to be able to count on retirement income from an IRA, 401(K), or other retirement savings account; 60% from income or money from savings and investments; 57% from an employer's pension, 48% from Social Security.

"America must make sure that Social Security continues as the foundation of our economic future for our families and that pensions and individual savings and investments supplement, not substitute for, Social Security benefits...."

Margaret A. Dixon
President, AARP, 1996–98
31 July 1997

Americans over 65 get 40% of their income from Social Security.

Social Security 2

Who gets benefits and how much? How have entitlement programs increased compared to other programs? How important is Social Security to the elderly?

?

Who gets benefits

Numbers and proportion of beneficiaries of all Social Security programs, and the average monthly benefit per category, December 1997.

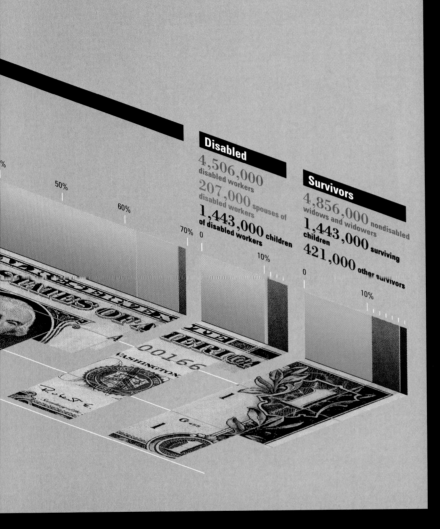

50%

60%

70%   0

Disabled

4,506,000 disabled workers

207,000 spouses of disabled workers

1,443,000 children of disabled workers

10%

Survivors

4,856,000 nondisabled widows and widowers

1,443,000 surviving children

421,000 other survivors

0

10%

Gender

In 1998, 42% of Americans receiving Social Security benefits were men and 58% were women.

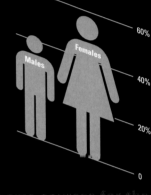

60%

40%

Males   Females

20%

0

Income sources for the over-65s

Social Security continues to be the largest source of income for the elderly, comprising over 40% of their income in 1997.

Earnings

Social Security

Assets

Retirement/pensions

Expectation and reality

Retirees have optimistic expectations of their retirement income. The greatest percentage expect that their most important source of income will be personal savings; in fact, it will be Social Security.

Anticipated and real source of greatest amount of retirement income, by percentage of retirees

Expectation   Reality

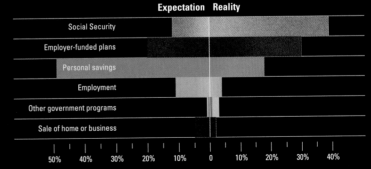

Social Security

Employer-funded plans

Personal savings

Employment

Other government programs

Sale of home or business

50%   40%   30%   20%   10%   0   10%   20%   30%   40%

○ FinanCenter: Personal Finance & Calculators. FinanCenter, Inc. www.financenter.com
A commercial web site designed to provide information and tools for consumers about home and auto loans, credit cards, and insurance, as well as other financial products.

Sources

U.S. Department of Commerce, Economics and Statistics Administration, Bureau of the Census. *Statistical Abstract of the United States,* 1998. Table N° 26.

Social Security Administration. *Annual Statistical Supplement to the Social Security Bulletin,* 1998.

Social Security Administration, Office of Research, Evaluation and Statistics. *Fast Facts and Figures about Social Security,* 1998.

Social Security Administration. *Income of the Population 55 or Older,* 1996.

AARP/Roper Starch. *Baby Boomers Envision their Retirement: An AARP Segmentation Analysis,* 1999.

U.S. Department of Commerce, Economics and Statistics Administration, Bureau of the Census. *Population Projections of the United States, 1995–2050,* 1996.

Only persons under 24 years old have a greater incidence of poverty than the national average.

The age group with the fewest number of people living in poverty is 55–64; the age group with the lowest rate of poverty is 45–54.

By the numbers

20% of Americans under 18 live in poverty,

1.5 times the national average.

14,000,000 Americans under 18 live in poverty,

3 times the number in the next largest group, 25–34, and

20 times more than Americans between 45 and 54.

Under-18s constitute **40%** of the poor, which is

almost **65%** more than their percentage of the population.

23 is the median age of Americans living in poverty.

On average, **2** children (and 1.7 adults) live in each poor household.

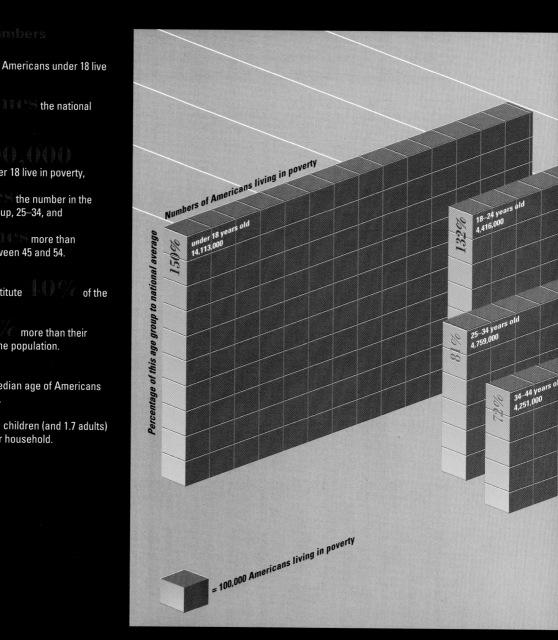

Numbers of Americans living in poverty

Percentage of this age group to national average

150% under 18 years old 14,113,000

132% 18–24 years old 4,416,000

81% 25–34 years old 4,759,000

72% 34–44 years old 4,251,000

☐ = 100,000 Americans living in poverty

The national view

Detroit has the highest proportion of people living in poverty (**32.4%**) among cities with over 200,000 residents.

New Hampshire has the country's lowest poverty rate, **6.9%**.

New Mexico has the country's highest poverty rate, **24.0%**.

The South and **the West** have the country's highest poverty rate, **14.6%**, but the South has 55% more people living in poverty than the West.

West Virginia has the country's lowest percentage of families with income above $100,000 (**less than 2%**).

Age and gender profiles of the U.S.

Composition of the poor by age and gender

Females Males

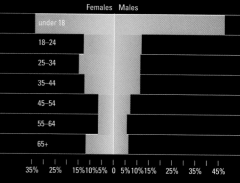

under 18

18–24

25–34

35–44

45–54

55–64

65+

35% 25% 15% 10% 5% 0 5% 10% 15% 25% 35% 45%

22.7% of adults in poor households are full-time workers.

The average annual income of Americans in the lowest income quintile is $3,200.

Among 18–24-year-old whites, the poverty rate for females is 41% greater than for males.

Among 18–24-year-old Blacks, the poverty rate for females is 88% greater than for males.

Among 18–24-year-old Hispanics, the poverty rate for females is 26% greater than for males.

The number of Americans 65 and older living in poverty has decreased by 10% since 1980. And because America is getting older, the percentage of the poor elderly in the total population has decreased by more than 31%.

Black and Hispanic children under 18 are more than 3½ times as likely to live in poverty as white children.

A person with a professional degree (MBA, JD, MD) earns more than six times as much as someone without a high school diploma.

Poverty by Age

How old are the poor? How does the age of the poor compare with the age of the country? What percentage of each age is poor? How does education affect income?

?

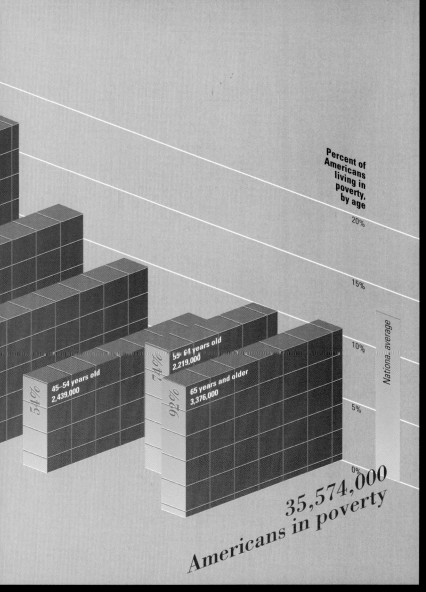

Percent of Americans living in poverty, by age

20%

15%

10%

5%

0%

Nationa-average

45–54 years old
2,439,000

54%

55–64 years old
2,219,000

74%

65 years and older
3,376,000

92%

35,574,000
Americans in poverty

Education and poverty

Not surprisingly, the poverty rate is much higher (actually, 10 times higher) and earnings much lower among high school dropouts compared to those with college and graduate degrees.

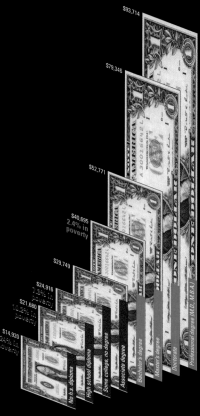

$93,714

$79,346

$52,771

$40,695
2.4% in poverty

$29,749

$24,916
5.4% in poverty

$21,680
10.2% in poverty

$14,920
24% in poverty

No h.s. diploma

High school diploma

Some college, no degree

Associate degree

Bachelor's degree

Master's degree

Doctorate

Professional degree (M.D. MBA)

Profile of the U.S. by age and gender

Females   Males

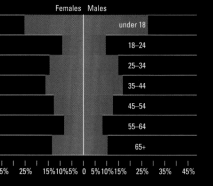

under 18

18–24

25–34

35–44

45–54

55–64

65+

45% 35% 25% 15%10%5% 0 5%10%15% 25% 35% 45%

Poverty. Census Bureau. Dept. of Commerce. U.S.
www.census.gov/hhes/www/poverty.html
Census data and reports on all aspects of poverty in U.S.

Sources

U.S. Department of Commerce, Economics and Statistics Administration, Bureau of the Census. *Statistical Abstract of the United States*, 118th Edition, 1998. Washington DC.

Wall Street Journal. *The Wall Street Journal Almanac*, 1999. New York.

U.S. Department of Commerce, Economics and Statistics Administration, Bureau of the Census; U.S. Department of Housing and Urban Development, Office of Policy Development and Research. *American Housing Survey for the United States in 1995.* Current Housing Reports H150/95RV. Washington DC.

Dalaker, Joseph and Mary Naifeh. U.S. Bureau of the Census, Current Population Reports, Series P60-201. *Poverty in the United States: 1997.* U.S. Government Printing Office, Washington DC, 1998.

For poverty rates and numbers by family composition, race, ethnicity, gender, geography, and national origin, see the following spread.

The number of whites living in poverty is almost as great as Blacks and Hispanics combined.

The poverty rate is greater outside metropolitan areas than within but more poor live in metropolitan areas than outside.

34% more women live in poverty than men; their risk of poverty is 28% greater.

Your chance of being **poor**:

1 in 2 if you are a member of a family headed by a Hispanic woman (no spouse present).

Hispanic mother in Willimantic CT. Photograph © Joel Katz.

1 in 2.7 if you are black, female, and under 18 years old.

1 in 4 if you are Native American.

1 in 5.3 if you live in the center of a city.

1 in 6.7 if you are female, but

1 in 8.6 if you are male.

1 in 7.1 if you are of Asian or Pacific Islander descent.

1 in 20.4 if you are a white male aged 54–59.

3.5 times greater if you live in New Mexico than if you live in New Hampshire.

Your chance of being **wealthy**:

1 in 8.3 if you live in Connecticut and

1 in 50 if you live in West Virginia or Mississippi.

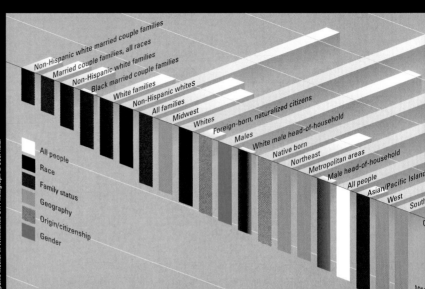

All people	
Race	
Family status	
Geography	
Origin/citizenship	
Gender	

Non-Hispanic white married couple families
Married couple families, all races
Non-Hispanic white families
Black married couple families
White families
Non-Hispanic whites
All families
Midwest
Whites
Foreign-born, naturalized citizens
Males
White male head-of-household
Native born
Northeast
Metropolitan areas
Male head-of-household
All people
Asian/Pacific Island
West
South

10%
20%
30%
40%

Poverty rates and numbers by selected characteristics

Poverty is a fascinating mix of "upstream" and "downstream" characteristics. For me, "upstream" relates to broad cultural and societal issues, best expressed in percentages; "downstream" has to do with delivery and quantifiable issues, best expressed by numbers.

The higher, in many cases strikingly higher, poverty rates among groups identifiable by race, ethnic origin, and gender are telling reminders of the distance we have yet to come to realize the American dream evenhandedly for all Americans.

The numbers of the poor among groups with the same characteristics are simply parallel to the makeup of the United States but of importance in planning for and delivering the services that the poor need.

Overall, these four types of aid to the poor have increased between 1980 and 1996, with the biggest increase in Medicaid. This graph shows the percentage of households receiving each type of aid and is therefore adjusted for increase in population.

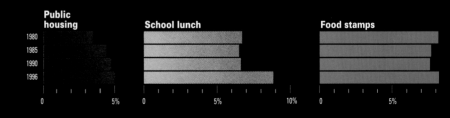

Public housing   **School lunch**   **Food stamps**

1980
1985
1990
1996

0   5%   0   5%   10%   0   5%

The average poverty thresholds in 1997 were:

$ 8,813 for one person

$10,743 for two people

$12,802 for three people

$16,400 for four people

$19,380 for five people

The thresholds are lower for individuals and two-person households over 65 years old.

The thresholds generally become lower as the number of children in a household increases.

The number of Black poor decreased 9.4% between 1996 and 1997; their poverty rate decreased 6.7%; their real median income increased 4.3%.

The rate of poverty for Black female heads-of-household decreased between 1996 and 1997 to 39.8% from 43.7%.

The poverty rate of foreign-born, naturalized citizens is half that of foreign-born non-citizens and lower than that of the native-born.

Poverty by Characteristic

What are our chances of being poor? Where do the poor live? Of what race and family composition are the poor?

?

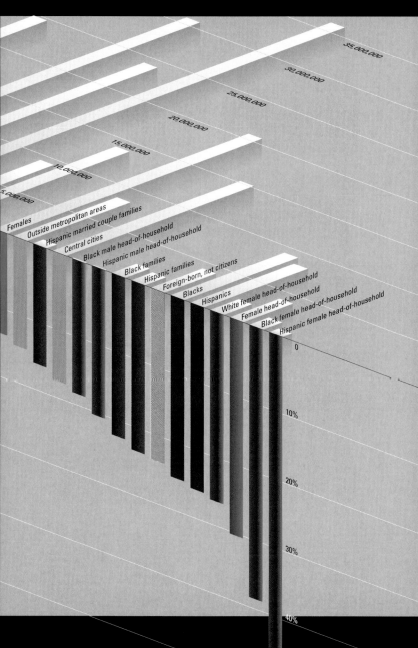

35,000,000
30,000,000
25,000,000
20,000,000
15,000,000
10,000,000
5,000,000

Females
Outside metropolitan areas
Hispanic married couple families
Central cities
Black male head-of-household
Hispanic male head-of-household
Black families
Hispanic families
Foreign-born, not citizens
Blacks
Hispanics
White female head-of-household
Female head-of-household
Black female head-of-household
Hispanic female head-of-household

0

10%

20%

30%

40%

50%

Counting Hispanics

In the 1990 census, all respondents were required to choose a race (white, Black, Asian/Pacific Islander, Native American/Aleut/Eskimo); specifying an ethnicity (Hispanic origin, for example) was optional. As a result, readily available data often double-counts persons of Hispanic origin. Based on the 1998 *Statistical Abstract,* 91.2% of Hispanics are double counted as white, 5.6% double counted as black, and 3.2% double counted as Asian/Pacific Islander or American Indian/Eskimo/Aleut. While this double counting has relatively little effect on statistics for Blacks, it has a significant effect on statistics for whites, increasing their poverty risk from 8.6% to 11.0%, a difference of 38%! The result is to reduce the perceived differential between non-Hispanic whites and other segments of the population. In the data presented in this section, classifications for whites include Hispanics unless otherwise stated.

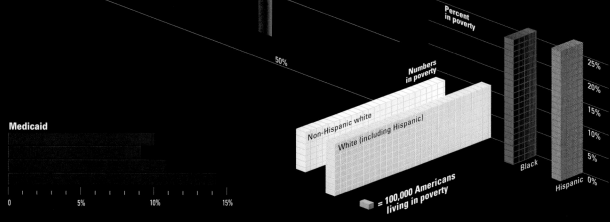

Percent in poverty

Numbers in poverty

Non-Hispanic white
White (including Hispanic)

25%
20%
15%
10%
5%
0%

Black
Hispanic

= 100,000 Americans living in poverty

Medicaid

0   5%   10%   15%

☞ *For poverty rates and numbers by age, see the preceding spread.*

Sources

U.S. Department of Commerce, Economics and Statistics Administration, Bureau of the Census. *Statistical Abstract of the United States,* 118th Edition, 1998. Washington DC.

Wall Street Journal. *The Wall Street Journal Almanac,* 1999. New York.

U.S. Department of Commerce, Economics and Statistics Administration, Bureau of the Census; U.S. Department of Housing and Urban Development, Office of Policy Development and Research. *American Housing Survey for the United States in 1995.* Current Housing Reports H150/95RV. Washington DC.

Dalaker, Joseph and Mary Naifeh. U.S. Bureau of the Census, Current Population Reports, Series P60-201. *Poverty in the United States: 1997.* U.S. Government Printing Office, Washington DC, 1998.

By the numbers

70% : the increase in residential mortgage debt between 1980 and 1997 adjusted for both inflation and population growth.

$1.36 trillion: residential mortgage debt in 1997 (up from $1.1 trillion in 1980).

14%: decrease in the residential mortgage delinquency rate between 1980 and 1997;

220% : increase in the residential foreclosure rate in the same time period.

The greatest growth in household type, both family and non-family, between 1970 and 1997 has been in **male-headed households**.

137% : increase in the percentage of after-tax income spent to support a home purchase between 1976 (24%) and 1997 (32.8%).

San Francisco: highest median price of home purchased, $289,700; highest average monthly payment for home purchase, $1,632; second highest percentage of after-tax income for monthly payment (after New York), 40.1%; longest time to save down payment, 4 years; highest average monthly apartment rent, $1,542; highest median household income, $86,600.

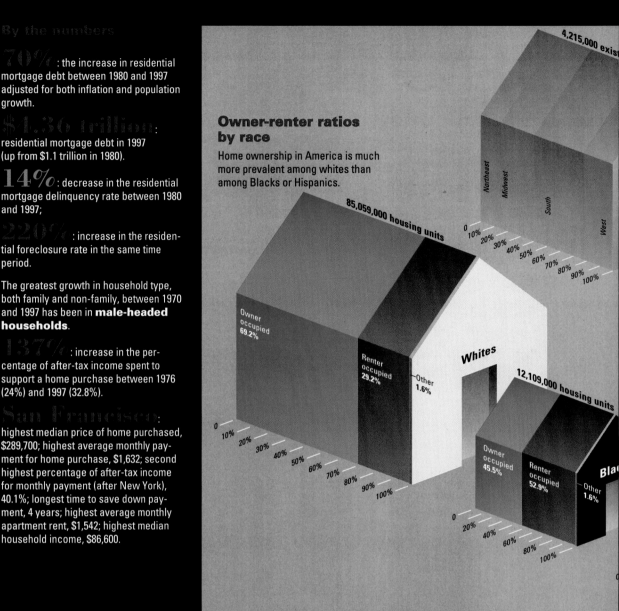

Owner-renter ratios by race

Home ownership in America is much more prevalent among whites than among Blacks or Hispanics.

85,059,000 housing units

Owner occupied 69.2%
Renter occupied 29.2%
Other 1.6%
Whites

12,109,000 housing units
Owner occupied 45.5%
Renter occupied 52.9%
Other 1.6%
Blac...

4,215,000 existing

Northeast | Midwest | South | West

The national view

San Francisco: $292,600 to buy an existing single-family home; **$1,601** to rent 3-bedroom housing; **$923** to rent 1-bedroom housing.

Residents of **Hawaii** would have to work **132 hours a week** at minimum wage to afford two-bedroom rental housing.[1]

Minnesota has the highest rate of home ownership, **75.4%**.

Kokomo is America's most affordable housing market.[2]

Oklahoma City: $77,000 to buy an existing single-family home; **$361** to rent 3-bedroom housing.

$620 to rent 3-bedroom housing in **Pittsburgh**.

Virginia has the highest percentage of renters **(53%)** unable to afford two-bedroom rental housing.

Where do we live?

Mostly in metropolitan areas, and mostly in the suburbs.

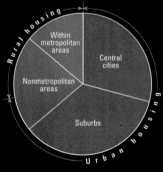

Rural housing | Urban housing
Within metropolitan areas
Central cities
Nonmetropolitan areas
Suburbs

Almost half the housing units in the United States were built between 1950 and 1979. The median age of housing units is 28 years.

The average sales price of a new one-family home is highest in the Northeast; the median sales price is highest in the West.

New housing is least expensive in the South; existing housing is least expensive in the Midwest.

2.8% of the total number of housing units in the United States are seasonal; 8% of year-round housing units are vacant. The vacancy rate of rental units is almost five times the rate for homeowner units.

Between 1970 and 1997, the average floor area of new single-family homes has grown from 1,500 to 2,150 square feet and the median floor area, from 1,385 to 1,975 square feet.

Housing Topics. Census Bureau. Dept. of Commerce. U.S. www.census.gov/hhes/www/housing.html Census data and reports on all aspects of U.S. housing market.

Housing costs, mean in dollars and as percentage of income

Rental housing is more costly as a percentage of income. Except among the elderly, owned housing is more expensive in dollars.

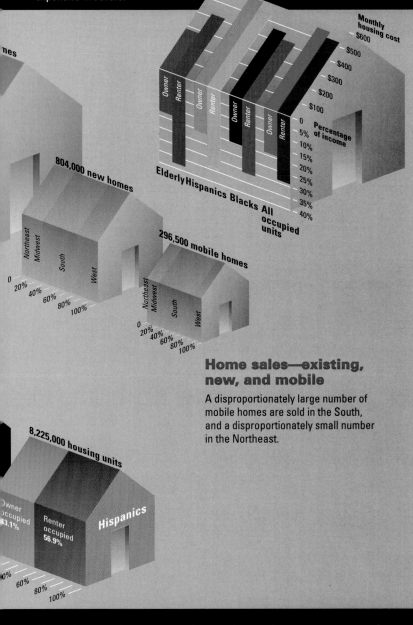

Monthly housing cost
- $600
- $500
- $400
- $300
- $200
- $100
- 0

Percentage of income
- 5%
- 10%
- 15%
- 20%
- 25%
- 30%
- 35%
- 40%

Elderly Hispanics Blacks All occupied units

Owner / Renter

804,000 new homes
Northeast Midwest South West
0 20% 40% 60% 80% 100%

296,500 mobile homes
Northeast Midwest South West
0 20% 40% 60% 80% 100%

Home sales—existing, new, and mobile

A disproportionately large number of mobile homes are sold in the South, and a disproportionately small number in the Northeast.

8,225,000 housing units
Owner occupied 43.1%   Renter occupied 56.9%   Hispanics
0% 60% 80% 100%

Housing debt by age

Freedom from housing debt increases with age. Mortgage and home equity debt peaks between the ages of 35 and 54 and decreases thereafter.

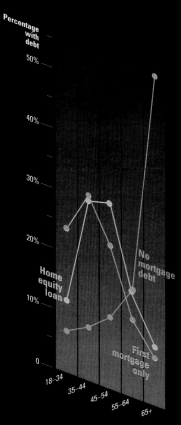

Percentage with debt
- 50%
- 40%
- 30%
- 20%
- 10%
- 0

Home equity loan
No mortgage debt
First mortgage only

18–34 35–44 45–54 55–64 65+

Housing unit type and number of rooms per unit

America is a single-family-house country; the mean number of rooms per housing unit is 5.1. The bars are colored to match the region of the country which has the highest percentage of each housing type and each room quantity.

Type of housing unit occupied

Single family detached	
Single family attached	
2–4 units	
5–9 units	
10–19 units	
20–49 units	
50 or more units	
Mobile home/trailer	

0 10% 20% 30% 40% 50% 60%

Number of rooms in housing units

1 room	
2 rooms	
3 rooms	
4 rooms	
5 rooms	
6 rooms	
7 rooms	
8 rooms or more	

0 10% 20%

☞ For a discussion of how persons of Hispanic origin are often double counted in many government statistical presentations, see *Poverty by Characteristic*.

☞ For additional information on age-related mortgage debt, see *Income and Debt*.

Notes

1 National Low Income Housing Coalition. *Out of Reach Report*, 1999.

2 Kokomo's #1 ranking in housing affordability—95.3—means that families earning the Kokomo median income of $46,900 could have purchased 95.3% of all the homes sold in the fourth quarter of 1997. The median sales price in Kokomo that quarter was $79,000. Source: National Association of Home Builders. From *The Wall Street Journal Almanac, 1999*.

Sources

U.S. Department of Commerce, Economics and Statistics Administration, Bureau of the Census. *Statistical Abstract of the United States*, 118th Edition, 1998. Washington DC.

Wall Street Journal. *The Wall Street Journal Almanac*, 1999. New York.

U.S. Department of Commerce, Economics and Statistics Administration, Bureau of the Census; U.S. Department of Housing and Urban Development, Office of Policy Development and Research. *American Housing Survey for the United States in 1995*. Current Housing Reports H150/95RV. Washington DC.

20–25% of the single adult homeless population suffers from persistent mental
illness[10], but only about a quarter of them
require institutionalization[11].

Age

Children under 18 account for 25% of
the urban homeless, the same percentage of the young in the general
population; unaccompanied minors
comprise 3%[5]. 51% of the homeless are
31–50 years old[1]. Other studies place
the percentage of homeless aged
55–60 at 2.5% to 19.4%[6].

Gender

Single adults are much more likely to
be male than female, with single men
comprising 45% of the urban homeless
population and single women, 14%[5].

Families

Families with children are considered
to be the fastest growing segment of
the homeless, comprising 38–40% of
the homeless[5,7], with higher proportions
in rural areas.

Race and ethnicity

The urban homeless population is considered to be 49% Black, 32% white,
12% Hispanic, 4% Native American,
and 3% Asian[5]. Not surprisingly, these
percentages vary widely with location:
the homeless in rural areas are much
more likely to be white; homelessness
among Native Americans and migrant
workers occurs largely in rural areas[8].

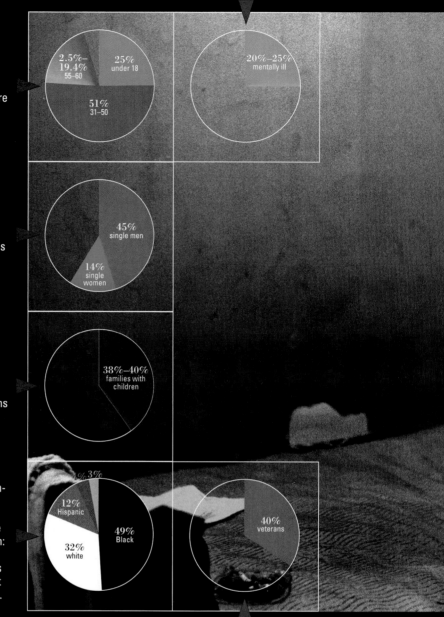

Veterans

40% of homeless men have
served in the armed forces, compared with 34% in the general
population[9]. In urban areas, 22%
of the homeless are veterans[5].

☞ For a discussion of how persons of Hispanic origin are
often double counted in many government statistical
presentations, see Poverty by Characteristic.

○ Homeless—Other Sources of
Information. Dept. of Housing and Urban
Development. U.S.
www.hud.gov/hmlother.html
HUD programs and policies that attempt to
alleviate the problems associated with
homelessness.

Notes

1 Burt, Martha. "Causes of the Growth of Homelessness
During the 1980s," in *Understanding Homelessness:
New Policy and Research Perspectives.* Fannie Mae
Foundation, 1991, 1997. Available free from the Fannie
Mae Foundation, 4000 Wisconsin Avenue, NW, North
Tower, Suite 1, Washington DC 20016.2804;
202.274.8074; fmpubs@fanniemaefoundation.org.

2 National Law Center on Homelessness and Poverty. *Out
of Sight—Out of Mind? A Report on Anti-Homeless Laws,
Litigation, and Alternatives in 50 United States Cities,*
1999. Available for $28 from the National Law Center on
Homelessness and Poverty, 918 F Street NW, Suite 412,
Washington DC 20004.1406; 202.638.2535.

3 Link, Bruce *et al.* "Life-Time and Five-Year Prevalence of
Homelessness in the United States" in *American Journal
of Public Health,* December 1994. Available from Dr. Bruce
Link, Columbia University, 100 Haven Avenue, Apt. 31-D,
New York NY 10032.2626.

Homelessness

Who are the homeless?
How many of them are there
and how are they counted?
How old, what gender,
family composition, and race
are they?

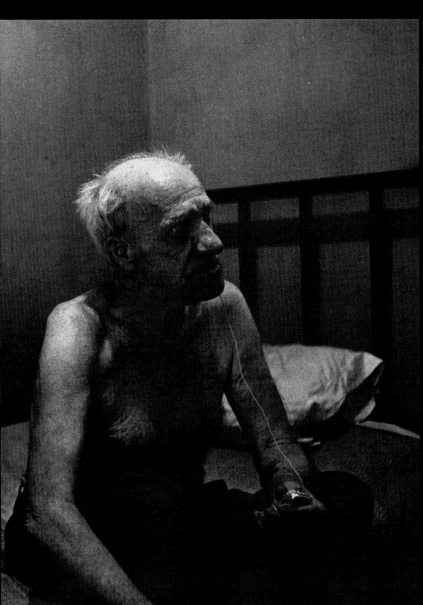

Homeless man in New Haven CT shelter. Photograph © Joel Katz.

Unseen, Uncounted

The National Coalition for the Homeless, the source of all the data used in this spread, discusses very articulately the difficulty and frustration of defining, and the virtual impossibility of quantifying, homelessness. It concludes that, since homelessness is a temporary condition, an appropriate measure of the problem is the number of people who experience homelessness over time rather than a number of "homeless people."

Most studies are limited to counting people on the street or in shelters. This can lead to significant underestimates of the magnitude of the problem:

1. In virtually every city, the estimated number of homeless greatly exceeded the capacity of emergency shelter and transitional housing spaces[11].

2. There are few or no shelters in rural areas of the U.S., and many people without housing live with relatives or friends in crowded, temporary arrangements and will not be counted.

3. A study of formerly homeless people found that 59.2% of them stayed in vehicles and 24.6% in tents, boxes, caves, or boxcars, and are unlikely to have been counted.

Below are summarized four national estimates of homelessness, none of which can really represent how many people are homeless.

1988[1]
500,000–600,000 = .20–.25%

1999[2]
700,000/night = .26%
2,000,000/year = .73%

1985–1990 averaged[3]
7,000,000 = 2.9% in 5 years

1994[4]
3% = 7,818,000

Housing costs

Declining wages and increasing rental costs have put housing out of the reach of minimum-wage workers. In the median state, a minimum-wage worker would have to work ___ hours a week to afford a two-bedroom apartment at 30% of his or her income, the Federal definition of affordable housing[12].

Principal Source

National Coalition for the Homeless
1012 14th Street NW, Suite 600
Washington DC 20005
202.737.6444
www.nch.ari.net

4   Culhane, Dennis *et al.* "Public Shelter Admission Rates in Philadelphia and New York City: Implications of Turnover for Sheltered Population Counts," in *Housing Policy Debate*, 5(1994)2: 107–140. Available free from the Fannie Mae Office of Housing Research, 3900 Wisconsin Avenue NW, Washington DC 20016; 202.752.7761.

5   U.S. Conference of Mayors. *A Status Report on Hunger and Homelessness in America's Cities: 1998.* Washington DC, 1998.

6   Institute of Medicine. *Homelessness, Health, and Human Needs.* Washington DC, National Academy Press, 1998.

7   Shinn, Marybeth and Beth Weitzman, "Homeless Families Are Different," in *Homelessness in America.* Washington DC, National Coalition for the Homeless, 1996.

8   U.S. Department of Agriculture, Rural Economic and Community Development. *Rural Homelessness: Focusing on the Needs of the Rural Homeless.* Washington DC, 1996.

9   Rosenheck, Robert *et al.* "Homeless Veterans," in *Homelessness in America.* Washington DC, Orex Press, 1996.

10 Koegel, Paul *et al.* "The Causes of Homelessness," in *Homelessness in America.* Washington DC, Orex Press, 1996.

11 Federal Task Force on Homelessness and Severe Mental Illness. *Outcasts on Main Street: A Report of the Federal Task Force on Homelessness and Severe Mental Illness.* Delmar NY, National Resource Center on Homelessness and Mental Illness, 1992.

12 National Coalition for the Homeless, 1012 14th Street NW, Suite 600, Washington DC 20005; 202.737.6444.

Disease & Illness
What kills us? Can diseases be eradicated?

Cancer
Who gets it? What kinds are there?
Are we winning the fight against it?

AIDS
Where is it? Who has it? What are the trends?

Disability
Who's disabled? How? How do the disabled support themselves?

Alternative Medicine
How popular is it? Is it for real?

Genetic Engineering
What is it? Where will it lead? What do we think about it?

Physical Fitness
How fat are we? How much exercise do we get?

Mental Health
What problems and effects are found in older Americans?
What are we doing about it?

The Cost of Health
Who pays? How much? Where does the money go?

The Business of Health
How much do doctors earn? What do we spend on hospitals?

Insurance
Who's covered? Who's not? Why?

2,900,000

people died from Tuberculosis in 1997.

Most common worldwide...

1. AIDS
2. Lyme Disease
3. Meningococcal infections
4. Escherichia Coli (E-Coli)
5. Malaria

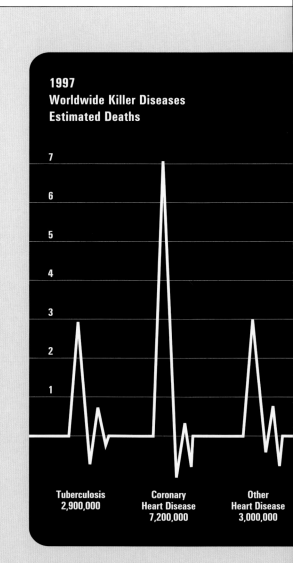

1997
Worldwide Killer Diseases
Estimated Deaths

Tuberculosis	Coronary Heart Disease	Other Heart Disease
2,900,000	7,200,000	3,000,000

Heart disease: The num

The facts

Men who have suffered clinical depression are more than twice as likely to develop heart disease as those who haven't.

Black smokers inhale more nicotine per cigarette than do white smokers. This may explain why they are 30% more likely to develop lung cancer.

Diesel exhaust fumes may pose a significant cancer risk even in low-level exposure, according to a draft EPA report.

Year of the virus

1977
Ebola Virus

1983
AIDS

1989
Hepatitis C

3
Killers

According to the table at left, these three diseases killed the most people worldwide in 1997.

**Coronary
Heart Disease
7.2 million**

**Cancer
6.58 million**

**Cerebrovascular
Disease
4.6 million**

We're back!

Diseases once considered outdated are making a comeback.

Cholera:
Caused by a bacterium spread principally through food and drinking water contaminated with human feces.

Malaria:
Caused by a parasite transmitted by the anopheles mosquito. Malaria has risen steadily during the 80s and 90s. Globally, about 300 to 500 million cases occur annually.

Tuberculosis:
This bacterial disease was predicted to be eliminated from the U.S. by the end of the century. According to the World Health Organization, Tuberculosis is the "world's most neglected health crisis."

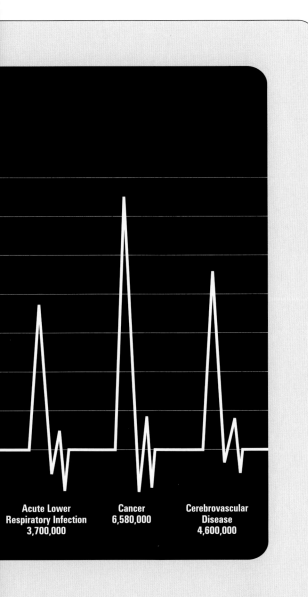

**Acute Lower
Respiratory Infection
3,700,000**

**Cancer
6,580,000**

**Cerebrovascular
Disease
4,600,000**

ber one killer in the U.S.

Between the periods 1976-80 and 1988-94, hypertension among adults age 20-74 declined sharply from 30 percent to 23 percent after remaining relatively stable over the previous 20 years.

Mortality from HIV infection declined 48 percent in 1997 following a 29 percent decline in 1996. This 2-year decline contrasts sharply with the period 1987-1994 when HIV mortality increased at an average rate of 16 percent per year.

● MEDLINEplus. National Library of Medicine. National Institutes of Health. Dept of Health and Human Services. U.S.
www.nlm.nih.gov/medlineplus/
The National Library of Medicine brings MEDLINEplus to the web as a source of information for health care professionals and consumers. Resources include databases, publications, links to health organizations, directories of doctors and hospitals, and a dictionary of medical terms.

1. Heart disease
3. Stroke

2.Cancer

A disease characterized by the unrestrained growth of cells, Cancer remains the second leading cause of death in the United States. In 1996, 539,533 deaths resulted from this disease.

Cancer afflicts people of all ages, races, and genders. It varies greatly in cause, symptoms, response to treatment, and possibility of cure.

1998

1998 marked the first drop in the number of new cancer cases in almost sixty years. In the 1930s, only one in four American cancer patients survived at least five years after diagnosis. In contrast, four out of ten who get cancer now will survive the five years following diagnosis.

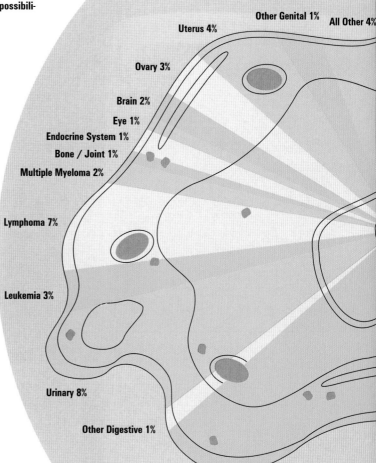

Other Genital 1%   All Other 4%

Uterus 4%

Ovary 3%

Brain 2%

Eye 1%

Endocrine System 1%

Bone / Joint 1%

Multiple Myeloma 2%

Lymphoma 7%

Leukemia 3%

Urinary 8%

Other Digestive 1%

Colon, Rectum, Anus 12

1,500 Americans

The facts

Common Cancers include blood and bone marrow, bone, lymph nodes, brain, sympathetic nervous system, kidneys and soft tissue.

In the U.S. 1 out of 4 deaths is due to Cancer. In 1999, about 1,221,800 new cancer cases are excepted to be diagnosed.

As a childhood disease, Cancer is rare.

1 in 2 men

A U.S. male has a 1 in 2 probability of developing invasive Cancer at some time during his life.

Cancer

Who gets it?
What kinds are there?
Are we winning the fight against it?

?

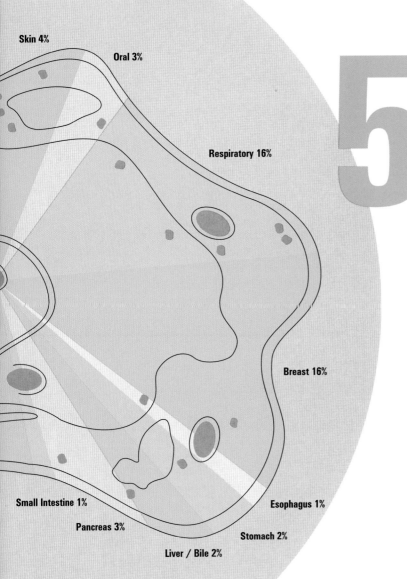

Skin 4%

Oral 3%

Respiratory 16%

Breast 16%

Small Intestine 1%

Pancreas 3%

Liver / Bile 2%

Stomach 2%

Esophagus 1%

5

Most common

The five leading types of Cancer and resulting deaths from each:

1. lung/bronchus
   160,000
2. colon/rectum
   56,500
3. breast (female)
   43,900
4. prostate (male)
   39,200
5. pancreas
   28,900

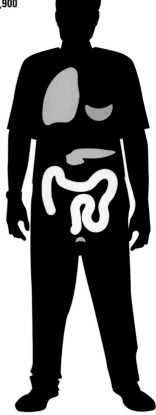

die daily

● CancerNet™. National Cancer Institute. National Institutes of Health. Dept of Health and Human Services. U.S. www.cancernet.nci.nih.gov/ CancerNet provides information, reviewed by oncologists, on cancer treatments, prevention, screening, and clinical trials for patients, health care professionals, basic researchers and the public.

Cancer is treated by surgery, radiation, chemotherapy, hormones and immunotherapy.

The National Institutes of Health estimate overall annual costs for cancer at 107 billion.

In the world

Of the 33.6 million people estimated to be infected with AIDS worldwide, nearly 70 percent reside in sub-Saharan Africa.

● Red areas of the map show regions of the world with the highest number of adults and children living with the virus.

● ● Pink areas indicate lesser numbers of infected.

33.6 mil

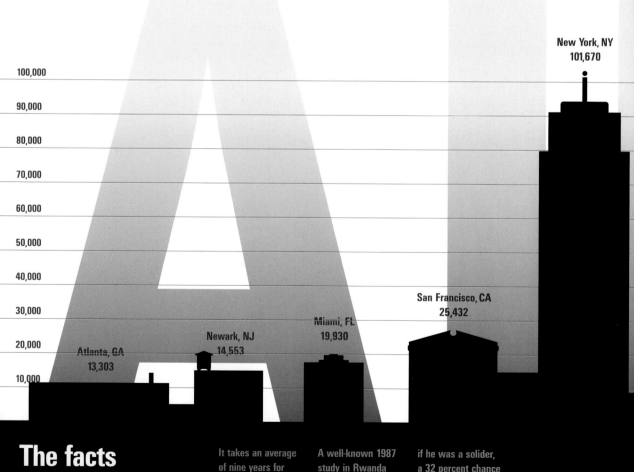

New York, NY
101,670

100,000

90,000

80,000

70,000

60,000

50,000

40,000

30,000

San Francisco, CA
25,432

Miami, FL
19,930

20,000

Newark, NJ
14,553

Atlanta, GA
13,303

10,000

The facts

It takes an average of nine years for HIV to progress to AIDS.

A well-known 1987 study in Rwanda showed that a woman had a 9 percent chance of infection if her husband was a farmer, a 22 percent chance

if he was a solider, a 32 percent chance if he was a white collar worker and a 38 percent chance if he was a government official.

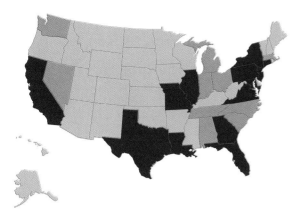

In America

- ● Red areas of the map to the left indicate 1,000 to 14,000 AIDS cases reported in the state.
- ● Dark pink areas indicate 500 to 1,000 cases reported.
- ● Light pink areas indicate 0 to 500 reported cases of the virus.

Where is it?
Who has it?
What are the trends?

?

Cases diagnosed annually

27,000
Black Americans are HIV positive.

10,394
Hispanic Americans are HIV positive.

20,188
White Americans are HIV positive.

lion

Infected
33.6 million people are estimated to be infected with AIDS worldwide. 860,000 are in North America.

In our Cities

American urban centers have become hotbeds for infection. In 1997 there were fourteen U.S. cities with over 10,000 HIV or AIDS infected people. New York City has by far the most infected, with more than the five next highest cities combined.

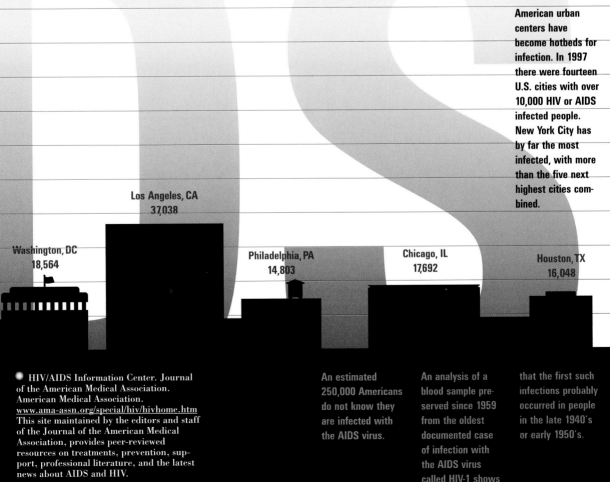

Los Angeles, CA
37,038

Washington, DC
18,564

Philadelphia, PA
14,803

Chicago, IL
17,692

Houston, TX
16,048

● HIV/AIDS Information Center. Journal of the American Medical Association. American Medical Association. www.ama-assn.org/special/hiv/hivhome.htm This site maintained by the editors and staff of the Journal of the American Medical Association, provides peer-reviewed resources on treatments, prevention, support, professional literature, and the latest news about AIDS and HIV.

An estimated 250,000 Americans do not know they are infected with the AIDS virus.

An analysis of a blood sample preserved since 1959 from the oldest documented case of infection with the AIDS virus called HIV-1 shows that the first such infections probably occurred in people in the late 1940's or early 1950's.

Worldwide, 859,000,000 people have some sort of disability. In the U.S. 54,000,000 people live with a disability, making them the single largest minority group in the country.

54 million Americans

Of the millions of people limited in their activities by long term disability, 73% are heads of households, 48% are principal shoppers, 46% are married, and 58% own their own homes.

1 in 5 homes
has a disabled person living there.

Learning impairments, mental retardation

Hearing impairment

Speech impairment

Paralysis

Orthopedic impairments

Absence of limb or other body part. Deformities in general

The facts

More than 7 million people employ mobility devices such as crutches, canes, walkers, wheelchairs and

It is estimated that at least one half of all non disabled adults have a disabled spouse, child, parent or friend.

About a third of adults with disabtiltties go to a restaurant at least once a week.

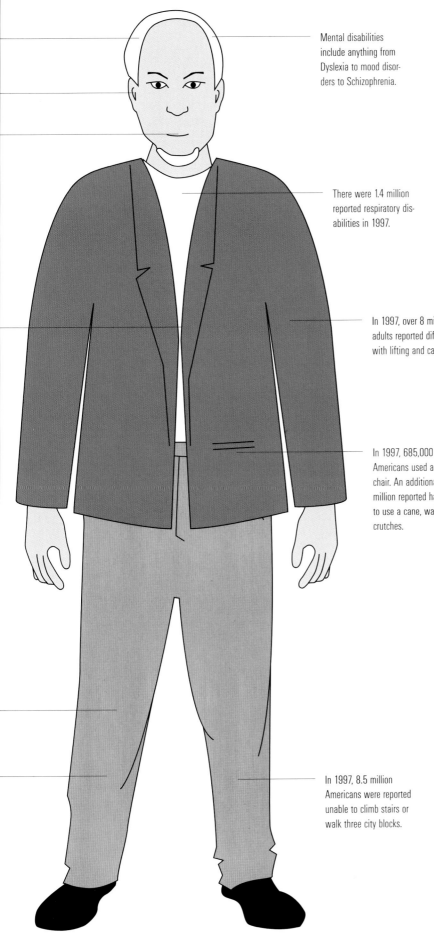

Mental disabilities include anything from Dyslexia to mood disorders to Schizophrenia.

There were 1.4 million reported respiratory disabilities in 1997.

In 1997, over 8 million adults reported difficulty with lifting and carrying.

In 1997, 685,000 Americans used a wheelchair. An additional 1.6 million reported having to use a cane, walker or crutches.

In 1997, 8.5 million Americans were reported unable to climb stairs or walk three city blocks.

Disability

Who's disabled? How? How do the disabled support themselves?

?

The pay scale

For persons without a disability, the employment rate is 80.5%. For those with a severe functional limitation, however, the employment rate is only 27.6%. The average monthly income for a non-disabled person is $2,446. For a person with a non-severe disability it is $2,006. A person with a severe disability only averages $1,562 per month.

1 in 6 people

One in every six Americans will be disabled sometime in his or her lifetime.

● National Institute on Disability and Rehabilitation Research. Office of Special Education. Dept. of Education. U.S. www.ed.gov/offices/OSERS/NIDRR/ Under the auspices of the Education Department, the National Institute on Disability and Rehabilitation Research coordinates research programs that aim to fully integrate and provide independent living for the disabled. Through their Doorways web site, consumers can access

The Americans with Disabilities Act gives civil rights protections to individuals with disabilities similar to those provided on the basis of race, color, sex, national origin, age, and religion. It guarantees equal opportunity for individuals with disabilities in public accommodations, employment, transportation, State and local government services and telecommunications.

Doctor or "Doctor"

Worldwide, only about 10 to 30% of health care is provided by conventional practitioners; the remaining 70 to 90% involves combinations with alternative practices. In the U.S. over 50% of all physicians use or refer patients to alternative treatments. 1 in 3 Americans uses some form of alternative medicine. 40% of Dutch physicians use homeopathy; 70% of German pain clinics use acupuncture.

80% of students in medical schools would like further training in alternative medicine. Currently, over 32 medical schools offer courses in complementary, alternative and unconventional medicine.

80%

80% of medical students would like further training in alternative medicine.

Often it is not the "magic bullets" developed in pharmacology, but combination approaches, that prove most useful for problems with complex causes. Usually these have fewer direct toxic side effects and may, if successful, cost less and therefore be preferable to patients.

50%

Over 50% of conventional physicians use some sort of alternative medicine.

42%

42% of all adults reported using some type of alternative medical therapy in 1997.

The facts

Alternative medicine comprises a wide variety of healing philosophies, approaches and therapies. It includes treatments practices not widely taught in medical schools, not generally used in hospitals, and not usually reimbursed by health insurance

healthfinder®. Dept. of Health and Human Services. U.S. www.healthfinder.gov healthfinder® is a gateway to consumer health information from various Federal Government agencies.

Medicinal herb sales in the U.S.

The U.S. herbal medicine industry is exploding. The graphic below shows total dollar amounts for specific medicinal herbs in 1997.

In addition to these, another $2.4 billion was spent on all other types of medicinal herbs.

Alternative Medicine

How popular is it?
Is it for real?

?

Ginseng
$210 million

Echinacea
$180 million

Gingko biloba
$160 million

200 Years

Homeopathy has essentially continued unchanged for over 200 years. In general, the history of alternative medicine is quite long. Acupuncture has been practiced for more than 2000 years and prayer, spiritualism, and shamanism have an estimated 20,000 year history.

Garlic
$150 million

St. John's Wort
$10 million

Funds

Congress created the Office of Alternative Medicine (OAM) in 1992. Funds allocated for the Office were $2 million in 1992 and 1993. In 1994 the budget was $3.5 million, $5.4 million in 1995 and $7.4 million in 1996.

Different strokes

Various U.S. alternative health services and the number of licensed practitioners in 1996.

Acupuncture
8,000

Chiropractic
55,000

Homeopathy
1,000

Massage Therapy
200,000

Naturopathy
1,500

Osteopathy
41,600

Health Topics A-Z. Centers for Disease Control and Prevention. Dept. of Health and Human Services. U.S. www.cdc.gov/health/diseases.htm An alphabetical approach, from Acute Care to Zoster, to finding information on diseases and other health topics is provided on this web site from the Centers for Disease Control and Prevention.

The OAM averages over a thousand inquiries per month about alternative and complementary medical practice and research.

Approximately one million Americans spend $500 million a year on acupuncture.

40%

According to a March of Dimes survey, more than 40% of Americans think it would be okay to make their children more attractive or more intelligent.

Where will it lead?

Plastic surgery was originally developed to correct facial deformities caused by war injuries, but was soon used as a means of esthetic perfection. Breast implants were developed to reconstruct breasts in women who lost theirs to mastectomy. Soon after they were inserted in women who simply wanted a larger cup size. Gene therapists foresee a time when something similar will happen with their technology too.

Genetics may account for about 20% of the U.S. Gross Domestic Product, or roughly $2 trillion, by the year 2025.

18%

18% of Americans believe it would be okay to use gene therapy to alter a child's aggression level or remove a disposition to alcoholism.

10%

10% of the U.S. population agrees that using gene therapy to prevent a child from becoming homosexual would be a good idea.

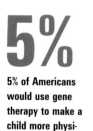

5%

5% of Americans would use gene therapy to make a child more physically attractive.

Few people question the value of correcting a gene for Sickle-Cell Anemia, Cystic Fibrosis, Alzheimer's, Heart Disease, or Cancer.

But altering genes for the sake of appearance requires much thought, debate, and ethical discussion.

The facts

Several companies are working on developing pigs with human genes in order to facilitate the use of the organs in humans. One day you may be able to own your own personal organ donor pig with your genes implanted. When one of your organs gives out, you have a back-up.

Human Genome Project Information. Dept. of Energy and National Institutes of Health. U.S. www.ornl.gov/hgmis
The 13-year Human Genome Project aims to identify the more than 80,000 human genes and determine the sequences of some 3 billion DNA subunits and make them available for biological study. Publications on the research, ethical and social issues, and more on genetics is found at this site.

Genetic Crossover

Genetic Engineering

What is it?
Where will it lead?
What do we think about it?

?

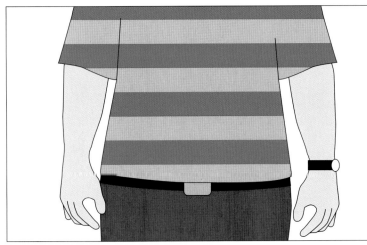

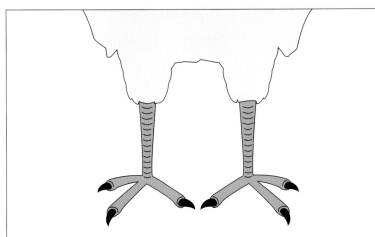

Plants

Soon, by means of genetic engineering, pheremones will be bred into plants as a means of pest control by luring insects and other pests away from their intended victims.

Humans

It is very possible that by the time our grandchildren reach adulthood, they could have almost complete control over exactly how their babies will look, think, and act.

Animals

Routine genetic programs will be used to enhance animals for food production, recreation, and even as pets.

Smart!

Plants will give higher yields and natural processes such as ripening will be enhanced and controlled.

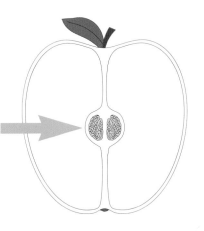

1

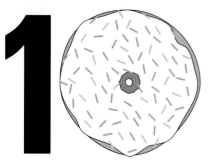

Fattest Cities:

New Orleans 37%

Norfolk 34%

San Antonio 33%

Kansas City 32%

Cleveland 32%

Detroit 31%

Columbus 31%

Cincinnati 31%

Pittsburgh 30%

Houston 29%

The list to the left shows the country's fattest cities with the percentage of overweight Americans residing in each. According to the Federal Obesity Guidelines, assessment of overweight involves evaluation of three key measures: body mass index (BMI), waist circumference, and a patient's risk factors for diseases and conditions associated with obesity. Overweight is defined as having a BMI of 25 to 29.9 and obesity as a BMI of 30 and above, which is consistent with the definitions used in many other countries.

Weight gain...

Between 1960 and 1994, the prevalence of obesity increased from nearly 13% to 22.5% of the U.S. adult population, with most of the increase occurring in the 1990's.

CLASS OF
'60

The average woman who considers herself overweight is 28 lbs. over her ideal weight. The average overweight man is 24 lbs. too heavy.

50% of all Americans ar

The facts

Even though more than half of Americans want to lose weight, fewer than one in five is on a diet. 62% of women want to lose weight, and only

3% want to gain, leaving only about 1/3 of all woman happy with their weight. Men are slightly happier: only 42% of men would like to lose

weight, and 10% would like to gain. That leaves almost half of adult men happy with their weight.

$33 billion
spent on the diet industry annually

Dieting is big business in America. Between fitness videos, multivitamin drinks, and prescription medication, the decision to lose weight has become a largely financial one.

Physical Fitness

How fat are we? How much exercise do we get?

CLASS OF **'94**

The average American woman is 5'4" tall and weighs 142 lbs. But she'd like to be 5'6" and weigh 129. The average man is 5'10" tall and weighs 180. He'd like to be 5'11" and weigh 171.

Couch Potatoes

- In the dark green areas, 30% of the population reported no regular exercise or physical activity.
- The lighter green areas were slightly more active.

e too fat.

The 28% of the population with no leisure physical activity is estimated to cost the U.S. economy $24 billion, accounting for 22 percent of heart disease, colon cancer and osteoporotic fractures, and 12% of diabetes. This represented about 2.4% of health care costs in 1995.
Source: Colditz, Graham. Medicine & Science in Sports & Exercise, American College of Sports Medicine.

Physical Activity and Health: A Report of the Surgeon General. Public Health Service. Dept. of Health and Human Services. U.S.
www.cdc.gov/nccdphp/sgr/sgr.htm
This report summarizes research on physical activity from physiologists, doctors, and behavioral scientists and concludes that exercise and physical activity can improve the quality of life and improve one's health.

Individuals who exercise regularly are less likely to develop:

Heart disease
Diabetes
High blood pressure
High cholesterol
Certain Cancers
Osteoporosis

Almost one in six elderly Americans suffer from serious, persistent symptoms of depression, and many have major clinical depression, an immobilizing disorder that can lead to

suicide. Depression increases the likelihood that a serious physical illness will develop or get worse and without treatment, greatly impacts the lives of the elderly as well as their families.

From 1980 to 1992, suicide rates rose by 9% among all Americans 65 and older, and by 35% among those aged 80 to 84. Only a small percentage of those deaths are believed to rep-

resent a calculated escape from an incurable illness. 40% of elderly suicide victims visit their doctors the week before. Rarely do the doctors detect the potential for suicide.

When the Utah division of Kennecott Copper Corporation provided mental health counseling for employees, its hospital medical and surgical costs decreased 48.9%.

The company claimed that costs dropped nearly 64.2%. In all, for every dollar spent on mental health care, the company saved $5.78.

5 million Americans, age 65 and over, suffer from serious depression.

The facts

Following are various categories of mental health problems and examples of the types of conditions in each.

Anxiety Disorders:
Panic Disorder
Social Phobia
Obsessive
Compulsive Disorder
Acute Stress Disorder

Childhood Disorders:
Conduct Disorder
Attention-Deficit
Disorder
Tourettes Disorder
Separation Anxiety

Cognitive Disorders:
Delirium
Dementia

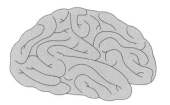

Mental Health

What problems and effects are found in older Americans? What are we doing about it?

?

For millions of people in the U.S. and around the world, Prozac and similar drugs have delivered freedom from depression and the opportunity for a more productive life. These drugs have not only helped those who are depressed, but also curbed suicide, hospitalization and mortality rates.

Therapy, in combination with antidepressant drug breakthroughs has yielded a decrease of 48.6% in the number of prescriptions written to senior citizens according to a recent Kaiser Permanente study. Other decreases included 47.1% in physician office visits, 45.3% in emergency room visits and 66.7% in frequency of hospitalizations.

As many as 90% of depressed elderly Americans are not receiving treatment.

Eating Disorders:	Mood Disorders:	Personality Disorders:	Psychotic Disorders:
Anorexia	Major Depressive	Paranoid Personality	Schizophrenia

In the United States, we spend each year an average of

$

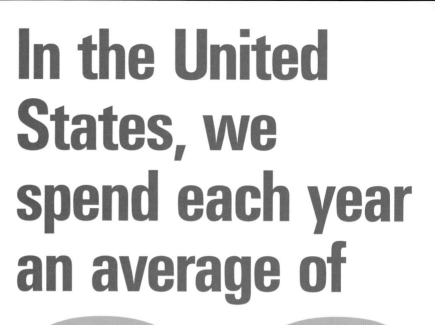

3,9

For the same amount we spend on health care, we could buy every man, woman and child in America a first class ticket from New York to Paris.

The average country spends $1,728 per person per year on health care, 7.5% of the gross domestic product. Turkey spends the least at

$260

per person on health care— the highest in the world.

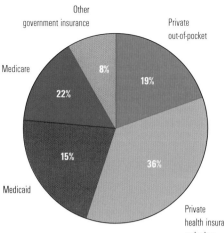

Who pays?

Of all industrialized countries, the U.S. has the lowest percentage of population with government-assured health insurance.

Other government insurance

Private out-of-pocket **19%**

Medicare **22%**

8%

Medicaid **15%**

36%

Private health insurance and other

The Cost of Health

Who pays?
How much?
Where does the money go?

?

Where it goes:

Hospitals 35%

Doctors 20%

Drugs 9%

Nursing Homes 8%

Home Care 3%

Dentists 5%

Vision Products 1%

Other 20%

Annual U.S. spending on health care now totals over

$1,100,000,000,000

13.5%

The U.S. also spends a higher percentage of its gross domestic product on health care than any other country, which means it has less to spend on other goods and services.

Health care spending is slowing, but it is still expected to double—to $2.2 trillion—by 2008.

● Household Health Expenditure and Population Projections. Medical Expenditure Panel Survey. Agency for Health Care Policy & Research. Dept. of Health and Human Services. U.S. www.meps.ahcpr.gov/nmes.htm Papers and data on health care cost trends and projected expenditures to 2005 are provided by the Agency for Health Care Policy and Research.

● Health Care Indicators. Health Care Financing Administration. Dept. of Health and Human Services. U.S. www.hcfa.gov/stats/indicatr/indicatr.htm Current data and analysis of health care spending, employment and prices are found in the Health Care Indicators.

● Health Information. National Institutes of Health Dept. of Health and Human Services. U.S. www.nih.gov/health/ Find consumer health information or conduct a literature search of the MEDLINE database of 11 million references at the Health Information page of the NIH web site.

737,764 U.S. Ph

Boys versus girls

In 1996 there were 580,377 practicing male physicians in the United States. There were 157,387 female physicians.

Of physicians under age 35 working in the U.S. in 1996, 64.4% were men and 35.6% were women.

20% of the Gross Domestic Product

15%

10%

5%

1960   1965   1970   1975

79%   21%

Prescription drug expenditures grew at double-digit rates during almost every year since 1980. In contrast, the growth of total national health expenditures actually decreased from 13% in 1980 to less than 5% in 1997.

A danger

The facts

Median annual incomes for selected medical specialties:

General / Family
$130,000

Surgery
$230,000

Anesthesiology
$215,000

Internal Medicine
$150,000

Radiology
$240,000

It is estimated that from 44,000 to 98,000 Americans die from errors in hospitals each year.

Source: Richardson, William. President W.K. Kellogg Foundation, Co-Author Institute of Medicine report.

ysicians

Strictly business

As shown below the health care industry has steadily become a solid part of the U.S. economy, representing close to 14% of the Gross Domestic Product. In 1996 there were 6,201 hospitals in the U.S., as compared to 6,125 in 1946. Such a figure seems disproportionate considering that medical expenses totaled $1.9 billion in 1946 and over $330 billion in 1996.

1980	1985	1990	1995

The states of medicine

California, New York, and Florida led the list of the states with the most practicing physicians in 1998.

87,593

71,718

39,715

The Blue Cross and Blue Shield System led the list of national managed care firms ranked by total HMO enrollment as of January 1999. Aetna-U.S. Healthcare, Kaiser Permanente and United HealthCare rounded out the top four.

Big HMO's

us shortage of nurses

The nation's hospitals are experiencing a shortage of registered nurses, especially the specialized, highly trained nurses who staff operating rooms, intensive care units and pediatric wards for high-risk babies. Driven in part by an aging population and the turmoil in managed care, the shortage began a year ago in California, and this year it has touched nearly all acute-care hospitals, where patients go with strokes, heart attacks, and major surgery and that employ nearly two-thirds of all registered nurses.

● Nancy M. Pindus and Ann Greiner. Effects of Health Care Industry Changes on Health Care Workers and Quality Patient Care: Summary of Literature and Research. Urban Institute. www.urban.org/health/pindus.htm This is a review of the literature and research on how the changing workforce and labor market effects the quality of patient care and safety of health care workers and how this information can be used to reform the health care industry.

In 1997,

43,40

Americans had no health insurance coverage.

Groups most likely to lack coverage include young adults, persons of Hispanic origin, part-time workers, and foreign-born people.

The facts

Among persons under age 65, 18.3% were uninsured in 1997, compared with 14.8% a decade earlier.

Because of Medicare, only 1% of persons ages 65 and older have no health insurance coverage.

● Medicare. Dept. of Health and Human Services. U.S. www.medicare.gov/ Medicare, administered by HCFA, provides health insurance to Americans over 65 and with certain disabilities and is the largest health insurance program in the United States. Their official web site contains reports, current and proposed health plans, contacts, and tips on how to avoid fraud.

16.5%
of the uninsured
were Black Non-
Hispanic Americans.

4.8%
were Asian/Pacific
Islanders.

Insurance

Who's covered?
Who's not?
Why?

?

0,000

1.2%
were American
Indians.

Covered at work

Employment is the leading source of health coverage for Americans. In 1997, 61.4% of the entire U.S. population had health insurance coverage obtained through an employer. Most people were covered by a private insurance plan for part or all of the year. Among the general population, 18- to 64-year old workers (both full- and part-time) are more likely to be insured than those who do not work. But, among the poor, workers are less likely to be covered than nonworkers. About 49.2% of poor full-time workers lacked insurance in 1997.

24.3%
of the uninsured
were Hispanic-
Americans.

Despite the
Medicaid program,

Poor people com-
prised 25.9% of all

Enacted jointly with
Medicare in 1965,

income persons.
In 1996, 36.1 million

Almost half of those
who are now 65

OLD GLORY
BRAND

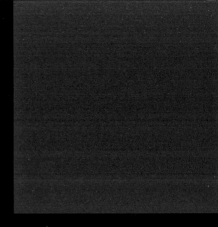

Kit Hinrichs

War
*What are the human and financial costs to the citizens of the
United States?*

Nuclear Arms
*What are the human and economic costs of nuclear weapons,
and what is the current threat to the world?*

Armaments
*The U.S. manufactures, stockpiles and distributes more
armaments than any other country. Has it made us more secure?
How big is the U.S. arsenal, what kind of weapons does it include
and how much does it cost?*

National Defense
*What are the human and financial costs of national defense to
the citizens of the United States?*

Terrorism
*How has the threat of terrorism changed our view of our
international neighbors and ourselves?*

Biochemical Weapons
*How dangerous are biochemical weapons? Who is at risk?
Are we prepared for an attack?*

Human Rights
*Where does the United States stand in the struggle for human
rights internationally and at home?*

International Affairs
Is the United States a good global citizen?

Intelligence Community
*Is the U.S. getting the most accurate, cost effective, relevant
information from its intelligence agencies?*

Hunger
*How does the U.S. stack up in the fight against domestic and
international hunger?*

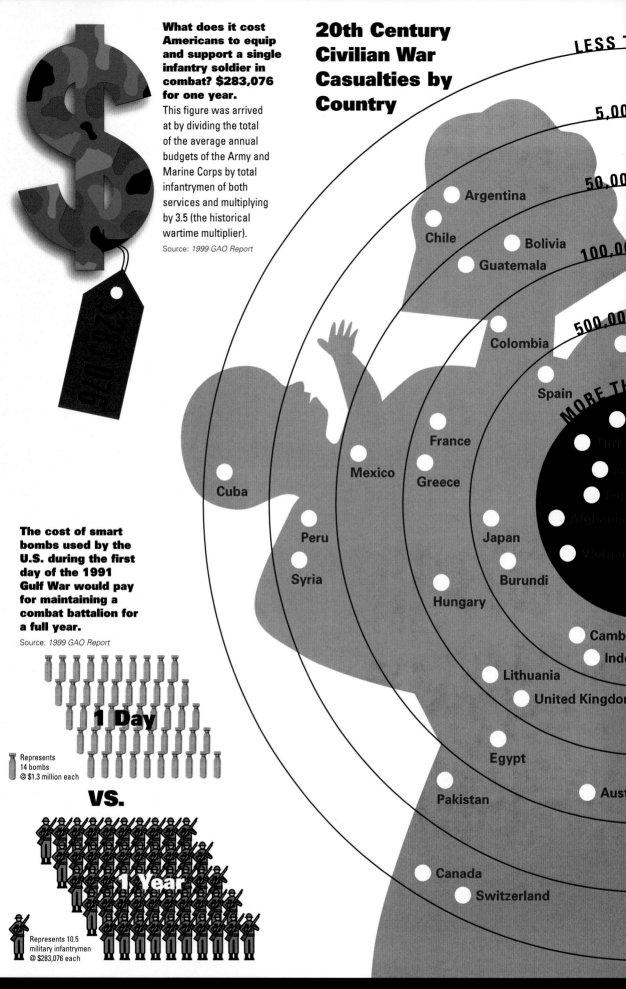

What does it cost Americans to equip and support a single infantry soldier in combat? $283,076 for one year.

This figure was arrived at by dividing the total of the average annual budgets of the Army and Marine Corps by total infantrymen of both services and multiplying by 3.5 (the historical wartime multiplier).

Source: *1999 GAO Report*

20th Century Civilian War Casualties by Country

LESS T

5,00

50,00

100,0

500,0

MORE TH

Argentina

Chile

Bolivia

Guatemala

Colombia

Spain

France

Mexico

Greece

Cuba

Japan

Peru

Burundi

Syria

Hungary

Lithuania

United Kingdo

Egypt

Camb

Ind

Pakistan

Aus

Canada

Switzerland

Turk

Afghani

Vietn

The cost of smart bombs used by the U.S. during the first day of the 1991 Gulf War would pay for maintaining a combat battalion for a full year.

Source: *1999 GAO Report*

1 Day

Represents 14 bombs @ $1.3 million each

VS.

1 Year

Represents 10.5 military infantrymen @ $283,076 each

How does war in the 20th century compare to the 19th century?

There have been six times as many deaths per war in the 20th century. No other century on record equals the 20th in uncivilized violence, number of conflicts waged, hordes of refugees created, or millions killed.

Source: Sivard. *World Military and Social Expenditures,* 1996

The U.S. ranks number one among 160 countries in military expenditures, military technology, worldwide military bases, military aid, combat aircraft, and arms exports.

Source: Sivard. *World Military and Social Expenditures,* 1996

Compared to the same 160 countries the U.S. ranks:

39th: Students per teacher
39th: Population per physician
19th: Contraceptive usage
8th: Public education spending per capita

Source: Sivard. *World Military and Social Expenditures,* 1996

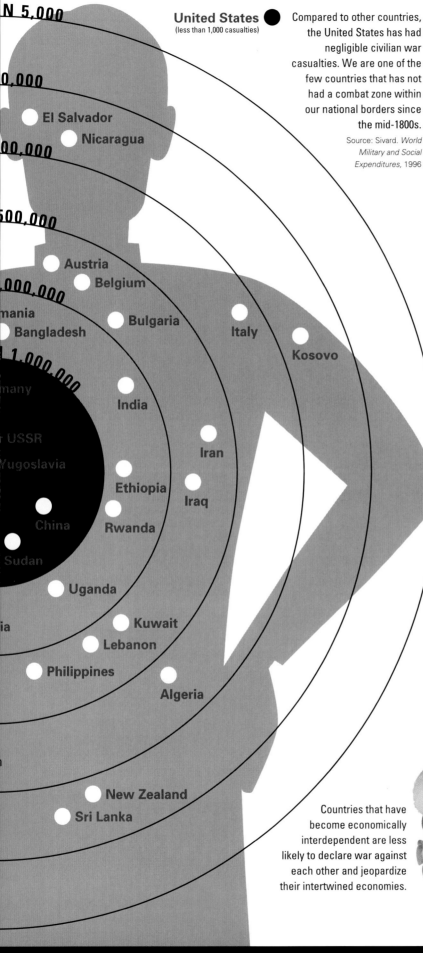

N 5,000

0,000

00,000

500,000

,000,000

1,000,000

United States ●
(less than 1,000 casualties)

El Salvador
Nicaragua

Austria
Belgium

mania
Bangladesh

Bulgaria

Italy

Kosovo

many

India

Iran

USSR
Yugoslavia

Ethiopia

Iraq

China

Rwanda

Sudan

Uganda

ia

Kuwait

Lebanon

Philippines

Algeria

New Zealand

Sri Lanka

Compared to other countries, the United States has had negligible civilian war casualties. We are one of the few countries that has not had a combat zone within our national borders since the mid-1800s.

Source: Sivard. *World Military and Social Expenditures*, 1996

War

What are the human and financial costs to the citizens of the United States?

?

Which countries suffered the worst civilian war casualties during the 20th century?

Increasingly, civilians are the major victims of war. An estimated 62 million civilians were killed worldwide over the past century – more than half of the estimated 110 million war-related deaths.

Source: Sivard. *World Military and Social Expenditures*, 1996

How many wars have been waged between countries that have at least one McDonald's franchise?

Source: McDonald's Corporation, 1997

0 CONFLICTS

Countries that have become economically interdependent are less likely to declare war against each other and jeopardize their intertwined economies.

Of the 27 major armed conflicts in 1998, only two - between India and Pakistan and between Eritrea and Ethiopia - were

World military expenditure in 1998 amounted to roughly $745 per person.

Every region in the world has experienced at least one major armed conflict in the last decade.

Nuclear Nations

United Kingdom: 185

China: 400

France: 450

United States: 10,925

How many nuclear weapons have been detonated worldwide since 1945?

Approximately 2,050 nuclear tests have been conducted since the end of WWII.

Source: The Brookings Institution, 1998

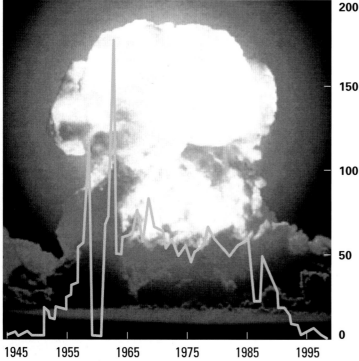

200	
150	
100	
50	
0	

1945 1955 1965 1975 1985 1995

Source: The Brookings Institution, 1998

What is the annual cost per capita of all U.S. nuclear weapons and related programs?

It costs each American approximately $130 per year for a total of $35.1 billion.

Estimated spending for 1998.
Source: *World Almanac,* 1999

How many nuclear arms are maintained around the world and which countries acknowledge possessing them?

Five nations acknowledge nuclear arsenals: Russia, United States, France, China and the United Kingdom. India and Pakistan are considered "Nuclear Threshold" countries, having tested but not deployed weapons.

Source: National Resources Defense Council; Congressional Budget Office

Since 1940, the United States has spent over $5.5 trillion on nuclear weapons. That is equivalent to the total national debt in 1998.

Source: The Brookings Institution, 1998

The world stockpile of nuclear weapons, after recent reductions, still represents over 700 times the explosive power used in the 20th Century's three major wars, which killed 44 million people.

Source: Sivard. *World Military and Social Expenditures,* 1998

Total land area occupied by U.S. nuclear weapons bases and facilities: 15,654 square miles.

Total land area of the District of Columbia, Massachusetts and New Jersey: 15,357 square miles.

Sources: *U.S. Nuclear Weapons Cost Study Project; Rand McNally Road Atlas and Travel Guide,* 1992

What is the largest U.S. nuclear explosion to date?

15 megatons on March 1, 1954

Source: U.S. Department of Energy

Russia: 20,000

Illustration: John Beckwith

*What are the human and
economic costs of nuclear
weapons, and what is the
current threat to the world?*

?

Where does the U.S. store its nuclear arsenal and how many missiles are in each state?

New Mexico	2,450
Georgia	2,000
Washington	1,685
Nevada	1,350
North Dakota	1,140

Source: National Resources Defense Council, 1998

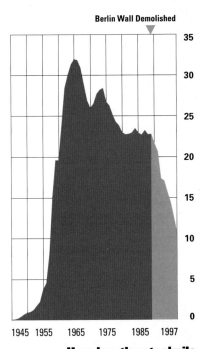

Berlin Wall Demolished

35	
30	
25	
20	
15	
10	
5	
0	

1945 1955 1965 1975 1985 1997

How has the stockpile of nuclear weapons changed since the fall of the Berlin Wall?

There has been a reduction of 4,390
weapons in nuclear stockpiles since 1989.

Source: The Brookings Institution, 1998

11 nuclear weapons have been lost by the
U.S. by accident and never recovered.

Source: U.S. Department of Defense; Center for
Defense Information; Greenpeace; *Lost Bombs,*
Atwood-Keeney Productions, Inc. 1997

Number of nuclear tests in the Pacific: 106.
Number of tests in Nevada: 911.
Total number of tests in Alaska, Colorado,
Mississippi and New Mexico: 10.

Source: Natural Resources Defense Council,
Nuclear Weapons Databook Project

The U.S. has paid $802,834,827 to the
Marshallese Islanders to compensate them
for damages from nuclear testing in 1956.

Source: U.S. Department of Justice, Torts
Branch, Civil Division

Today's American soldier is the most lethal in U.S. history – with a destructive force over 332 times greater than a Revolutionary War soldier.

Source: Dupuy, *Evolutions of Weapons and Warfare*, 1987

Equipping America's Fighting Man 1776–1999

Revolutionary War
Musket and support of one cannon per 750 men. Food for 2-3 days.

Civil War
Rifled musket and one cannon per 500 men. Hardtack biscuit, bacon and bread. Supplies for one week.

WWI
Bolt action, breech/magazine loading rifle, grenades, support of machine gun and artillery. Supplies from depots in rear areas.

WWII
Semi-automatic and automatic rifles, grenades, land mines, machine guns, medium and long-range artillery. Supplies for 3-5 days of combat. Close air support contributes to firepower.

1970
Automatic rifles, grenades, land mines, machine guns, medium and long-range artillery, rocket artillery, anti-tank guided missiles (ATGMs). Supplies for 2-3 days of intensive combat. Close air support contributes greatly to ground firepower.

During President Clinton's first year in office, U.S. arms sales more than doubled. From 1993 to 1997, the U.S. government sold, approved, or gave away $190 billion in weapons to virtually every nation on earth.

Source: MoJo Wire (Mother Jones Online) 1999

The U.S. has over 50% of the world arms sales market.

Source: MoJo Wire (Mother Jones Online) 1999

The U.S. has not been shy about arming potential foes in regional conflicts. For example, two of America's biggest arms customers are Greece and Turkey, which have been threatening to go to war with each other for decades over the tiny Mediterranean island of Cyprus.

Source: MoJo Wire (Mother Jones Online) 1999

1999

Automatic rifles, grenades, land mines, machine guns, artillery, airpower, ATGMs, smart munitions, Individual GPS navigational system, laser targeting systems,

infrared night vision devices. Today's soldier can carry supplies for 2 days of combat – the same as a WWII soldier – due to the high rate of fire/rapid ammunition consumption of current weapons. Helicopters and tracked vehicles make it much easier to supply infantrymen.

Infantry Illustrations: Jeffery West

Armaments

The U.S. manufactures, stockpiles and distributes more armaments than any other country. Has it made us more secure?

?

The U.S. is the leading manufacturer and exporter of arms – 4 times greater than its next largest competitor.

Top ten exporters of armaments worldwide

1 United States

2 United Kingdom   **3** Russia   **4** France

5 Sweden   **6** Germany   **7** Israel

8 China   **9** Canada   **10** Netherlands

Top ten importers of armaments worldwide

1 Saudi Arabia

2 Japan   **3** Egypt   **4** Turkey

5 South Korea   **6** Taiwan   **7** United Kingdom

8 Australia   **9** Kuwait   **10** United States

Source: U.S. States Department, *WMEAT* 1997

Number of Weapons in the U.S. Arsenal

226 Warships

1,072 Ballistic Missiles

The M-16 is the military's primary infantry rifle. There are approximately 350,000 active M-16 rifles in U.S. military circulation. Unit replacement cost is $586/gun.

350,000 M-16 Rifles

Estimated U.S. stockpile of Anti-Personnel Landmines. In 1997, President Clinton announced that by 2006 the U.S. will no longer use Anti-Personnel Landmines.

Source: 1999 Human Rights Watch; *1997 White House Fact Sheet*

11 million Landmines

Over 90% of all conflict casualties worldwide are caused by light weapons. Only 3 of the 49 major conflicts in the 1990s have used major weapon systems.

Source: Center for Defense Information

The Navy has requested $3 billion for the F/A -18 E/F jet in fiscal 2000 though the plane is underperforming and over budget, while veteran's groups estimate that the fiscal 2000 budget is almost $3 billion less than is needed to adequately address the health care needs of our nation's veterans

Half the world's governments spent more to guard their citizens against military attack than to protect them against all the enemies of good health.

Source: Sivard. *World Military and Social Expenditures. 1996*

In World War II, a torpedo fired from a submarine could travel a distance of six miles; today's sea-launched cruise missile can hit the bull's eye 1,500 miles away.

Source: Sivard. *World Military and Social Expenditures. 1996*

Includes aircraft carriers, cruisers, destroyers and frigates. Additionally, the Navy has 84 submarines.

Includes bombers, fighter and attack planes in all divisions.

How big is the U.S. arsenal, what kind of weapons does it include and how much does it cost?

?

Missiles with nuclear warheads including the Minuteman and Peacekeeper. The U.S. arsenal also contains hundreds of thousands of other missiles (surface-to-surface; surface-to-air; air-to-ground).

8,480 Airplanes

In 1999, the U.S. Department of Defense spent $48.9 billion on weapons procurement.

Weapons with calibre of 100mm and above. Includes guns, Howitzers, rocket launchers and mortars.

$1.9 billion

Budgeted cost of ammunition for U.S. armed forces for 1999.

12,566 Artillery Weapons

8,369 Tanks

Includes heavy and light tanks and armored vehicles.

Sources: CDI 1999; 1999 ADR; *Department of Defense Budget FY 2000/2001; The Military Balance 1998–1999; FAS 1999*

Unmanned missiles, carrying enough explosive power to destroy a large city, can now reach any point on the globe in less than 30 minutes.

Source: Sivard. *World Military and Social*

$2.6 billion will buy the following:
Three DDG-51 Aegis Destroyers, used in multi-threat environments that include air, surface and sub-surface threats.
OR
Immunization program with added vaccines

President Clinton approved an increase for the Pentagon of $112 billion over 6 years, the same amount the General Accounting Office has estimated that it would cost to renovate and upgrade our schools.

United States

VS.

Russia

France

Japan

Germany

China

United Kingdom

How large are the combined active U.S. armed forces?
1,437,600 total military personnel, including the U.S. Coast Guard.

Source: *The Military Balance*: 1998/1999; The International Institute for Strategic Spending

Number of active personnel in the Army: 479,400
Of this, 15% are women.

How much of the U.S. defense dollar does it take to maintain each service?
28 cents for the Army

How does the U.S. compare to other countries in defense spending?
The annual expenditure of the U.S. defense spending is equal to the combined expenditure of Russia, France, Japan, Germany, China and the United Kingdom.

Source: *The Military Balance*, 1997–98; International Institute for Strategic Studies

Source: *The Military Balance:* 1998/1999; The International Institute for Strategic Studies

U.S. ARMY

Uncle Sam was Samuel Wilson, an honest, hardworking meat packer from Troy, New York. He supplied meat to the U.S. Army during the war of 1812.

Source: The Lemmelson-MIT Awards Program's Invention Dimension website

The American flag was designed by a naval flag designer named Francis Hopkinson, whom the U.S. Government did not compensate for his services. Old Glory has inspired several other flags, including those of Chile, Liberia, Malaysia, and Puerto Rico.

Between 1980 and 1990, the armed forces discharged an average of 1,500 service members annually for being gay.

Since the end of the Cold War, active duty troops in the U.S. military have been reduced by about one-third, from 2.1 million in 1987, to 1.4 million in 1997.

Source: Public Agenda 1999

Number of active personnel in the Navy: 380,600

Of this, 14% are women.

Number of active personnel in the Air Force: 370,300

Of this, 18% are women.

Decrease in defense spending since the fall of the Berlin Wall:

Nearly 40%, from $400 billion to $250 billion.

Source: Public Agenda 1999

Number of active personnel in the Marines: 171,300

Of this, 5% are women.

32 cents for the Navy

35 cents for the Air Force

5 cents for the Marine Corps

U.S. NAVY

U.S. AIR FORCE

U.S. M.C.

What percentage of the American public fears a foreign-sponsored terrorist attack?

Source: *Princeton Survey*/Pew Research Center, 9/97

54% fear a foreign-sponsored terrorist attack

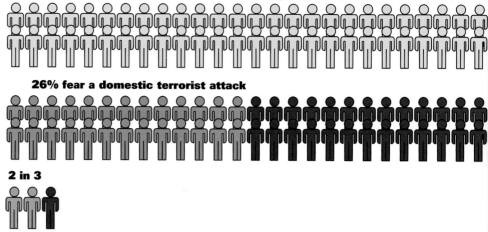

What percentage of the American public fear a domestic terrorist attack?

Source: *Princeton Survey*/Pew Research Center, 9/97

26% fear a domestic terrorist attack

Between 1982–1994, what percentage of terrorist attacks in the U.S. were domestic?

Source: Federal Bureau of Investigation

2 in 3

Illustration: John Beckwith

How many acts of terrorism occur each year worldwide?

In 1998, there were 273 international terrorist attacks. Of these, 40 percent were directed against U.S. targets.

Source: U.S. State Department, *1998 Report on Global Terrorism*

Cyberterrorism is a threat. The U.S. is at risk of cyberterrorist attacks that could shut down utilities, air traffic control and other services. U.S. law enforcement agencies are 5-10 years behind international criminals in electronic capabilities.

Source: Center for Strategic and International Studies, 1998

How many U.S. cities have received training and equipment in the event of a nuclear, biological or chemical attack?

At the end of 1998, 40 cities had received training. Each city receives $300,000 in conjunction with training from the Department of Defense for personal protection, decontamination and detection equipment.

In 1998, 40 percent of the 273 terrorist attacks worldwide were directed against U.S. targets.

Source: Brookings Institution, 1998

By percentage, what are the most commonly used weapons in terrorist attacks?

Includes attacks against U.S. facilities and attacks in which U.S. citizens suffered casualties.

Source: *1998 Patterns of Global Terrorism*, State Department Report

Bombing 85%	Firebombing 5%	Armed Attack 5%	Kidnapping 4%	Arson 1%

Terrorism

How has the threat of terrorism changed our view of our international neighbors and ourselves?

?

Terrorist attacks kill more civilians than military personnel by a ratio of 4 to 1.

Source: DCI Counterterrorist Center, 1998

VS.

Worldwide, what are the odds that an American will be killed in a terrorist attack?

Of the 741 people killed in terrorist attacks in 1998, only 3 percent were Americans.

Source: U.S. State Department, *1998 Report on Global Terrorism*

What percentage of Americans believe that it is likely that terrorists will explode a nuclear bomb within the next ten years in the United States?

Very likely to happen	23%
Fairly likely	27%
Fairly unlikely	24%
Very unlikely	23%

Source: Gallup Organization, 6/98

What regions of the world have the highest incidents of terrorism against the U.S.?

Latin America	87
Western Europe	13
Middle East	5
Africa	3
Eurasia	3

Source: U.S. State Department, *1998 Report on Global Terrorism*

The bombing of the Federal Building in Oklahoma City on April 19, 1995, killing 168 people and wounding hundreds, was the largest act of domestic terrorism in U.S. history.

Source: Federal Bureau of Investigation, *1997 Terrorism in the United States*

What would it cost to launch a major attack against a civilian population?

It would cost as little as $1 to disperse a deadly biological agent over 1 square kilometer.

ONE SQUARE KM

As a threat to human life, biological weapons are on a scale comparable to nuclear weapons as a means of mass destruction.

Source: *Crimes of War*, Gutman & Reiff

What percentage of police departments nationwide have had training in biological weapon attacks?

A sampling of police departments revealed that only 1.12 percent of police personnel have had biological weapons training.

Source: Center for Nonproliferation Studies, Monterey Institute of International Studies, 1999

Which biological agents pose the greatest threat to the United States?

Anthrax and smallpox are recognized as the agents of choice for terrorists. Anthrax is very durable and persistent in the environment and fatal if inhaled. Smallpox is highly contagious and there is no known medical treatment.

Source: Office of the Surgeon General, U.S. Army, 1977

ANTHRAX

Spies and satellites are only marginally helpful for ferreting out biological gear as small as kitchen cookware that is easy to hide and whose purpose can be peaceful (unlike the nuclear arms, bombers, ships, and missiles of the Cold War).

Source: New York Times, *The Threat of Germ Weapons is Rising. Fear, Too*. Broad and Miller, 12/27/98

18 acts of biochemical terrorism were reported to law enforcement officials in the U.S. between 1960-1998.

Source: Center for Nonproliferation Studies, Monterey Institute of International Studies.

The U.S. military is vaccinating all troops against anthrax and has begun a $322 million program to build stockpiles for 18 other vaccines, including one to combat smallpox.

Source: New York Times, *The Threat of Germ Weapons is Rising. Fear, Too*. Broad and Miller, 12/27/98

Biochemical Weapons

How dangerous are biochemical weapons? Who is at risk? Are we prepared for an attack?

?

Which nations have stockpiled chemical or biological weapons?

Countries known to possess or to be actively seeking some form of biochemical weapons capability: China, Iran, Iraq, Israel, Libya, North Korea, Russia, South Korea, Syria, Taiwan and the United States.

Source: Center for Defense Information; 1999

What are the deadliest biological agents?

Anthrax, Cholera, Plague, Botulism (Botulinum Toxin), Tularemia, Variola (Smallpox), Ricin (Toxin), Q Fever, Staphylococcal Enterotoxin B (Toxin), Brucellosis, Venezuelan Equine Encephalitis, Tricothecene

Source: Biological Agent Information Papers,
U.S. Army Institute of Infectious Diseases

What percentage of U.S. ground personnel suffer from the effects of Gulf War Syndrome?

1 in 7. Although the Persian Gulf War ended in 1991, approximately 100,000 American veterans continue to experience unexplained health problems.

Source: CNN Interactive, 1999

What is VX?

The chemical agent VX is one of the deadliest nerve agents known to humankind, especially when applied to the skin. A 10-milligram drop on the skin can kill an adult human in 15 minutes.

Source: *New York Times*

How many arrests are made in America each year for possession or threatened use of biological weapons?

This information is difficult to obtain due to its sensitivity. In 1995, there were 3 arrests made for possession of a biological agent.

Source: FBI Threat Assessment

What percentage of the Pentagon's daily Gulf War records of soldiers' chemical exposure is missing?

76 percent.

Source: Gulf War Research Foundation

Basic Human Rights Performance Ranking by Country

1. Sweden
2. Finland
3. Switzerland
4. Netherlands
5. Norway
6. Denmark
7. Japan
8. Canada
9. West Germany
10. Australia
11. France
12. United Kingdom
13. Belgium
14. Austria
15. Hong Kong
16. Irish Republic
17. New Zealand
18. Spain
19. Greece
20. **United States**
21. Portugal
22. Israel
23. Italy
24. Uruguay
25. Costa Rica
26. Mauritius
27. Argentina
28. Hungary
29. Venezuela
30. Dominican Republic
31. Trinidad
32. Panama
33. Ecuador
34. Jamaica
35. Botswana
36. East Germany
37. Kuwait
38. Singapore
39. Congo
40. Senegal
41. Gambia
42. Sierra Leone
43. Algeria
44. Czechoslovakia
45. Bulgaria
46. Brazil
47. South Korea
48. Jordan
49. Saudi Arabia
50. Cameroon

Source: World Bank, *World Development Report* (1986); World Bank, *World Tables, 1985–1986*

Human Rights Abuses

Asylum-seekers detained

Since 1996, there has been a 75% increase in immigration detainees in the U.S., over 6,000 of whom are held in local jails. For many, their sole crime is travelling without papers.

Source: The Lancet, *Human Rights in the U.S.A.: Land of the Free?* 1998

Police Brutality

Every year there are thousands of reports of assault and ill-treatment by police. There is no reliable national data, but inquiries into some of the largest urban police departments have uncovered systematic brutality.

Amount of annual U.S. trade with countries cited for torture

$400,000,000,000. Mexico, South Korea and China are among the largest traders cited.

Source: State Department/Statistical Abstract of the United States, Commerce Department

Mexico

Of 62 foreigners on death-row in the U.S., most were effectively denied access to consular assistance, in violation of the Vienna Convention on Consular Relations.

Source: Amnesty International Report 1998

Cincinnati's human rights ordinance has the nation's only provision forbidding discrimination against Appalachian Americans.

American Friends Service Committee
www.afsc.org/
A Quaker organization which includes people of various faiths who are committed to social justice, peace and humanitarian service.

Human Rights

Human rights abuses are known to occur throughout the world, including in the U.S. However, hard evidence and quantifiable statistics have been difficult to gather, and human rights groups have relied primarily on anecdotal accounts.

Where does the United States stand in the struggle for human rights internationally and at home?

?

Treatment of Prisoners

Restraint chairs – specially designed chairs to immobilize inmates – are widely used in U.S. prisons despite known dangers.

Death Penalty

In 1998, 68 people were executed in the U.S., bringing the total number executed since 1977 to 500. More than 100 countries have abolished the death penalty.

Children in Jail

No official statistics are available, but it is believed that at least 3,500 juveniles (18 and under) are being held with the U.S. general prison population.

Source: *Amnesty International Report,* 1999
Illustration: John Beckwith

States or districts which have enacted laws banning discrimination on the basis of sexual orientation (listed by date of enactment):

**District of Columbia
Wisconsin
Massachusetts
Connecticut
Hawaii
California
New Jersey
Vermont
Minnesota
Rhode Island
New Hampshire
*Maine**

*Maine enacted and then rescinded its law.
Source: National Gay and Lesbian Task Force

76% of Black Americans and 61% of White Americans feel that the civil rights movement has had a positive effect on the United States.

76%

61%

South Korea

China

The Federal Government will spend over $1.7 trillion in 1999. Of that amount, $19.5 billion (.01% of the total) will go to international affairs.

Source: U.S. Budget for FY 2000 Historical Tables

What percentage of U.N. peacekeeping forces are U.S. military personnel?

Source: United Nations

4%

Visas

Entries/*Entrées*   Departures/*Sorties*

GLOBAL DIPLOMACY

THE UNITED STATES GOVERNMENT POLICY

In 1999 United States budgeted $1.04 billion for diplomatic security/law enforcement cooperation and worldwide security upgrades.
Source: Diplomatic & Consular Programs Activities Summary.

DIPLOMATIC **SECURITY** U.S. EMBASSIES

PASSPORTS **1998** ISSUED

6,539,864

In the past 20 years, the number of passports issued by the U.S. has increased by more than 200% to 6,539,864 in 1998.

16

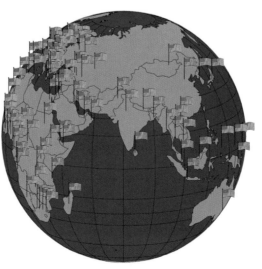

How many embassies, and consulates does the United States maintain around the world?
155 posts in six regional groupings.
Estimated figure for 1999.
Source: Embassy World, 1999

In 50 years of peacekeeping, over 750 military and civilian personnel from 118 countries have served in 49 operations.

Source: *SIPRI Yearbook 1999* (Stockholm International Peace Research Institute)

Over 52 million Americans traveled overseas in 1995.

Source: *1998 Statistical Abstract of the United States,* U.S. Census

Total U.S. payments to the U.N. are less than one-quarter of one percent of the federal budget.

Source: United Nations

Visas

Entries / Entrées   Departures / Sorties

The budget for U.S. diplomatic relations (arms control, political & economic reporting, trade, global environmental and scientific reporting) is $345 million.

Source: 1999 Budget of the United States Government; U.S. State Department;

U.S. Passport Services employs over 800 people in the U.S.

The 1999 budget estimate for U.S. consular relations (passports, visas, services to American citizens overseas) is $347 million.

17

International Affairs

Is the United States a good global citizen?

?

How much do we spend on worldwide refugees vs. peacekeeping forces?

The U.S. spends $670 million on refugees and $231 million on peacekeeping forces, a 3 to 1 ratio.

VS.

Estimated figure for 1999. Source: *Where do U.S. Diplomats Work/Summary of Positions,* State Department.

1999 Export-Import Figures

U.S. Imports

U.S. Exports

$97.2 (in billions)

$77.5 (in billions)

25%

What percentage of the total annual U.N. budget is assessed to the U.S.?

The United States is only responsible for 25% of the U.N.'s regular peacekeeping budget. To date, the U.S. owes the U.N. over 1.3 billion dollars in dues.

Source: United Nations

Arms Control and International Security. Dept. of State. U.S.
www.acda.gov
The missions of arms control, nonproliferation, and political-military affairs will be

There are over 85 million fingerprints in the FBI's files that belong to people who have never been convicted of a crime. That is one in every 3 Americans.

Source: Federal Bureau of Investigation

How many years of legal action did it take to get the CIA to release the annual U.S. intelligence budget in 1997?

Source: Tim Weiner, *Blank Check: The Pentagon's Black Budget,* Warner Books/Center for National Security Studies/Central Intelligence Agency

30 Years

What was the number of federal wiretap warrants granted for criminal investigations in 1996?

Source: *Legal Times/* Federal Bureau of Investigation

581 Warrants

How many warrants were granted for espionage investigations by the U.S. Foreign Intelligence Surveillance Court?

Source: *Legal Times/* Federal Bureau of Investigation

839 Warrants

How many U.S. government agencies and organizations carry out intelligence activities?

Source: Director of Central Intelligence, 1999

13 Agencies

Zero

How many U.S. citizens were officially spied on by the CIA?

Source: Central Intelligence Agency

Number of DNA samples collected from convicted serial criminals: 6,000.

Estimated number of federal fugitives eligible for the FBI's Ten Most Wanted list is more than 6,000.

1,000 Informants

How many CIA informants have been laid off since 1995?

Source: Central Intelligence Agency

Ratio of the number of CIA employees to the number of U.N. employees, worldwide: 4 to 3

Source: Jeffrey T. Richelson, *The U.S. Intelligence Community*/ United Nations

$26.7 Billion

What was the budget for all U.S. government intelligence and intelligence-related activities in 1998?

Source: Central Intelligence Agency

The CIA has requested exemptions for 2 out of 3 documents scheduled to be declassified under the Freedom of Information Act in 2000.

Source: Central Intelligence Agency

The U.S. intelligence budget in 1998 was roughly equivalent to the gross domestic product of Zimbabwe – a country of 11.1 million inhabitants.

Source: *1999 Central Intelligence Agency Factbook*

Click a button on the
UN Hunger Site and
somewhere in the
world a hungry person
gets a meal. The
food is paid for by
corporate sponsors.

Source: www.thehungersite.com

12 percent of the world is starving.

Source: P. Singer, *Practical Ethics* 1994;
United Nations

Worldwide, every three seconds a child dies of hunger.

That's equivalent to a
Hiroshima-sized bomb being
dropped on the world's
children every three to
four days.

Source: *Hunger In America;*
Freedom from Hunger website

Number of U.S. households that experience hunger:

In 1995, hunger existed in
4.2 million households, or
4.1% of all households

Source: *Could There Be Hunger*

4.1%

It is impossible to talk about hunger
without talking about poverty. More than
36 million Americans are poor; most of
them are children.

Source: *Hunger in America*

Inequality exists not only between
countries, but also within countries between
the wealthy and poor. In the U.S., 29% of
children are hungry or at risk of hunger,
and the child poverty rate is double that of
any other industrial country.

4.4 billion people live in developing
countries and one third survive on less
than $1 per day.

Source: *The State of Food Insecurity in the
World,* 1998; 1998 BBC News

If all the world's undernourished people were gathered together (into a new country), it would be the third most populous nation just behind China and India.

Source: *The State of Food Insecurity in the World*, 1998; 1998 BBC News

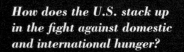

Hunger

How does the U.S. stack up in the fight against domestic and international hunger?

?

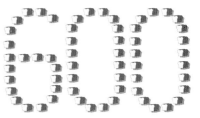

U.S. shipments of surplus food abroad include more than 2 million metric tons of bread and flour yearly, enough to bake about 600 loaves of bread a year for every hungry child in the United States.

Source: *World Hunger: 12 Myths,* Lappe, Collins, Rosset, 1998

54 percent of Americans are overweight and more than 20 percent are obese.

Science Magazine: "Environmental Contributions to the Obesity Epidemic" Hill & Peters, 29 May 1998

51% are children and seniors

What percentage of food bank clients are children and seniors?
About half of the U.S. households that report experiencing hunger receive food assistance from the federal government. 51% of food bank clients are children and seniors.

Source: *Could There Be Hunger*

The 6 billion people of the world today have, on average, 15% more food per person that the global population of 4 billion had 20 years ago.

Source: *Report of the Inter-sessional*

● Food Assistance in Disaster Situations: Frequently Asked Questions. Dept. of Agriculture. U.S.
www.fns.usda.gov/fdd/menu/ administration/disaster/disaster.htm
As part of the Federal Emergency Response

● Food for Peace Program. Agency for International Development. U.S.
gaia.info.usaid.gov/hum_response/ffp/
The U.S. federal government agency that implements America's foreign economic and humanitarian assistance programs.

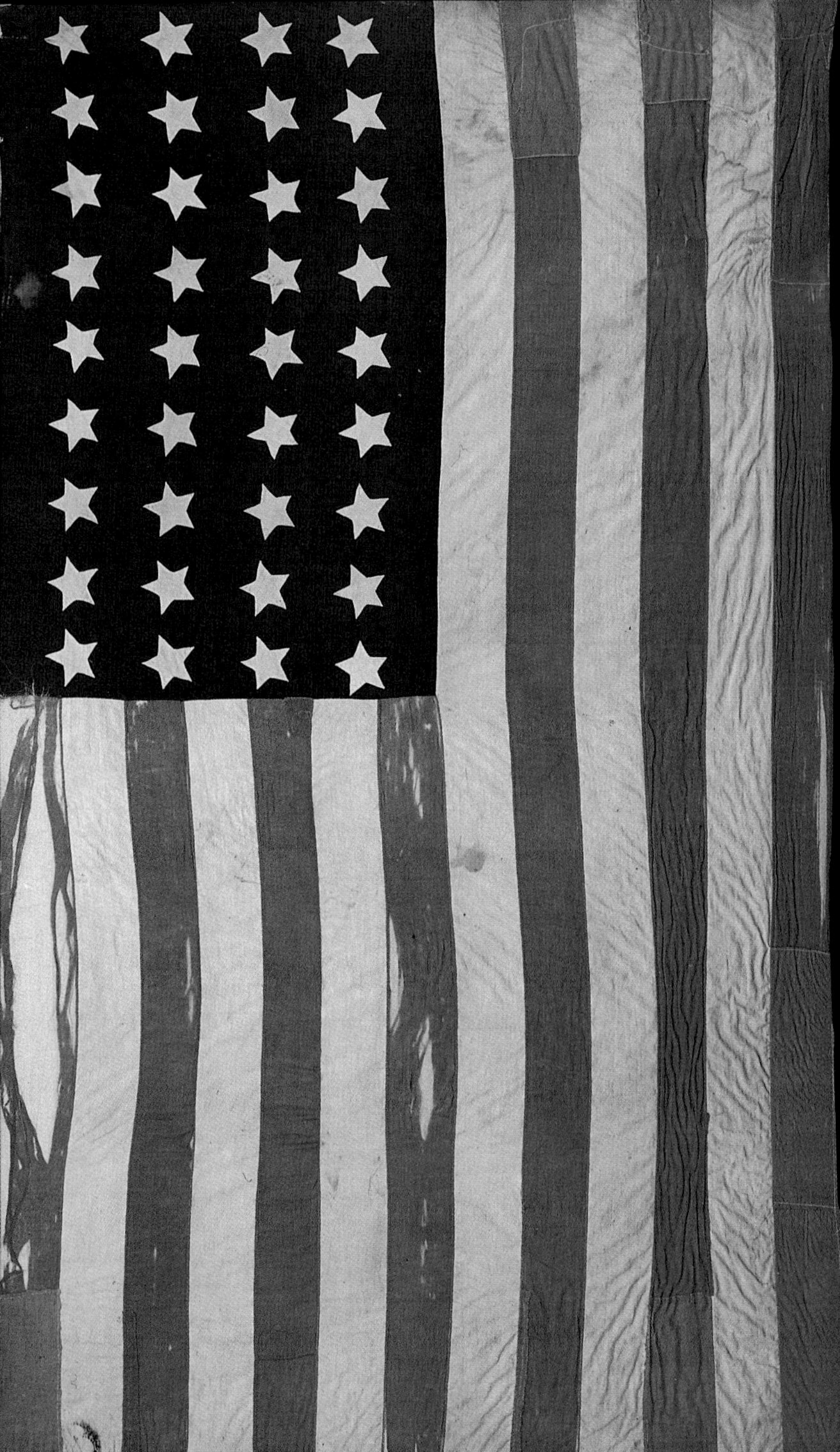

Greenberg

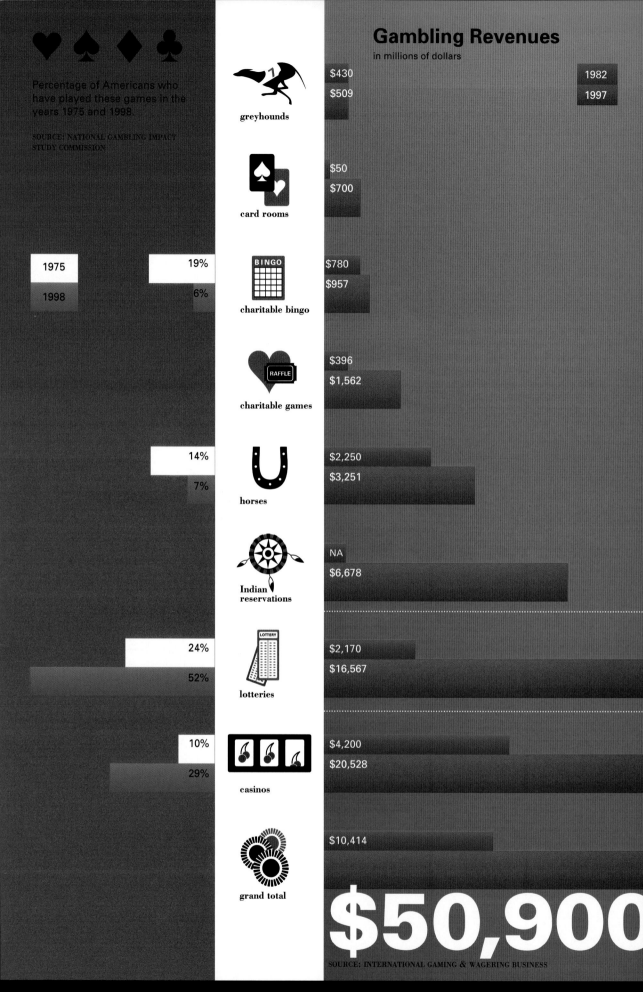

Percentage of Americans who have played these games in the years 1975 and 1998.

SOURCE: NATIONAL GAMBLING IMPACT STUDY COMMISSION

Gambling Revenues

in millions of dollars

1982
1997

	greyhounds	$430 / $509
	card rooms	$50 / $700
	charitable bingo	$780 / $957
	charitable games	$396 / $1,562
14% / 7%	horses	$2,250 / $3,251
	Indian reservations	NA / $6,678
24% / 52%	lotteries	$2,170 / $16,567
10% / 29%	casinos	$4,200 / $20,528
	grand total	$10,414

1975 — 19%
1998 — 6%

$50,900

SOURCE: INTERNATIONAL GAMING & WAGERING BUSINESS

Fun and Games?

More than 5% of all adults develop a gambling problem at some time. There are approximately 40 gambling treatment programs located in 24 states.

5,000,000

Americans are problem or pathological gamblers...

15,000,000

are at risk.

Gambling

How much do Americans spend on gambling?

?

Americans will spend $700 billion in legal wagers this year.

Revenues from legal betting have increased by 1,600% in the past 25 years. And the average percentage of personal income devoted to gambling has more than doubled.

SOURCE:
THE ATLANTA JOURNAL-CONSTITUTION, 1999

38 states currently operate lotteries.

Top Lottery Prize States
(in billions)

$1.7 Massachusetts

$1.6 Texas

$1.0 Ohio

$1.0 Florida

38 gambling establishments are owned and run by Native American tribes.

Per capita income for each tribe member:

$1,300

Gambling interests contributed $5 million to national political races in '97 and '98.

40% DEM

REP 60%

000,000

1997 GRAND TOTAL GAMBLING REVENUES: $51 BILLION

1,800,000

Adults are said to exhibit severe pathological gambling behavior each year.

1,100,000

Children between the ages of 12 and 17 exhibit severe pathological gambling behavior each year.

Two out of three children have gambled at least once.

● National Gambling Impact Study Commission
www.ngisc.gov
The NGISC was created to study the social and economic impacts of gambling on various levels of government, communities, and social institutions. The Final Report and recommendations of the Commission are the culmination of a two year investigation and they are available on this web site along with subject-focused staff reports.

Marijuana is by far the most prevalent illicit drug.
In 1996, nearly 5% of the population age 12 and older
(over 10 million) used marijuana or hashish.

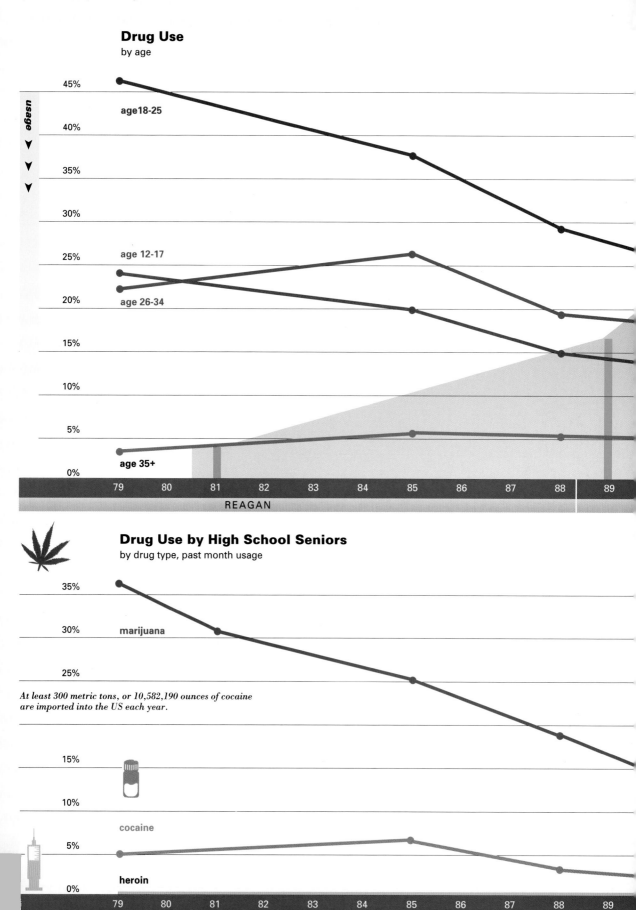

Drug Use
by age

usage

▼
▼
▼

45%

age18-25

40%

35%

30%

25%   age 12-17

20%   age 26-34

15%

10%

5%

0%   age 35+

| 79 | 80 | 81 | 82 | 83 | 84 | 85 | 86 | 87 | 88 | 89 |

REAGAN

Drug Use by High School Seniors
by drug type, past month usage

35%

30%   marijuana

25%

At least 300 metric tons, or 10,582,190 ounces of cocaine
are imported into the US each year.

15%

10%

cocaine

5%

heroin

0%

| 79 | 80 | 81 | 82 | 83 | 84 | 85 | 86 | 87 | 88 | 89 |

74 million, or 35% of Americans age 12 and older, reported use of an illicit drug at least once in their lifetime.

Federal Spending
in millions of dollars

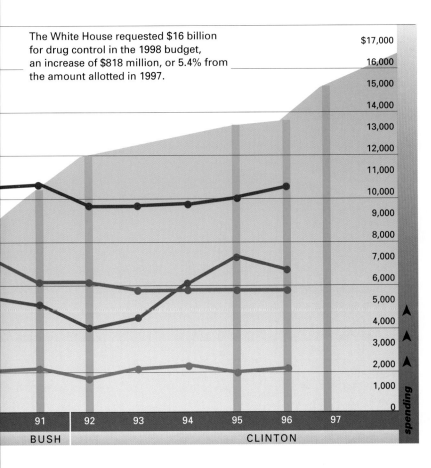

The White House requested $16 billion for drug control in the 1998 budget, an increase of $818 million, or 5.4% from the amount allotted in 1997.

	$17,000
	16,000
	15,000
	14,000
	13,000
	12,000
	11,000
	10,000
	9,000
	8,000
	7,000
	6,000
	5,000
	4,000
	3,000
	2,000
	1,000
	0

spending

| 91 | 92 | 93 | 94 | 95 | 96 | 97 |

BUSH   CLINTON

The FBI reported an estimated 1,506,200 state and local arrests for drug law violations in 1996.

In the same year, the National Institute of Justice's Drug Use Forecasting program found that the percentage of adult male arrestees testing positive for drugs at the time of arrest ranged from 48% in San Jose to 82% in Chicago. Adult female arrestees testing positive ranged from 35% in New Orleans to 83% in Manhattan.

Juvenile male detainees testing positive ranged from 38% in Portland to 67% in D.C.

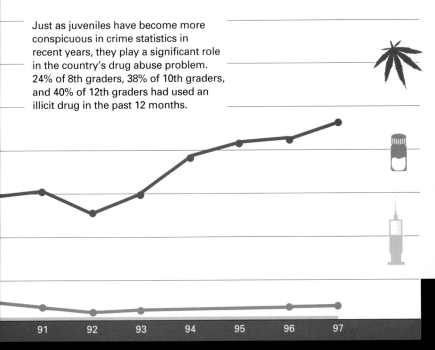

Just as juveniles have become more conspicuous in crime statistics in recent years, they play a significant role in the country's drug abuse problem. 24% of 8th graders, 38% of 10th graders, and 40% of 12th graders had used an illicit drug in the past 12 months.

Reported use of marijuana by high school seniors during the past month peaked in 1978 at 37% and declined to its lowest level in 1992 at 12%. The use of marijuana has increased since then, back up to 24% in 1997.

Reported use of cocaine by high school seniors during the past month increased from 2% to 6% between 1975 and 1981. The highest level was 7% in 1985. In 1997, 2.5% of high school seniors used cocaine.

Heroin use by high school seniors ranged from .2% to a high of .6% in 1985.

| 91 | 92 | 93 | 94 | 95 | 96 | 97 |

National Clearinghouse for Alcohol and Drug Information.
www.health.org/pubs/nhsda/index
The National Clearinghouse for Alcohol and Drug Information brings to the web the annual Household Survey on Drug Abuse dating from 1993.

Bankruptcy filings
from 1900 to 1910:
173,298

Bankruptcy filings
from 1900 to 1997:
7,915,796

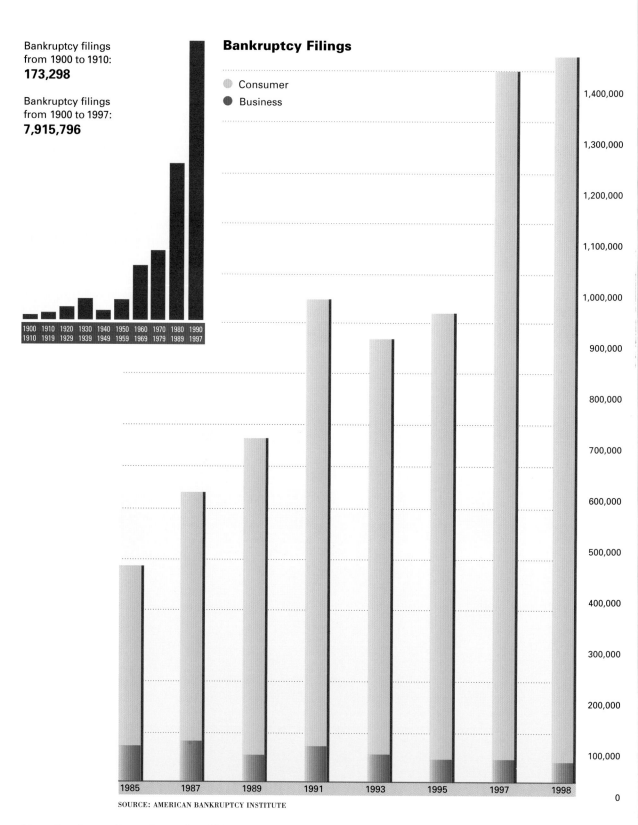

Bankruptcy Filings

- ● Consumer
- ● Business

1900	1910	1920	1930	1940	1950	1960	1970	1980	1990
1910	1919	1929	1939	1949	1959	1969	1979	1989	1997

1,400,000

1,300,000

1,200,000

1,100,000

1,000,000

900,000

800,000

700,000

600,000

500,000

400,000

300,000

200,000

100,000

1985   1987   1989   1991   1993   1995   1997   1998

0

SOURCE: AMERICAN BANKRUPTCY INSTITUTE

Two in three American families use credit cards.

**About 52% always pay off their balances, 20% sometimes
pay them off, and 28% hardly ever pay them off.**

**The estimated 60 million households with revolving
credit card balances carried an average of $7,000
of credit card debt per household. This costs an average
of more than $1,000 in interest and fees per year,
per household.**

Bankruptcy

How many Americans are filing for bankruptcy?

?

The rise in bankruptcies is due to many factors including easily available credit, the expansion of legalized gambling, the divorce rate, simpler bankruptcy laws, unrecovered medical claims, and widespread advertising by bankruptcy attorneys.

SOURCE: HOUSTON CHRONICLE 7/98

1,442,600
bankruptcy filings in 1998

97%
are consumer bankruptcy filings

SOURCE: AMERICAN BANKRUPTCY INSTITUTE

Bankruptcy Rate
by state, per 100,000

Highest		Lowest	
TN	983	NC	352
GA	839	IA	345
NV	800	ME	340
AL	791	VT	324
MI	706	SD	320
OK	680	ND	306
CA	649	SC	299
VA	640	AK	225

The greatest increase in bankruptcy filings has occurred in New England. Massachusetts leads all states with a 961% rise from 1984 to 1997.

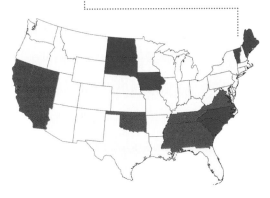

Credit card debt doubled from 1990 to 1996. By the end of 1997, the total was

$455,000,000,000

On the Job Surveillance

63% of organizations surveyed practiced ar least one form of surveillance. Of these:

26%
video taped
employee performance

15%
stored and reviewed
e-mail messages

14%
stored and reviewed
computer files

10%
taped and reviewed
voice mail

5%
taped **telephone**
conversations

Increase in the number of workers under surveillance since 1991:

275%

Data Collection on the Web

A recent study of consumer privacy on the Internet shows that nearly two-thirds of all commercial web sites display some type of warning if they collect personal information.

The study found that 93% collect some type of personal information. A Web vendor can track which pages you visit, what you buy, where you have linked from and where you go after you leave.

Consumer Profiling

The buying and selling of consumers' personal information is big business. Information is gathered from the Web, applications, subscriptions, and credit card purchases.

Posted earnings of one information broker: $281,000,000

Percentage of Web Sites that Collect Personal Information

TYPE OF WEB SITE	FINANCIAL	CHILDREN	RETAIL	HEALTH
E-mail address	93	96	100	100
Name	73	74	77	53
Postal address	65	49	70	51
Telephone #	59	24	67	47
Fax #	27	26	31	13
Birth date	17	46	7	12
Social Security #	20	1	6	3
Credit card #	7	0	31	8
Gender	4	25	2	8
Occupation	21	3	5	3
Education	6	7	7	2
Income	20	3	3	0
Interests	1	18	5	3
Hobbies	1	9	0	1

People who don't use the Internet frequently cite privacy concerns as their prime reason for staying offline.

Cost of installing one traffic surveillance camera: $7,500 to $12,000

Spent on purchasing surveillance cameras last year: $1,000,000,000

SOURCE: ELECTRONIC MONITORING & SURVEILLANCE, 1997 AMA SURVEY

The word "privacy" does not appear in the United States Constitution.

The Supreme Court has ruled that there is a limited right to privacy in matters of marriage, procreation, child rearing and education. However, information held by third parties such as financial records or telephone calling records are not protected. New technologies make it ever easier to capture, store, analyze, share and act upon data.

Personal Identification

Three conventional forms of identification are cards (usually with a magnetic strip or photograph), passwords (PIN), and biometrics (fingerprint, voice).

Biometric technology has attained great sophistication and accuracy in recent years, surpassing all other forms of identification:

Chance of mistaken identity via
retinal scanning:

1 in 1,000,000,000,000,000

Chance of mistaken identity via
fingerprint scanning:

1 in 1,000

Privacy

Do we have a right to privacy?

?

Wiretapping

Wiretaps placed on cell phones, pagers, e-mail and other electronic communication devices nearly tripled last year. Police wiretaps on cell phones and pagers now outnumber wiretaps on telephones connected to conventional phone lines.

In 1998, state and federal judges authorized 1,329 wiretaps, a 12% increase over 1997. State and local drug investigations accounted for the increase; about 75% of all wiretaps were requested in drug cases.

Wiretap investigations conducted in 1998 led to 3,450 arrests and 897 convictions.

The federal government and New York accounted for more than 70% of all wiretaps in 1998.

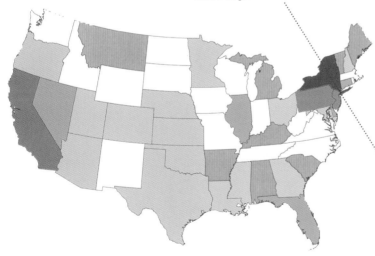

SOURCE: THE ADMINISTRATIVE OFFICE OF THE U.S. COURTS

- 0 wiretaps
- 1-10 wiretaps
- 10-50 wiretaps
- 50-100 wiretaps
- 100+ wiretaps
- states without wiretap laws

If you don't want to be caller ID'd, dial *67 before making your call.

● Electronic Privacy Information Center
www.epic.org/
Established in 1994 to conduct public interest research and advocate privacy and First Amendment rights in an electronic environment. Their web site contains reports and current news on privacy issues.

Weapons Used in Crimes*

weapon	1980	1990	1996
Guns	**101**	**94**	**82**
Strongarm	95	108	78
Knife	32	30	18
Other	23	25	24

*robbery and property crimes only

SOURCE: FEDERAL BUREAU OF INVESTIGATION

Gun Deaths by State

states with lowest percentage		states with highest percentage	
North Dakota	17%	**District of Columbia**	80%
Delaware	31%	**Mississippi**	79%
Iowa	31%	**Louisiana**	78%
Hawaii	33%	**Maryland**	78%
Wisconsin	42%	**West Virginia**	76%
		Tennessee	76%

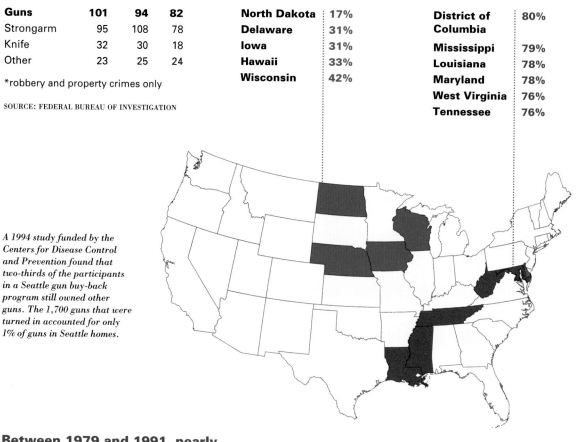

A 1994 study funded by the Centers for Disease Control and Prevention found that two-thirds of the participants in a Seattle gun buy-back program still owned other guns. The 1,700 guns that were turned in accounted for only 1% of guns in Seattle homes.

Between 1979 and 1991, nearly 50,000 children were killed by guns—that's more than the number of Americans killed during our 25 years in Vietnam.

	Revolvers		Pistols		Rifles	
	Manufactured	Exported	Manufactured	Exported	Manufactured	Exported
1986	**734,650**	103,900	**693,000**	16,650	**970,550**	37,250
1997	**370,428**	63,656	**1,036,000**	44,200	**1,251,350**	76,600

According to the Bureau of Alcohol, Tobacco and Firearms, the U.S. manufactured 1,406,505 handguns in 1997, 77,972 less than in 1996, and 316,425 less than in 1995. The U.S. imported 474,182 handguns in 1997— 16,372 less than in 1996, and 231,911 less than in 1995.

Gun violence is statistically on the decline. However, after a season of sensational killings, the debate over the place of guns in our society rages on.

Weapons

What impact do guns have on America's crime problem?

?

Gun Deaths by Country

per 100,000 people (selected countries)

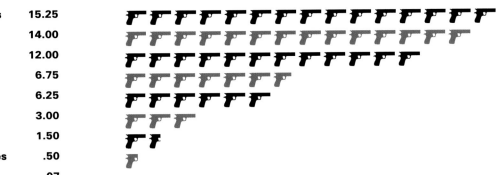

United States	15.25
Brazil	14.00
Mexico	12.00
Finland	6.75
France	6.25
Australia	3.00
Germany	1.50
England/Wales	.50
Japan	.07

The United States and Finland have the two highest rates of per capita gun ownership, and the two highest rates of gun suicide, in the world.

Murders by Guns
in thousands

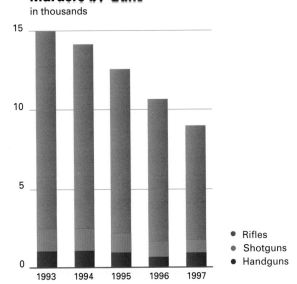

- Rifles
- Shotguns
- Handguns

SOURCE: NEWSWEEK MAGAZINE, 8/99

	Shotguns		Machine Guns	
	Manufactured	Exported	Manufactured	Exported
1986	**641,500**	59,000	**41,500**	25,000
1997	**916,000**	86,250	**67,900**	20,900

Policy.com Issue of the Week
For Week 3/29/99: Gun Control Under Fire
www.policy.com/issuewk/1999/0329_65/index.html
Policy.com is a nonpartisan policy news and information service that highlights research, opinions, and events relating to public policy issues. This Issue of the Week examines gun control, the Second Amendment, and reform alternatives.

		Violent Crime					Property Crime			
	Total	total	murder	forcible rape	robbery	aggravated assault	total	burglary	larceny theft	vehicle theft
1996 rate per 100,000 population	5,079	634	7	36	202	388	4,445	943	2,976	526
% change 1986 to 96	-7	3	-14	-5	-10	12.2	-9	-30	-1	3.6
Metropolitan areas	5,512	715	8	38	244	424	4,798	993	3,188	616
Other cities	5,328	461	5	35	72	350	4,867	935	3,695	238
Rural areas	2,050	222	5	24	16	177	1,828	620	1,083	126

Highest Crime Rates
Total crimes reported for cities with the highest crime rates, 1996

● = 3,316

● = 2,500

● = 1,900

• = 1,130

In surveys of 12 cities in 1998, the percentage of residents who said they were fearful of crime in their neighborhood ranged from 20% in Madison, WI to 48% in Washington, DC.

Violent offenses include

murder
non-negligent manslaughter
rape
sexual assault
robbery
assault
extortion
intimidation
criminal endangerment

Property offenses include

burglary
larceny
motor vehicle theft
fraud
possession and selling of stolen property
destruction of property
trespassing
vandalism
criminal tampering

Drug offenses include

possession
manufacturing
trafficking

Public-order offenses include

commercialized prostitution
morals and decency charges
liquor law violations
weapons
drunk driving
escape to avoid prosecution
court offenses
obstruction

1998

Violent crimes

8,100,000

Property crimes

22,900,000

Total crimes

31,300,000

Highest Crime Rates

	index	total
Atlanta	**17,070**	**3,316**
St. Louis	15,129	2,728
Miami	13,746	3,115
Oklahoma City	12,159	1,130
Baltimore	12,001	2,723
Detroit	11,991	2,319
Washington, DC	11,889	2,470
Kansas City	11,662	1,981
Albuquerque	11,308	1,469
Minneapolis	11,291	1,883
Nashville	11,219	1,890
Memphis	11,127	1,985

SOURCE: U.S. BUREAU OF JUSTICE STATISTICS.
CRIMINAL VICTIMIZATION 1996

In 1998, Americans experienced approximately 31.3 million crimes.

73% were property crimes, 26% were crimes of violence.
For every 1,000 persons age 12 and older, there were two rapes
or sexual assaults, three assaults with serious injury and four
robberies. Murder was the least frequent violent crime—about
seven murder victims per 100,000 persons in 1997.

SOURCE: 1998 NATIONAL CRIME VICTIMIZATION SURVEY

Victim/Offender Relationship

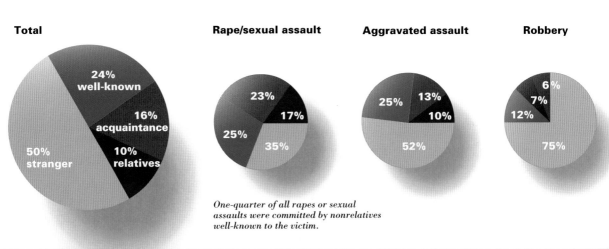

Total

24% well-known
16% acquaintance
50% stranger
10% relatives

Rape/sexual assault

23%
17%
25%
35%

*One-quarter of all rapes or sexual
assaults were committed by nonrelatives
well-known to the victim.*

Aggravated assault

13%
25%
10%
52%

Robbery

6%
7%
12%
75%

- stranger
- relatives
- well-known
- casual acquaintance

● Uniform Crime Reports
Federal Bureau of Investigation
www.fbi.gov/ucr/ucreports.htm
The statistics in the UCR are provided
through a national reporting system and the
resulting publications provide an overview
of crime in the U.S. The web reports date
from 1995 and include statistics on murder
and manslaughter, forcible rape, robbery,
aggravated assault, burglary, larceny theft,
auto theft, arson and hate crime.

Crime Rates

property crime by region per 100,000 population

- 2,000-2,999
- 3,000-3,999
- 4,000-5,499
- 5,500-6,500

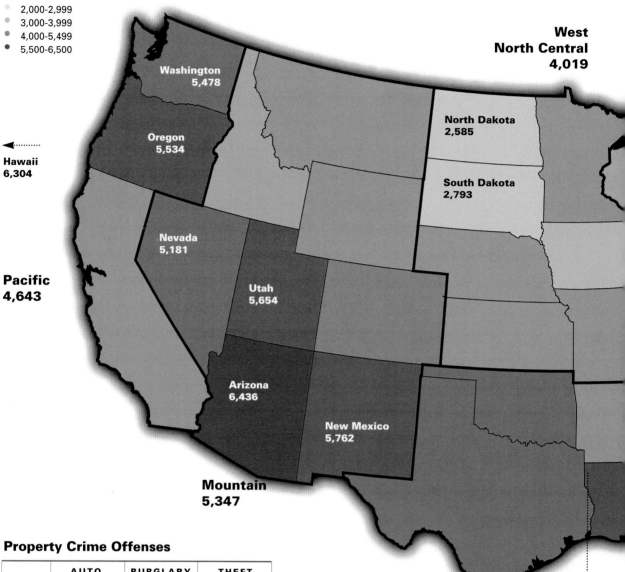

West North Central
4,019

Washington
5,478

North Dakota
2,585

Oregon
5,534

South Dakota
2,793

Hawaii
6,304

Nevada
5,181

Pacific
4,643

Utah
5,654

Arizona
6,436

New Mexico
5,762

Mountain
5,347

Louisiana
5,910

West South Central
5,113

Property Crime Offenses

	AUTO	BURGLARY	THEFT
1960	328,000	912,000	1,855,500
1965	497,000	1,282,500	2,572,500
1970	928,500	2,205,000	4,226,000
1975	1,009,500	3,265,500	5,978,000
1980	1,132,000	3,795,000	7,137,000
1985	1,103,000	3,073,500	6,926,600
1990	1,636,000	3,074,000	7,946,000
1991	1,662,000	3,157,000	8,142,000
1992	1,611,000	2,980,000	7,915,000
1993	1,563,000	2,835,000	7,821,000
1994	1,539,000	2,713,000	7,880,000
1995	1,472,500	2,594,000	7,998,000
1996	1,395,000	2,501,500	7,894,500

The Smithsonian displayed George Washington's false teeth until they were stolen in 1981.

53% of state prison inmates, 74% of jail inmates, and 87% of federal inmates were imprisoned for offenses which involved neither harm, nor the threat of harm, to a victim.

SOURCE: DEPARTMENT OF JUSTICE

Property Crime

Are property crime rates increasing or decreasing?

?

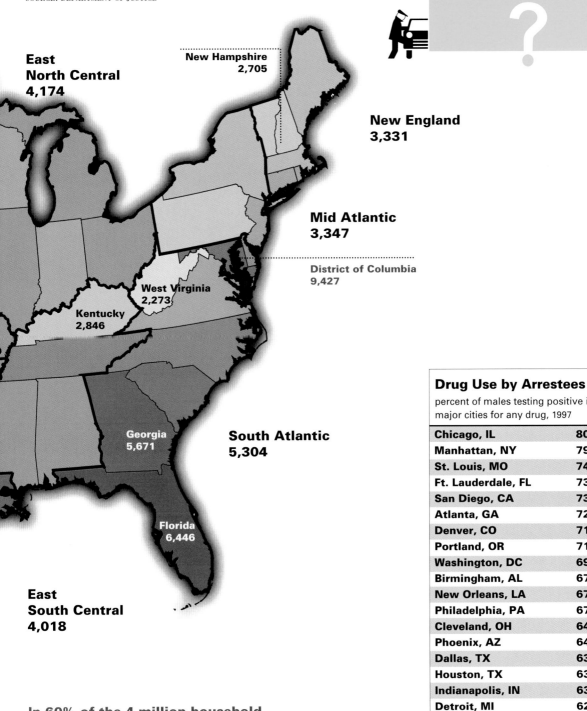

East
North Central
4,174

New Hampshire
2,705

New England
3,331

Mid Atlantic
3,347

District of Columbia
9,427

West Virginia
2,273

Kentucky
2,846

Georgia
5,671

South Atlantic
5,304

Florida
6,446

East
South Central
4,018

In 60% of the 4 million household burglaries in 1998, the burglar gained entry through an unlocked door or window.

Drug Use by Arrestees	
percent of males testing positive in major cities for any drug, 1997	
Chicago, IL	80%
Manhattan, NY	79%
St. Louis, MO	74%
Ft. Lauderdale, FL	73%
San Diego, CA	73%
Atlanta, GA	72%
Denver, CO	71%
Portland, OR	71%
Washington, DC	69%
Birmingham, AL	67%
New Orleans, LA	67%
Philadelphia, PA	67%
Cleveland, OH	64%
Phoenix, AZ	64%
Dallas, TX	63%
Houston, TX	63%
Indianapolis, IN	63%
Detroit, MI	62%
Omaha, NE	62%
Miami, FL	61%
Los Angeles, CA	59%

SOURCE: US NATIONAL INSTITUTE OF JUSTICE

Drugs and Crime
National Institute of Justice.
Department of Justice.
www.ojp.usdoj.gov/nij/drugdocs.htm
The National Institute of Justice makes available via its web site many reports on drug use and crime dating from 1994.

From 1992 to 1996, the number of U.S. homicides declined by 20%, yet the number of murders reported on the ABC, CBS and NBC evening news increased by 721%.

TV Crime Time
minutes on ABC, CBS and NBC

- O.J. case/trial
- All other crime
- Guns/gun control

The PursuitWatch Network, in San Dimas, CA, is a paging service that informs its customers whenever a high-speed chase is televised.

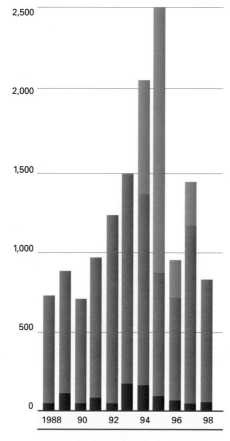

SOURCE: MEDIA STUDIES CENTER

Domestic Violence

Domestic violence is a pattern of assault and coercion, including physical, sexual, and psychological attacks, as well as economic coercion, used against one's intimate partner.

Researchers have long known of the link between domestic violence and child abuse. Each year, more than one million children are confirmed as victims of child abuse and neglect. As a result of this treatment, three children die every day.

95% of assaults on spouses or ex-spouses are committed by men against women.

SOURCE: THE U.S. DEPARTMENT OF JUSTICE

when?

55%

of all violent crimes occur between the hours of 6 am and 6 pm.

where?

40%

of all rapes and/or sexual assaults occur at or near the victim's home or lodging.

how?

91%

of all rapes and/or sexual assaults occur while the offender has no weapons.

Homicide Rate
per 100,000 residents population, 1995

black male

black female

white male

white female

Atheists and agnostics suffered the fewest— only 2— religion-related hate crimes in 1996.

Violence

If the crime rate is dropping, why do Americans feel more threatened by crime?

?

Hate Crimes

The largest categories of reported hate crimes included:

Anti-Black	**3,945**
Anti-White	**1,554**
Anti-Jewish	**1,236**
Anti-Male Homosexual	**937**

The most hate crimes against lesbians and gays reported in 1995 were in:

New York City	**625**
San Francisco	**324**
Los Angeles	**256**
Minneapolis/St. Paul	**218**

The violent acts in descending frequency were:

Intimidation	**4,048**
Simple Assault	**1,796**
Aggravated Assault	**1,268**
Murder	**20**
Forcible Rape	**12**

The FBI claims that 75% of the U.S. population is represented in these data. However, less than half of law enforcement agencies report hate crimes and only 1,150 actually record incidents.

7,947 hate crimes were reported to local authorities in 1995.

Workplace Violence

Occupations with high risk of work-related homicides, 1996

Occupation	homicide rate per 100,000	homicides
Taxi drivers	23	46
Guards	6	50
Police & Detectives	5.5	54
Sales counter clerks	5.5	11
Food & Lodging Managers	4.5	61
Bartenders	3.5	11
Sales supervisors & proprietors	3.5	147
Cashiers	3	85
Stock handlers	1	12
Truck drivers	1	27

● homicide rate per 100,000

🧍 = one homicide

SOURCE: U.S. BUREAU OF LABOR STATISTICS

● Center for the Study and Prevention of Violence. University of Colorado. www.colorado.edu/cspv/index.html
The Center has a three-fold mission: to collect and make available resources on the causes and prevention of violence, to provide technical assistance in developing and assessing prevention programs, and to conduct research.

A child is arrested for a violent crime every 5 minutes.

That's 288 arrests per day, 105,000 per year.

SOURCE: THE CHILDREN'S DEFENSE FUND

More than half (27) of the U.S. states have no restrictions for prosecuting juveniles as adults. 42 states have created laws that hold parents responsible for their children's behavior— of those, 17 make parents criminally liable.

Juvenile Crime
by sex and race, per 1,000 youth

	1986	1995
Male total	**72**	**92**
Property Crime	44	47
Violent Crime	12	20
Drug Offenses	5	10
Public Order Offenses	12	17
Female total	18	27
Property Crime	10	14
Violent Crime	3	7
Drug Offenses	1	2
Public Order Offenses	4	5
White total	40	50
Property Crime	25	27
Violent Crime	5	10
Drug Offenses	3	5
Public Order Offenses	7	9
Black total	**80**	**123**
Property Crime	44	53
Violent Crime	20	34
Drug Offenses	4	13
Public Order Offenses	12	24
Other races total	**30**	**44**
Property Crime	20	26
Violent Crime	4	9
Drug Offenses	2	2
Public Order Offenses	5	7

Male youth are at 7.3 times greater risk of fatal firearm injuries and 6.0 times greater risk of nonfatal firearm injuries than female youth.

12 am	1 am	2 am	3 am	4 am	5 am	6 am	7 am	8 am	9 am	10 am	11 am

4,223 children were killed by firearms in 1997— that's one child every two hours.

Student Gun-Related Expulsions

number of students expelled per 100,000 for States with highest rates in 1997-98

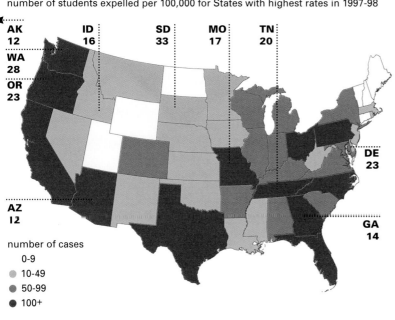

AK	ID	SD	MO	TN
12	16	33	17	20

WA
28

OR
23

DE
23

AZ
12

GA
14

number of cases
- 0-9
- 10-49
- 50-99
- 100+

3,930 students were expelled during the 1997-98 school year for bringing firearms to school—down about 30% from the previous year.

The main reason given by adolescents for obtaining or carrying guns is self-protection.

SOURCE: NATIONAL CENTER FOR JUVENILE JUSTICE, JUVENILE COURT STATISTICS

Juvenile crime has spiked upward while adult crime rates have remained flat or declined. It is now more likely for a 15-year-old than a 30-year-old to commit a violent crime.

Between 1985 and 1995, the juvenile arrest rate for violent crimes rose 69%; for murders, it rose 96%.

Police made about 2.7 million arrests of juveniles in 1995, 19% of them for violent crimes—murder, forcible rape, armed robbery and aggravated assault. That translates into an arrest for one in every 200 people between the ages of 10 and 17.

Juveniles were involved in 32% of all robbery arrests, 23% of weapons arrests, and 15% of arrests for murder and aggravated assault.

pm	1 pm	2 pm	3 pm	4 pm	5 pm	6 pm	7 pm	8 pm	9 pm	10 pm	11 pm

○ National Criminal Justice Reference Service. Department of Justice.
www.ncjrs.org
The Justice Information Center is the most extensive clearinghouse of crime, criminal justice, and juvenile justice information in the world. Find reports and statistics online or search the database for government and non-government publications and articles from professional journals.

States With Highest Incarceration Rates

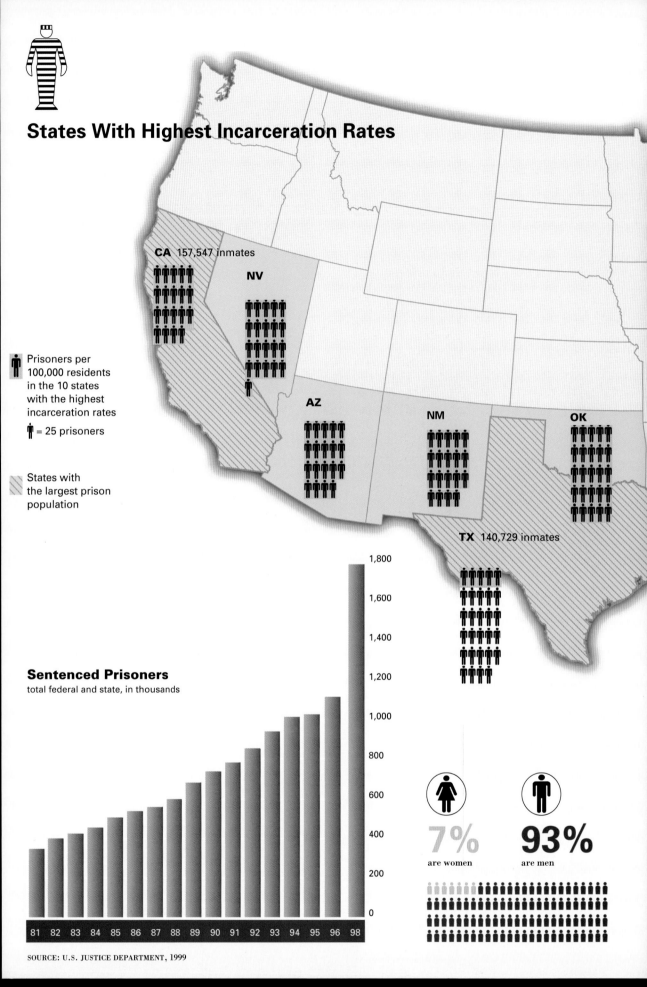

CA 157,547 inmates

NV

Prisoners per 100,000 residents in the 10 states with the highest incarceration rates

♦ = 25 prisoners

States with the largest prison population

AZ

NM

OK

TX 140,729 inmates

Sentenced Prisoners
total federal and state, in thousands

| 1,800 |
| 1,600 |
| 1,400 |
| 1,200 |
| 1,000 |
| 800 |
| 600 |
| 400 |
| 200 |
| 0 |

81 82 83 84 85 86 87 88 89 90 91 92 93 94 95 96 98

7%
are women

93%
are men

SOURCE: U.S. JUSTICE DEPARTMENT, 1999

From 1978 to 1996, the number of violent offenders entering prisons doubled (from 43,733 to 98,672 inmates); the number of nonviolent offenders tripled (from 83,721 to 161,796 inmates) and the number of drug offenders increased sevenfold (from 14,241 to 114,071 inmates).

If incarceration rates remain unchanged, one in every 20 people (5.1%) will serve time in a prison during their lifetime.

*The number of prisoners
has more than tripled in
the last twenty years
from 500,000 to 1.8 million.
Prison populations now
exceed the combined
populations of Wyoming,
Alaska and North Dakota.*

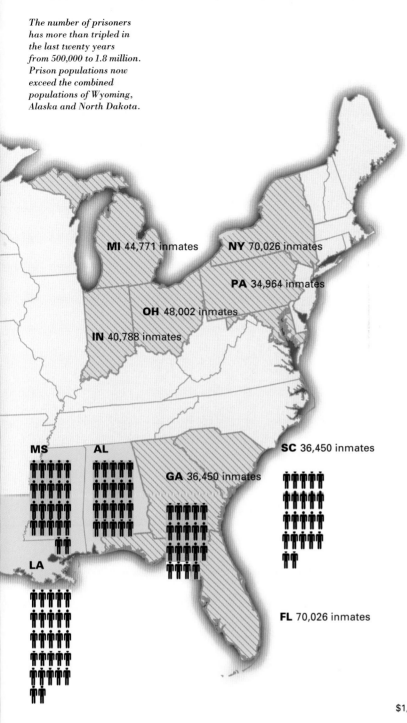

MI 44,771 inmates   **NY** 70,026 inmates

PA 34,964 inmates

OH 48,002 inmates

IN 40,788 inmates

MS **AL** **GA** 36,450 inmates **SC** 36,450 inmates

LA

FL 70,026 inmates

In 1997 a record 5.7 million Americans were under "correctional supervision"— jail, prison, probation, or parole.

SOURCE: BUREAU OF JUSTICE STATISTICS

1,800,000

Prison population in 1999

$20,000-$40,000

Average annual cost per prisoner

$31 billion

Combined prison and jail budgets for 1997

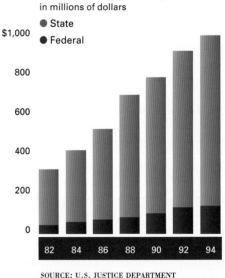

Justice System Expenditures
in millions of dollars
- State
- Federal

| | 82 | 84 | 86 | 88 | 90 | 92 | 94 |

SOURCE: U.S. JUSTICE DEPARTMENT

**More than 7 of every 10
jail inmates had sentences
prior to probation or
incarceration.**

**Prison spending increased
faster than funding for
colleges between 1977
and 1995. Spending
growth for prisons was
823% compared to 374%
for higher education.**

for 1999: **3,549**

Prisoners under Death Sentence

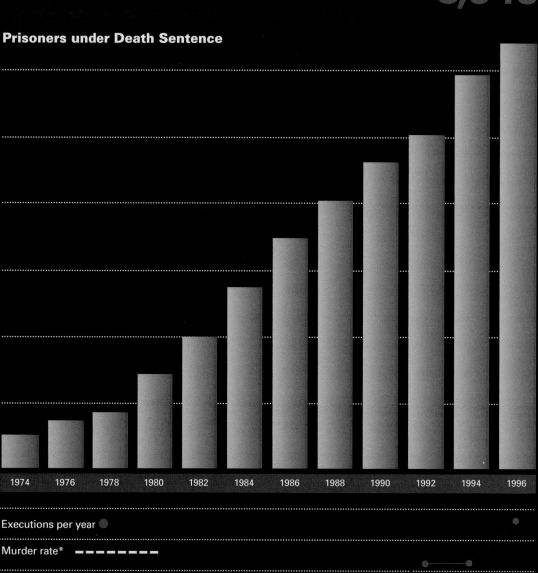

| | 1974 | 1976 | 1978 | 1980 | 1982 | 1984 | 1986 | 1988 | 1990 | 1992 | 1994 | 1996 |

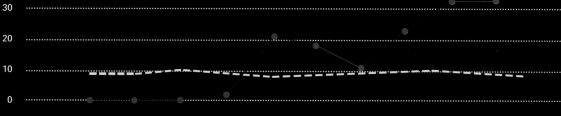

Executions per year ●

Murder rate* ━ ━ ━ ━ ━ ━ ━

*per 100,000 population

The number of executions has not affected national murder rates

Since the death penalty was reinstated in 1976, the number of executions has substantially increased. During this same period, there is virtually no change in the national murder rate.

SOURCE: FBI UNIFORM CRIME REPORTS

| 1974 | 1976 | 1978 | 1980 | 1982 | 1984 | 1986 | 1988 | 1990 | 1992 | 1994 | 1996 |

Executions by race

● White
● Black

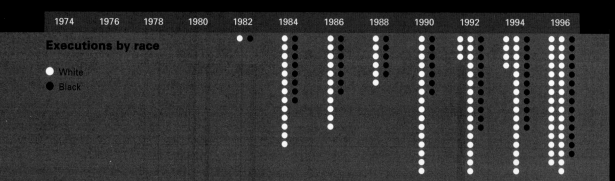

Race of Death Row Inmates

○ **White 47%**   ● Black 42%   ● Hispanic 8%   ● Other 3%

Race of Victims

○ **White 83%**   ● Black 11%   ● Hispanic 4%   ● Other 2%

Race of District Attorneys*

22 Hispanic DAs =    22 Black DAs =

1,794 White DAs =

* chief prosecuting official with discretionary power
to determine charging levels in death penalty states

Death Penalty

*Is capital punishment a
deterrent to murder?*

?

The United States is the only Western industrialized nation that allows capital punishment.

From 1930 to 1996, 4,217 executions
were carried out under state
or federal authority. 3,859 occurred
before 1972, when the Supreme
Court ruled capital punishment
unconstitutional.

Since the Court reinstated the death
penalty in 1976, an additional
566 executions have been carried out;
82 inmates have been exonerated.

**83% of capital cases
involve white victims,
even though nationally
only 50% of murder
victims are white.**

SOURCE: NAACP LDP DEATH ROW

Prisoners executed in 1996 had been on death row for an average of
10 years. A positive aspect of this lengthy wait is that it allows some death
row prisoners to prove their innocence before they face execution.

However, 36 of the 38 states that have capital punishment have a statute of
limitations for evidence presented after conviction.

SOURCE: DEATH PENALTY INFORMATION CENTER

● **Death Penalty Information Center**
www.essential.org/dpic
This non-profit organization that favors
the abolition of the death penalty provides
numerous reports on issues surrounding
the use of capital punishment.

Crochet and appliqué flag, circa 1920 from the collection of Kit Hinrichs

Hani Rashid / Lise Anne Couture

Sex & Sexuality
Who is sexually active? What forms of birth control are being used?

Stock Market
How many Americans invest in stocks? What kinds of stock do they prefer?

Transportation
How do Americans get around?

Space Program
How much is spent on America's space program?

Cities
What are the average earnings in America's biggest cities? What are the growth rates of these cities?

Race
What percentage of Americans is represented by each race? How is each race doing in terms of employment?

Marriage & Divorce
What percentage of Americans is married? Divorced? How does our divorce rate compare to that of other countries?

Families
How big is the average American family? Who is supporting these families?

American Demographics
How do our characteristics relate?

Datascaping USA
How can we better understand America's characteristics?

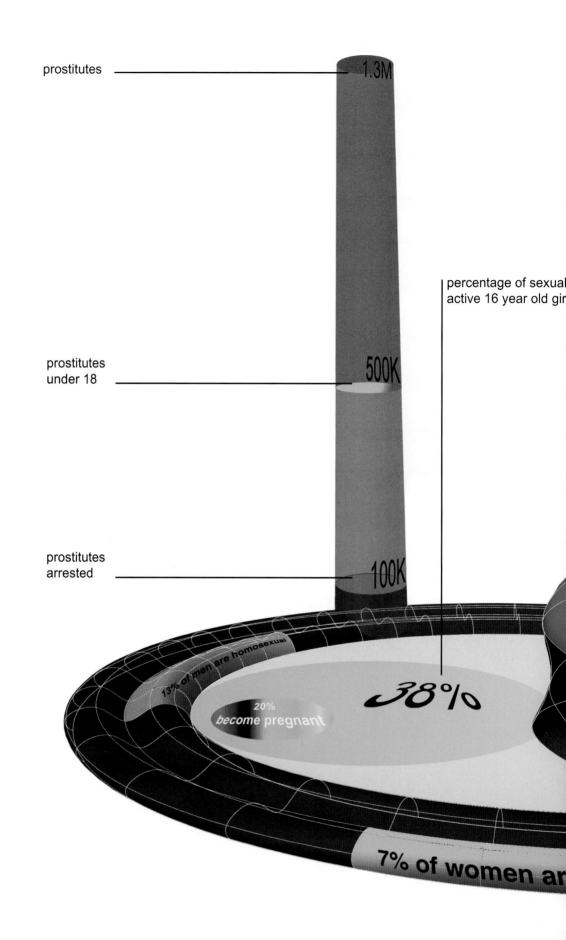

prostitutes —————————————— 1.3M

percentage of sexual
active 16 year old gir

prostitutes
under 18 ————————————— 500K

prostitutes
arrested ————————————— 100K

13% of men are homosexual

20%
become pregnant

38%

7% of women ar

Sexual activity

On average American adults have
1.49 sexual partners each year.

The average American has sex 59.6
times annually.

Married people age 18-29 have the
most sex (111.4 times a year) .

Teen sex

65% of female teenagers and 68% of
male teenagers in the U.S. are sexually active.

25% of sexually active teens
acquired an STD in 1997.

Diseases

Each year 12 million cases of sexually transmitted diseases are reported.

Every year 31,130 Americans die of
HIV/AIDS.

Sex & Sexuality

Who is sexually active?
What forms of birth control
are being used?

female
sterilization

condoms

male sterilization

birth control pill

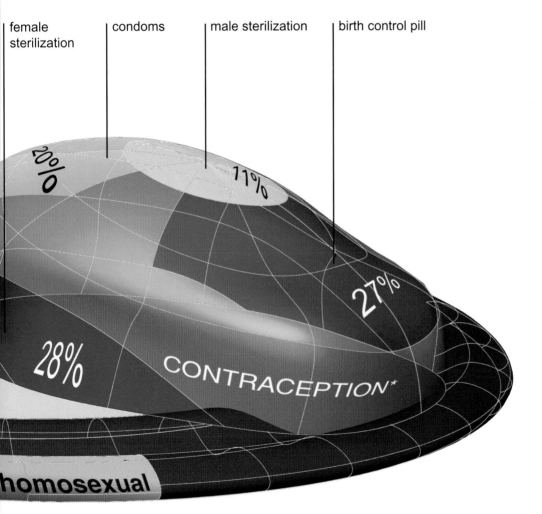

20%

11%

27%

28%

CONTRACEPTION*

homosexual

Pregnancy

Nearly half of the 6.3 million
pregnancies in the United States
each year are unintended.

13% of all U.S. births are to teens,
78% of these are not planned.

Fertility

In 1940, the average number of
sperm per human male ejaculation
was 100 million. In 1990, it was 50
million.

Each year 4.5 million couples experience infertility.

*methods of contraception

Statistics for contraception
represent use by fertile and
sexually active women who are
15 to 44 years old. This equals
69% of the female population.

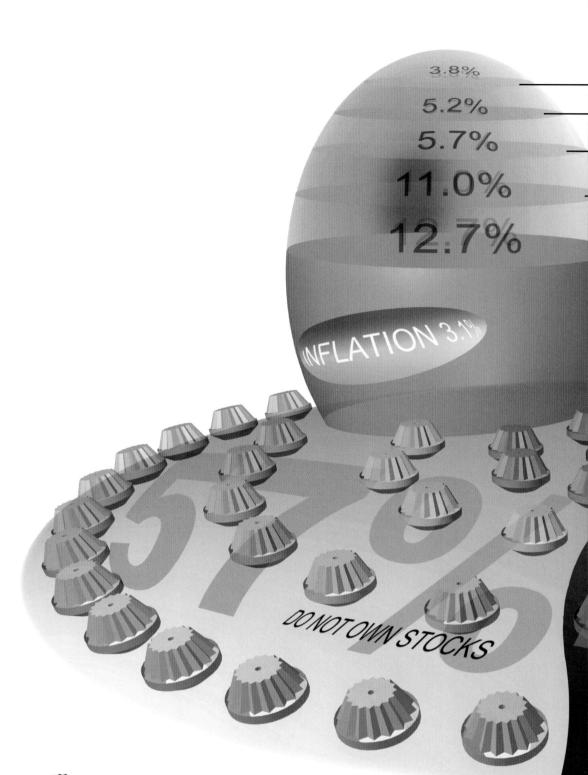

3.8%

5.2%

5.7%

11.0%

12.7%

INFLATION 3.1%

57%

DO NOT OWN STOCKS

 $1,608 tax exempt money market

$8,981 taxable money market

$10,315 bond & income

$23,993 equity funds

$44,897 mutual funds

total annual amount (in $100M) of assets invested in funds

Investment club members	**The most popular stocks with investment clubs:**	**The price for a seat on the NYSE**
65.3% are women, 34.7% are men.	Number of clubs with stock	1997 high price: $ 1,750,000 low price: $ 1,175,000
46% hold an undergraduate college degree.	Pepsi Co. Inc. 11,338 Intel Corp. 11,019	
	Motorola, Inc. 9,863	1965
86% have a family income of $35K or more.	Tricon Global 9,168 Merck & Co. Inc. 8,687	high price: $ 250,000 (+700%) low price: $ 190,000 (+620%)

Stock Market

How many Americans invest in stocks? What kinds of stock do they prefer?

?

annual rates of return (1926-1997)

treasury bills

long term government bonds

long term corporate bonds

S&P 500

small company stocks

NYSE volume daily average

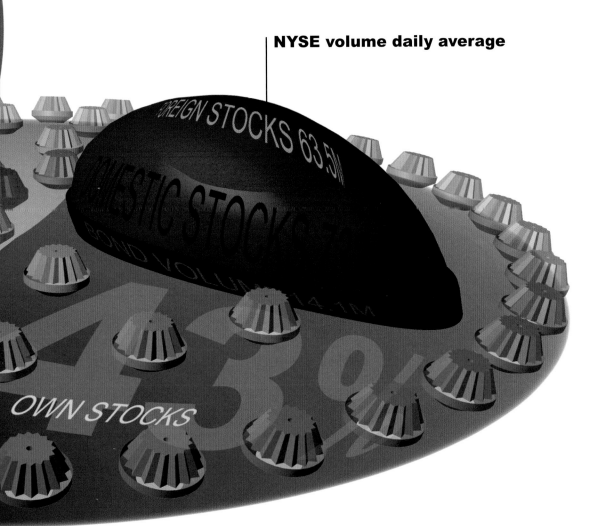

FOREIGN STOCKS 63.5M

DOMESTIC STOCKS

BOND VOLUME 14.1M

43%

OWN STOCKS

Profile of stock owners

60% of Americans who own mutual funds have holdings in excess of $10,000.

59% of Americans with individual stocks have holdings in excess of $10,000.

Almost half of stockholders have household incomes between $30,000 and $75,000.

20% of stock owners are retired.

85% of stockholders are white.

persons employed in transportation occupations

number and type of vehicles

occupants killed in vehicle accidents

number and type of vehicles

130,000,000 passenger cars
69,000,000 light trucks
7,000,000 commercial trucks
697,000 buses

208M mo

90.4%

7.6%

2.6%

5.4%

4,024,000 motor vehicles

70,000 water transportation

116,000 rail transportation

241,000 air transportation

persons employed in
transportation occupations

Fuel consumption for transportation purposes		States with highest number of motor vehicles	Motor vehicles per household
fuel	gallons	California has the highest number of motor vehicles by more than double the number in the next highest state (CA -15,398,720, FL - 7,285,563).	In 1969 the average household had one car. In 1995 the average household had two cars, and 19% of all households owned three or more cars.
Total	148,298,767,000		
Gasoline	120,125,000,000		
Diesel	27,825,950,000		
Replacement fuel	3,711,500,000		
Alternative fuels	321,389,000		

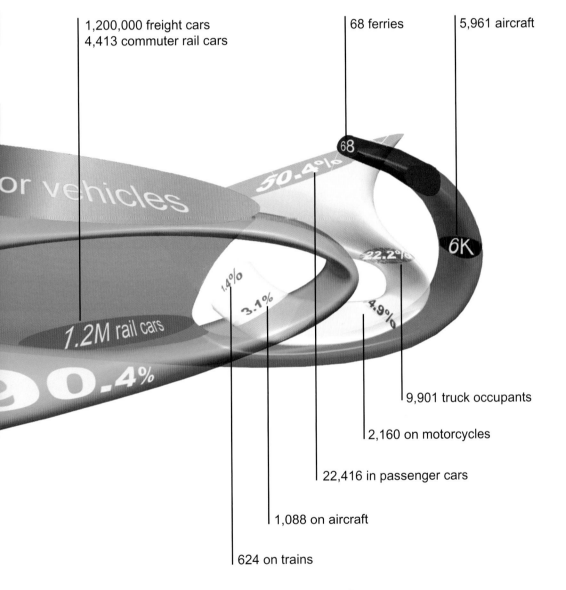

1,200,000 freight cars
4,413 commuter rail cars

68 ferries

5,961 aircraft

or vehicles

50.4%

68

22.2%

6K

1.4%

3.1%

4.9%

1.2M rail cars

0.4%

9,901 truck occupants

2,160 on motorcycles

22,416 in passenger cars

1,088 on aircraft

624 on trains

**occupants killed
in vehicle accidents**

Transportation Expenditure

$847 billion or 11% of the Gross
Domestic Product was spent on
transportation in 1996.

Length of public roads in the U.S.

Interstate highways	46,036 miles	1%
National highway system	112,467 miles	3%
Other	3,760,947 miles	96%

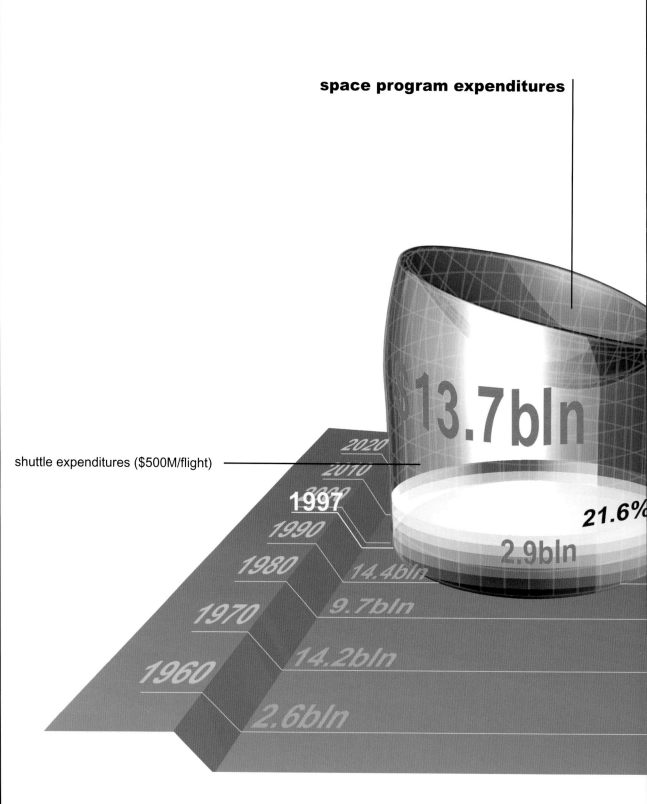

shuttle expenditures ($500M/flight)

$13.7bln

2020
2010
1997
1990
1980   14.4bln
1970   9.7bln
1960   14.2bln
        2.6bln

21.6%
2.9bln

Successful space launches

U.S.	1124
Soviet Union / CIS	2548
Japan	52
European Space Agency	96
China	49
France	10
India	8
Israel	3

Tax dollars at work

The NASA budget of $13.7 billion is 0.825% of the total $1.653 trillion in federal budget.

NASA employs 17,913 civil servants.

Public opinion

44% of Americans say they would travel in space given the chance.

44% of registered voters believe in intelligent life on other planets.

57% of Americans believe that space exploration impacts daily life.

Space Program

How much is spent on America's space program?

?

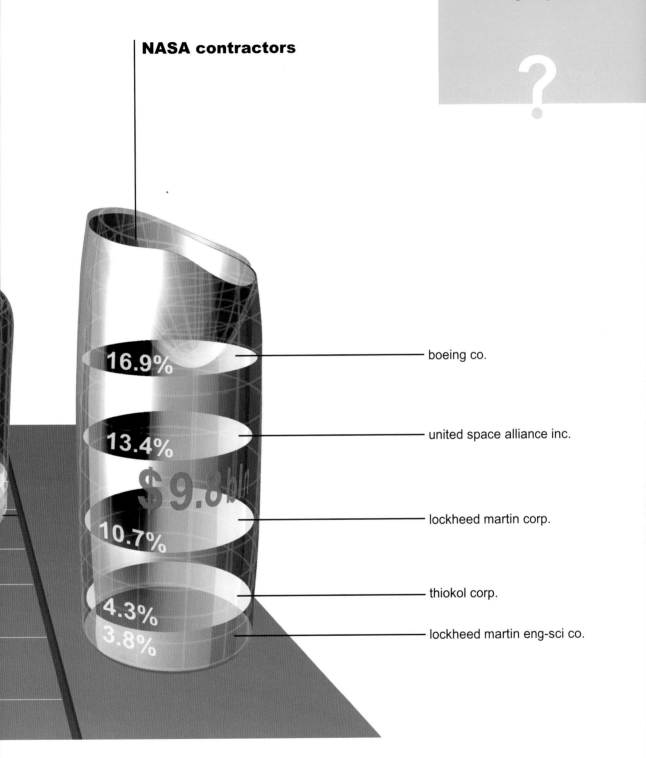

NASA contractors

16.9% — boeing co.

13.4% — united space alliance inc.

$9.8bln

10.7% — lockheed martin corp.

4.3%
3.8%

thiokol corp.

lockheed martin eng-sci co.

Future

The anticipated bill for a manned international space station is $35 billion to $45 billion.

Space tourism

It costs $4,000 per pound to lift a payload into orbit. An optimistic assumption of $200 per pound would price a ticket into space at no less than $50,000.

● National Aeronautics and Space Administration. U.S. www.nasa.gov/NASA_homepage.html/ Principal federal agency committed to spreading the unique knowledge that flows from its aeronautics and space research.

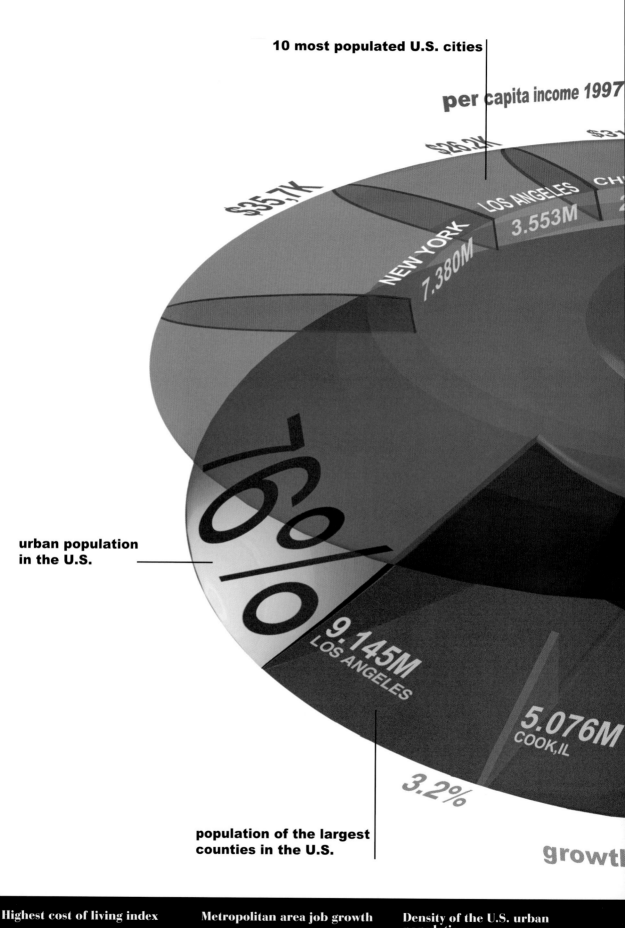

10 most populated U.S. cities

per capita income 1997

$26.2K

$3...

$35.7K

NEW YORK
7.380M

LOS ANGELES
3.553M

CH...

urban population
in the U.S.

76%

9.145M
LOS ANGELES

5.076M
COOK,IL

3.2%

population of the largest
counties in the U.S.

growth

Highest cost of living index		Metropolitan area job growth		Density of the U.S. urban population:
	Index	Sarasota, FL	8.44%	
San Francisco	134.8	McAllen-Mission, TX	6.74%	There are 29.5 people per square
New York	122.4	Phoenix, AZ	5.92%	kilometer in the U.S.
Boston	121.4	Dallas, TX	5.91%	

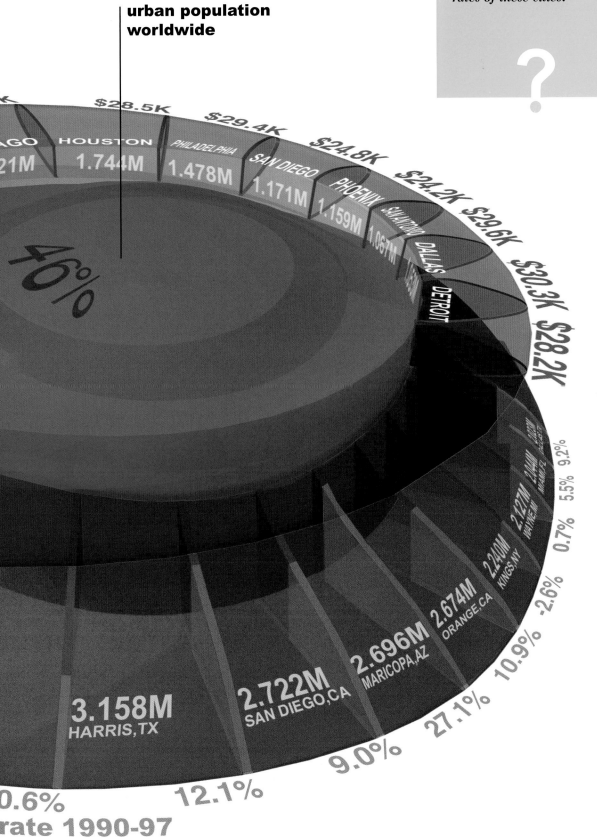

Cities

What are the average earnings in America's biggest cities? What are the growth rates of these cities?

?

urban population worldwide

$28.5K

$29.4K

$24.8K

$24.2K $29.6K

$30.3K $28.2K

AGO   HOUSTON   PHILADELPHIA

21M   1.744M   1.478M   SAN DIEGO   PHOENIX   SAN ANTONIO   DALLAS

1.171M   1.159M   1.067M

DETROIT

46%

9.2%

5.5%

0.7%

-2.6%

10.9%

27.1%

9.0%

12.1%

0.6%

rate 1990-97

3.158M
HARRIS, TX

2.722M
SAN DIEGO, CA

2.696M
MARICOPA, AZ

2.674M
ORANGE, CA

2.240M
KINGS, NY

2.127M
WAYNE, MI

Distribution of housing units

32% in central cities
24% in non-metropolitan areas
44% in suburbs

National Urban Institute
www.urbaninstitute.org/
The Urban Institute investigates social and
economic problems confronting the nation
and analyzes efforts to solve these
problems.

Urban Land Institute
www.uli.org
ULI research is geared to assist in solving
the land use issues of our society.

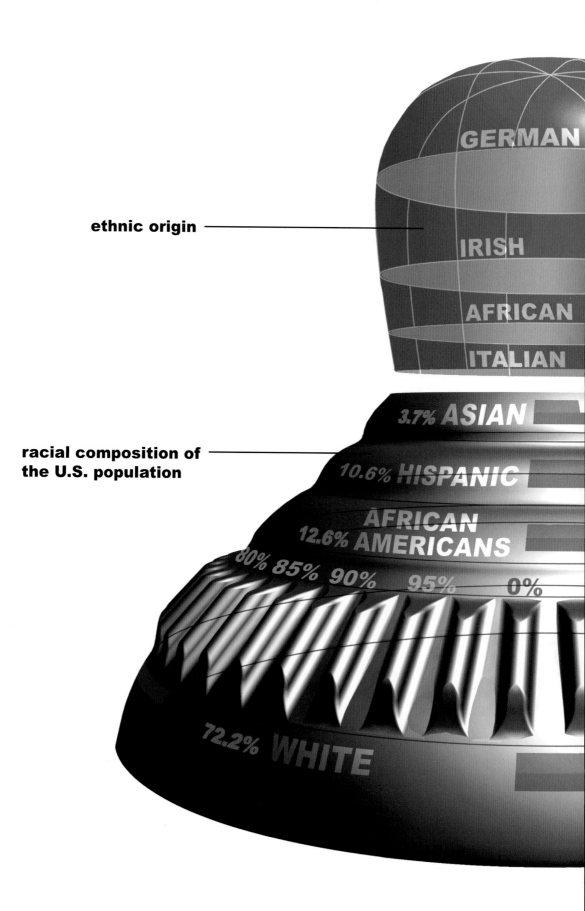

ethnic origin

GERMAN

IRISH

AFRICAN

ITALIAN

racial composition of the U.S. population

3.7% ASIAN

10.6% HISPANIC

AFRICAN
12.6% AMERICANS

80% 85% 90% 95% 0%

72.2% WHITE

Average income

$37,005 is the median household income in the U.S.

Whites earn $38,972 on average, African Americans earn $25,050, and Hispanics earn $26,628.

Technology

Among families earning $15,000 to $35,000 per year, more than 32% of whites own computers, but only 19% of blacks and Hispanics in this income range have computers at home.

Business ownership

Minorities own 12.5% of U.S. business.

Race

What percentage of Americans is represented by each race? How is each race doing in terms of employment?

?

42.9%

28.6%

17.6%

10.8%

5%   10%   15%   20%

 unemployment rate according to race

racial and ethnic composition of workforce

Home ownership

71.7% of white families own their own homes compared to 46% of black families and 43% of Hispanic families.

808,163 people in America live on reservations.

Infant mortality rates

blacks   14.6
Hispanics   6.3
whites   6.3   per 1000 live births

● Institute on Race & Poverty. University of Minnesota Law School.
www1.umn.edu/irp/
Addresses the underlying causes of the problems created at the intersection of racial segregation and poverty.

marital status

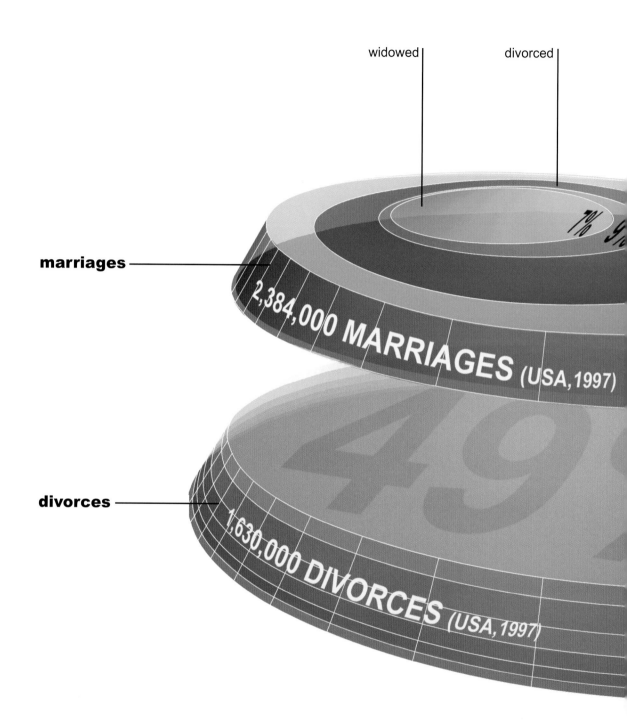

widowed | divorced |

marriages —— 2,384,000 MARRIAGES (USA, 1997)

7% 9

divorces —— 1,630,000 DIVORCES (USA, 1997)

Median age of men and women when married for the first time:			Divorced population:	Unmarried couple households:	
1976:	men	23.8 years	The number of divorced people has more than quadrupled from 1970 with 4.3 million to 18.3 million in 1996.	Age of couples	
	women	21.3 years		Under 25	20%
				25-44 yrs	60%
1996:	men	27.1 years		45-64 yrs	15%
	women	24.8 years		65 and over	5%

Marriage & Divorce

What percentage of Americans is married? Divorced? How does our divorce rate compare to that of other countries?

?

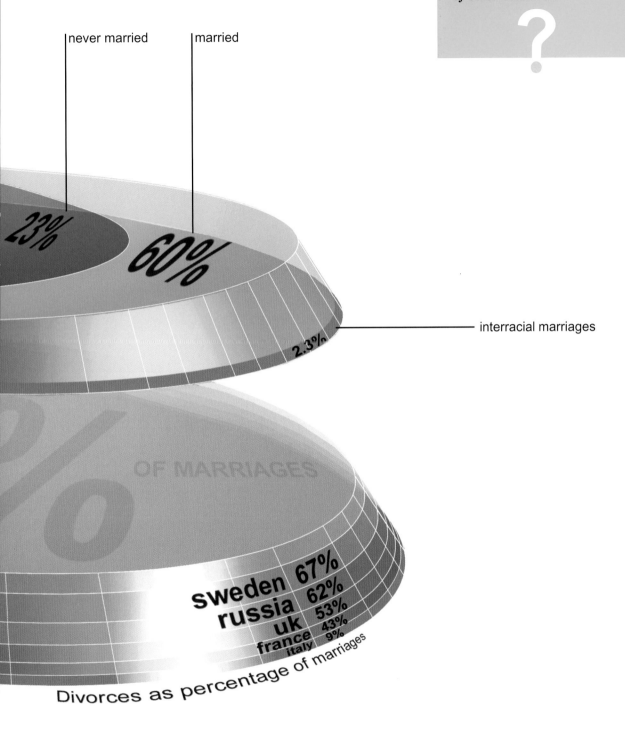

never married

married

23%

60%

2.3% — interracial marriages

OF MARRIAGES

sweden 67%
russia 62%
uk 53%
france 43%
italy 9%

Divorces as percentage of marriages

Never married adults:

In 1996 44.9 million adults had never been married, more than twice the number in 1970 (21.4M).

⬤ Policy.com. Issue of the Week.
6/21/99:Marriage: the State of the Union
www.policy.com/issuewk/1999/0621_78/
index.html
A commercial news service offering policy
information and news reports.

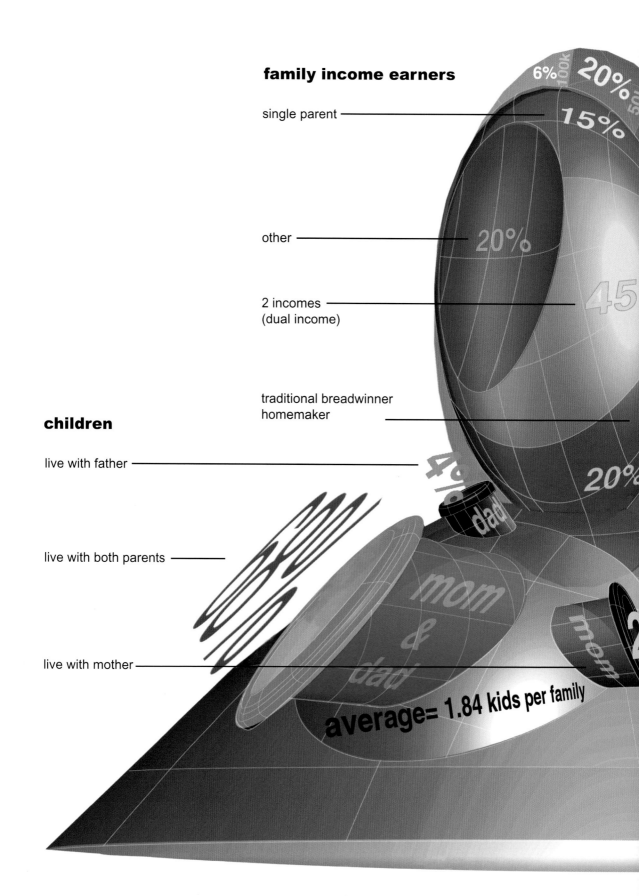

family income earners

single parent

other

2 incomes
(dual income)

traditional breadwinner
homemaker

6% 100k 20% 50
15%
20%
45
20%
40 dad

children

live with father

live with both parents

live with mother

mom
&
dad

mom
2

average= 1.84 kids per family

Poverty thresholds		Financial assistance	Single mothers
Size of family	1997 income	4,564,000 Americans receive	From 1980 to 1997 the population of
		unemployment compensation.	American single mothers rose by
1 person	$ 8,183		60% to 10 million.
2 persons	$10,473	4,932,000 Americans receive	
3 persons	$12,802	educational assistance.	
4 persons	$16,400		
5 persons	$19,380		

Families

How big is the average American family? Who is supporting these families?

?

31.1%

25k

26.5%

10k

16%

——————— **annual family incomes**

+6%

21%

23%

3

of couples have no children

——————— **size of families**

2 persons 43%

Child abuse

In 1997 126,095 incidents of sexual abuse of children were recorded.

In 1997 244,903 incidents of physical abuse were recorded.

Preschool child care

Care in child's home	33%
Care in a relative's home	15.9%
Care in another home	15.4%
Daycare center	21.6%
Nursery or Preschool	7.8%
With mother at work	5.5%

The average number of children per family is 1.84.

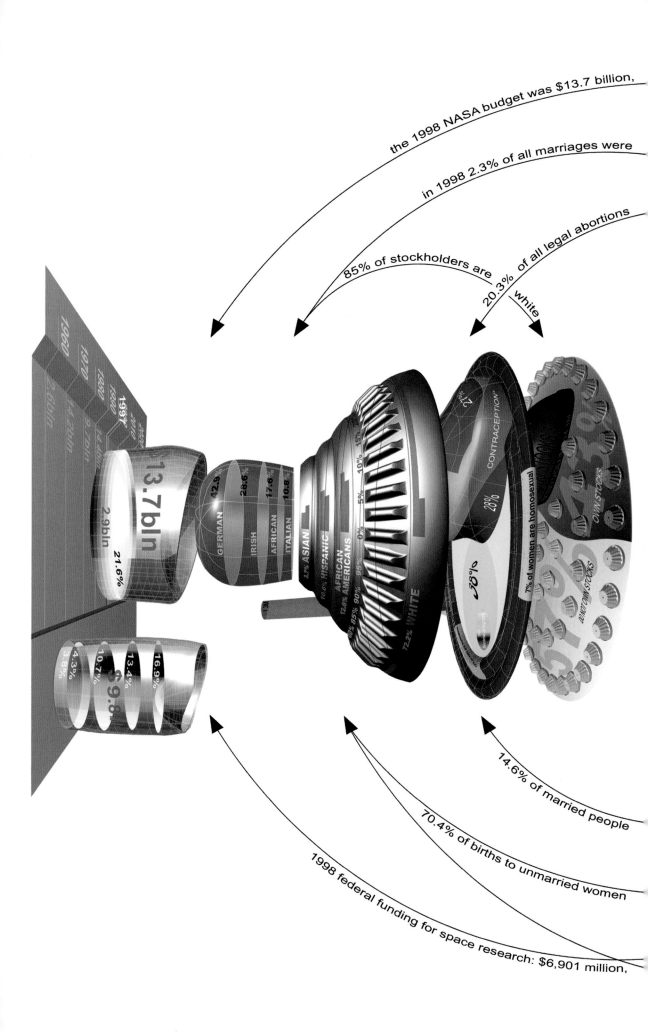

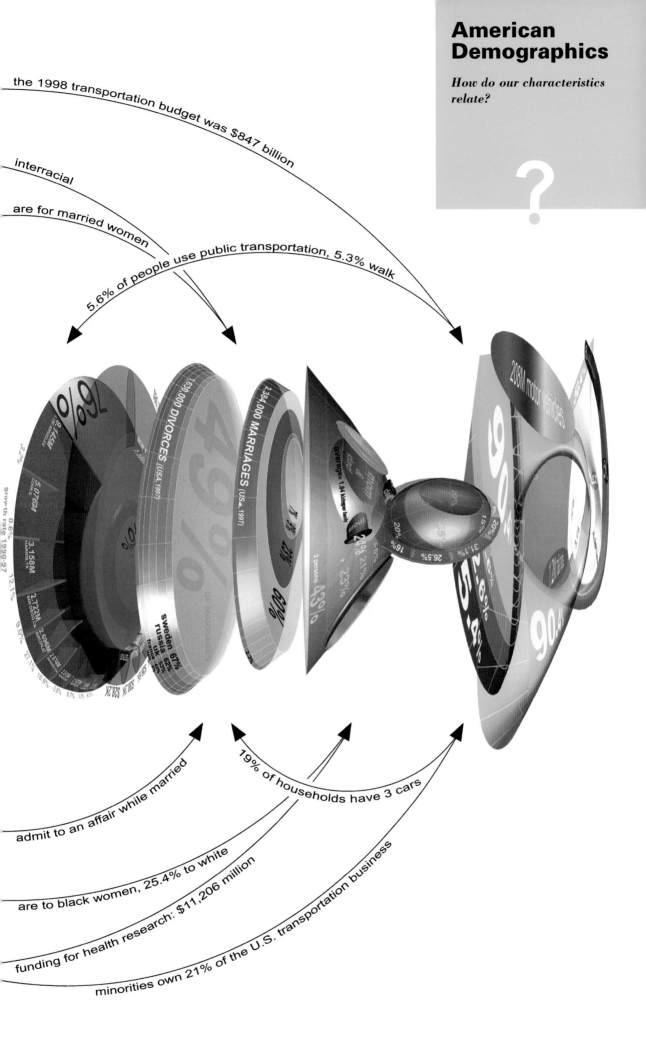

the 1998 transportation budget was $847 billion

interracial

are for married women

5.6% of people use public transportation, 5.3% walk

admit to an affair while married

19% of households have 3 cars

are to black women, 25.4% to white

funding for health research: $11,206 million

minorities own 21% of the U.S. transportation business

Sex and Sexuality   1,300,000 prostitutes   500,000 arrested   under eighteen 100,000   38% of 16 year old girls are sexually a

  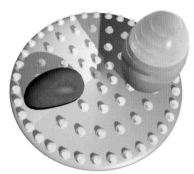

Stock Market   43% of Americans own stock   annual rate of return for S&P 500 1926-97 11%   for small company stocks 12.7%   in

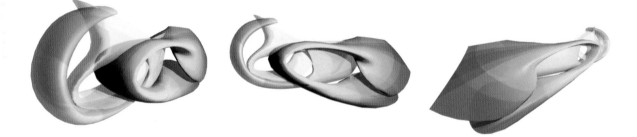

Transportation   over 208 million motor vehicles in the US including 130 million passenger cars   over 22,000 automobile occupants kille

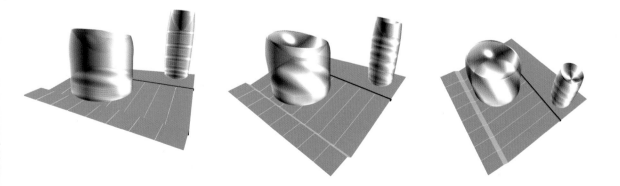

Space Program   the overall NASA budget is $13.7 billion   independent contractors receive $9.8 billion   NASA spends $2.9 billio

20% of these become pregnant   13% of men and 7% of women are homosexual

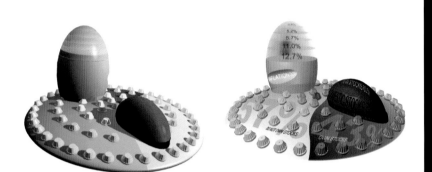

eraged 3.1%   NYSE daily average stock volume $796.6M for bonds 14.1M

lly   241,000 persons employed in air transportation occupations

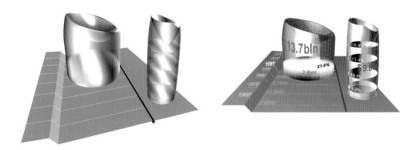

lly on space shuttle flights which cost an average of $500 million per flight

The eight models contained on these pages created by Asymptote, exist as Virtual Reality Markup Language (VRML) models that are accessible and operable on the Internet. The models can be found at the **TED**X website www.understandingusa.com. Each three dimensional model can be manipulated and adjusted according to certain criteria allowing for different readings and means of understandings. The adjustability and transformative aspects of these data entities allow for each subject to be analyzed and scrutinized from different viewpoints. These are different 'vantage' points one can assume in order to reference information in a variety of ways. *Timelining*, for example allows for certain adjustments of the data to be made where one can reverse or fast forward a timeline to see how the datascape alters and transforms. By choosing one element in the data model and adjusting it according to some criteria, other items that are related can also be re-configured and adjusted accordingly. Here various correlations can be made on data that might otherwise be missed or misconstrued. This new method of reading, recording and gathering information creates a much richer and deeper understanding of information in contrast to conventional graphing and charting systems.

The datascapes consist of three main components that allow them to be interactive entities for eventual porting over the web. They were initially modeled as rudimentary wireframes in Maya software and kept 'lightweight'

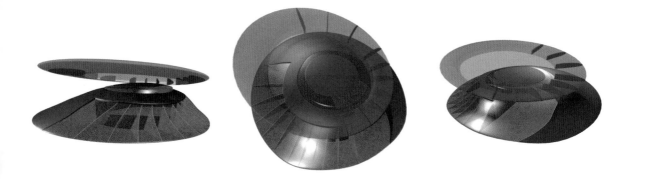

Cities

a76% of the American population lives in urban areas   the urban population worldwide is 46%   New York is the largest city with 7,3

Race

ethnic origin: 42.9% German 28.6% Irish 17.6% African 10.8% Italian   racial composition: 72.2% White 12.6% African American 10.6% H

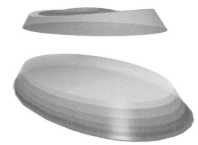

Marriages and Divorces

23% of American adults have never married   60% are married   9% are divorced   the number o

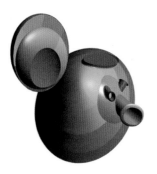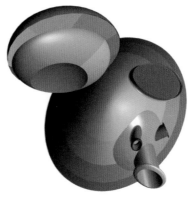

Families

6% of families have 5 or more persons   45% of families have dual incomes   53% of couples do not have children under 18 year

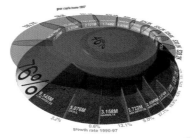

in order to allow them to be efficiently read despite the bandwidth restrictions of the Internet as the technology exists today.

After the design refinement in Maya and the exporting of the models as VRML 2.0, the wireframes are re-configured and the design continues in Cosmo Worlds, software produced by Silicon Graphics. At this juncture the models are attributed with various features including animation, interactive components and motion sensors. The models are also texture mapped in Cosmo Worlds in order to give them tectonic characteristics including lighting and shading. The moving texture maps are key framed animations that are placed on the wireframes and give the datascapes their 'live' feedback capability when accessed and manipulated over the Internet.

The models are completely updatable and resident in a virtual real estate that can be infinitely transformed. This capability for the models to be updated continuously implies that these data entities could be 'current' indefinitely. Also, as a certain period of time elapses and new data is incorporated, these entities become valuable as mnemonic containers of information. They are effectively a living record of all of the past data inputs. A record of data captured through time (from various points of view) would form a very significant means to understanding junctures, milestones, thresholds and correlations over time.

inhabitants   the largest county is Los Angeles with 9,145,000

3.7% Asian   unemployment: Black 10% Hispanic 7.7% White 4.2%

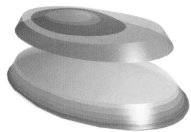

es annually equals 49% of marriages   in 1997 there were 1,630,000 divorces

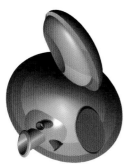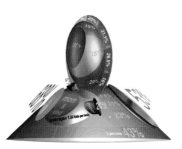

e   68% of children live with both parents   24% live with only the mother

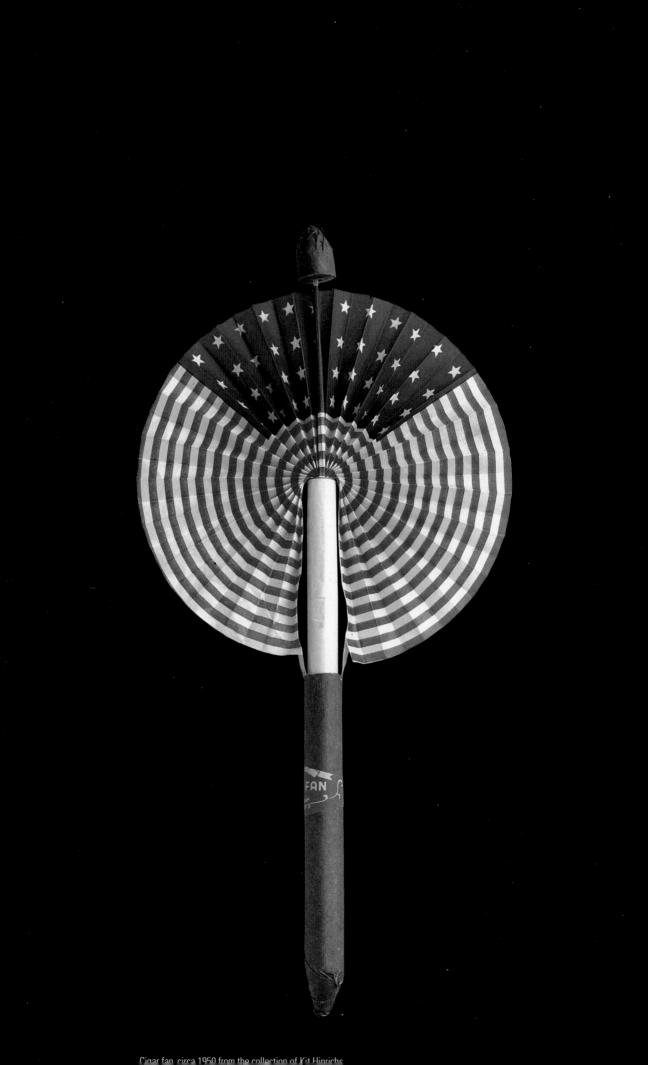

Cigar fan, circa 1950 from the collection of Kit Hinrichs

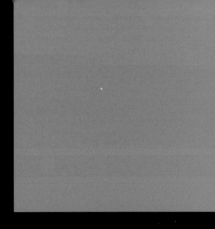

Ramana Rao

Consumption & Consequences
How are we using the Earth? What does it mean for our future well being?

Energy
What are our sources of energy? How has this changed since 1900?

Water
Where do we get fresh water? How do we use it?

Food
How did food production keep pace with population growth? How much of what kinds of proteins do we consume?

Materials
How has material production grown in the last few decades? How does the U.S. compare to the rest of the world?

Land Use / Degradation
How is the Earth's land used by humans? How much of the Earth's forest remains? How extensive is land degradation?

Pollution
What are the main types and sources of pollution? How extensive is air, water, and atmospheric pollution?

Biodiversity
How many species of what types of animals and plants are there? What are the causes of extinction and how does the current rate compare to the past?

Climatic Change
How has global temperature changed in recent times? What climate changes and consequences could be triggered?

Links & Resources
How are the topics connected? Where can I find more information?

Organizations
What governmental and research organizations provide information and data? What organizations focus on environmental issues?

To live, humans like all other species of life, consume resources from the environment and thereby alter it. Many times in the history of human civilizations, humans, ever-adaptable, ever-inventive, amassed in thriving populations. They ratcheted up their consumption to levels of marked impact on their ecosystem. As this impact crossed a threshold, consequences threatened the future of that civilization. This in turn propelled a need for action. In some cases, action was in time. In others, it was not. In the past, the impact on the planet and consequences to humans were first local and then regional. Now the region is the entire planet and the civilization is all of humanity. Our impact is global: no place on Earth is free of the marks of human civilization.

1

CONSUMPTION: We have animal needs: food, water, shelter, as well as humans needs—understanding, entertainment, challenge. As our numbers and affluence increase and as the power and variety of our technology magnifies, so does our consumption and impact on the planet.

ENERGY

WATER

FOOD

MATERIALS

HUMAN ACTION: Our problems are global, so we cannot adapt locally or regionally. We must balance the needs of the industrial and developing worlds. We can fail to adapt because we do not see what is happening or because we do not act accordingly. The earth will survive. The question is about us.

4

When we hear the debate we see what is wrong in each side and dismiss the topic!

Cornucopians seeing the upsides of consumption celebrate human ingenuity and the ability of economies to drive attention to the right problems. As price goes up, more of many resources can be found. And when not, other ways of meeting the same need or fulfilling the same want can be found. We are clever!

CONSUMPTION

Human impact on Earth is a function of population, affluence, and technology: more people, richer consumption, more varied assault, the greater the impact.

During the next decade, India and China will each add about ten times as many people as the U.S. will. The stress on the natural world by new Americans may exceed that by new Indians and Chinese combined.

WORLD POPULATION

1900
1960
1999

1.5B
3.0B
6.0B

Population growth is currently at about 80 million people per year. This is adding a New York each month, a Mexico each year, and an India each decade.

The hunter-gatherer consumed 2,500 calories each day, all of it food. The modern human consumes 31,000 calories, most of it as fossil fuel. An American consumes 6 times this amount.

Consumption & Consequences

How are we using the Earth? What does it mean for our future well being?

?

2

IMPACTS ON EARTH: We are changing the face of the earth. Our economy moves natural and artificial materials in massive flows of trade. We return by-products of our consumption to the earth's waters and air which circulate these elements globally. We are swamping the capacities of earth's ecosystems to absorb.

DEFORESTATION/DESERTIFICATION

POLLUTION

BIODIVERSITY

CLIMATIC CHANGE

CONSEQUENCES: As all places are degraded, as natural resources are exhausted, as material flows surpass ecosystem capacities, as even the climate changes, we face prospects of cataclysmic human conflicts, serious threats to our health, degradation of our lives, destructive natural disasters, and devastation of other forms of life.

3

How can we see what is right in each side and use our attention productively? ?

CONSEQUENCES

Catastrophists seeing the downsides of consequences warn of human hubris and the devastation that narrow economic models are inflicting on the earth and on human future. History is full of examples of human societies that destroyed themselves by patterns of overconsumption. The sky is falling!

Human domination of nature is evident in many indicators of how much of the world's resources are used:

>40% of world's "primary productivity," annual production of the plants consumed
>40% of all land has been transformed
>65% of ocean fisheries past their limits
>50% of accessible freshwater is used

Species are going extinct at a rate estimated by scientists to be hundreds or even thousands times the "background" rate.

Only one-fifth of the world's original forests cover remains in large tracts of relatively undisturbed forest.

2 billion hectares of land have been degraded by humans, 15% of all land.

CO_2 levels in the atmosphere are the highest they have been in 160,000 years.

The 14 warmest years since 1866 have occurred since 1980.

1998 storm-related weather damage was almost 50% above the record of 1996, and more than the total for all of the 1980s.

Without energy nothing would move. Modern civilization has been powered by the harnessing of fossil fuels. First the harnessing of coal in the 18th and 19th centuries, and then oil in the 20th century. Annual flows of oil have grown by a factor of almost 175 since the century's beginning, and after adjusting for inflation, are sold for about 10 percent less.

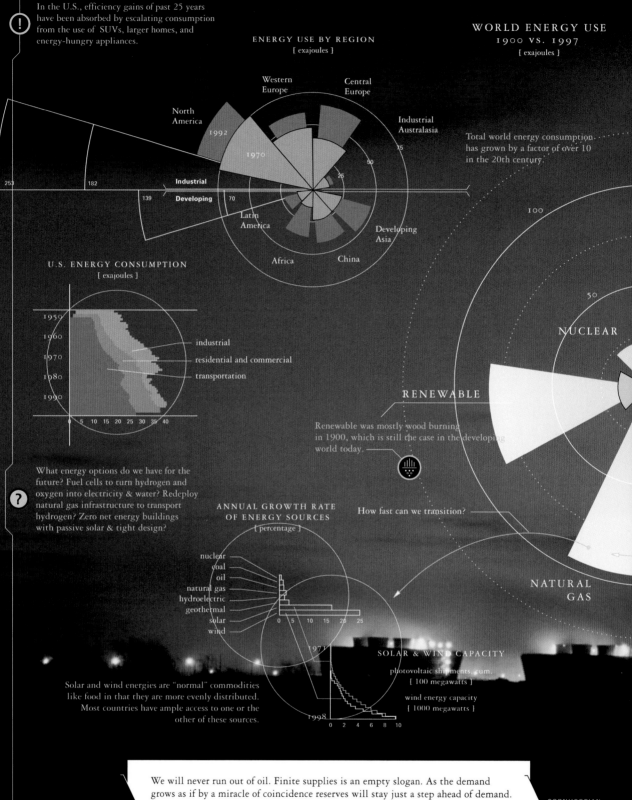

(!) In the U.S., efficiency gains of past 25 years have been absorbed by escalating consumption from the use of SUVs, larger homes, and energy-hungry appliances.

ENERGY USE BY REGION
[exajoules]

WORLD ENERGY USE
1900 VS. 1997
[exajoules]

Western Europe

Central Europe

North America

1992

Industrial Australasia

75

1970

80

25

Total world energy consumption has grown by a factor of over 10 in the 20th century.

253   182

Industrial

139   Developing   70

Latin America

Developing Asia

Africa   China

100

U.S. ENERGY CONSUMPTION
[exajoules]

1950
1960
1970
1980
1990

industrial

residential and commercial

transportation

0   5   10   15   20   25   30   35   40

50

NUCLEAR

RENEWABLE

Renewable was mostly wood burning in 1900, which is still the case in the developing world today.

What energy options do we have for the future? Fuel cells to turn hydrogen and oxygen into electricity & water? Redeploy natural gas infrastructure to transport hydrogen? Zero net energy buildings with passive solar & tight design?

(?)

ANNUAL GROWTH RATE
OF ENERGY SOURCES
[percentage]

How fast can we transition?

nuclear
coal
oil
natural gas
hydroelectric
geothermal
solar
wind

0   5   10   15   20   25

NATURAL GAS

1971

SOLAR & WIND CAPACITY

photovoltaic shipments, cum.
[100 megawatts]

Solar and wind energies are "normal" commodities like food in that they are more evenly distributed. Most countries have ample access to one or the other of these sources.

wind energy capacity
[1000 megawatts]

1998

0   2   4   6   8   10

We will never run out of oil. Finite supplies is an empty slogan. As the demand grows as if by a miracle of coincidence reserves will stay just a step ahead of demand. Just consider how the global reserve, in number of years of current production, has continued to grow to now well over 40 years.

CORNUCOPIAN

Energy is the capacity to perform work. Scientist measure it in joules, which is the amount of energy used by a tiny burning candle or a hummingbird's flight in a second. An exajoule is a billion billion joules.

Power is the ability to produce energy over time so it is measured in joules/second called watts. Human power is 50–90 watts, the typical range of incandescent bulbs.

A kilowatt-hour, equivalent to 3,600,000 joules, is another common unit of energy.

Percentage of energy consumed
by richest fifth of world: 58
by poorest fifth of world: 4
by the U.S.: 25

Ratio of United States to Europe's per capita energy consumption: 2

People lacking modern fuels or electricity:
2 Billion

Additional people lacking modern amenities such as refrigeration, hot water:
2 Billion

The entire global Internet requires less electricity than New York City uses.

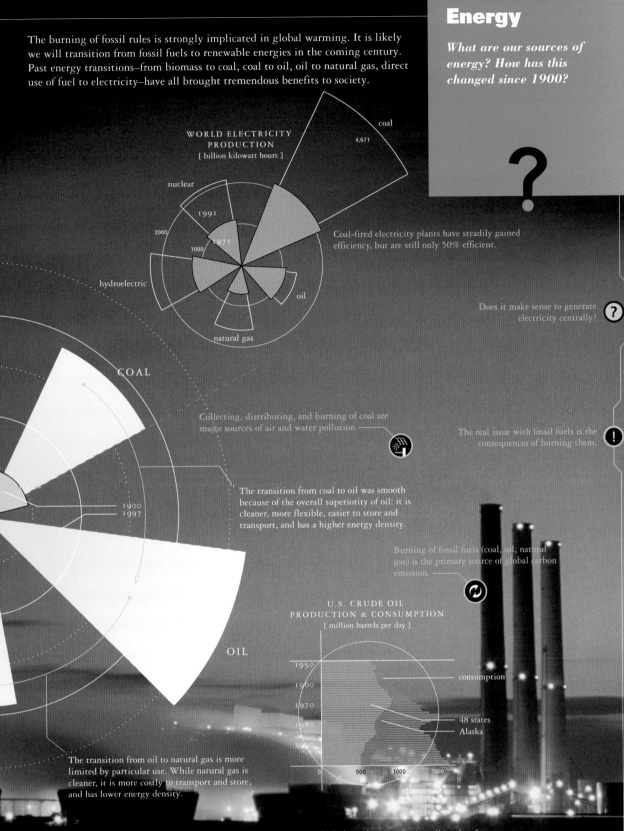

Energy

What are our sources of energy? How has this changed since 1900?

?

The burning of fossil rules is strongly implicated in global warming. It is likely we will transition from fossil fuels to renewable energies in the coming century. Past energy transitions–from biomass to coal, coal to oil, oil to natural gas, direct use of fuel to electricity–have all brought tremendous benefits to society.

WORLD ELECTRICITY PRODUCTION
[billion kilowatt hours]

coal
4,671

nuclear

1991

2000

1971

1000

hydroelectric

oil

natural gas

Coal-fired electricity plants have steadily gained efficiency, but are still only 50% efficient.

Does it make sense to generate electricity centrally? **?**

COAL

Collecting, distributing, and burning of coal are major sources of air and water pollution.

The real issue with fossil fuels is the consequences of burning them. **!**

The transition from coal to oil was smooth because of the overall superiority of oil: it is cleaner, more flexible, easier to store and transport, and has a higher energy density.

1900
1997

Burning of fossil fuels (coal, oil, natural gas) is the primary source of global carbon emission.

OIL

U.S. CRUDE OIL PRODUCTION & CONSUMPTION
[million barrels per day]

1950
1960
1970
1980
1990

consumption

48 states
Alaska

0   500   1000   1500

The transition from oil to natural gas is more limited by particular use. While natural gas is cleaner, it is more costly to transport and store, and has lower energy density.

U.S. dependence on foreign oil is a key factor in U.S. foreign policy and international affairs in general.

CATASTROPHIST

Based on a standard forecasting tool, oil production will peak in 2010-2020. But more important than bounded supplies is the consequences of burning fossil fuels. They are the major source of atmospheric carbon. The full costs of burning fossil fuels should be taken into account. We must convert immediately.

Fossil Energy Online. Dept. of Energy. U.S.
www.fe.doe.gov
Federal reports and programs dealing with coal, oil, and natural gas.

In 1997, BP Chairman John Browne announced that his company takes global warming seriously and would step up investments in solar energy.

"We've embarked on the beginning of the last days of the age of oil."
— Mike Bowlin, Chairman/CEO, ARCO

SOURCES: VACLAV SMIL'S ENERGIES, VACLAV SMIL'S COMMUNICATIONS, WORLDWATCH INSTITUTE'S STATE OF THE WORLD 1999 & VITAL SIGNS 1999

DATA: WORLDWATCH INSTITUTE'S DATA DISKS, US DEPT. OF ENERGY'S ENERGY INFORMATION ADMINISTRATION

Unlike other resources, fresh water has no substitute for most of its uses. Though we live on a planet where there is "water, water, everywhere," a very small portion is available as fresh water at the right time and the right place. A global water cycle of evaporation from the oceans and precipitation to the land provides us with our renewable supplies. The capacity of this vast solar-powered water pump is fully consumed in many places. Increasing population and consumption is pushing more and more countries into occasional or constant states of water crisis.

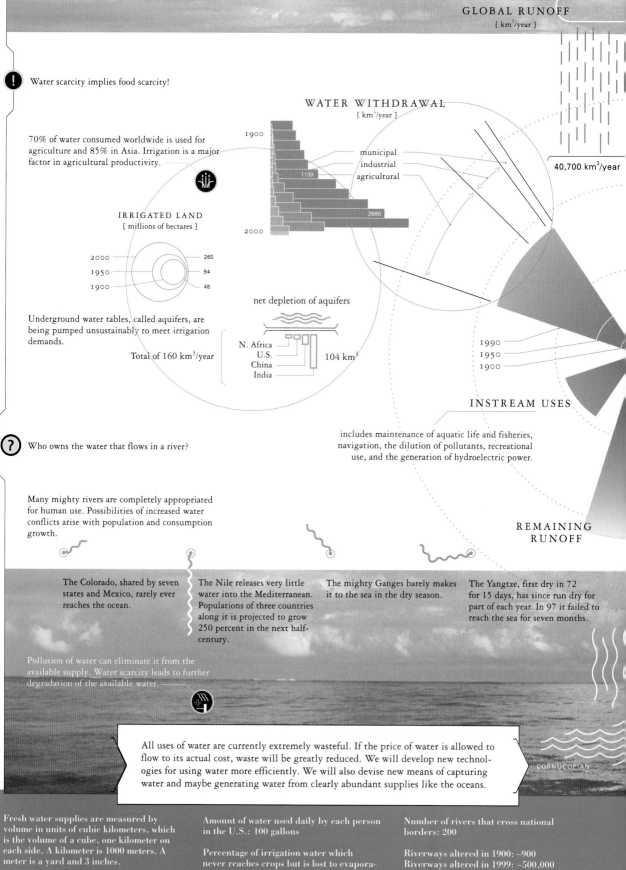

GLOBAL RUNOFF
[km³/year]

! Water scarcity implies food scarcity!

WATER WITHDRAWAL
[km³/year]

70% of water consumed worldwide is used for agriculture and 85% in Asia. Irrigation is a major factor in agricultural productivity.

1900

municipal
industrial
agricultural

1130

40,700 km³/year

2680

2000

IRRIGATED LAND
[millions of hectares]

2000		260
1950		94
1900		48

net depletion of aquifers

Underground water tables, called aquifers, are being pumped unsustainably to meet irrigation demands.

Total of 160 km³/year

N. Africa
U.S.
China
India

104 km³

1990
1950
1900

INSTREAM USES

? Who owns the water that flows in a river?

includes maintenance of aquatic life and fisheries, navigation, the dilution of pollutants, recreational use, and the generation of hydroelectric power.

Many mighty rivers are completely appropriated for human use. Possibilities of increased water conflicts arise with population and consumption growth.

REMAINING RUNOFF

The Colorado, shared by seven states and Mexico, rarely ever reaches the ocean.

The Nile releases very little water into the Mediterranean. Populations of three countries along it is projected to grow 250 percent in the next half-century.

The mighty Ganges barely makes it to the sea in the dry season.

The Yangtze, first dry in 72 for 15 days, has since run dry for part of each year. In 97 it failed to reach the sea for seven months.

Pollution of water can eliminate it from the available supply. Water scarcity leads to further degradation of the available water.

All uses of water are currently extremely wasteful. If the price of water is allowed to flow to its actual cost, waste will be greatly reduced. We will develop new technologies for using water more efficiently. We will also devise new means of capturing water and maybe generating water from clearly abundant supplies like the oceans.

CORNUCOPIAN

Fresh water supplies are measured by volume in units of cubic kilometers, which is the volume of a cube, one kilometer on each side. A kilometer is 1000 meters. A meter is a yard and 3 inches.

A cubic kilometer would cover all of Manhattan to a height of 18 meters, roughly the height of a spacious 4 story building.

Amount of water used daily by each person in the U.S.: 100 gallons

Percentage of irrigation water which never reaches crops but is lost to evaporation or runoff: 60–75

Percentage of irrigated area in which salination reduces crop yields: 10

Number of rivers that cross national borders: 200

Riverways altered in 1900: ~900
Riverways altered in 1999: ~500,000

Annual "recharge" rate of Ogallala aquifer, extending from Texas to South Dakota and from Colorado to Kansas, as percent of annual withdrawal: 25–40 percent

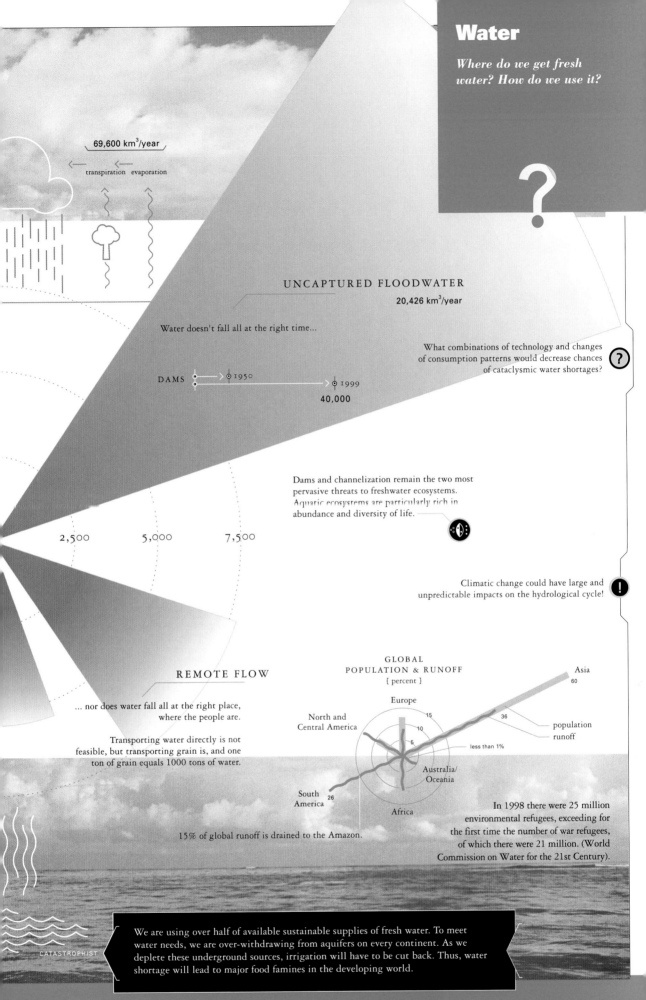

Water

Where do we get fresh water? How do we use it?

?

69,600 km³/year

transpiration evaporation

UNCAPTURED FLOODWATER

20,426 km³/year

Water doesn't fall all at the right time...

What combinations of technology and changes of consumption patterns would decrease chances of cataclysmic water shortages? **(?)**

DAMS |———> 1950 ———————> 1999

40,000

2,500   5,000   7,500

Dams and channelization remain the two most pervasive threats to freshwater ecosystems. Aquatic ecosystems are particularly rich in abundance and diversity of life.

Climatic change could have large and unpredictable impacts on the hydrological cycle! **!**

REMOTE FLOW

... nor does water fall all at the right place, where the people are.

Transporting water directly is not feasible, but transporting grain is, and one ton of grain equals 1000 tons of water.

GLOBAL POPULATION & RUNOFF
[percent]

Asia
60

Europe

North and Central America

15

10

5

36

less than 1%

population
runoff

Australia/
Oceania

South America
26

Africa

15% of global runoff is drained to the Amazon.

In 1998 there were 25 million environmental refugees, exceeding for the first time the number of war refugees, of which there were 21 million. (World Commission on Water for the 21st Century).

CATASTROPHIST

We are using over half of available sustainable supplies of fresh water. To meet water needs, we are over-withdrawing from aquifers on every continent. As we deplete these underground sources, irrigation will have to be cut back. Thus, water shortage will lead to major food famines in the developing world.

○ Environment. Bureau of Oceans and International Environmental and Scientific Affairs. Dept. of State. U.S. www.state.gov/www/global/oes/envir.html OES is the Department of State's focal point for foreign policy formulation and implementation in global environment, science, and technology issues.

Number of people who lack safe drinking water worldwide: 1 Billion

Number of people living in countries facing absolute water scarcity by 2025: 1 Billion

The World Bank estimates that the costs for tapping new supplies of water will be 2–3 times that of existing supplies.

SOURCES: S. POSTEL ET AL. IN *SCIENCE*, VOL. 271, STATE OF THE WORLD AND VITAL SIGNS 1999, INTERNATIONAL RIVERS NETWORK, INTERNATIONAL WATER MGMT. INSTITUTE, WORLD RESOURCES INSTITUTE

DATA: WORLDWATCH INSTITUTE 99 DATA DISKS, WORLDWATCH MAGAZINE, 12(6)

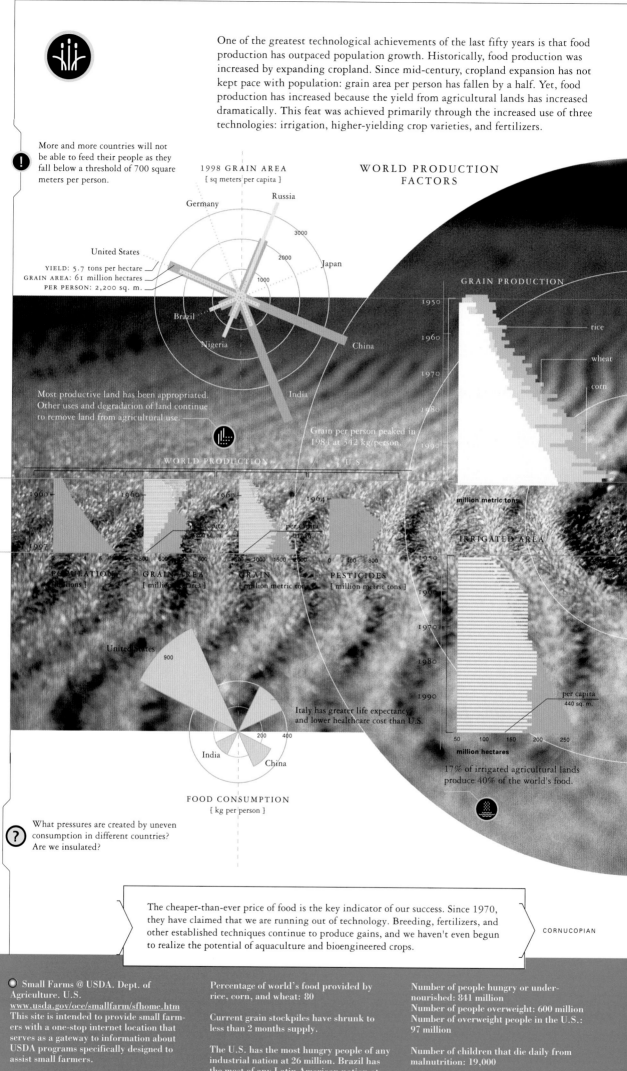

One of the greatest technological achievements of the last fifty years is that food production has outpaced population growth. Historically, food production was increased by expanding cropland. Since mid-century, cropland expansion has not kept pace with population: grain area per person has fallen by a half. Yet, food production has increased because the yield from agricultural lands has increased dramatically. This feat was achieved primarily through the increased use of three technologies: irrigation, higher-yielding crop varieties, and fertilizers.

More and more countries will not be able to feed their people as they fall below a threshold of 700 square meters per person.

1998 GRAIN AREA
[sq meters per capita]

WORLD PRODUCTION FACTORS

Germany

Russia

United States
YIELD: 5.7 tons per hectare
GRAIN AREA: 61 million hectares
PER PERSON: 2,200 sq. m.

Japan

3000

2000

1000

Brazil

Nigeria

China

India

GRAIN PRODUCTION

1950

1960

1970

1980

1990

rice

wheat

corn

Most productive land has been appropriated. Other uses and degradation of land continue to remove land from agricultural use.

Grain per person peaked in 1984 at 342 kg/person.

WORLD PRODUCTION

U.S.

1960

1960

1960

1964

1997

million metric tons

IRRIGATED AREA

1950

1960

POPULATION
[millions]

GRAIN AREA
[million hectares]

GRAIN
[million metric tons]

PESTICIDES
[million metric tons]

per capita
2200 sq. m.

per capita
3170 g

2   3   4   5   500 600 700 800   500 1000 1500 2000   0   400   800

1970

1980

1990

United States

900

Italy has greater life expectancy and lower healthcare cost than U.S.

per capita
440 sq. m.

50   100   150   200   250

million hectares

India

China

200   400

17% of irrigated agricultural lands produce 40% of the world's food.

FOOD CONSUMPTION
[kg per person]

What pressures are created by uneven consumption in different countries? Are we insulated?

The cheaper-than-ever price of food is the key indicator of our success. Since 1970, they have claimed that we are running out of technology. Breeding, fertilizers, and other established techniques continue to produce gains, and we haven't even begun to realize the potential of aquaculture and bioengineered crops.

CORNUCOPIAN

Small Farms @ USDA. Dept. of Agriculture. U.S.
www.usda.gov/oce/smallfarm/sfhome.htm
This site is intended to provide small farmers with a one-stop internet location that serves as a gateway to information about USDA programs specifically designed to assist small farmers.

Percentage of world's food provided by rice, corn, and wheat: 80

Current grain stockpiles have shrunk to less than 2 months supply.

The U.S. has the most hungry people of any industrial nation at 26 million. Brazil has the most of any Latin American nation at 10 million.

Number of people hungry or under-nourished: 841 million
Number of people overweight: 600 million
Number of overweight people in the U.S.: 97 million

Number of children that die daily from malnutrition: 19,000

Percentage of children under five in South Asia stunted by malnutrition: >60

Food

How did food production keep pace with population growth? How much of what kinds of proteins do we consume?

?

The gains from these past advances are diminishing rapidly. The increasing yield, which grew 2.1 percent per year from 1950 to 1990, has dropped to 1.1 percent per year in the 1990s. 1984 was the peak year for grain production per person. Meanwhile, increased affluence is driving increasing production of various protein sources, many of which are bumping up against their own limits.

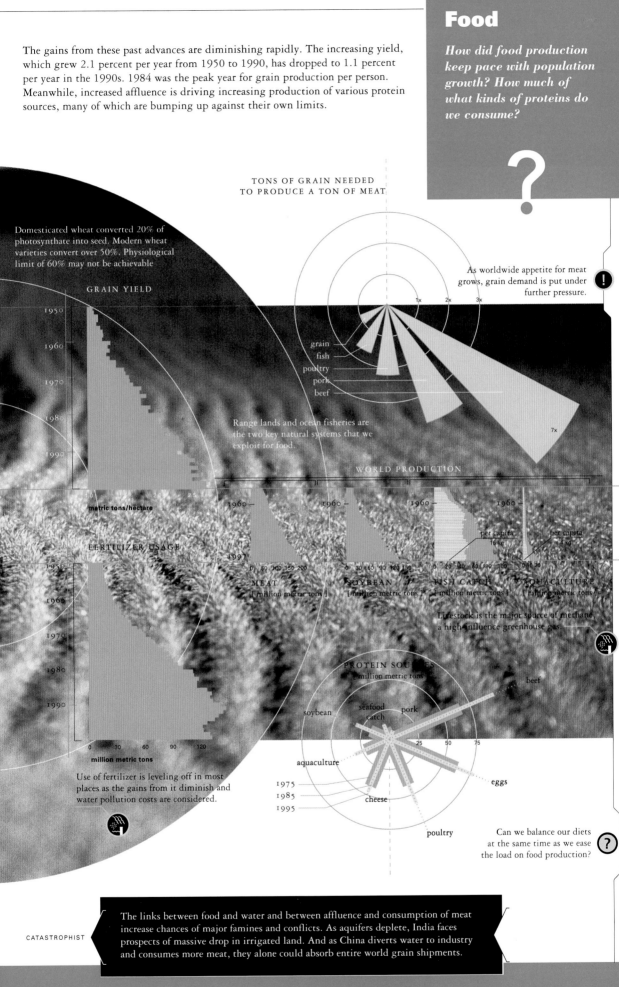

TONS OF GRAIN NEEDED
TO PRODUCE A TON OF MEAT

Domesticated wheat converted 20% of photosynthate into seed. Modern wheat varieties convert over 50%. Physiological limit of 60% may not be achievable

GRAIN YIELD

As worldwide appetite for meat grows, grain demand is put under further pressure.

grain
fish
poultry
pork
beef

Range lands and ocean fisheries are the two key natural systems that we exploit for food.

WORLD PRODUCTION

metric tons/hectare

FERTILIZER USAGE

MEAT
[million metric tons]

SOYBEAN
[million metric tons]

FISH CATCH
[million metric tons]

AQUACULTURE
[million metric tons]

per capita
16 kg

per capita
1 kg

Livestock is the major source of methane, a high-influence greenhouse gas.

million metric tons

Use of fertilizer is leveling off in most places as the gains from it diminish and water pollution costs are considered.

PROTEIN SOURCES
million metric tons

beef

soybean

seafood catch

pork

aquaculture

eggs

1975
1985
1995

cheese

poultry

Can we balance our diets at the same time as we ease the load on food production?

CATASTROPHIST

The links between food and water and between affluence and consumption of meat increase chances of major famines and conflicts. As aquifers deplete, India faces prospects of massive drop in irrigated land. And as China diverts water to industry and consumes more meat, they alone could absorb entire world grain shipments.

Number of insect species genetically resistant to pesticides: 550
Species of diseases: 230
Species of weeds: 220

Bioengineered "transgenic" crops are being used to combat pests. The area planted in transgenic crops grew 15 times between 96 and 98 to 28 million hectares, about an eighth of the area planted in wheat.

Increase in meat consumption in last population doubling: 4 times

Percentage of all grain fed to livestock: 40

Number of 15 major oceanic fisheries in decline because of overfishing: 11

Number of disputes between countries over ocean fisheries in 1997: >100

SOURCES: STATE OF THE WORLD 1999, VITAL SIGNS 1999, L. BROWN ET AL. BEYOND MALTHUS, WORLD RESOURCES INSTITUTE'S WORLD RESOURCE 1998-99

DATA: WORLDWATCH INSTITUTE'S DATA DISK., U.S. EPA, U.S. DEPT. OF AGRICULTURE, U.N. FOOD & AGRICULTURE ORGANIZATION

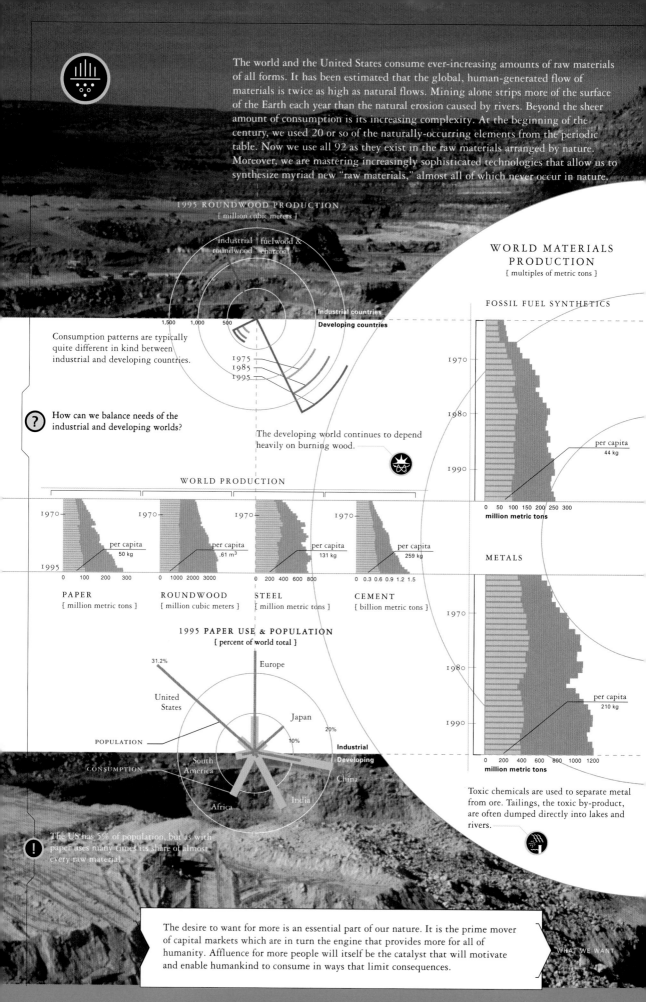

The world and the United States consume ever-increasing amounts of raw materials of all forms. It has been estimated that the global, human-generated flow of materials is twice as high as natural flows. Mining alone strips more of the surface of the Earth each year than the natural erosion caused by rivers. Beyond the sheer amount of consumption is its increasing complexity. At the beginning of the century, we used 20 or so of the naturally-occurring elements from the periodic table. Now we use all 92 as they exist in the raw materials arranged by nature. Moreover, we are mastering increasingly sophisticated technologies that allow us to synthesize myriad new "raw materials," almost all of which never occur in nature.

1995 ROUNDWOOD PRODUCTION
[million cubic meters]

industrial roundwood | fuelwood & charcoal

Industrial countries
Developing countries

1,500   1,000   500

1975
1985
1995

Consumption patterns are typically quite different in kind between industrial and developing countries.

(?) How can we balance needs of the industrial and developing worlds?

The developing world continues to depend heavily on burning wood.

WORLD MATERIALS PRODUCTION
[multiples of metric tons]

FOSSIL FUEL SYNTHETICS

1970

1980

per capita
44 kg

1990

0   50 100 150 200 250 300
million metric tons

METALS

1970

1980

per capita
210 kg

1990

0   200 400 600 800 1000 1200
million metric tons

Toxic chemicals are used to separate metal from ore. Tailings, the toxic by-product, are often dumped directly into lakes and rivers.

WORLD PRODUCTION

1970

1995

0   100   200   300

per capita
50 kg

PAPER
[million metric tons]

1970

0 1000 2000 3000

per capita
.61 m³

ROUNDWOOD
[million cubic meters]

1970

0 200 400 600 800

per capita
131 kg

STEEL
[million metric tons]

1970

0 0.3 0.6 0.9 1.2 1.5

per capita
259 kg

CEMENT
[billion metric tons]

1995 PAPER USE & POPULATION
[percent of world total]

31.2%

Europe

United States

Japan

20%

10%

Industrial
Developing

China

POPULATION

CONSUMPTION

South America

Africa

India

The US has 5% of population, but as with paper uses many times its share of almost every raw material.

The desire to want for more is an essential part of our nature. It is the prime mover of capital markets which are in turn the engine that provides more for all of humanity. Affluence for more people will itself be the catalyst that will motivate and enable humankind to consume in ways that limit consequences.

WHAT WE WANT

Materials are typically measured by weight in units of metric tons. A metric ton is 1000 kilograms which is about 2200 lbs, or about 10% more than a U.S. ton.

Materials are also often measured by volume, as in the case of roundwood, using the unit of cubic meters, which is about 1/3 more than a cubic yard. A cord of wood is 3.6 cubic meters.

Percentage of Americans who believe that "most of us buy and consume far more than we need": 82

Per-capita U.S. usage of materials excluding food and energy: >100 kg

Increase in materials usage if entire world lived at same intensiveness as Americans: 7 times

Number of chemical compounds developed since 1930: 100,000

Number of automobiles worldwide: 500 million

Percentage of cars consumed by industrial nations: 87
Percentage of people: 20

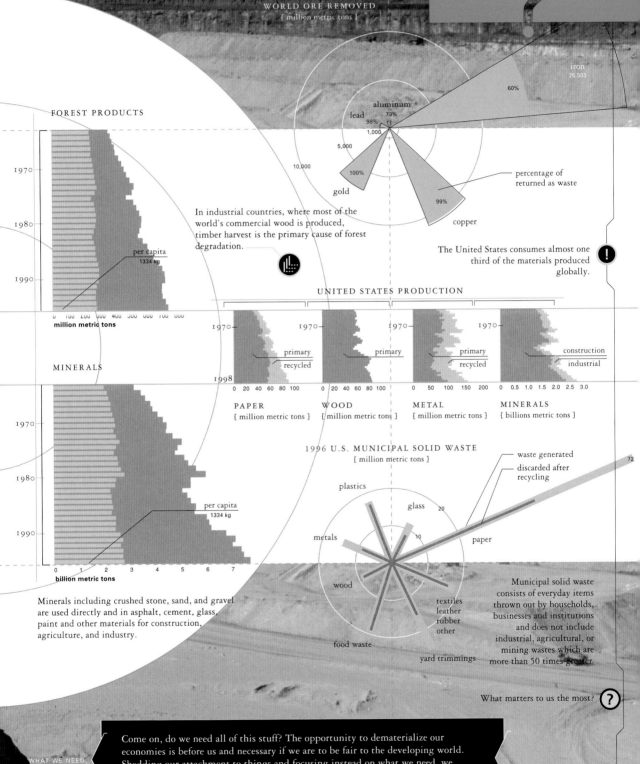

Materials

How has material production grown in the last few decades? How does the U.S. compare to the rest of the world?

?

WORLD ORE REMOVED
[million metric tons]

iron 25,503

60%

aluminum 70%
lead 98%
1,000
5,000
10,000
gold 100%
copper 99%

percentage of returned as waste

FOREST PRODUCTS

1970
1980
1990

per capita 1334 kg

0 100 200 300 400 500 600 700 800
million metric tons

In industrial countries, where most of the world's commercial wood is produced, timber harvest is the primary cause of forest degradation.

The United States consumes almost one third of the materials produced globally.

!

MINERALS

1970
1980
1990

per capita 1334 kg

0 1 2 3 4 5 6 7
billion metric tons

Minerals including crushed stone, sand, and gravel are used directly and in asphalt, cement, glass, paint and other materials for construction, agriculture, and industry.

UNITED STATES PRODUCTION

1970
primary
recycled
1998

1970
primary

1970
primary
recycled

1970
construction
industrial

0 20 40 60 80 100
PAPER
[million metric tons]

0 20 40 60 80 100
WOOD
[million metric tons]

0 50 100 150 200
METAL
[million metric tons]

0 0.5 1.0 1.5 2.0 2.5 3.0
MINERALS
[billions metric tons]

1996 U.S. MUNICIPAL SOLID WASTE
[million metric tons]

waste generated
discarded after recycling

plastics
glass 20
metals 10
wood
food waste
yard trimmings
textiles leather rubber other
paper
72

Municipal solid waste consists of everyday items thrown out by households, businesses and institutions and does not include industrial, agricultural, or mining wastes which are more than 50 times greater.

What matters to us the most? (?)

WHAT WE NEED

Come on, do we need all of this stuff? The opportunity to dematerialize our economies is before us and necessary if we are to be fair to the developing world. Shedding our attachment to things and focusing instead on what we need, we might be remembered in a 100 years as the most durable civilization in history.

Mining requires removing both ore and "overburden", the earth that covers the ore. Amount of overburden and ore removed to produce one ton of copper: 220 tons

Waste generated in production of 2 gold wedding rings: 6 tons

Length of rivers and streams in the U.S. polluted by mining: 19,000 kilometers

The U.S. EPA lists 40,000 "Superfund" hazardous waste sites. Cleaning up just 1400 priority sites will cost $31B. It will cost $32–72 billion to clean up toxic damages at thousands of abandoned mines:

Municipal solid waste generated by each American annually: 1600 lbs
Amount of paper: 600 lbs

SOURCES: STATE OF THE WORLD 1999, CONSUMPTION OF MATERIALS IN THE UNITED STATES 1900–1995, GRECIA MATOS, USGS

DATA: WORLDWATCH INSTITUTE'S DATA DISK, U.S. ENVIRONMENTAL PROTECTION AGENCY, CARBON DIOXIDE INFORMATION ANALYSIS CENTER

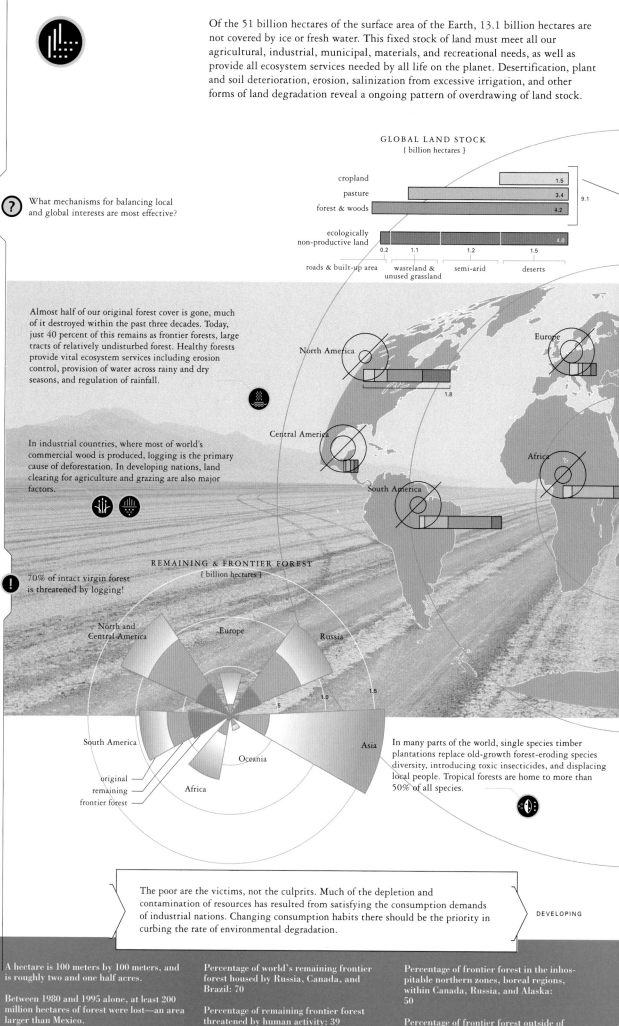

Of the 51 billion hectares of the surface area of the Earth, 13.1 billion hectares are not covered by ice or fresh water. This fixed stock of land must meet all our agricultural, industrial, municipal, materials, and recreational needs, as well as provide all ecosystem services needed by all life on the planet. Desertification, plant and soil deterioration, erosion, salinization from excessive irrigation, and other forms of land degradation reveal a ongoing pattern of overdrawing of land stock.

What mechanisms for balancing local and global interests are most effective?

GLOBAL LAND STOCK
{ billion hectares }

cropland	1.5
pasture	3.4
forest & woods	4.2

9.1

ecologically non-productive land				4.0
0.2	1.1	1.2	1.5	
roads & built-up area	wasteland & unused grassland	semi-arid	deserts	

Almost half of our original forest cover is gone, much of it destroyed within the past three decades. Today, just 40 percent of this remains as frontier forests, large tracts of relatively undisturbed forest. Healthy forests provide vital ecosystem services including erosion control, provision of water across rainy and dry seasons, and regulation of rainfall.

Europe

North America

In industrial countries, where most of world's commercial wood is produced, logging is the primary cause of deforestation. In developing nations, land clearing for agriculture and grazing are also major factors.

Central America

Africa

South America   1.8

REMAINING & FRONTIER FOREST
{ billion hectares }

70% of intact virgin forest is threatened by logging!

North and Central America

Europe

Russia

1.5
1.0
.5

South America

Oceania

Asia

Africa

original
remaining
frontier forest

In many parts of the world, single species timber plantations replace old-growth forest-eroding species diversity, introducing toxic insecticides, and displacing local people. Tropical forests are home to more than 50% of all species.

The poor are the victims, not the culprits. Much of the depletion and contamination of resources has resulted from satisfying the consumption demands of industrial nations. Changing consumption habits there should be the priority in curbing the rate of environmental degradation.

DEVELOPING

A hectare is 100 meters by 100 meters, and is roughly two and one half acres.

Between 1980 and 1995 alone, at least 200 million hectares of forest were lost—an area larger than Mexico.

In 1998, heavy rains brought record-setting floods to many deforested regions in India, Bangladesh, Mexico, and China.

Percentage of world's remaining frontier forest housed by Russia, Canada, and Brazil: 70

Percentage of remaining frontier forest threatened by human activity: 39

Percentage of frontier forest falling entirely within the temperate zone (e.g. most of the U.S. and Europe): 3

Percentage of frontier forest in the inhospitable northern zones, boreal regions, within Canada, Russia, and Alaska: 50

Percentage of frontier forest outside of boreal regions that is threatened: 75

Top 150 non-wood forest products, such as rattan, cork, nuts, oils, and medicinals, are worth more than $11B a year.

How is the Earth's land used by humans? How much of the Earth's forest remains? How extensive is land degradation?

?

A key notion is the carrying capacity: how many people can be supported by a given amount of land indefinitely. A related notion of ecological footprint inverts this notion asking how much land is needed to supply the materials and absorb the wastes of a given population. Either way, with the population at 6 billion people, consuming by current patterns and technologies, it appears we have surpassed the capacity of available land.

What tools can we use to weigh the impacts of consumption options? ?

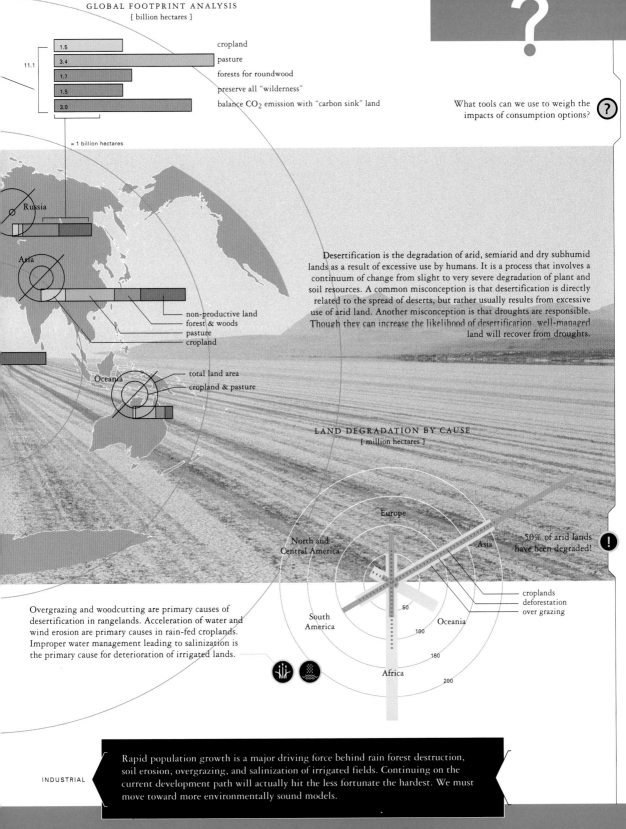

GLOBAL FOOTPRINT ANALYSIS
[billion hectares]

11.1

1.5	cropland
3.4	pasture
1.7	forests for roundwood
1.5	preserve all "wilderness"
3.0	balance CO_2 emission with "carbon sink" land

= 1 billion hectares

Russia

Asia

non-productive land
forest & woods
pasture
cropland

Oceania

total land area
cropland & pasture

Desertification is the degradation of arid, semiarid and dry subhumid lands as a result of excessive use by humans. It is a process that involves a continuum of change from slight to very severe degradation of plant and soil resources. A common misconception is that desertification is directly related to the spread of deserts, but rather usually results from excessive use of arid land. Another misconception is that droughts are responsible. Though they can increase the likelihood of desertification, well-managed land will recover from droughts.

LAND DEGRADATION BY CAUSE
[million hectares]

Europe

North and Central America

Asia

50% of arid lands have been degraded! !

croplands
deforestation
over grazing

South America

Oceania

50

100

150

Africa

200

Overgrazing and woodcutting are primary causes of desertification in rangelands. Acceleration of water and wind erosion are primary causes in rain-fed croplands. Improper water management leading to salinization is the primary cause for deterioration of irrigated lands.

Rapid population growth is a major driving force behind rain forest destruction, soil erosion, overgrazing, and salinization of irrigated fields. Continuing on the current development path will actually hit the less fortunate the hardest. We must move toward more environmentally sound models.

INDUSTRIAL

Percentage of all land that is dryland: 41
Percentage degraded: 25

Percentage of land that is dryland in Africa: 66
Percentage degraded: 73

Percentage of land that is dryland in North America: 33
Percentage degraded: 74

Rate that arable land in the drylands is being degraded: 10 million hectares/year

An "ecological footprint" analysis of North America, which accounts for materials and energy usage and waste generation, shows that the world would need to be 3 times as big to support the current population at same level of consumption as North Americans.

SOURCES: OUR ECOLOGICAL FOOTPRINT, WACKERNAGEL & REES, WORLD RESOURCES INSTITUTE'S FRONTIER FOREST INITIATIVE, STATE OF THE WORLD 1999

DATA: WORLDWATCH INSTITUTE'S DATA DISK, U.N. FOOD & AGRICULTURE ORGANIZATION (FAO)

All biological and economic activities by their very nature absorb resources from and return wastes to the environment. When wastes alter the ongoing functioning of natural processes and produce undesirable environmental or health effects, they are characterized as pollution. Anything can be a pollutant if too much of it is introduced into a given setting. Not just modern human materials, so-called non-biodegradables like plastics, synthetic organic chemicals, and radioactive compounds, but also natural compounds essential to life like fixed nitrogen, plant nutrients, carbon dioxide, and even soil. At current population levels and with rapidly expanding demand for food, water, materials, and energy, human activity is producing a broad range and variety of pollution. Locally to globally, pollution is pervasively impacting ecosystems, human health and quality of life, and the workings of the planet.

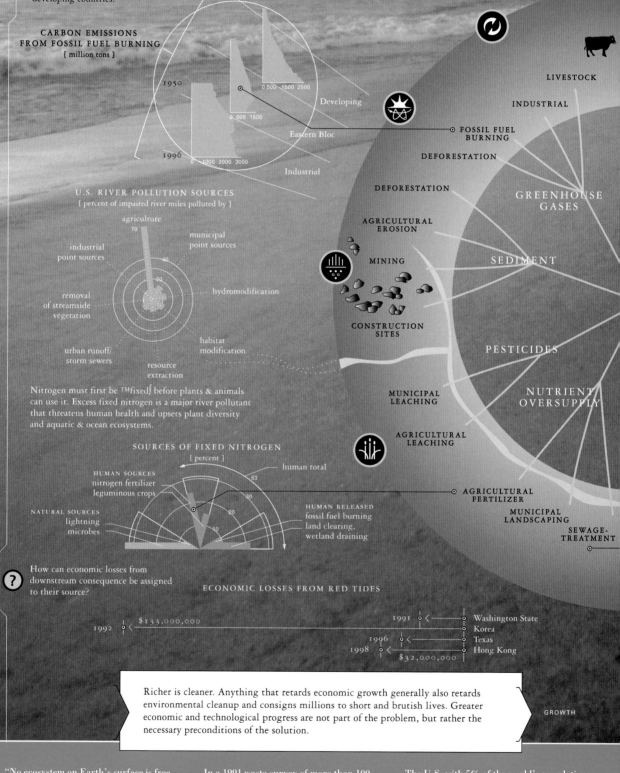

! Per-capita carbon emission in industrial countries! Absolute carbon emission in developing countries!

CARBON EMISSIONS
FROM FOSSIL FUEL BURNING
[million tons]

1950
0 500 1500 2500
Developing
0 600 1500
Eastern Bloc
1996
0 1000 2000 3000
Industrial

FOSSIL FUEL
BURNING

LIVESTOCK
INDUSTRIAL
DEFORESTATION
GREENHOUSE
GASES
DEFORESTATION
AGRICULTURAL
EROSION
MINING
SEDIMENT
CONSTRUCTION
SITES
PESTICIDES
MUNICIPAL
LEACHING
NUTRIENT
OVERSUPPLY
AGRICULTURAL
LEACHING
AGRICULTURAL
FERTILIZER
MUNICIPAL
LANDSCAPING
SEWAGE-
TREATMENT

U.S. RIVER POLLUTION SOURCES
[percent of impaired river miles polluted by]
agriculture
70
municipal
point sources
industrial
point sources
40
20
hydromodification
removal
of streamside
vegetation
habitat
modification
urban runoff/
storm sewers
resource
extraction

Nitrogen must first be ™fixed‖ before plants & animals can use it. Excess fixed nitrogen is a major river pollutant that threatens human health and upsets plant diversity and aquatic & ocean ecosystems.

SOURCES OF FIXED NITROGEN
[percent]
human total
HUMAN SOURCES
nitrogen fertilizer
leguminous crops
63
30
NATURAL SOURCES
lightning
microbes
20
10
HUMAN RELEASED
fossil fuel burning
land clearing,
wetland draining

? How can economic losses from downstream consequence be assigned to their source?

ECONOMIC LOSSES FROM RED TIDES

1992 $133,000,000
1991 Washington State
Korea
1996 Texas
1998 Hong Kong
$32,000,000

Richer is cleaner. Anything that retards economic growth generally also retards environmental cleanup and consigns millions to short and brutish lives. Greater economic and technological progress are not part of the problem, but rather the necessary preconditions of the solution.

GROWTH

"No ecosystem on Earth's surface is free of pervasive human influence."
— Vitousek et al. in Science

"It's not that we're running out of stuff. What we're running out of is what the scientists call 'sinks', places to put the by-products of our large appetites."
— Bill McKibben in Atlantic Monthly

In a 1991 waste survey of more than 100 nations, 90% that responded agreed that uncontrolled dumping of industrial wastes is a problem, 66% that hazardous industrial waste is disposed of at uncontrolled sites, and nearly 25% that they dumped industrial waste directly into oceans.

More than 20,000 rivers, lakes and estuaries across the U.S. are polluted.

The U.S. with 5% of the world's population is responsible for 20% of carbon emission.

85–90 percent of pesticides used in agriculturally and municipally never reach their targets.

The "Dead Zone" in the Gulf of Mexico caused by nutrient runoff is eleven times the size of Lake Ontario.

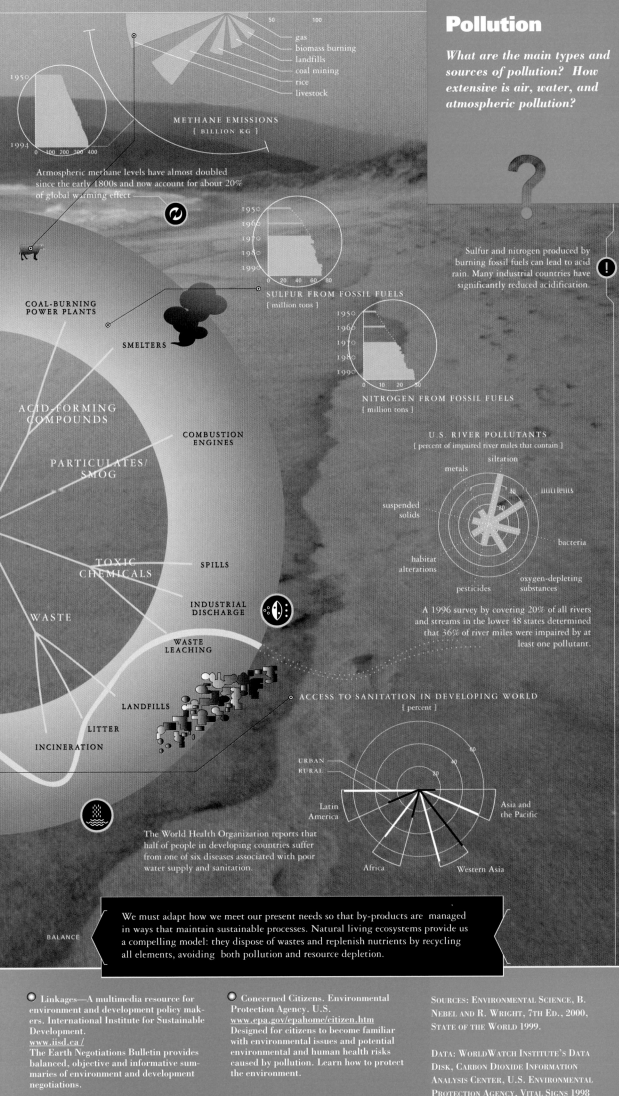

Pollution

What are the main types and sources of pollution? How extensive is air, water, and atmospheric pollution?

METHANE EMISSIONS
[BILLION KG]

- gas
- biomass burning
- landfills
- coal mining
- rice
- livestock

50   100

1950
1994

0 100 200 300 400

Atmospheric methane levels have almost doubled since the early 1800s and now account for about 20% of global warming effect

1950
1960
1970
1980
1990

0 20 40 60 80

SULFUR FROM FOSSIL FUELS
[million tons]

COAL-BURNING
POWER PLANTS

SMELTERS

Sulfur and nitrogen produced by burning fossil fuels can lead to acid rain. Many industrial countries have significantly reduced acidification.

1950
1960
1970
1980
1990

0 10 20 30

NITROGEN FROM FOSSIL FUELS
[million tons]

ACID-FORMING
COMPOUNDS

PARTICULATES/
SMOG

COMBUSTION
ENGINES

U.S. RIVER POLLUTANTS
[percent of impaired river miles that contain]

siltation
metals
nutrients
suspended
solids
bacteria
habitat
alterations
pesticides
oxygen-depleting
substances

TOXIC
CHEMICALS   SPILLS

WASTE

INDUSTRIAL
DISCHARGE

A 1996 survey by covering 20% of all rivers and streams in the lower 48 states determined that 36% of river miles were impaired by at least one pollutant.

WASTE
LEACHING

ACCESS TO SANITATION IN DEVELOPING WORLD
[percent]

LANDFILLS

LITTER

INCINERATION

URBAN
RURAL

60
40
20

Latin
America

Asia and
the Pacific

The World Health Organization reports that half of people in developing countries suffer from one of six diseases associated with poor water supply and sanitation.

Africa

Western Asia

BALANCE

We must adapt how we meet our present needs so that by-products are managed in ways that maintain sustainable processes. Natural living ecosystems provide us a compelling model: they dispose of wastes and replenish nutrients by recycling all elements, avoiding both pollution and resource depletion.

Linkages—A multimedia resource for environment and development policy makers. International Institute for Sustainable Development.
www.iisd.ca /
The Earth Negotiations Bulletin provides balanced, objective and informative summaries of environment and development negotiations.

Concerned Citizens. Environmental Protection Agency. U.S.
www.epa.gov/epahome/citizen.htm
Designed for citizens to become familiar with environmental issues and potential environmental and human health risks caused by pollution. Learn how to protect the environment.

SOURCES: ENVIRONMENTAL SCIENCE, B. NEBEL AND R. WRIGHT, 7TH ED., 2000, STATE OF THE WORLD 1999.

DATA: WORLDWATCH INSTITUTE'S DATA DISK, CARBON DIOXIDE INFORMATION ANALYSIS CENTER, U.S. ENVIRONMENTAL PROTECTION AGENCY, VITAL SIGNS 1998

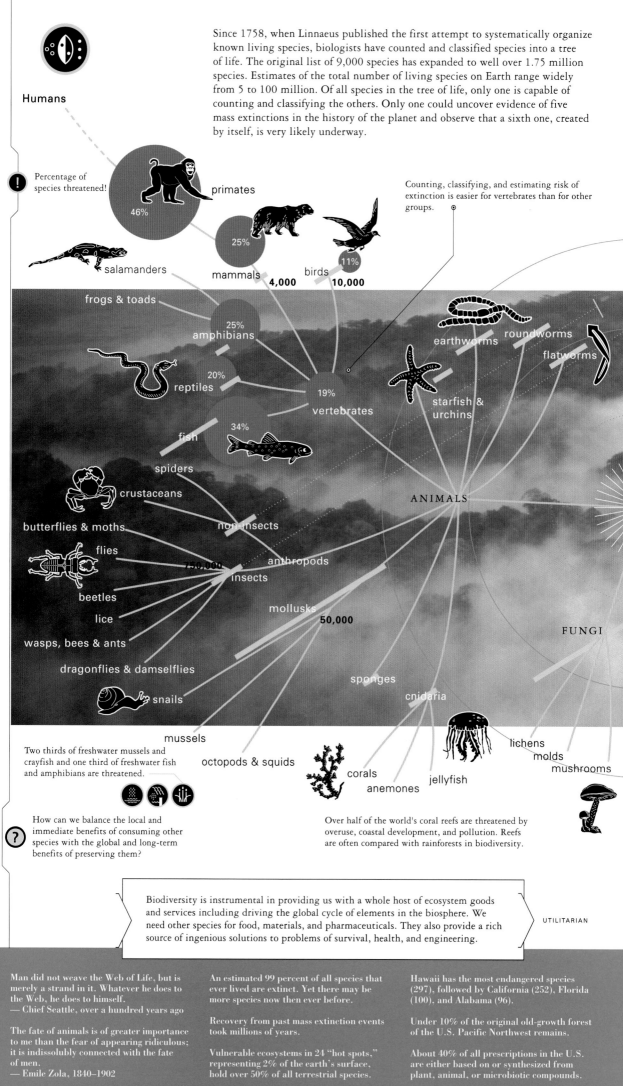

Humans

Since 1758, when Linnaeus published the first attempt to systematically organize known living species, biologists have counted and classified species into a tree of life. The original list of 9,000 species has expanded to well over 1.75 million species. Estimates of the total number of living species on Earth range widely from 5 to 100 million. Of all species in the tree of life, only one is capable of counting and classifying the others. Only one could uncover evidence of five mass extinctions in the history of the planet and observe that a sixth one, created by itself, is very likely underway.

Percentage of species threatened!

primates 46%

Counting, classifying, and estimating risk of extinction is easier for vertebrates than for other groups.

25% mammals **4,000**

11% birds **10,000**

salamanders

frogs & toads

25% amphibians

earthworms   roundworms
flatworms

20% reptiles

starfish & urchins

19% vertebrates

fish 34%

spiders

crustaceans

ANIMALS

butterflies & moths

non-insects

flies

anthropods

750,000

beetles

insects

lice

mollusks **50,000**

FUNGI

wasps, bees & ants

dragonflies & damselflies

snails

sponges

cnidaria

mussels

lichens
molds
mushrooms

Two thirds of freshwater mussels and crayfish and one third of freshwater fish and amphibians are threatened.

octopods & squids

corals
anemones

jellyfish

How can we balance the local and immediate benefits of consuming other species with the global and long-term benefits of preserving them?

Over half of the world's coral reefs are threatened by overuse, coastal development, and pollution. Reefs are often compared with rainforests in biodiversity.

Biodiversity is instrumental in providing us with a whole host of ecosystem goods and services including driving the global cycle of elements in the biosphere. We need other species for food, materials, and pharmaceuticals. They also provide a rich source of ingenious solutions to problems of survival, health, and engineering.

UTILITARIAN

Man did not weave the Web of Life, but is merely a strand in it. Whatever he does to the Web, he does to himself.
— Chief Seattle, over a hundred years ago

The fate of animals is of greater importance to me than the fear of appearing ridiculous; it is indissolubly connected with the fate of men.
— Emile Zola, 1840–1902

An estimated 99 percent of all species that ever lived are extinct. Yet there may be more species now then ever before.

Recovery from past mass extinction events took millions of years.

Vulnerable ecosystems in 24 "hot spots," representing 2% of the earth's surface, hold over 50% of all terrestrial species.

Hawaii has the most endangered species (297), followed by California (252), Florida (100), and Alabama (96).

Under 10% of the original old-growth forest of the U.S. Pacific Northwest remains.

About 40% of all prescriptions in the U.S. are either based on or synthesized from plant, animal, or microbiotic compounds.

Biodiversity

How many species of what types of animals and plants are there? What are the causes of extinction and how does the current rate compare to the past?

?

CAUSES OF EXTINCTIONS SINCE 1600
[percent]

habitat destruction

Converting wild land to human uses, altering the balance of habitats through harvesting and pollution, and reshaping and fragmentation of large patches of natural ecosystems.

other

36
10
20
30
39

+17 inches

overuse

Over-harvesting of species by hunting, fishing, logging, and collecting of food, raw materials, skins, furs, ivory, now-rare woods.

+4 inches

Introduced into an ecosystem from elsewhere often thrive unchecked by natural controls, throwing off the balance of the ecosystem and destroying many native species.

exotic species

MARINE FAMILIES
[Cambrian Era to the present]

millions of years ago

now

CENOZOIC — Quaternary — Tertiary

76% of species lost

Cretaceous

100

MESOZOIC — Jurassic

200

76% — Triassic

96% — Permian

Carboniferous

300

82% — Devonian

PALEOZOIC — 85% — Silurian

Ordovician

400

500

Cambrian

1000 800 600 400 200 0

BACTERIA

ferns

mosses

conifers

PLANTS

14%

250,000

seed plants

flowering plants

The tree of life is an artificial structure which is created by humans to understand life. It is constantly changing as species appear and disappear and as human knowledge of the realities it represents evolves.

PROTISTA

By examining the fossil record, paleontologist have identified five mass extinctions in the past. It is hard to identify species in the fossil record so extinction rates are determined only for families. However, the numbers of species that went extinct in each extinction event have been estimated and reveal a more dramatic loss of biodiversity.

algae

protozoa

BIODIVERSITY IN THE TREE OF LIFE
[number of described species & percent at risk]

Means number, variety, and variability of living organisms and the ecosystems that contain them. Counting species is a very common method for measuring biodiversity.

How can we effectively plant the the effort to preserve biodiversity in the workings of our civilization? **(?)**

DEONTOLOGICAL

Life has intrinsic value and has no greater value in one form than in another. We alone carry the ability to make moral judgments and thus responsibility toward other species. The diversity of life is an image of great beauty and deep truths that can lift us to new heights on our quest for cultural and spiritual enlightenment.

The World Wide Fund for Nature (WWF) publishes the Living Planet Index (LPI), an indicator of the state of Earth's natural ecosystem. The LPI is based on measures of forest cover and fresh water and marine species. The LPI declined 30 percent from 1970 to 1995.

A "cascade effect" can be triggered by the loss of "keystone" species in an ecosystems.

"We are in the midst of one of the greatest extinction spasms of geological history."
— E.O. Wilson

In 1998, the majority of biologists polled in the U.S. agreed that the world is in the midst of a mass extinction. The majority thought 20% of all species will become extinct within 30 years, while a third of scientists predicted a 50% extinction rate.

SOURCES: CONSERVATION AND BIODIVERSITY, ANDREW DOBSON, WORLD RESOURCE INSTITUTE'S BIODIVERSITY PROGRAMME, NATIONAL GEOGRAPHIC, FEB 1999

DATA: IUCN RED LISTS, UC BERKELEY'S MUSEUM OF PALEONTOLOGY, UNIVERSITY OF ARIZONA TREE OF LIFE PROJECT.

Climate is the essential foundation of all systems on the earth. A rapid change of climate would have widespread and devastating effects on human civilization, as well as all life and the natural world. Human activity, particularly carbon dioxide emission, is strongly implicated in a global warming trend which may in turn upset the global climate. The atmosphere, oceans, and land form a giant weather machine, fueled by the Sun and shaped by the rotation of the Earth. The oceans play a central role as the major source of water for the hydrological cycle as well as for their innate capacity to absorb heat. Furthermore, the giant ocean conveyor belt which moves heat in huge masses of warm water plays an enormous role in global climate. The conveyor completes a cycle over a period of 1000 years.

The Earth's climate has done abrupt flip-flops often!

ATMOSPHERIC CONCENTRATIONS OF CARBON DIOXIDE (CO_2)

The North Atlantic current, with the flow of 100 Amazons, keeps Europe 9-18 degrees Fahrenheit warmer than other land of comparable latitudes.

CO_2 concentrations and temperatures are measured for periods prior to instrumental and historical records in many ways. Scientists analyze ice cores, tree density, tree rings, lake bed sediment, and corals.

CO_2 concentrations are now at their highest levels in 160,000 years, while global temperatures are at at their highest since the Middle Ages.

Concentrations have increased primarily because of fossil fuel burning and deforestation.

MONTHLY CO_2 CONCENTRATIONS MEASURED AT MAUNA LOA, HAWAII

1959

1998

300   320   340   360

May

250   300   350
parts per million by volume

The seasonal rise and fall of carbon dioxide shows the "breath" of life on the planet. Levels rise from fall to spring as plant matter releases carbon dioxide. Levels fall from spring to fall as carbon dioxide is consumed by growing plants through photosynthesis.

Warm shallow current

Cold, salty

deep current

Scientist still disagree on how climate works and what may lead to what. Meanwhile, proposed corrective environmental policies would have minuscule impact, while risking global economic growth. Since wealthier is healthier, ill-conceived policies may themselves have the exact opposite of their intended effect.

CAUTIONARY

"The balance of evidence suggests that there is a discernible human influence on global climate."
— U.N. Panel of Scientists in 1995

Global average temperature has risen about 1 degree Fahrenheit since 1860. Future warming is predicted to be 2 to 6 degrees by 2100 compared to 5 to 9 degrees since the depth of the last ice age.

Stabilizing atmospheric CO_2 concentrations at safe levels will require a 60–80 percent cut in carbon emissions.

The climate seems to have been remarkably stable since the last ice age ended 10,000 years ago. As far as scientists can tell, global temperature varied by less than one degree since the dawn of civilization.

Global Warming. Union of Concerned Scientists.
www.ucsusa.org/warming/index
The Union of Concerned Scientists works to ensure that all people have clean air and energy, as well as safe and sufficient food.

Mount Everest rises to 29,035 feet, seven feet higher than the altitude recognized for 45 years. Source: Bradford Washburn, 89, Millennium Expedition to Mount Everest.

Climatic Change

How has global temperature changed in recent times? What climate changes and consequences could be triggered?

?

The conveyer is driven by the flow of warm salty water to the North Atlantic. There, cold dry Arctic winds cools the water and evaporates water from the surface, making it saltier and denser. It drops down 4000 meters and flows back to the tip of Africa and the Indian and Pacific oceans. More rainfall or melting ice in the North Atlantic, as predicted for global warming, could introduce more water that could disrupt the "flushing" effect of falling dense, salty water that draws in warm waters to the far north. A failure of the conveyer like this could trigger a climate flip-flop, leading to the next ice age.

Are we investing enough in understanding the global weather machine? **?**

Many documented trends confirm projected consequences of global warming including receding glaciers, rising sea levels, dying coral reefs, and migrating plants and animals.

A global temperature shift would have profound effects on natural ecosystems, especially when compounded with pollution and habitat destruction. For example, the present sites of many nature preserves may not support the species for which they were established.

GLOBAL AVERAGE TEMPERATURE
1866-1998

1900

1950

58   57   56   55
degrees Fahrenheit

Both Economy and Ecology are highly weather-dependent! **!**

Warm shallow current

Cold, salty deep current

Human society has made great investments aligned with the climate as it is. For example, half of all people live in coast cities. Rises in sea level would flood many coastal areas and make them more prone to storm damage. Similarly, agricultural investments are aligned with current weather patterns.

ECONOMIC LOSSES
from Weather-Related Natural Disasters

1960

1998

100   80   60   40   20   0
billion dollars

The record heat of 1998 unleashed widespread natural disasters: droughts in 45 countries; massive fires in tropical and subtropical forest from Mexico to Indonesia, which blackened 3,500 square km; floods in China and Bangladesh, which dislodged 80 million people; severe storms and epidemics in Africa and all the Americas including Hurricane Mitch, which killed 18,000 people in Central America; and heat waves in the U.S., India, and Southern Europe.

PRECAUTIONARY

Where there are threats of serious or irreversible damage, lack of scientific certainty should not be used as a reason for postponing cost-effective measures to prevent environmental degradations. Employing these measures is like taking insurance: we must avoid highly costly even if uncertain outcomes.

Mean sea level has risen by 4 to 10 inches over the last 100 years. Models project that sea levels will rise another 6 to 40 inches by 2100 with a best estimate of 25 inches. Two Pacific Island atolls have been totally submerged.

Butterflies in Europe are migrating 20–150 miles north. They are very delicate creatures, our canaries in a coal mine.

Endangered Species Home Page. Fish and Wildlife Service. Dept. of Interior. U.S.
www.fws.gov/r9endspp/endspp
Protecting endangered and threatened species and restoring them to a secure status in the wild is the primary objective of the endangered species program. Includes reports and other data.

SOURCES: THE GREAT CLIMATE FLIP-FLOP, WILLIAM CALVIN, ATLANTIC MONTHLY, JANUARY 1998, BERNARD NEBEL & RICHARD WRIGHT, ENVIRONMENTAL SCIENCE, 2000

DATA: WORLDWATCH INSTITUTE'S DATA DISK, C. KEELING, T. WHORF, SCRIPP'S MAUNA LOA OBSERVATORY IN HAWAII

Vaclav Smil, *Energies*, 1999

Christopher Flavin and Seth Dunn, Reinventing the
Energy System, *State of the World* 1999

U.S. Dept of Energy, www.doe.gov

Green Energy Guide site, www.repp.org/greene/greeneduhome.html

Union of Concerned Scientists Energy site, www.ucsusa.org/energy/

Centre for Renewable Energy and Sustainable Technology,
www.crest.org

Policy.com list of energy sites,
www.policy.com/community/bytopic/issuecatorg13.html

Sandra Postel, *Pillars of Sand: Can the Irrigation Miracle Last?*, 1999

Paul Simon, *Tapped Out: The Coming World Crisis in Water and
What We Can Do About It*, 1999

Sandra Postel, et al., Human Appropriation of
Renewable Fresh Water, *Science*, Vol 271

International Rivers Network, www.irn.org

U.S. Geological Survey's Water Division, water.usgs.gov

International Water Management Institute,
www.cgiar.org/iwmi/

The World's Waters site, www.worldwater.org

Lester Brown, Feeding Nine Billion, *State of the World* 1999

Gordon Conway, *The Doubly Green Revolution*, 1997

Frances Moore Lappe, *Diet for a Small Planet*, 1992

P.A. Matson, et al., Agricultural Intensification
and Ecosystem Properties, *Science*, Vol 277

United Nations's Food & Agriculture Organization (FAO),
www.fao.org

Consultative Group on International Agricultural Research,
www.cgiar.org

U.S. Department of Agriculture, Agricultural Fact Book,
www.usda.gov/news/pubs/fbook98/content.htm

Union of Concerned Scientist's Agriculture site,
www.ucsusa.org/agriculture/

Michael Brower & Warren Leon, *The Consumer's Guide
to Effective Environmental Choices*, 1999

Gary Gardner and Payal Sampat, Forging a Sustainable
Materials Economy, *State of the World* 1999

Grecia Matos and Lorie Wagner, Consumption of Materials
in the United States 1900-1995,
greenwood.cr.usgs.gov/pub/min-info-team/ann-rev/ar-23-107/

World Resources 98-99, www.wri.org

U.S. Geological Survey's Mineral Information,
www.minerals.usgs.gov/minerals/

FAO Forestry Programme,
www.fao.org/forestry/forestry.htm

Bernard Nebel & Richard Wright,
Environmental Science, 2000

Andrew Goudie, *The Human Impact on the
Natural Environment*, 1994

Vaclav Smil, *Cycles of Life*, 1997

Worldwatch Institute,
State of the World 1999, 1999

Michael Brower & Warren Leon,
*The Consumer's Guide to Effective
Environmental Choices*, 1999

Ronald Bailey, editor,
The True State of the Planet, 1995

Paul Ehrlich & Anne Ehrlich,
Betrayal of Science and Reason, 1996

Julian Simon, *Ultimate Resources 2*, 1998

Ed Ayres, *God's Last Offer*, 1999

Lester Brown, Gary Gardner, & Brian
Halweil, *Beyond Malthus*, 1999

Herman Daly, *Beyond Growth*, 1996

Bill McKibben, A Special Moment in
History, *Atlantic Monthly*, May 1988

Links &
Resources

*How are the topics
connected? Where can I
find more information?*

?

Mathis Wackernagel & William Rees, *Our Ecological Footprint*, 1996

Janet Abramovitz and Ashley Mattoon,
Reorienting the Forest Products Economy,
State of the World 1999

World Resource Institute, The Last Frontier
Forests: Ecosystems and Economies on the Edge,
www.wri.org/ffi/lff-eng/

FAO Forestry Programme, www.fao.org/forestry/forestry.htm

FAO's The State of the World's Forest,
www.fao.org/forestry/sofo/sofo99/default.htm

WWF's Forests for Life Program,
www.panda.org/forests4life/

World Resource Institute's Forest site, www.wri.org/forests/

Desertification of Arid Land, H. E. Dregne,
infoserver.ciesin.org/docs/002-193/002-193.html

United Nations Convention to Combat Desertification,
www.unccd.ch

The Nature Conservancy, www.tnc.org

Bernard Nebel & Richard Wright, *Environmental Science*, 2000

Peter Vitousek et al., Human Alteration of Global Nitrogen
Cycle: Causes and Consequence, esa.sdsc.edu/tilman.pdf

PIRG's Report on Toxic Releases into America's Waterways,
www.pirg.org/enviro/toxics/waters98/

U.S. Environmental Protection Agency Superfund
Cleanup Information, www.epa.gov/superfund/

EPA's Office of Water, www.epa.gov/ow/

EPA's Office of Air & Radiation, www.epa.gov/oar/

EPA's Surf Your Watershed site, www.epa.gov/surf/

Andrew Dobson, *Conservation and Biodiversity*, 1998

Edward Wilson, *The Diversity of Life*, 1993

David Quammen, Planet of Weeds, *Harper's*, Oct 98

World Conservation Monitoring Center, Biodiversity
Overview, www.wcmc.org.uk/infoserv/biogen/biogen.html

World Resource Institute's Biodiversity Site,
www.wri.org/biodiv

The Tree of Life, phylogeny.arizona.edu/tree/

UC Berkeley Museum of Paleontology,
www.ucmp.berkeley.edu/exhibit/phylogeny.html

The World's Conservation Union (IUCN) Species
Survival Commission, www.iucn.org/themes/ssc/index.htm

World Wide Fund for Nature (WWF), www.panda.org

Conservation International, www.conservation.org

William Calvin, The Great Climate Flip-Flop,
Atlantic Monthly, January 1998

Climate Change Information Kit, www.unfcc.de/resource/iuckit

Intergovernmental Panel on Climate Change, www.ipcc.ch

UN Convention on Climate Change, www.unfccc.de/index.html

UN World Meteorological Organization, www.wmo.ch/

EPA's Global Warming site, www.epa.gov/globalwarming/

World Resources Institute Climate Change site, www.wri.org/climate/

Peter Vitousek, et al., Human Domination
of Earth's Ecosystems, *Science* 277

Vaclav Smil, Nature's Services, Human
Follies, *Population and Development
Review*, June 99

Mark Sagoff, Do We Consume Too Much?,
Atlantic Monthly, June 1997

Atlantic Monthly environmental articles,
www.theatlantic.com/politics/environ/
environ.htm

Worldwatch Institute's Vital Signs and
Data Disks yearly series,
www.worldwatch.org

World Resource Institute, World Resources
biennial series, www.wri.org

WWF's Living Planet Report,
www.panda.org/livingplanet/lpr99/

Policy.com, list of environmental sites,
www.policy.com/community/bytopic/
issuecatorg14.html

Rocky Mountain Institute, www.rmi.org

Union of Concerned Scientists,
www.ucsusa.org

GOVERNMENTAL AGENCIES:

U.N. Environmental Programme
www.unep.org

U.N. Food and Agricultural Organization
www.fao.org

U.N. World Meteorological Organization
www.wmo.ch

U.S. Department of Energy
www.doe.gov

U.S. Department of Agriculture
www.usda.gov

U.S. Environmental Protection Agency
www.epa.gov

U.S. Geological Survey
www.usgs.gov

RESEARCH AND INFORMATION:

Center for International Earth Science Information Network
infoserver.ciesin.org

Consultative Group on International Agricultural Research
www.cgiar.org

International Water Management Institute
www.cgiar.org/iwmi

International Food Policy Research Institute
www.cgiar.org/ifpri

Island Press, Eco-Compass
www.islandpress.com

Public Interest Research Groups
www.pirg.org

Rocky Mountain Institute
www.rmi.org

Resources for the Future
www.rff.org

World Conservation Monitoring Centre
www.wcmc.org.uk

World Resources Institute
www.wri.org

The World's Waters site
www.worldwater.org

Worldwatch Institute
www.worldwatch.org

Union of Concerned Scientists
www.ucsusa.org

Radial Grids

Table Lens

Photography: Corbis—Craig Aurness, CRD Photo, Michael Cuthbert, Robert Landau, Jim Richardson; Graphis Stock—Gary Faye, Gildo Nicolo Spandoni, Adam Woolfitt; Swan Stock—Peter Goin.

Advisors: Daniel Russell, Vaclav Smil, Kevin Mullet, Hector Moll-Carillo.

⊙ Center for Environmental Information and Statistics. Environmental Protection Agency. U.S.
www.epa.gov/ceis
CEIS is the U.S. Environmental Protection Agency's (EPA) new one-stop source of data and information on environmental quality, status and trends.

⊙ EPA Global Warming Site. Environmental Protection Agency. U.S.
www.epa.gov/globalwarming
The U.S. Global Change Research Program (USGCRP) coordinates the world's most extensive research effort on climate change.

Organizations

What governmental and research organizations provide information and data? What organizations focus on environmental issues?

?

ENVIRONMENTAL ORGANIZATIONS:

American Rivers, Inc.,
www.amrivers.org

Centre for Renewable Energy and Sustainable Technology
www.crest.org

Conservation International
www.conservation.org

Coral Reef Alliance
www.coral.org

Environmental Defense Fund
www.edf.org

Earthwatch Expeditions, Inc.
www.earthwatch.org

Greenpeace
www.greenpeace.org

Global Action Plan
www.globalactionplan.org

International Rivers Network
www.irn.org

National Environmental Education and Training Foundation
www.neetf.org

National Resources Defense Counsel
www.nrdc.org

National Audubon Society
www.audubon.org

National Parks and Conservation Association
www.npca.org

National Wildlife Federation
www.nwf.org

Nature Conservancy
www.tnc.org

Sierra Club
www.sierraclub.org

Rain Forest Action Network
www.ran.org

W. Alton Jones Foundation
www.wajones.org

Wilderness Society
www.tws.org

World Conservation Union (IUCN)
www.iucn.org

World Wide Fund for Nature (WWF)
www.panda.org

Maps

Hyperbolic Trees

Maps

○ Natural Hazards. Dept. of Interior. U.S.
www.doi.gov/nathaz/index.html
Page outlines information, descriptions, programs and policies involving such natural hazards as wildfires, earthquakes, floods, etc.

○ National Biological Information Infrastructure. U.S.
www.nbii.gov/
The NBII is an electronic gateway to biological data and information maintained by federal, state, and local government agencies; private sector organizations; and other partners around the nation and the world.

○ President's Council on Sustainable Development. U.S.
www.whitehouse.gov/PCSD
PCSD has advised President Clinton on sustainable development and develops bold,, new approaches to achieve economic, environmental, and equity goals.

Tom Wood

Life in America
Is the quality of life better or worse than it was fifty years ago?

American Family
Is the quality of life for your family better or worse than it was fifty years ago?

American Society
Is the quality of life for others better or worse than it was fifty years ago?

Social Issues
Have social issues and trends had an impact on your life?

American Technology
Have inventions and technology had an influence on your life?

American Achievement
What are America's greatest achievements?

American Failure
What are America's greatest failures?

American Ingenuity
What factors contribute to America's success?

Collective Memory
What world events are most memorable to Americans? What world events are most memorable to Americans old enough to remember?

Historical Context
How well do Americans remember history?

What's life in the United States like today? Is it better than it was 50 years ago? Has it stayed the same or gotten worse?

Here are 10 questions and answers from a recent survey, conducted by the Pew Research Center under the direction of Andrew Kohut, that explore some of the topics concerning the past century in America. There are no conclusions, just reactions that show how the average American generally feels about the quality of his, her or someone else's life.

For a number of social, economic, political and technological reasons, Americans think that life is generally getting better.

When asked if life is better now for them and their families,
Americans responded.

63% *better* **25%** *same* **12%** *worse*

When asked if life was better for Americans overall,
they responded with quite a different answer.

44% *better* **26%** *same* **30%** *worse*

ABOUT THE SURVEY
The principal findings
of the Pew Research
Center are the result
of a national survey of
1,546 adults conducted
in April of 1999.

Americans generally see the Twentieth Century as a time of significant economic, social and technological progress. As individuals, as families and as members of various demographic groups, nearly two-thirds of Americans surveyed— men and women, whites and blacks, young and old—say that their lives are better today than were the lives of their families fifty years ago.

Family

How Americans view the quality of life for their families today.

Gender
	better
MEN	63%
WOMEN	62

Age
AGE 18-34	59%
AGE 35-54	66
AGE 55-64	66
AGE 65 OR OLDER	57

Race
WHITE	62%
BLACK	67
HISPANIC	57

Income
$50,000 OR MORE	69%
$30,000-$49,999	65
$20,000-$29,999	60
$20,000 OR LESS	47

Education
COLLEGE GRADUATE	67%
HIGH SCHOOL GRADUATE	60
SOME HIGH SCHOOL	58

Depression Generation
born in 1929 or before

World War II Generation
born before 1933

Swing Generation
born 1933-1945

Baby Boom Generation
born 1946-1964

Generation X
born 1965-1976

Generation Y
born 1977-2000

THE GOOD
40% of those who see their lives as better cite prosperity, higher pay and financial security as reasons for improvement. This is true of all major demographic groups.

THE BAD
16% of Americans say the pace of life is to blame for life being worse in America.

THE UGLY
Americans who say their lives are worse today blame the breakdown of family values, moral decay, crime and drugs in equal numbers as the primary reasons.

same   worse

4   33
4   34

7   34
4   30
4   34
3   40

4   34
4   29
4   39

3   28
4   31
4   36
3   49

4   29
5   35
4   38

INCOME
The perception that life is better today is especially strong among the wealthy and well educated. Almost **70%** of people with incomes of more than $50,000 and a similar number of those with college degrees hold this view. Americans with incomes of less than $20,000 are the rare group who say their lives are no better than they were fifty years ago.

YOUTH
Children don't necessarily want more time with their parents, but they would like their parents to make more money, according to a recent study.

Although a majority of Americans say that their lives are better today than they were fifty years ago, a parallel story is not nearly as optimistic. Misgivings about America today are focused on the declining moral climate, with people from all walks of life looking skeptically at how the country has changed culturally and spiritually.

Others

How Americans view the quality of life for other groups.

overall survey results

Demographic groups	better
WOMEN	83%
DISABLED PEOPLE	82
AFRICAN AMERICANS	81
HISPANICS	65
WORKING CLASS	60
SENIOR CITIZENS	61
GAYS AND LESBIANS	61
WHITE MALES	53
MEN	51
MIDDLE CLASS	51
RELIGIOUS PEOPLE	46%
CHILDREN	46
TEENAGERS	33
UNION MEMBERS	35
FARMERS	20 ... 15

WOMEN AT WORK
In 1955, **36%** of women were in the work force, compared to **60%** today. In 1955, **85%** of men were in the work force, compared to **75%** today.

AFRICAN AMERICANS
68% of blacks say their lives are better today than fifty years ago, compared to **83%** of whites who feel the lives of blacks have improved.

MINORITY BUSINESS
The number of minority businesses has increased substantially. There are **46%** more black-owned firms, **76%** more Hispanic and **56%** more Asian-owned companies.

UNION MEMBERS
Union membership accounted for **16%** of the work force in 1990 with over 6.5 million members.

SENIORS
81% of seniors are more likely to say that their lives have improved as compared to **57%** of the younger generation.

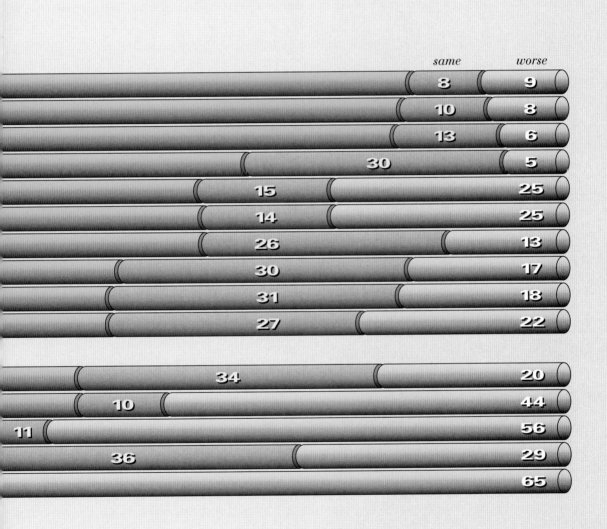

same | worse

8 | 9
10 | 8
13 | 6
30 | 5
15 | 25
14 | 25
26 | 13
30 | 17
31 | 18
27 | 22
34 | 20
10 | 44
11 | 56
36 | 29
| 65

YOUTH
56% of the public say the lives of teenagers are worse today, and **44%** view children's lives as difficult. Parents with children have a particularly dim view of their future.

FARMERS
65% of Americans say that farmers' lives are worse today than they were fifty years ago. Only **20%** of Americans say farmers' lives are better today.

FARMS
In 1950 there were more than 5.5 million farms with an average of 213 acres. Currently there are 2 million farms with an average of 471 acres.

RELIGION
The Moral Majority, founded in 1990, was the first evangelical group to become active politically, advocating conservative moral and political positions.

USA.FYI
The work week in 1973 was 40.6 hours, and the average time spent on leisure was 26.2 hours. Today the work week averages 51 hours with 19.5 hours of leisure time.

Social trends of the past decade get mixed reviews. Two societal shifts of the late Twentieth Century—the civil rights movement and women in the workplace—are woven into our cultural identity and viewed favorably by nearly everyone. The benefits of other changes, such as the growth of suburbs, spending habits and even popular music, are more ambiguous to the public, and few recent trends are seen as improvements by a clear majority of Americans.

Trends

How social issues and trends impact American life.

overall survey results

Issues and trends of the decade — better

MUTUAL FUNDS	69%
HOME SCHOOLING	43
GAY RIGHTS	39
LOTTERIES	35
HMO/MANAGED CARE	31
TELEMARKETING	21
RAP MUSIC	14

Issues and trends of the century

CIVIL RIGHTS MOVEMENT	84%
WOMEN IN THE WORKPLACE	83
GROWTH OF SUBURBS	52
ROCK AND ROLL	45
LEGALIZED ABORTION	34
ACCEPTANCE OF DIVORCE	30
CREDIT CARD USE	22 · · · 10

MUTUAL FUNDS
Americans say mutual funds have been a change for the better, but a range of other developments fail to get positive ratings from even a majority of the public.

RAP MUSIC
Americans have a mixed opinion of rap music. **26%** of blacks say it is a change for the better; **12%** of whites agree. **47%** of blacks say rap is actually worse, and **55%** of whites agree.

CIVIL RIGHTS
Blacks are no more likely than whites to say the civil rights movement has been a change for the better.

THE OFFICE
87% of women say women in the work-place has been a change for the better; **78%** of men agree.

Social Issues

Have social issues and trends had an impact on your life?

?

DEMOGRAPHIC GROUP RESULTS
Positive response to social trends and issues

$75,000 or more	82%	$75,000 or more	20%	Blacks	36%	Blacks	26%
$20,000-29,999	53%	$20,000-29,999	40%	Whites	18%	Whites	12%
College Graduate	78%	College Graduate	22%	Age 18-34	27%	Age 18-34	24%
High School	52%	High School	44%	Age 65+	15%	Age 65+	6%

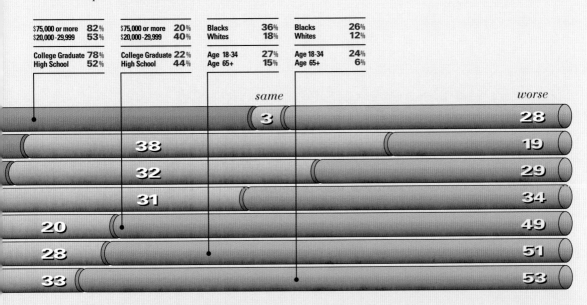

same · *worse*

same	worse
3	28
38	19
32	29
31	34
20	49
28	51
33	53

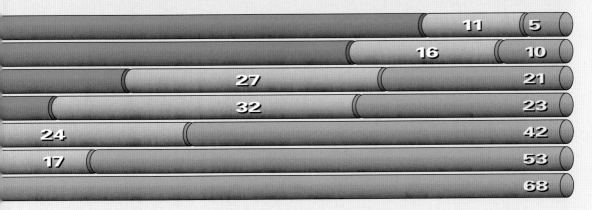

same	worse
11	5
16	10
27	21
32	23
24	42
17	53
	68

SUBURBIA
63% of those who live in the suburbs say the growth of these areas has been a good thing, compared to **53%** of those living in cities and **42%** of those in rural areas.

HOME SCHOOLING
Home schooling has become more popular with over 300,000 students educated at home, most for religious reasons.

SCHOOL COSTS
The average annual expenditure per student in public schools was $260 in 1950, $955 in 1970 and $5,532 in 1990.

GAY RIGHTS
45% of Democrats say that the gay rights movement made things better, compared to **31%** of Republicans.

USA.FYI
According to a recent study, the fastest growing professions are homemaker, computer science, special education and sales representatives.

Science and technology are seen as catalysts for the century's economic prosperity. Americans celebrate the inventions and conveniences of the Twentieth Century and point to advancements in these fields as principal reasons for improvements in their families' well-being. Inventions ranging from the automobile to birth control pills to the Internet are credited with improving the quality of life in America.

Technology

How technology impacts American life.

overall survey results

Technology of the decade	*better*	
E-MAIL	71%	
THE INTERNET	69	
CELLULAR PHONES	66	
CABLE TELEVISION	62	
FERTILITY DRUGS	43	
PROZAC	40	
VIAGRA	36	
CLONING OF SHEEP	15	36

Technology of the century		
RADIO	96%	
AUTOMOBILE	91	
HOME COMPUTER	87	
HIGHWAY SYSTEM	84	
AIRLINE TRAVEL	77	
TELEVISION	73	
BIRTH CONTROL PILLS	72	
SPACE EXPLORATION	72	
NUCLEAR ENERGY	48	
NUCLEAR WEAPONS	19	18

NEW TECHNOLOGY
Americans express the greatest enthusiasm for communications technologies, such as e-mail, the Internet and cellular phones.

INTERNET
75% of those under the age of fifty say the Internet is a change for the better, compared to **51%** of those 65 years and older.

AT HOME
Pole results for the most innovative home technology
#1 Personal computer
#2 Television
#3 Refrigerator
(www.technocopia.com)

DEVELOPMENTS
1954 RCA produces first color television set.
1967 Public broadcasting established.
1978 Cell phone first developed by Bell Labs.
1992 The Internet is introduced to the public.

TELEVISION
74% of the American households have more than one television; **74%** have cable and **84%** have VCRs.

TELEVISION VIEWING
Average weekly television viewing time per household in 1970 was 42 hours. It was 46 hours in 1980, 48.5 in 1990 and 50.5 today.

American Technology

Have inventions and technology had an influence on your life?

?

DEMOGRAPHIC GROUP RESULTS

Positive response to technology having an impact

$75,000 or more	86%	$75,000 or more	81%	Men	65%	$75,000 or more	73%
$20,000 or less	57%	$20,000 or less	56%	Women	68%	$20,000 or less	53%
18-34 years	82%	18-34 years	76%	18-34 years	72%	18-34 years	58%
65+ years	47%	65+ years	51%	65+ years	57%	55+ years	67%
College Graduate	78%	College Graduate	81%	Blacks	77%	East Coast	69%
High School	64%	High School	59%	Whites	65%	West Coast	55%

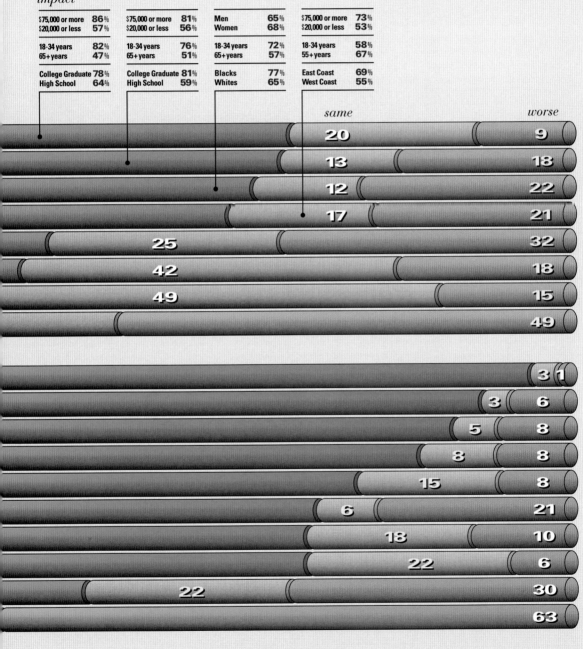

same — *worse*

same	worse
20	9
13	18
12	22
17	21
25	32
42	18
49	15
	49

same	worse
	3 1
3	6
5	8
8	8
15	8
6	21
18	10
22	6
22	30
	63

MEDICINE
Prozac, Viagra and fertility drugs get mixed reviews by the public, who are uneasy about recent breakthroughs in pharmacology and biotechnology.

CLONING
49% of Americans see the cloning of sheep as a change for the worse. **62%** of women say it is a change for the worse, compared to just **36%** of men.

SCIENCE
The public does not embrace all scientific advances. Just **48%** say nuclear energy is a change for the better, and nuclear weapons are viewed as a step forward by only **19%**.

USA.FYI
In 1997 there were 48,000 Americans admitted to hospital emergency rooms with skateboard-related injuries, **33%** more than the previous year.

USA.FYI
Of all cable channels, ESPN and CNN are tied for having the largest number of subscribers, 71 million.

Americans name the country's strong economy, social programs, advances in science, medicine and the space program in particular as America's greatest achievements. But nothing comes close to technological progress when evaluating America's greatest achievements—not winning the World Wars or the Cold War, not the civil rights movement and not even the Social Security System that lifted so many out of poverty.

Achievements

America's greatest accomplishments.

overall survey results

FREEDOM AND LIBERTY
CIVIL RIGHTS
ENDING SEGREGATION
WOMEN'S RIGHTS
EQUAL RIGHTS

5%

CIVIL RIGHTS

SPACE PROGRAM
TECHNOLOGY
TRANSPORTATION
COMPUTERS
SCIENCE
COMMUNICATIONS

EDUCATION
DEMOCRACY
FREEDOM

12%

OTHER FACTORS

41%

TECHNOLOGY / SCIENCE

Over **40**% cite technological advances and specifically the space program as America's most outstanding accomplishments.

1958 NASA established to conduct research and space exploration.
1961 First American space voyage.
1981 The first space shuttle *Columbia* completes mission.

1955 IBM introduces first business computer.
1956 Computer language introduced.
1975 Development of first personal computer.
1981 First portable computer produced.

International and social policies are considered by many as America's greatest achievements of the century. Victories in World War II and the Cold War are cited by only **7**% of the public.

In 1956 the Dow Jones Industrial average index hit 500 points. In 1972 it reached 1,000 points, 2,000 in 1987, 5,000 in 1995, and in 1999 it broke 10,000 points.

American Achievement

What are America's greatest achievements?

?

The top five of **The Learning Channel's** Countdown 100: Greatest Achievements of the 20th Century: (1) Exploration of Space, (2) Electricity, (3) End of World War II, (4) Education for the Masses, (5) Civil Rights Movement.

STANDARD OF LIVING
STABLE ECONOMY
BETTER JOBS
LOWER UNEMPLOYMENT
SOCIAL SECURITY
WELFARE

5%

ECONOMY

MEDICAL ADVANCEMENTS
HEALTH CARE

7%

MEDICINE

23%

NOT SURE

PEACE
WINNING WORLD WAR II
END OF THE COLD WAR
DIPLOMACY
WORLD POWER

7%

WAR / PEACE

CIVIL RIGHTS
Advances in civil rights and programs that lifted so many out of poverty, such as Social Security and welfare, are ranked as significant American achievements.

1960 Civil Rights Act is authorized by Congress.
1972 Equal Rights Amendment approved.
1981 Sandra Day O'Conner is the first woman appointed to the Supreme Court.

MEDICINE
1964 **Medicare Act is** passed, establishing government-run health care for senior citizens and the poor.

1953 First open heart surgery is performed.
1966 First artificial heart implant.
1967 First human heart transplant performed.

USA.FYI
M&Ms were created for the United States military in 1940.

When they were asked to name the nation's greatest failures of the Twentieth Century, Americans were split almost equally between war, morality and politics. The use of force tops the list of disappointments, followed by war, a decline in moral values and problems with politics and government.

Failures

America's greatest failures.

overall survey results

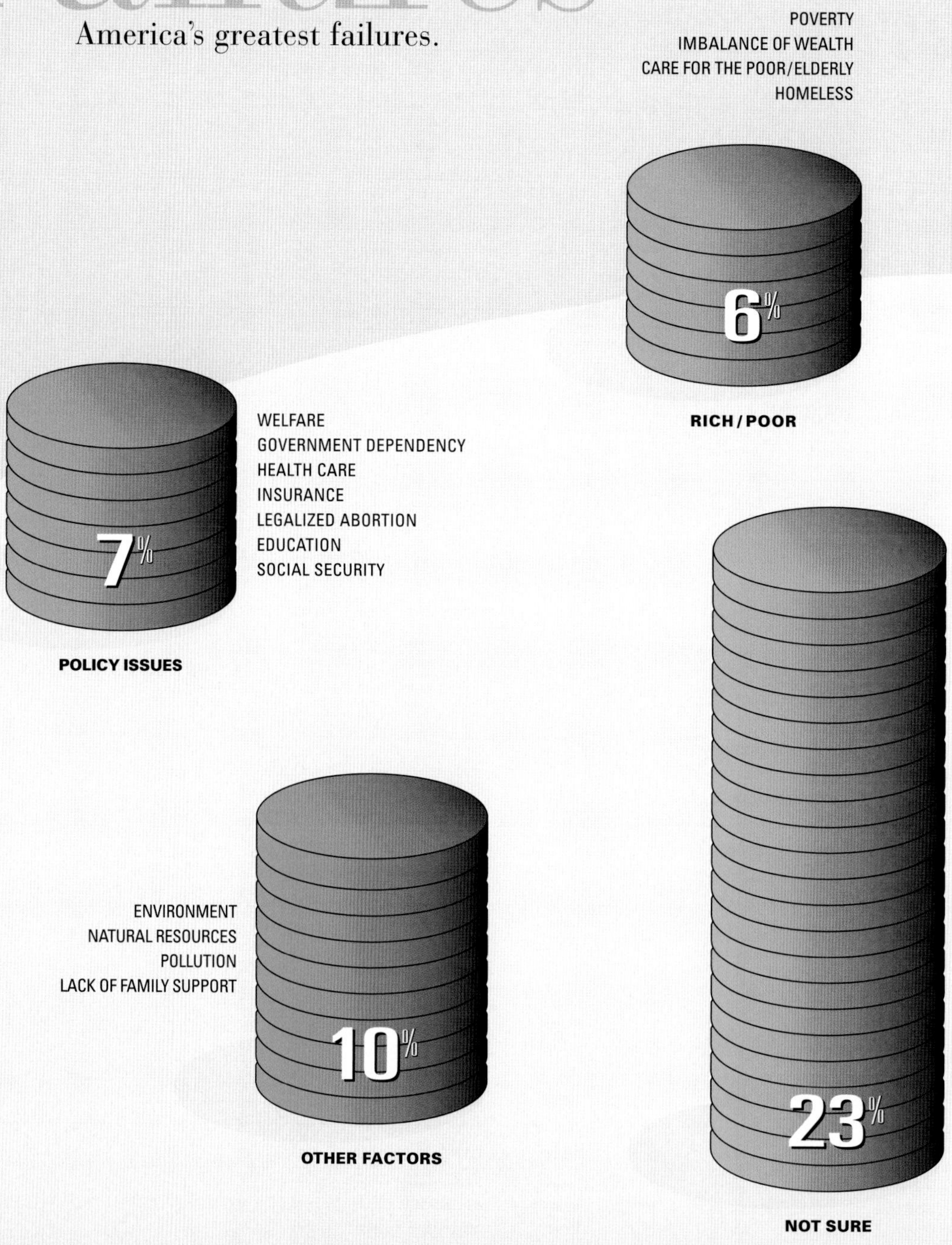

POVERTY
IMBALANCE OF WEALTH
CARE FOR THE POOR/ELDERLY
HOMELESS

6%

RICH/POOR

WELFARE
GOVERNMENT DEPENDENCY
HEALTH CARE
INSURANCE
LEGALIZED ABORTION
EDUCATION
SOCIAL SECURITY

7%

POLICY ISSUES

ENVIRONMENT
NATURAL RESOURCES
POLLUTION
LACK OF FAMILY SUPPORT

10%

OTHER FACTORS

23%

NOT SURE

WAR
25% of men cite war as the nation's greatest calamity; **10%** of women agree. Conversely, **18%** of women think that moral breakdown is the greatest failure; **10%** of men agree.

VIETNAM
Twenty-four years after the fall of Saigon, Vietnam still haunts Americans. It is the most often mentioned national failure and the government's greatest mistake of the century.

50,000 conscientious objectors are believed to have left the country during the Vietnam conflict. 250,000 never registered for the draft, and 110,000 burned their draft cards in protest.

POLICY ISSUES
Americans feel certain policy areas, such as welfare, health care or education, are the government's greatest failures; paradoxically, these are some of the same issues that were cited as the greatest achievements of the Twentieth Century.

RACE RELATIONS
CIVIL RIGHTS
WOMEN'S RIGHTS
EQUAL RIGHTS

CRIME
VIOLENCE
INEFFECTIVE JUSTICE SYSTEM
WAR ON DRUGS
PRISON SYSTEM

GOVERNMENT CORRUPTION
DISTRUST OF GOVERNMENT
LACK OF MORALS
GOVERNMENT TOO LARGE
ETHICS AND SCANDALS
BUDGET AND DEFICIT
TAXES

6%

CIVIL RIGHTS

6%

JUSTICE SYSTEM

10%

GOVERNMENT

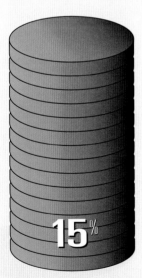

MORAL DECLINE
LACK OF VALUES
FAMILY BREAKDOWN
LACK OF ETHICS
LACK OF RELIGION

VIETNAM
INVOLVEMENT IN WARS
WORLD POLICING
FOREIGN POLICY
WORLD INFLUENCE
USE OF POWER

17%

WAR

15%

MORALS

CIVIL RIGHTS
Blacks place the treatment of minorities and intolerance at the top of their list of America's failures. **21%** of blacks hold this view, compared to just **6%** of whites.

MORALITY
Nearly the same number of Americans describe Clinton's lack of ethics and the Vietnam War as the nation's most significant failures.

ETHICS
Watergate, considered the most significant political scandal in American history, led to the resignation of Richard Nixon, the only president to resign.

ENVIRONMENT
Established in 1973, the Environmental Protection Agency was created to monitor the nation's environmental health.

USA.FYI
College expenses hit a record high in 1990 with an Ivy League education costing more than $20,000 a year. It is expected to cost at least $35,000 in the year 2000.

Americans are nearly unanimous in crediting the country's social and political system for its achievements, despite today's cynicism for the government and the news media. The Constitution, free elections and the free enterprise system are viewed as the major reasons for America's success, and the country's natural resources, cultural diversity and character of the people are also cited as key factors.

Ingenuity

Factors that contribute to America's success.

Government

CONSTITUTION	**85%**
FREE ELECTIONS	**84**
TWO-PARTY SYSTEM	**49**

Society

FREEDOM OF THE PRESS	**69%**
FREE ENTERPRISE SYSTEM	**81**
CULTURAL DIVERSITY	**71**
AMERICAN PEOPLE'S CHARACTER	**69**
NATURAL RESOURCES	**78**
GEOGRAPHIC ISOLATION	**53**

Religion

SEPARATION OF CHURCH & STATE	**41%**
JUDEO-CHRISTIAN BELIEFS	**41**
GOD'S WILL	**65**
GOOD LUCK	**25**

Blacks **41**%
Whites **41**%

Blacks **39**%
Whites **41**%

Blacks **82**%
Whites **63**%

Blacks **26**%
Whites **25**%

One of the greatest differences between demographic groups is their evaluation of the free enterprise system. **85%** of men label free enterprise as a major reason for America's success, compared to **77%** of women. **84%** of 35 and older and **74%** of 18-34 years agree, compared to **83%** of whites and **66%** of blacks.

The total amount of United States currency in circulation totals $450,612,505,753. In 1998 there were 189 billionaires in the United States.

IMMIGRATION
Immigration has been a major factor in the growth of the United States. The number of arrivals surged around the turn of the century and, in the last decade, has risen sharply.

From 1991 to 1996 alone, over 6 million people entered this country. Today there are 5 million people living in the United States illegally.

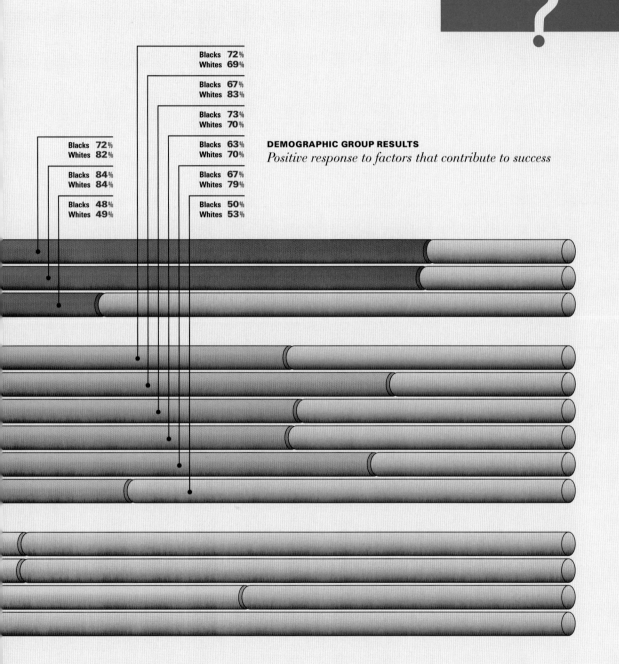

Blacks **72**%
Whites **69**%

Blacks **67**%
Whites **83**%

Blacks **73**%
Whites **70**%

Blacks **72**%
Whites **82**%

Blacks **63**%
Whites **70**%

DEMOGRAPHIC GROUP RESULTS
Positive response to factors that contribute to success

Blacks **84**%
Whites **84**%

Blacks **67**%
Whites **79**%

Blacks **48**%
Whites **49**%

Blacks **50**%
Whites **53**%

IN GOD WE TRUST
91% of black women credit God's will as a key factor in America's success, and **69**% of white women agree. **72**% of black men and **57**% of white men also think this is true.

PARTY SYSTEM
Seniors citizens are enthusiastic about the importance of the two-party system and geographic isolation, prominent theories of an earlier era.

MALL MANIA
In 1964 there were 7,600 shopping centers with a total of $78 billion in sales. Today there are 43,000 malls with more than $1 trillion in sales annually.

USA.FYI
The United States is the leading exporter of wheat and corn and is second only to Thailand in exporting rice.

USA.FYI
The United States government's annual budget for 1999 was $1.7 trillion, compared to $68 billion in 1955.

> **Memories** that are shared by a majority of Americans are largely of recent events with little historical significance. An example of this would be the death of Princess Diana. These common memories, however, are central to America's cultural identity, and it is in cultural terms that Americans reflect on the various decades of the century.

Memory

Events specifically recalled by all Americans.

Since 1990

PRINCESS DIANA'S DEATH	**87**% *international event*
OKLAHOMA CITY BOMBING	**86** *national event*
BEGINNING OF GULF WAR	**75**

Before 1990

TIANANMEN SQUARE MASSACRE	**41**%
CHALLENGER EXPLOSION	**78**
REAGAN SHOT BY HINCKLEY	**67**
NIXON'S RESIGNATION	**53**
ARMSTRONG MOON WALK	**54**
MARTIN LUTHER KING ASSASSINATION	**43**
JOHN F. KENNEDY ASSASSINATION	**53**
KOREAN WAR	**15**

Before 1950

END OF WORLD WAR II	**21**%
FRANKLIN ROOSEVELT'S DEATH	**17**
ATTACK ON PEARL HARBOR	**18**
PARIS FALLING TO THE NAZIS	**7**
1929 STOCK MARKET CRASH	**4**

REMEMBERING
The power of the Pearl Harbor and JFK's death are striking given that Princess Diana's fatal car accident and the terrorist blast in Oklahoma City are events of this decade.

The lives and deaths of other American leaders remain vivid in the minds of most who are old enough to remember, though less compelling than the death of Kennedy.

The public remembers John Hinckley's attack on Ronald Reagan, Franklin Roosevelt's death, Richard Nixon's resignation, and the assassination of Martin Luther King.

Collective Memory

*What world events are most
memorable to Americans?*

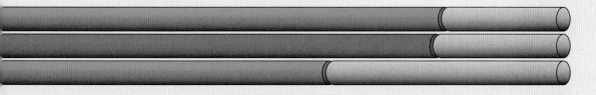

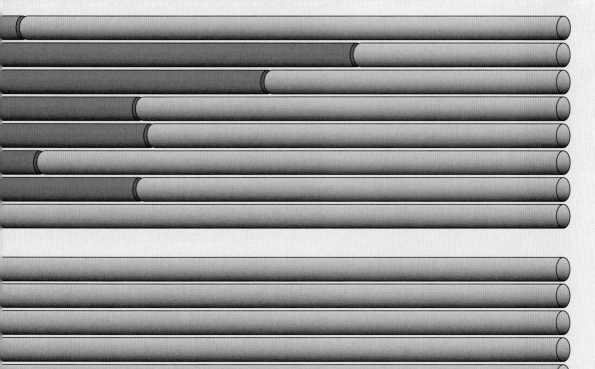

SPACE PROGRAM
Triumphs and tragedies
of the space program
are remembered with
equal strength. **80%**
remember where they
were in 1969 when
Armstrong walked on
the moon. **82%** of
the adults surveyed
remember what they
were doing when
they heard about the
Challenger explosion
in 1986.

SPIRIT OF ST. LOUIS
Charles Lindbergh
completes the first
non-stop transatlantic
flight from New York
to Paris in 1927.

USA.FYI
Mickey Mouse is
introduced in 1928
in the Walt Disney
animated film
Steamboat Willie.

USA.FYI
Americans are more
aware of national events
than world events,
and studies have
found that men follow
international news more
closely than women.

(Events and people that shaped the nation's history in the Twentieth Century, such as the stock market crash, the Great Depression, Franklin Roosevelt's death and World War II, are remembered personally by very few Americans today. The country is generally united in its recollections of more recent events.

Memory

Events specifically recalled by Americans old enough to remember.

Since 1990

PRINCESS DIANA'S DEATH	**87**% *international event*
OKLAHOMA CITY BOMBING	**86** *national event*
BEGINNING OF GULF WAR	**76**

Before 1990

TIANANMEN SQUARE MASSACRE	**42**%
FALL OF BERLIN WALL	**60**
CHALLENGER EXPLOSION	**82**
REAGAN SHOT BY HINCKLEY	**72**
NIXON'S RESIGNATION	**67**
ARMSTRONG MOON WALK	**80**
MARTIN LUTHER KING ASSASSINATION	**67**
JOHN F. KENNEDY ASSASSINATION	**90**
KOREAN WAR	**43**

Before 1950

END OF WORLD WAR II	**79**%
FRANKLIN ROOSEVELT'S DEATH	**71**
ATTACK ON PEARL HARBOR	**85**
PARIS FALLING TO THE NAZIS	**38**
1929 STOCK MARKET CRASH	**38**

AGE 18 TO 34
This generation can remember when they heard about the bombing in Oklahoma City (85%), the Challenger disaster (81%) and the Gulf War (74%). The attempt on the life of Ronald Reagan (61%) is remembered by only slightly more than those who recall the fall of the Berlin Wall (55%).

AGE 35 TO 54
Oklahoma City (88%) is remembered as clearly as the death of John F. Kennedy (86%), even though some in this age group were not born when Kennedy was shot. Many remember hearing about the Challenger explosion (86%) and the Moon Walk (80%). Most recall learning of Hinckley's attempt on Reagan's life (80%) and the Gulf War (75%).

AGE 55 TO 64
Almost everyone in this generation remembers exactly when they heard about the assassination of Kennedy (98%). Other events of the late 1960s and early 1970s are especially memorable for this generation, such as learning of Armstrong's historic Moon Walk (89%) and the death of Martin Luther King (82%). The Oklahoma City bombing (87%) and the Challenger disaster (83%) are also strong memories.

DEMOGRAPHIC GROUP RESULTS
How well different age groups remember specific

Age 18-34		Age 35-54		Age 55-64		Age 65	
Oklahoma City	85%	Oklahoma City	88%	JFK Assassination	98%	JFK Assassination	93%
Challenger Disaster	81%	JFK Assassination	86%	Moon Walk	89%	Pearl Harbor	91%
Gulf War	74%	Challenger Disaster	86%	Oklahoma City	87%	World War II Ends	89%
Reagan Shot	61%	Moon Walk	80%	Challenger Disaster	83%	Moon Walk	87%
Berlin Wall	55%	Gulf War	75%	MLK Assassination	82%	FDR Death	85%

AGE 65 AND OLDER
For senior citizens, memories of the past several decades pale in comparison to events from their younger years. Most seniors remember hearing of Kennedy's assassination (93%), the attack on Pearl Harbor (91%) and the end of World War II (89%). Equal numbers recall hearing about the Moon Walk (87%) and Franklin Roosevelt's death (85%).

USA.FYI
Theodore Roosevelt was the youngest president at the age of 42. Ronald Reagan was the oldest at 69.

Americans do well when it comes to placing major national events in chronological order. Typically, older Americans follow the news more closely and are generally more knowledgeable about politics and history than younger adults. Those who experience a particular event during their early adulthood are best able to put it in historical context.

History

How well Americans know world events.

World War II *or* **Korean War**

78% know that World War II came before the Korean War.

94% of the **World War** and the **Depression** generations can correctly identify the historical sequence of many major political and social events of the Twentieth Century.

Panama Canal *or* **Interstate Highways**

70% of the public's knowledge extends beyond American wars, scandals and politics.

83% of the **World War** and the **Depression** generations know that construction of the Panama Canal began before the Interstate Highway System.

Which came first?

| WORLD WAR II | **78**% *correct* |
| KOREAN WAR | **14** *incorrect* |

Which came first?

| PANAMA CANAL OPENS | **70**% |
| INTERSTATE HIGHWAY SYSTEM | **17** |

Which came first?

| NATO ESTABLISHED | **24**% |
| BERLIN WALL BUILT | **52** |

Which came first?

| BROWN V. BOARD OF EDUCATION | **72**% |
| ROE V. WADE | **10** |

Which came first?

| CUBAN MISSILE CRISIS | **63**% |
| NIXON VISIT TO CHINA | **17** |

Which came first?

| WATERGATE SCANDAL | **74**% |
| IRAN CONTRA SCANDAL | **13** |

This period is thought of as a time of optimism. The Model T is introduced, the Food and Drug Administration is established and **60%** of Americans are living in rural areas.

The Panama Canal is completed, the Sixteenth Amendment permits income tax . America, having vowed not to interfere in the domestic affairs of other nations, enters World War I.

Almost one-third of Americans see this period of time as swinging and carefree. Economic descriptions include references to both the boom and bust of these years.

The harsh economic conditions of the time painted a clear picture in the public's mind. The Great Depression and economy top all other references.

This decade is dominated by World War II, which is mentioned by over one-third of the public. Many refer to economic rebuilding, and coming out of the Depression.

Most think of rock and roll music, Elvis, cars, great fun and general prosperity. Those who actually lived during this era focused more on progress, peace and modernization.

DEMOGRAPHIC GROUP RESULTS

How well different age groups know their history

NATO *or*
Berlin Wall

This question stumped the public with only **24**% responding correctly.

37% of the **Silent Generation** was especially knowledgeable about the Cold War and can place the NATO alliance before the Berlin Wall. This group were young adults when one or both of these events occurred.

Brown v. Board of Education *or* **Roe v. Wade**

72% of the population knew the 1954 Brown v. Board of Education anti-segregation decision occurred before the 1973 Roe v. Wade ruling that legalized abortion.

80% of **Generation X** is especially clear on the political clashes over affirmative action and abortion rights.

Cuban Missile Crisis *or* **Nixon in China**

63% of Americans got this right.

74% of **Baby Boomers** remember the timing of President Richard Nixon's 1972 visit to China with clarity and correctly place it after the 1962 Cuban missile crisis.

Watergate *or* **Iran-Contra**

74% of Americans know this one.

80% of **Baby Boomers** know that Watergate, one of the defining events of their young adulthood, came before Iran-Contra. No other generation scored as well as this group.

Age 18 to 34 .... **69**%
Age 35 to 54 .... **76**%
Age 55 to 64 .... **90**%

Age 18 to 34 .... **59**%
Age 35 to 54 .... **70**%
Age 55 to 64 .... **79**%

Age 18 to 34 .... **22**%
Age 55 to 64 .... **37**%
Age 65 + ... **28**%

Age 35 to 54 .... **76**%
Age 55 to 64 .... **69**%
Age 65 + ... **49**%

Age 18 to 34 .... **49**%
Age 55 to 64 .... **72**%
Age 65 + ... **58**%

Age 18 to 34 .... **69**%
Age 55 to 64 .... **72**%
Age 65 + ... **70**%

Terms such as hippies, flower children, drugs, music and free love are used. Significant numbers also spoke of civil and political unrest and characterize this decade as a troubled and turbulent time.

The Vietnam War, Watergate, Nixon's resignation and legalized abortion are crowded out by references to disco, drugs, John Travolta and a sense of fun.

References include music and culture, materialism, greed and economics. Politics takes a back seat to cultural memories; only **2**% mention Ronald Reagan or Reaganomics.

High-tech, fast-paced, stress and progress top the list to describe this final decade. The Gulf War conflict was not cited. Young Elvis was named the most popular United States commemorative stamp.

USA.FYI
In 2019 space travel will enter a new era when NASA launches a manned mission to the planet Mars.

Silk quilt flag, circa 1910 from the collection of Kit Hinrichs

Nancye Green / Michael Donovan

Moore's Law
Where do we begin?

Information Technology
*What is 100100110011101000110100111110100101001
0110000011010100100100111001111?*

The Internet
What does it look like?

E-Commerce
How far and how fast? What's all the fuss?

Computer Crime
What should we fear?

Internet Users
Who's online? What are they doing?

Employment
Who's on the next shift?

Information Anxiety
How much is too much?

Information Overload
How do we feel about it?

MOORE'S LAW states that

the speed and performance of computer chips doubles every 18 to 24 months, thereby expanding computational power in exponential leaps. Computers are about one hundred million times more powerful than they were a half century ago, yet their prices are *decreasing*.

Two Hundred Million CPS (Laptop)

There are **one hundred thousand dots** shown here. Each dot alone represents **two hundred billion CPS,** of which five thousand (the speed of ENIAC) would be

one forty-millionth of a dot (not visible to the naked eye)!

20,000,000,0

THE COMPUTING POWER OF THE HUMAN BF

1946
ENIAC:
Five Thousand CPS

This computer conducted mathematical calculations and occupied 1,000 square feet—approximately the size of one quarter of a basketball court. **Memory (in RAM) possessed by ENIAC: 0 MB.**[*]

[*] Although ENIAC possessed rudimentary storage capacity in its 20 "accumulators," it had no RAM.

UNLESS OTHERWISE NOTED, SOURCES FOR THIS PAGE ARE: KURZWEIL, RAY, *THE AGE OF SPIRITUAL MACHINES*, 1999; PORT, KURTIS, "MACHINES WILL BE SMARTER TH

Glossary

CPS
abbreviation for calculations per second

ENIAC
abbreviation for Electrical Numerical Integrator and Computer

MB
abbreviation for megabyte

MEGABYTE
a unit of computer memory or disk storage space

RAM
abbreviation for Random Access Memory

RANDOM ACCESS MEMORY
the primary working memory in a computer, used for the temporary storage of programs and data, in which data can be accessed directly and modified

Encarta World English Dictionary, St. Martin's Press, 1999.

Merriam Webster's Collegiate Dictionary, Tenth Edition, Merriam-Webster, Inc., 1997.

"If the automobile industry had made as much progress [as the computer industry] in the past fifty years, a car today would cost a hundredth of a cent and go faster than the speed of light."

KURZWEIL, RAY, *THE AGE OF SPIRITUAL MACHINES*, 1999.

1998
LAPTOP:
Two Hundred Million CPS

A Pentium® II Processor ran a typical laptop in 1998. It was approximately the size of a dime. **Memory (in RAM) possessed by a typical laptop: approximately 60 MB.**

00,000,000 CPS

= 20 MILLION BILLION CALCULATIONS PER SECOND

4.5"

5.75"   13"

2020
MASSIVELY PARALLEL NEURAL NET COMPUTER:
Twenty Million Billion CPS

By the year 2020, experts predict that the density of computer circuits will have increased such that the raw processing power of a human brain will fit into a shoebox. **Memory (in RAM) possessed by the brain: approximately 1 million billion MB.**

However, even Gordon Moore, author of Moore's Law, believes that the development trend **cannot be sustained and will reach "finite limits" in "several years."**
WWW.CNET.NEWS.COM.

RE," *BUSINESS WEEK*, AUG. 30, 1999; WWW.LIBRARY.UPENN.EDU; AND WWW.INTEL.COM/INTEL/MUSEUM/25ANNIV.

Facts

Your personal computer will be able to simulate the brain power of the entire U.S. population by 2048.

Ray Kurzweil, *The Age of Spiritual Machines*, 1999. Page 105

An average electronic toothbrush has 3,000 lines of computer code.

Hafner, Katie, "Honey, I Programmed the Blanket," *The New York Times*, May 27, 1999.

Note

Because technology evolves so quickly, our attempts to understand it are constantly challenged. Data and analyses, studies and even predictions, are often eclipsed before they reach publication. Therefore, our explanation of information technology is not a snapshot of a specific moment, but rather a perspective of what has happened and a glimpse of what might await.

IT (INFORMATION TECHNOLOGY)

is a te
use of computer, electronics, and telecommunication
distributing information in digital form. This distribu
networking of industries to individualized services, in

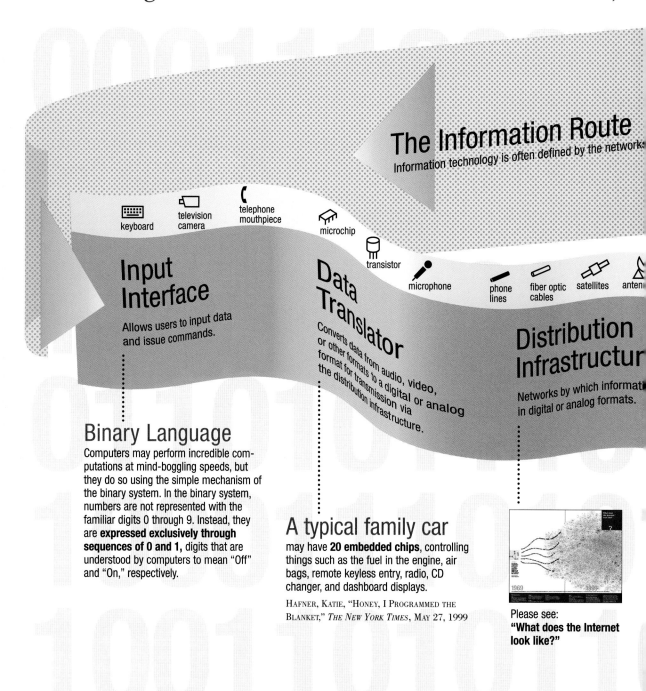

The Information Route
Information technology is often defined by the network

keyboard
television camera
telephone mouthpiece
microchip
transistor
microphone
phone lines
fiber optic cables
satellites
anten

Input Interface
Allows users to input data and issue commands.

Data Translator
Converts data from audio, video, or other formats to a digital or analog format for transmission via the distribution infrastructure.

Distribution Infrastructur
Networks by which informati in digital or analog formats.

Binary Language
Computers may perform incredible computations at mind-boggling speeds, but they do so using the simple mechanism of the binary system. In the binary system, numbers are not represented with the familiar digits 0 through 9. Instead, they are **expressed exclusively through sequences of 0 and 1,** digits that are understood by computers to mean "Off" and "On," respectively.

A typical family car
may have **20 embedded chips,** controlling things such as the fuel in the engine, air bags, remote keyless entry, radio, CD changer, and dashboard displays.

HAFNER, KATIE, "HONEY, I PROGRAMMED THE BLANKET," *THE NEW YORK TIMES,* MAY 27, 1999

Please see:
"What does the Internet look like?"

Glossary

ANALOG
relating to a system or device that represents data variation by a measurable physical quality

DIGITAL
representing a varying physical quantity by means of signals that are interpreted as numbers (usually in the binary system)

FIBER OPTICS
the technology of transmitting information through thin, flexible, glass or plastic tubes (optical fibers) using modulated light waves

MICROCHIP
a tiny complex of electronic components and their connections that is contained in or on a small, flat piece of material (usually silicon)

MICROPROCESSOR
the central processing unit, consisting of an integrated circuit and a single chip, that performs the basic operations in a microcomputer

ROUTER
a computer-switching program that transfers incoming messages to outgoing pathways via the most efficient route possible

n that is broadly applied to the quipment for processing and n ranges from worldwide iding cable TV and e-mail.

tems and hardware through which it operates.

Tom Starnes, an analyst at Dataquest, notes that 4.8 billion embedded processors were sold in 1998, and only 2.5% were intended for use in personal computers.

HAFNER, KATIE, "HONEY, I PROGRAMMED THE BLANKET," *THE NEW YORK TIMES*, MAY 27, 1999

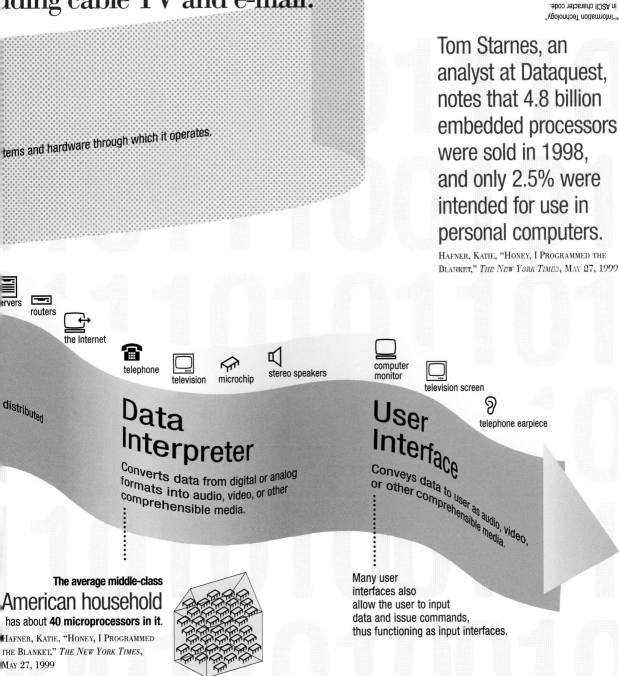

ervers

routers

the Internet

telephone

television

microchip

stereo speakers

computer monitor

television screen

distributed

telephone earpiece

Data Interpreter

Converts data from digital or analog formats into audio, video, or other comprehensible media.

User Interface

Conveys data to user as audio, video, or other comprehensible media.

The average middle-class
American household
has about **40 microprocessors in it**.

HAFNER, KATIE, "HONEY, I PROGRAMMED THE BLANKET," *THE NEW YORK TIMES*, MAY 27, 1999

Many user interfaces also allow the user to input data and issue commands, thus functioning as input interfaces.

SERVER
the computer in a network that stores application programs and data files that are accessed by other computers in the network

TRANSISTOR
a small electronic device that is used to control the flow of electricity in electronic devices and is frequently incorporated into microchips

Encarta World English Dictionary, St. Martin's Press, 1999.

Merriam Webster's Collegiate Dictionary, Tenth Edition, Merriam-Webster, Inc., 1997.

Note

While "free" thought and an informed populace are the underpinnings of democracy, information itself is a valued commodity—as much so as a patented invention or copyrighted performance. Ironically, our own attempts to illustrate the value of IT were complicated by the fact that information *about information* can be proprietary and therefore costly.

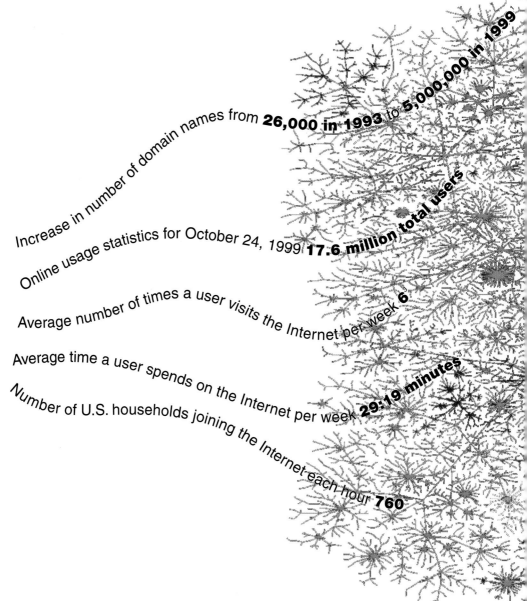

Increase in number of domain names from **26,000 in 1993** to **5,000,000 in 1999**[1]

Online usage statistics for October 24, 1999 **17.6 million total users**[2]

Average number of times a user visits the Internet per week **6**[3]

Average time a user spends on the Internet per week **29:19 minutes**[3]

Number of U.S. households joining the Internet each hour **760**[4]

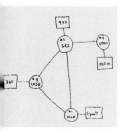

ARPANET

The world's first computer network, created by linking four computers across California and Utah. This original, four-node ARPANET evolved into our modern-day, billion-site Internet.

COMPUTER MUSEUM HISTORY CENTER, 1999

1969

1. U.S. DEPARTMENT OF COMMERCE/NETCRAFT 2. HOT OFF THE NET (NIELSEN/NETRATINGS) ©1999 NETRATINGS, INC. 3. HOT OFF THE NET (NIELSEN/NETRATINGS FOR

Glossary

ARPA
abbreviation for the Advanced Research Projects Agency, a group established by the Department of Defense in 1957 in order to promote science and technology during the Cold War

DOMAIN
The sequence of words, phrases, abbreviations, or characters that identifies a specific computer or network on the Internet and serves as its address

INTERNET
a network that links computer systems all over the world by satellite and telephone, connecting users with service networks such as e-mail and the World Wide Web

NETWORK
a system of two or more computers, terminals, or communications devices linked by wires, cables, or a telecommunications system in order to exchange information

ONLINE
attached to or available through a central computer or computer network

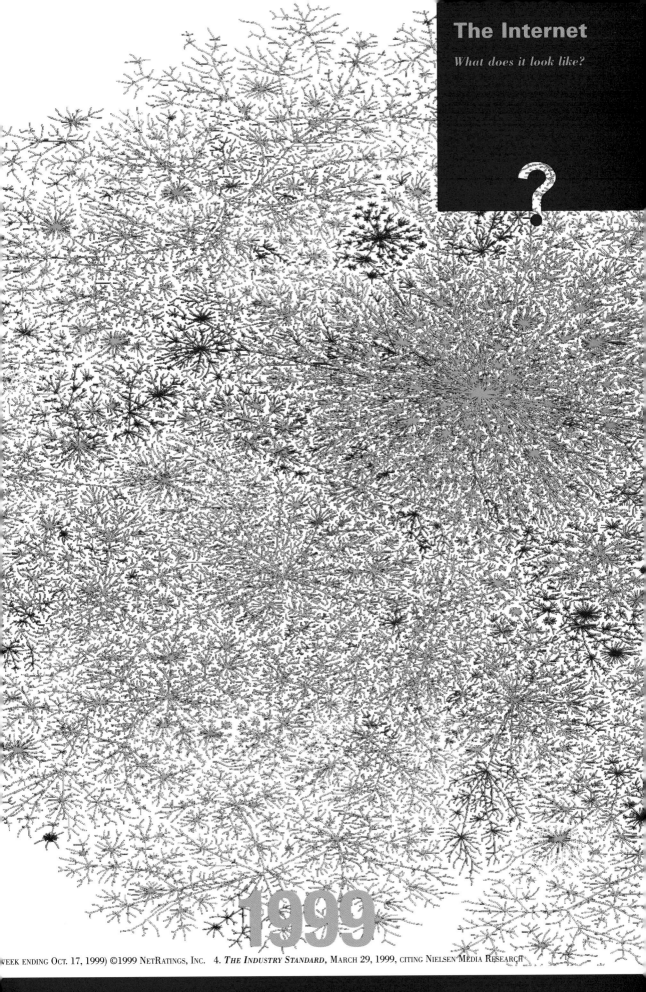

The Internet

What does it look like?

?

1999

URL
abbreviation for Uniform Resource Leader; an address identifying the location of a file on the Internet

WORLD WIDE WEB
a large set of linked documents and other files, located on computers connected through the Internet, that is used to access, manipulate, and download data and programs

Encarta World English Dictionary, St. Martin's Press, 1999.

Information:

About the Internet map (above)
This image shows the potential path of an e-mail message originating in the United States and traveling through each of the world's 95,800 registered networks. The lines branch at each network or switch along the way.

It was made by recording the shortest path taken by test messages sent on May 3, 1999, from a computer in Murray Hill, New Jersey, to each of the 95,800 registered networks, and then graphed using special software to plot each route.

From browsing online...

5,187.1 miles ...

Richardson-Dallas	**16.5 miles**
Dallas-Washington, D.C.	**1548.6 miles**
Washington, D.C.-New York	**233.9 miles**
New York-New Jersey	**24.8 miles**
New Jersey-Tennessee	**893.8 miles**
Tennessee-New York	**904.1 miles**
New York-Dallas	**1548.6 miles**
Dallas-Richardson	**16.5 miles**
TOTAL	**5187.1 miles**

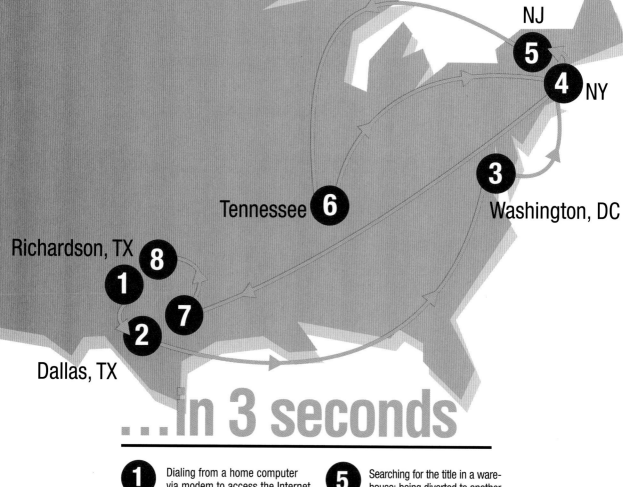

NJ

5

4 NY

3 Washington, DC

Tennessee **6**

Richardson, TX **8**

1

7

2

Dallas, TX

...in 3 seconds

1 Dialing from a home computer via modem to access the Internet

2 Connecting with the ISP and navigating to a Website featuring an online bookstore; selecting a book

3 Channeling through the network hub in Washington, D.C.

4 To New York City, where the Website is hosted

5 Searching for the title in a warehouse; being diverted to another city for additional searching

6 Finding the book; being returned to the Website in New York City

7 Relaying information through the ISP again

8 Displaying results on the home computer

...to buying online

During 1998, sales of books online rose 300% to an estimated

$650 million

from $150 million in 1997.

"*Book Industry Trends 1999: Covering the Years 1993–2003,*" The Statistical Service Center, 1999.

E-Commerce
How far and how fast?

?

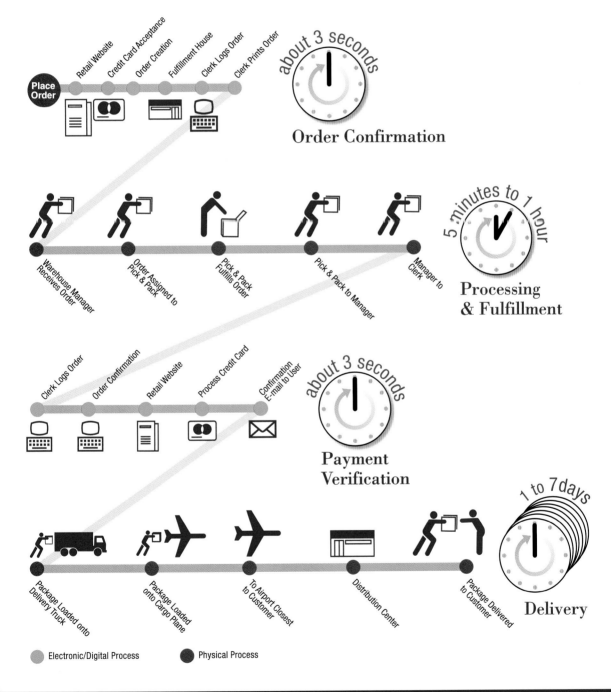

Place Order → Retail Website → Credit Card Acceptance → Order Creation → Fulfillment House → Clerk Logs Order → Clerk Prints Order

about 3 seconds
Order Confirmation

Warehouse Manager Receives Order → Order Assigned to Pick & Pack → Pick & Pack Fulfills Order → Pick & Pack to Manager → Manager to Clerk

5 minutes to 1 hour
Processing & Fulfillment

Clerk Logs Order → Order Confirmation → Retail Website → Process Credit Card → Confirmation E-mail to User

about 3 seconds
Payment Verification

Package Loaded onto Delivery Truck → Package Loaded onto Cargo Plane → To Airport Closest to Customer → Distribution Center → Package Delivered to Customer

1 to 7 days
Delivery

- Electronic/Digital Process
- Physical Process

WEBSITE
a group of related Web pages

WEB PAGE
a computer file written in HTML that contains text, graphics files, and sound files and is accessible via the World Wide Web

Encarta World English Dictionary St. Martin's Press, 1999.

- **Government Electronic Commerce Policy. U.S.**
www.ecommerce.gov/
Designed to introduce and explain the wide variety of policy initiatives in place to foster the spread of electronic commerce.

- **Understanding the Digital Economy.**
www.digitaleconomy.gov/
Based on a conference held by the U.S. Department of Commerce, the site reviews recent research on implications of the digital economy and examines the agenda for future research needs.

IMPACT OF E-COMMERCE BY INDUSTRY, 2000–2005
Estimates of online shares.

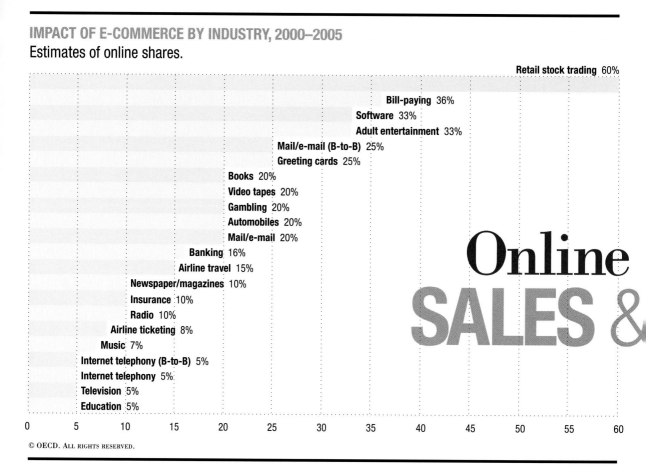

Retail stock trading 60%
Bill-paying 36%
Software 33%
Adult entertainment 33%
Mail/e-mail (B-to-B) 25%
Greeting cards 25%
Books 20%
Video tapes 20%
Gambling 20%
Automobiles 20%
Mail/e-mail 20%
Banking 16%
Airline travel 15%
Newspaper/magazines 10%
Insurance 10%
Radio 10%
Airline ticketing 8%
Music 7%
Internet telephony (B-to-B) 5%
Internet telephony 5%
Television 5%
Education 5%

Online SALES &

0   5   10   15   20   25   30   35   40   45   50   55   60

The market value for the Forbes 500 increased by 27% from 1997 to 1998. The typical company rose by 10% in value, though Internet companies such as Dell Computer and Amazon.com enjoyed much greater wealth creation, with increases of 164.1% and 1,030%, respectively.

FORBES, "MARKET VALUE," APRIL 19, 1999

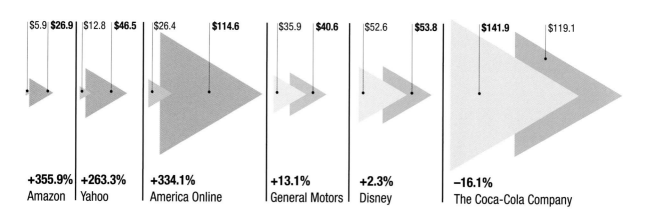

$5.9 $26.9 $12.8 $46.5 $26.4 $114.6 $35.9 $40.6 $52.6 $53.8 $141.9 $119.1

+355.9% +263.3%   +334.1%   +13.1%   +2.3%   −16.1%
Amazon | Yahoo   America Online   General Motors | Disney   The Coca-Cola Company

MARKET VALUE: E-COMPANIES COMPARED TO TRADITIONAL COMPANIES
$ Billions, from Sept. 1998 to Sept. 1999

STANDARD AND POOR'S COMPUSTAT, 1999

Glossary

E-COMMERCE
abbreviation for electronic commerce

ELECTRONIC COMMERCE
business transactions that take place via the Internet

INTERNET
a network that links computer systems all over the world by satellite and telephone, connecting users with service networks such as e-mail and the World Wide Web

BENCHMARK
a standard against which something can be measured or assessed

B-TO-B
abbreviation for business-to-business

BUSINESS-TO-BUSINESS
describing communications, transactions, or other interactions between businesses

ONLINE
attached to or available through a central computer or computer network

E-commerce is transforming American business—both the way we do it and the means we use to measure it. The bulls and bears of the market now depend on the mouse.

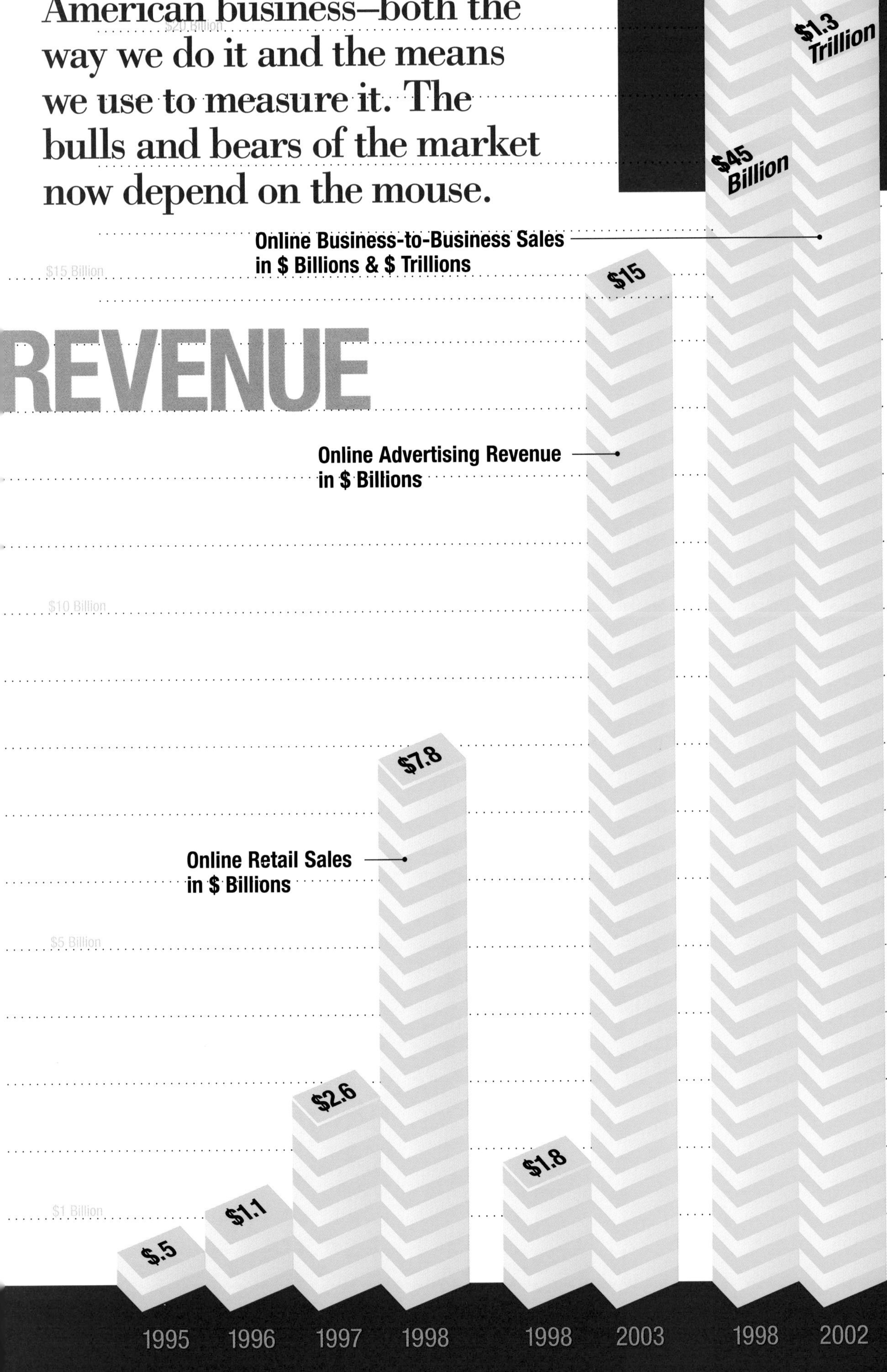

E-Commerce
What's all the fuss?

$1.3 Trillion

$45 Billion

Online Business-to-Business Sales in $ Billions & $ Trillions

REVENUE

$15

Online Advertising Revenue in $ Billions

$7.8

Online Retail Sales in $ Billions

$2.6

$1.8

$1.1

$.5

$20 Billion

$15 Billion

$10 Billion

$5 Billion

$1 Billion

| 1995 | 1996 | 1997 | 1998 | 1998 | 2003 | 1998 | 2002 |

THE EMERGING DIGITAL ECONOMY II (6/22/99), U.S. DEPARTMENT OF COMMERCE

TELEPHONY
the science, technology, or system of communication by telephone

WEB MEDIA PROPERTY
a company that specializes in the development, formatting, and publishing of online information

GENERAL SOURCE: ENCARTA WORLD ENGLISH DICTIONARY, ST. MARTIN'S PRESS, 1999

SPECIFIC SOURCE: INVESTOR RELATIONS, JUNE 1998

During the Gulf War, Dutch hackers **stole information about U.S. troop movements** from U.S. Defense Department computers and tried to sell it to the Iraqis, who thought it was a hoax and turned it down.

WWW.CNN.COM/TECH/SPECIALS/HACKERS

Hacker Kevin Mitnick is allegedly responsible for intruding into the networks of Sun Microsystems, Motorola, Fujitsu, Novell, Colorado Supernet, Netcom, Nokia, and the Well.

Kevin also reputedly stole proprietary source codes for operating systems or cellular phones from half a dozen companies. Included in his escapades was **the pilfering of the Netcom customer credit card database, which contained information about almost 20,000 card accounts.**

WWW.AVIARY-MAG.COM

The Federal Trade Commission won a federal injunction against an international porn ring that cloned 25 million Web pages and "hijacked" unsuspecting visitors to its smut sites. In another incident, a gang calling itself gH, or Global Hell, **defaced the White House Website with a picture of flowered panties.**

WWW.ZDNET.CO.UK/NEWS/1999/NEWS

MOTIVES

There are no "typical" computer-related crimes and no "typical" motives for committing such crimes, but common motives include:

THE AMERICAN CRIMINAL LAW REVIEW, SUMMER 1999.

EXHIBITING TECHNICAL EXPERTISE

HIGHLIGHTING WEAKNESSE

PUNISHMENT O

ASSERTING A BELIEF IN OPE

DIVERSITY OF THE CRIME: DOLLAR AMOUNT OF ANNUAL LOSSES BY TYPE

This chart shows the relative costs of these computer crimes. It is based on a representative survey of over 520 U.S. corporations, government agencies, financial institutions, and universities, of which 163 could quantify their losses for 1999.

$50 million
$40 million
$30 million
$20 million
$10 million

Insider access · Theft of proprietary information · Telecom fraud · Financial fraud · Virus · Laptop theft · Insider net abuse · Denial of service · Sabotage · System penetration · Telecom eavesdropping · Active wiretapping

Glossary

BIOMETRICS
a system that automatically recognizes a person by identifying distinguishing traits
www.biometrics.org/html/introduction.html

DENIAL OF SERVICE
illegal use of computer-related technology that prevents another individual from accessing financial, telecommunications, other services

ENCRYPTION
the use of a key to convert computer data or messages into something incomprehensible, such that it can only be reconverted by an authorized recipient holding a matching key

FIREWALLS
a piece of computer software intended to prevent unauthorized access to system software or data

HACK
to use computer expertise to gain entry and explore the computer system of another for the purpose of understanding how it works or stealing data

HACKER
a person who uses computers to gain restricted information secretly and illicitly by circumventing the established security protocols

Using his personal computer and modem, a juvenile hacked into the NYNEX (now Bell Atlantic) telephone system that serviced the Worcester, Massachusetts, area. The hacker shut down telephone service to 600 customers in the local community.

The resulting disruption **affected all local police and fire 911 services, as well as the ability of incoming aircraft to activate the runway lights** at the Worcester airport. Telephone service was out at the airport tower for six hours.
NIPC CYBER THREAT ASSESSMENT, OCT 1999.

Computer Crime

What should we fear?

?

SABOTAGE

COMPUTER VOYEURISM

N COMPUTER SECURITY SYSTEMS

ETALIATION

CCESS TO COMPUTER SYSTEMS

There are approximately

100,000

hackers worldwide.

WHO ARE THE HACKERS?

Potential professional hackers for hire (corporate spies) **9.9%**

World-class cybercriminals **.1%**

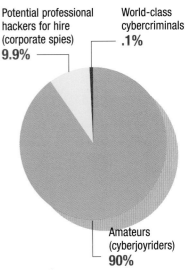

Amateurs (cyberjoyriders) **90%**

IBM GLOBAL SECURITY ANALYSIS LAB, YORKTOWN HEIGHTS, NY

THE GROWING INTRUSION-DETECTION MARKET

The market for intrusion-detection products is growing. According to International Data Corp., the market has **grown from about $20 million in 1997 to about $100 million in 1999 and is projected to hit $528 million by 2005.**

$600 million

$300 million

1997   1999   2005

"GETTING THE DROP ON NETWORK INTRUDERS," WWW.CNN.COM, OCT. 11, 1999.

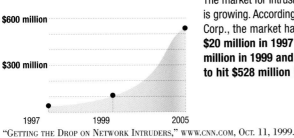

Americans are getting in line to get online —at home and at work, with friends and from school, when shopping and while watching TV.

By gender, online Americans are . . .	
Men	**52%**
Women	**48%**
	1

By age, online Americans are . . .	
Under 30	**30%**
30–49	**50%**
50–64	**15%**
65+	**4%**
	2

American college freshmen who use the Internet to do research or homework	**83%**
American college freshmen who e-mail	**66%**
	3

There are **7** new **people** on the **Internet** every **second.** 4

Although fewer **seniors** than young adults are currently online, it is the seniors who are spending more time online. Users 55 and older **spend more time online** than their younger 18–24-year-old counterparts.5

36% of American college students have **created their own Websites** or home pages.6

Glossary

CHAT ROOM
a facility in a computer network (such as the Internet) in which participants exchange comments or information in real time

E-MAIL
a communication system for transmitting data from one computer to another, using a telephone connection and modems; a message sent via this system

HOME PAGE
the opening page on a Website; also, somebody's personal Website

HYPERTEXT MARKUP LANGUAGE
the notations used to indicate formatting and programming instructions for the World Wide Web

HTML
an abbreviation for HyperText Markup Language

In fact, the Internet reached as many Americans in its first six years as the telephone did in its first four decades.[7]

36% of online users say they go online for news at least once a week. The favorite news topics include . . .

Weather	**64%**	International	**47%**
Technology	**59%**	Health	**46%**
Entertainment	**58%**	Science	**43%**
Business	**58%**	Politics	**43%**
Sports	**47%**	Local News	**42%**

8

Percent of America's racial groups online:

White, Non-Hispanic	**38%**
Black, Non-Hispanic	**19%**
Native American Indian/Eskimo	**30%**
Asian Pacific Islander	**36%**
Hispanic	**17%**

9

49% of online users believe that **Internet news** is actually **more accurate** than traditional news sources.[10]

A **child** in a low-income **white** family is **3 times** as likely to have Internet access as a child in a comparable **black** family.[11]

INTERNET
a network that links computer systems all over the world by satellite and telephone, connecting users with service networks such as e-mail and the World Wide Web

ISP
abbreviation for Internet Service Provider

INTERNET SERVICE PROVIDER
a business that provides access to the Internet, usually for a monthly fee

ONLINE
attached to or available through a central computer or computer network

REAL TIME
the ability of certain computer systems to process, update, and respond to data as soon as it is received

SURF
to go on the Internet or watch television for recreation, frequently changing the site or channel

Of American Internet users, the percent who go online . . .

Percent of all Americans who . . .

. . . own a computer

36% 1995
43% 1998

. . . use the Internet

14% 1995
41% 1998

. . . use e-mail [13]

10% 1995
35% 1998

Number of American kids ages 2 to 12 online

20 million
15 million
10 million
5 million

1997   2002

14

American single-parent households with Internet access **15%**

American dual-parent households with Internet access **39%**

15

Favorite online activities of kids, ages 7-14	Boys	Girls	Total
Gather information	66%	69%	67%
Play games	44%	56%	49%
Creative activities	49%	57%	48%
Download stuff	54%	38%	46%

16

23% of American **parents** worry what their kids might see on the **Internet**. **35%** of American parents worry what their kids might see on **TV**.[17]

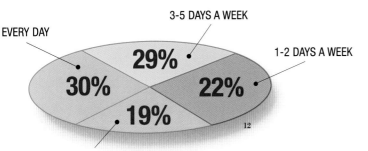

EVERY DAY
3-5 DAYS A WEEK
1-2 DAYS A WEEK

29%
30%
22%
19%

LESS OFTEN / DON'T KNOW

12

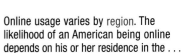

E-mail is being used for:	1995	1998
Work	31%	12%
Personal	30%	41%
Both	38%	47%

18

By education level, online Americans are . . .	
College graduates	39%
Have some college	31%
High school graduate	25%
Less than high school	4%

19

Online usage varies by region. The likelihood of an American being online depends on his or her residence in the . . .

West	36%
Midwest	35%
Northeast	33%
South	30%

20

Employees are using their Internet access to surf for **sports news, stock trading, job hunting.**[21]

40% of the users who went online during 1998 **never attended college—** twice the number from the previous year.[22]

However, **urban** households in all parts of the country have **higher usage** rates than **rural** households of similar income, education, and racial identification.[23]

1, 2, 8, 10, 12, 13, 17, 18, 19, 22. The Pew Research Center for the People and the Press, Jan. 1999.

3. *The New York Times*, Jan. 25, 1999.

4. www.internetindicators.com/facts.html

5. American Demographics, website 6/98.

6. www.channelseven.com/adinsight/market-insight/archive/1998/199809

7. W. Michael Cox, Federal Reserve Bank of

SHIFTING FROM...

FARMING/FISHING/FORESTRY

The farming, fishing, and forestry industries employed 28% of the entire American workforce in 1913. By 2005, they will employ only 2.5%.

30%   **1913**

20%

10%   **2005**

BUREAU OF LABOR STATISTICS

8,000,000 workers—one in sixteen working Americans—became displaced during the period of January 1995 to December 1997. **A little less than half (3,600,000) were long-tenured workers** who had been with their employers for three or more years.

BUREAU OF LABOR STATISTICS, 1998

U.S. UNION MEMBERSHIP AS PERCENTAGE OF LABOR FORCE

18.8%   20%

13.9%

10%

1984   1998   0%

John Sweeney, president of the A.F.L.-C.I.O. (American Federation of Labor and Congress of Industrial Organizations), notes that the fastest-growing industries—such as finance, child-care, retail trade, and airlines—added 26 million new jobs to the economy from 1984 through 1997, but produced very few new union members.

The A.F.L.-C.I.O. cites that only 1 out of every 20 of those new workers joined a union.

The New York Times, Oct. 13, 1999

OCCUPATIONS WITH THE GREATEST DECLINE

Projected percentage of decrease from 1996 ○ to 2006 ●

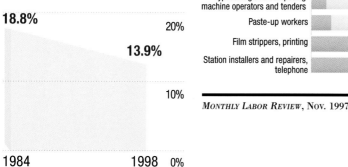

Typesetting and composing machine operators and tenders	-75%
Paste-up workers	-75%
Film strippers, printing	-75%
Station installers and repairers, telephone	-74%

10,000   20,000   30,000   40,000

MONTHLY LABOR REVIEW, NOV. 1997

MEAN ANNUAL WAGES BY OCCUPATION 1997

Musicians $36,190

Kindergarten Teachers $34,150

Registered Nurses $41,400

BUREAU OF LABOR STATISTICS

Glossary

CHIEF INFORMATION OFFICER (CIO)
the highest-ranking IT professional within a company or corporation, responsible for the overall management of all technology-related decisions

DATABASE
a systematically arranged collection of computer data, structured so that it can be automatically retrieved or manipulated

DATABASE ADMINISTRATOR
person responsible for maintaining the structure and integrity of a database by coordinating changes, upgrades, maintenance, and testing[1]

DISPLACED WORKERS
people who have lost or left their jobs because their employers closed or moved, lacked sufficient work, or abolished their position or shift[2]

IT PROFESSIONAL
a person who designs, produces, or utilizes information technology

SHIFTING TO...

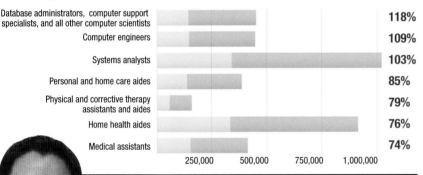

"**By 2006,** **50%** of all American workers will be employed in IT positions or within industries that intensively utilize information technology, products, and services."

U.S. DEPARTMENT OF COMMERCE, "THE EMERGING DIGITAL ECONOMY II," JUNE 1999

FASTEST-GROWING OCCUPATIONS

Projected percentage of increase from 1996 ● to 2006 ●. Of the seven fastest-growing occupations, three are "high-tech" and four are "hands-on".

Database administrators, computer support specialists, and all other computer scientists	118%
Computer engineers	109%
Systems analysts	103%
Personal and home care aides	85%
Physical and corrective therapy assistants and aides	79%
Home health aides	76%
Medical assistants	74%

250,000   500,000   750,000   1,000,000

MONTHLY LABOR REVIEW, NOV. 1997

Computer Systems Managers $68,600

Systems Analysts $51,400

Computer Support Specialists $39,000

U.S. DEPARTMENT OF COMMERCE,
"THE EMERGING DIGITAL ECONOMY II,"
JUNE 1999

AVERAGE SALARIES

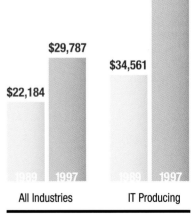

	All Industries	IT Producing
1989	$22,184	$34,561
1997	$29,787	$52,920

U.S. DEPARTMENT OF COMMERCE, "THE EMERGING DIGITAL ECONOMY II," JUNE 1999

IT PRODUCING
devoted to the design and/or creation of information technology

SYSTEM ANALYST
person who determines which functions and requirements are necessary for new or existing information systems or technology to perform specific tasks[1]

SYSTEM ARCHITECT
person responsible for conceptualizing and designing the ways in which computer hardware, software, and peripherals interact in order to perform necessary functions

WEBMASTER
somebody who creates, organizes, or updates the information content of a Website

General Source:
Encarta World English Dictionary, St. Martin's Press, 1999

Specific Source:
[1]Bureau of Labor Statistics
[2]Bureau of Labor Statistics

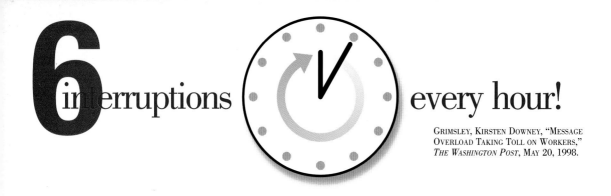

6 interruptions every hour!

GRIMSLEY, KIRSTEN DOWNEY, "MESSAGE OVERLOAD TAKING TOLL ON WORKERS," THE WASHINGTON POST, MAY 20, 1998.

AVERAGE NUMBER OF MESSAGES RECEIVED IN A DAY BY THE TYPICAL U.S. OFFICE WORKER:

Phone Calls	52
E-mail	36
Voice Mail	23
Postal Mail	18
Inter-office	18
Fax	14
Post-it™	13
Pager	8
Cell Phone	4
Express Mail™	3

INCREASE IN THE NUMBER OF DAILY ADVERTISING MESSAGES, 1971 TO 1991

Americans were exposed to **six times more advertising messages** by the end of this 20-year period.

3,000

1991

2,000

1,000

1971

SHENK, DAVID, "WHY YOU FEEL THE WAY YOU DO," INC. BOSTON, JAN. 1999.

Glossary

DIGITAL
processing, operating on, storing, transmitting, representing, or displaying data in the form of numerical digits, as in a digital computer

EXPRESS MAIL™
a trademark for the overnight delivery service of the United States Postal Service

INFORMATION AGE
a common name for the current period of human history, characterized by the widespread use of electronics to access information, particularly with respect to computers and the Internet

PAGER
a small electronic message-receiving device, often with a small screen, that beeps, flashes, or vibrates to let the user know that somebody is trying to contact him or her

Encarta World English Dictionary, St. Martin's Press, 1999.

STRESS

Stress is a common phenomenon in our Information Age. It contributes to cardiovascular disease, depression, and gastro-intestinal disorders. The National Mental Health Association reports that **75% to 90% of all visits to physicians are stress-related**.
NMHA, 1997.

Job stress is estimated to cost U.S. industry

$200 billion to $300 billion annually in absenteeism,
diminished productivity, employee turnover, accidents, worker's compensation, and direct medical, legal, and insurance fees.
FISCHER, AARON, "IS YOUR CAREER KILLING YOU?" *DATA COMMUNICATIONS*, FEB. 1998.

Information Anxiety
How much is too much?

?

" **information overload has replaced information scarcity as an important new emotional, social, and political problem.**"
SHENK, DAVID, "WHY YOU FEEL THE WAY YOU DO," *INC. BOSTON*, JAN. 1999.

A.D.D.

The defining characteristics of Attention Deficit Disorder **(inattention, inability to concentrate, hyperactive or impulsive behavior)** are increasingly prevalent in our society. Although some researchers believe that A.D.D. has a purely biochemical basis, others—such as Dr. Theodore Gross—believe that A.D.D. can be influenced by environmental factors such as our

current "information explosion."

"WHY YOU FEEL THE WAY YOU DO"

CELL PHONES AND ACCIDENTS

There are approximately **170,000,000** automobile drivers in the U.S. and **80 million** cell phones—a sometimes dangerous combination. In North Carolina, for example, the number of cellular phone-related crashes has been projected to double in a five-year period.

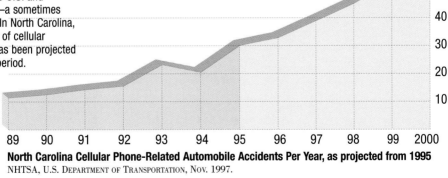

North Carolina Cellular Phone-Related Automobile Accidents Per Year, as projected from 1995
NHTSA, U.S. DEPARTMENT OF TRANSPORTATION, NOV. 1997.

AMERICANS WHO SAY THESE TECHNOLOGICAL INNOVATIONS AND INFORMATION TECHNOLOGY DEVICES HAVE MADE LIFE . . .

	Better	Worse	No Difference
Radio	96%	1%	3%
Computer	87%	8%	5%
E-Mail	71%	9%	20%
Internet	69%	18%	12%
Cell Phone	66%	22%	12%
Cable TV	62%	21%	17%

THE INSTITUTE FOR THE FUTURE WITH THE GALLUP ORGANIZATION FOR PITNEY BOWES, INC.

CHANGES IN HOURS PER PERSON PER YEAR USING CONSUMER MEDIA

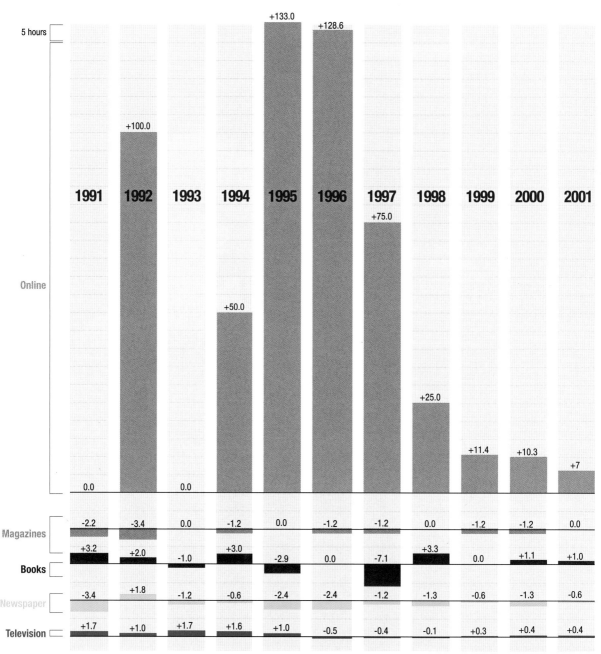

5 hours

Online

	1991	1992	1993	1994	1995	1996	1997	1998	1999	2000	2001
Online	0.0	+100.0	0.0	+50.0	+133.0	+128.6	+75.0	+25.0	+11.4	+10.3	+7
Magazines	-2.2	-3.4	0.0	-1.2	0.0	-1.2	-1.2	0.0	-1.2	-1.2	0.0
Books	+3.2	+2.0	-1.0	+3.0	-2.9	0.0	-7.1	+3.3	0.0	+1.1	+1.0
Newspaper	-3.4	+1.8	-1.2	-0.6	-2.4	-2.4	-1.2	-1.3	-0.6	-1.3	-0.6
Television	+1.7	+1.0	+1.7	+1.6	+1.0	-0.5	-0.4	-0.1	+0.3	+0.4	+0.4

U.S. CENSUS BUREAU, THE OFFICIAL STATISTICS™ STATISTICAL ABSTRACT OF THE UNITED STATES: 1998 SEP. 25, 1998

Glossary

CELL PHONE
wireless telephone that operates via
cellular technology

CELLULAR
in telecommunications, refers to the
arrangement of radio communications

into small areas, or cells, each utilizing
a separate transmitter

E-MAIL
a communication system for transmitting
data from one computer to another,
using a telephone connection and
modems; a message sent via this system

PC
abbreviation for personal computer

PERSONAL COMPUTER
a computer with its own operating
system and a wide selection of software,
used by an individual

Encarta World English Dictionary, St. Martin's Press, 1999.

41% of Americans believe our greatest achievements of the 20th century have been in science and technology, followed by medical advances.

THE PEW RESEARCH CENTER,
"TECHNOLOGY TRIUMPHS, MORALITY FALTERS" 1999

Information Overload

How do we feel about it?

?

AS OF JULY 1999, HOME PC USE HAS SURPASSED

1,000,000,000 HOURS

PER WEEK, AND 53% OF THAT TIME IS BEING SPENT ONLINE.

INTERNET.COM'S CYBER ATLAS, CYBERATLAS.INTERNET.COM/BIG-PICTURE/TRAFFIC-PATTERNS/0,1323,5931,00.HTML

Online time is significant and growing...

PERCENT OF TIME PER WEEK SPENT ON VARIOUS MEDIA, 1998.

Online time in 2003 24%
10.2 hrs

Online 17%
7.1 hrs.

TV 37%
15.6 hrs

Magazines 7%
3.1 hrs.

Newspapers 9%
4 hrs.

Radio 30%
12.6 hrs.

40% of adults enjoy using a PC at home, compared to **60% of kids** ages 4–11.

MTV NETWORKS LEISURE TIME STUDY

JUPITER AND JUPITER ANALYSIS
©1999 JUPITER COMMUNICATIONS

Dried flower flag, circa 1986 created by Amy Hoffman Selfe

First things first: **media organizations**

The seven companies on these two pages generate most of what we see
on TV or at the movies, and what we read.

And if it seems as though they are competing for our attention ...

The chart below shows that the Big Seven are competitors
in almost all the major areas of content production.

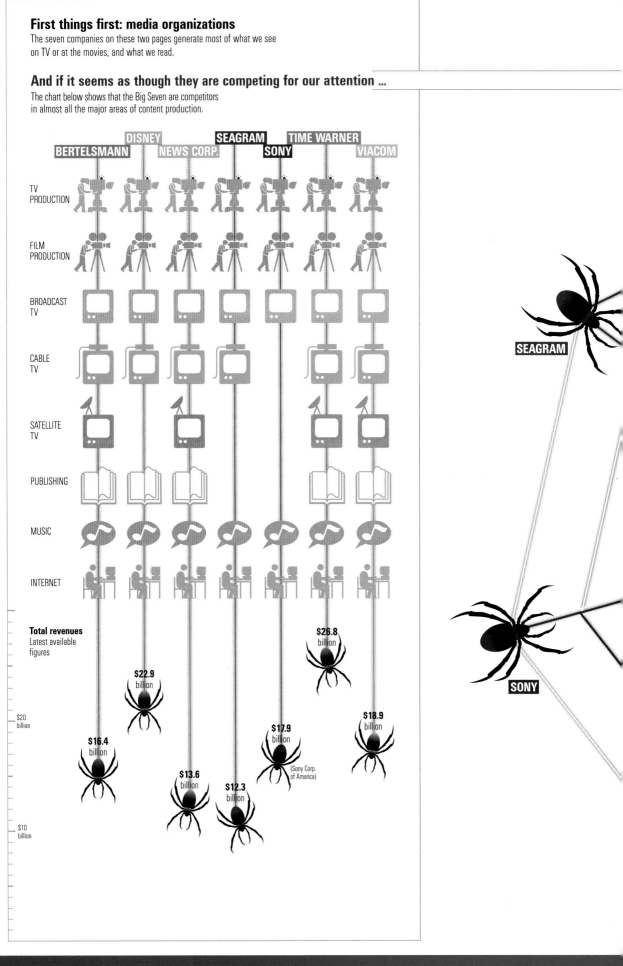

DISNEY   SEAGRAM   TIME WARNER

BERTELSMANN   NEWS CORP.   SONY   VIACOM

TV PRODUCTION

FILM PRODUCTION

BROADCAST TV

CABLE TV

SATELLITE TV

PUBLISHING

MUSIC

INTERNET

Total revenues
Latest available figures

$26.8 billion

$22.9 billion

$20 billion

$16.4 billion

$13.6 billion

$12.3 billion

$17.9 billion
(Sony Corp. of America)

$18.9 billion

$10 billion

SEAGRAM

SONY

Sources: Individual companies' Annual Reports; *The Economist*; *The New York Times*; *Time*

The **Federal Communications Commission** has strict regulations that could force the newly formed **Viacom-CBS** media giant to sell some of its local stations. One of the **F.C.C.** rules is that any single company cannot have TV coverage of more than 35% of the country. The new **Viacom** would have about 44%.

In 1998, there were 2,393 country music radio stations (both AM and FM) in the U.S. Way behind in second place after country was adult contempory music with 1,562 stations, news and talk radio with 1,356 stations, and religion with 1,075 stations.

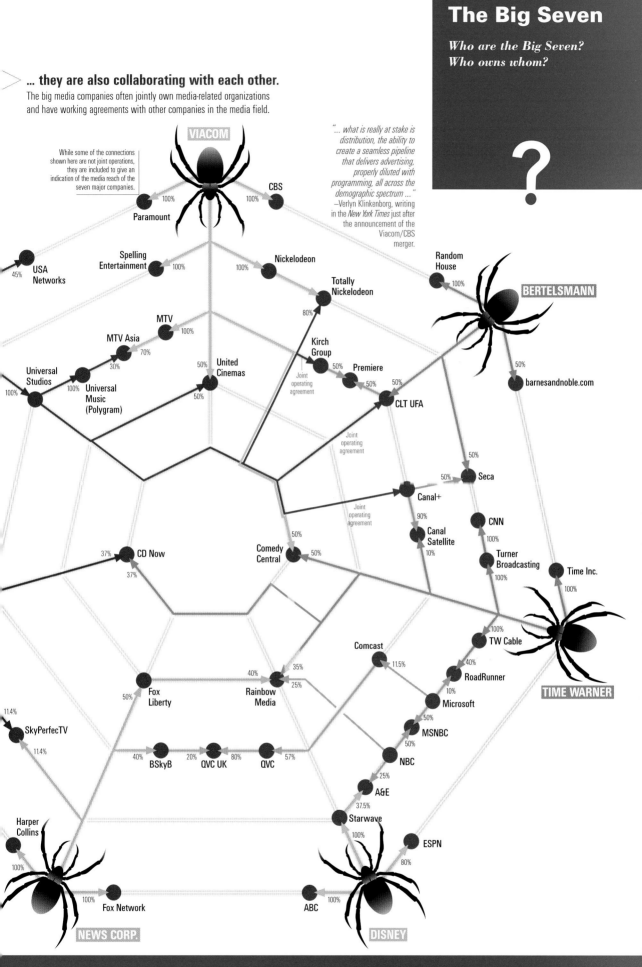

The Big Seven

Who are the Big Seven?
Who owns whom?

?

... they are also collaborating with each other.

The big media companies often jointly own media-related organizations and have working agreements with other companies in the media field.

While some of the connections shown here are not joint operations, they are included to give an indication of the media reach of the seven major companies.

"... what is really at stake is distribution, the ability to create a seamless pipeline that delivers advertising, properly diluted with programming, all across the demographic spectrum ..."
—Verlyn Klinkenborg, writing in the *New York Times* just after the announcement of the Viacom/CBS merger.

VIACOM

CBS
100%
Paramount 100%

USA Networks 45%
Spelling Entertainment 100%
Nickelodeon 100%

Totally Nickelodeon 80%

Random House 100%
BERTELSMANN

MTV 100%
MTV Asia 70%
30%
Universal Studios 100%
Universal Music (Polygram) 100%

United Cinemas 50%
50%

Kirch Group 50%
Joint operating agreement
Premiere 50%
50%
CLT UFA

50%
barnesandnoble.com

Joint operating agreement

Seca 50%
50%

Canal+
Joint operating agreement
90%
Canal Satellite 10%

CNN 100%
Turner Broadcasting 100%

Time Inc. 100%

CD Now 37%
37%

Comedy Central 50%
50%

TW Cable 100%
100%

Comcast 11.5%
RoadRunner 40%
TIME WARNER

Fox Liberty 50%
40%
Rainbow Media 35%
25%

Microsoft 10%

MSNBC 50%

SkyPerfecTV 11.4%
11.4%
BSkyB 40%
QVC UK 20%
80% QVC 57%
NBC 50%

A&E 25%

Starwave 37.5%
100%

ESPN 80%

Harper Collins 100%

Fox Network 100%
NEWS CORP.

ABC 100%
DISNEY

But increasingly, power in U.S. media belongs to companies that are not considered part of the traditional media establishment. They fall into two broad categories: companies that provide the technical means to publish or broadcast, and financial organizations that provide venture capital for start-ups, or actively finance mergers and acquisitions.

The companies in this diagram are the top 100 chosen by *New Media* magazine for their influence in the converging fields of media, communications and computers. As you can see, the center of this whirling universe is the internet.

While financial clout and market reach are important, *New Media* weighed these two questions before publishing their list:

1. Which companies should we be paying attention to?

2. Which companies are potential partners or competitors?

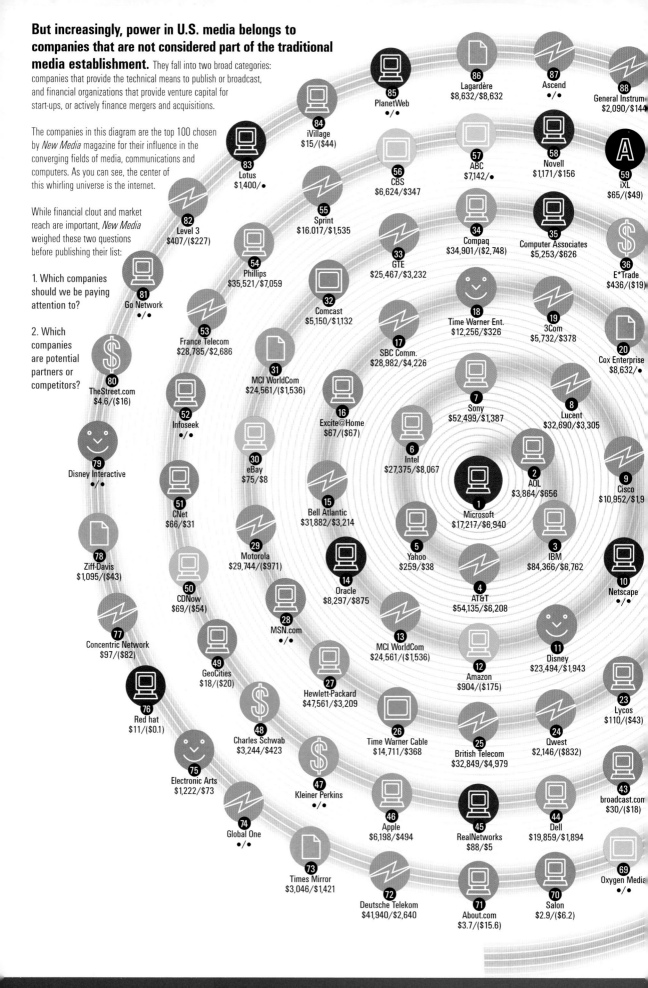

85 PlanetWeb •/•

86 Lagardère $8,632/$8,632

87 Ascend •/•

88 General Instrum $2,090/$144

84 iVillage $15/($44)

83 Lotus $1,400/•

56 CBS $6,624/$347

57 ABC $7,142/•

58 Novell $1,171/$156

59 iXL $65/($49)

82 Level 3 $407/($227)

55 Sprint $16.017/$1,535

33 GTE $25,467/$3,232

34 Compaq $34,901/($2,748)

35 Computer Associates $5,253/$626

36 E*Trade $436/($19)

81 Go Network •/•

54 Phillips $35,521/$7,059

32 Comcast $5,150/$1,132

18 Time Warner Ent. $12,256/$326

19 3Com $5,732/$378

20 Cox Enterprise $8,632/•

80 TheStreet.com $4.6/($16)

53 France Telecom $28,785/$2,686

31 MCI WorldCom $24,561/($1,536)

17 SBC Comm. $28,982/$4,226

7 Sony $52,499/$1,387

8 Lucent $32,690/$3,305

79 Disney Interactive •/•

52 Infoseek •/•

16 Excite@Home $67/($67)

6 Intel $27,375/$8,067

2 AOL $3,864/$656

9 Cisco $10,952/$1,9

78 Ziff-Davis $1,095/($43)

51 CNet $66/$31

30 eBay $75/$8

1 Microsoft $17,217/$6,940

77 Concentric Network $97/($82)

50 CDNow $69/($54)

29 Motorola $29,744/($971)

15 Bell Atlantic $31,882/$3,214

5 Yahoo $259/$38

3 IBM $84,366/$6,762

10 Netscape •/•

76 Red hat $11/($0.1)

28 MSN.com •/•

14 Oracle $8,297/$875

4 AT&T $54,135/$6,208

11 Disney $23,494/$1,943

75 Electronic Arts $1,222/$73

49 GeoCities $18/($20)

27 Hewlett-Packard $47,561/$3,209

13 MCI WorldCom $24,561/($1,536)

12 Amazon $904/($175)

23 Lycos $110/($43)

48 Charles Schwab $3,244/$423

26 Time Warner Cable $14,711/$368

25 British Telecom $32,849/$4,979

24 Qwest $2,146/($832)

44 Dell $19,859/$1,894

43 broadcast.com $30/($18)

74 Global One •/•

47 Kleiner Perkins •/•

46 Apple $6,198/$494

45 RealNetworks $88/$5

73 Times Mirror $3,046/$1,421

72 Deutsche Telekom $41,940/$2,640

71 About.com $3.7/($15.6)

70 Salon $2.9/($6.2)

69 Oxygen Media •/•

Source: *New Media Magazine*

The U.S. has 65 million cable subscribers. The next most wired nations are **Germany** (17 million), **The Netherlands** (6 million), **Belgium** (4.5 million) and **Britain** (3 million)

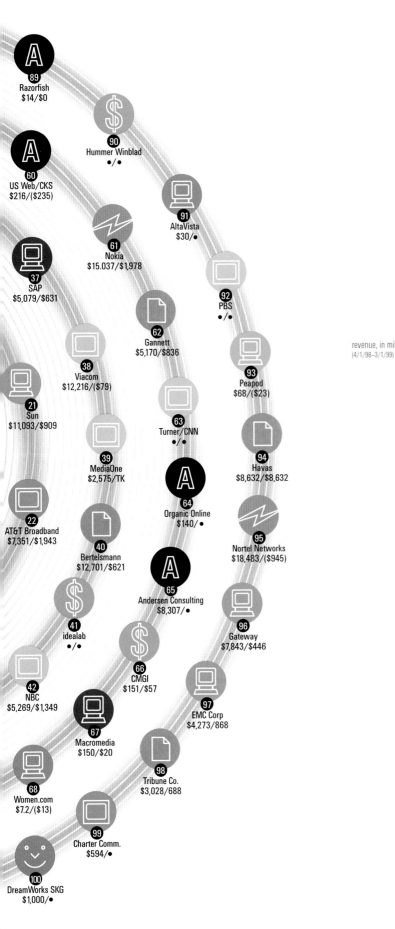

89 Razorfish $14/$0

90 Hummer Winblad •/•

91 AltaVista $30/•

60 US Web/CKS $216/($235)

61 Nokia $15.037/$1,978

92 PBS •/•

37 SAP $5,079/$631

62 Gannett $5,170/$836

93 Peapod $68/($23)

38 Viacom $12,216/($79)

63 Turner/CNN •/•

94 Havas $8,632/$8,632

21 Sun $11,093/$909

39 MediaOne $2,575/TK

64 Organic Online $140/•

95 Nortel Networks $18,483/($945)

22 AT&T Broadband $7,351/$1,943

40 Bertelsmann $12,701/$621

65 Andersen Consulting $8,307/•

41 idealab •/•

96 Gateway $7,843/$446

42 NBC $5,269/$1,349

66 CMGI $151/$57

97 EMC Corp $4,273/868

67 Macromedia $150/$20

98 Tribune Co. $3,028/688

68 Women.com $7.2/($13)

99 Charter Comm. $594/•

100 DreamWorks SKG $1,000/•

KEY

New Media ranking

↓

1
Microsoft

revenue, in millions (4/1/98–3/1/99) → $17,217/$6,940 ← net income, in millions (4/1/98–3/1/99)

• ← wholly owned subsidiaries and private or multiple-ownership companies

- Software
- Internet services
- Computer technology
- E-commerce
- Communications Services & Technology
- Financial Services
- Entertainment
- Print
- TV carriers
- TV programming
- Agencies

How many hours a week do we watch TV?

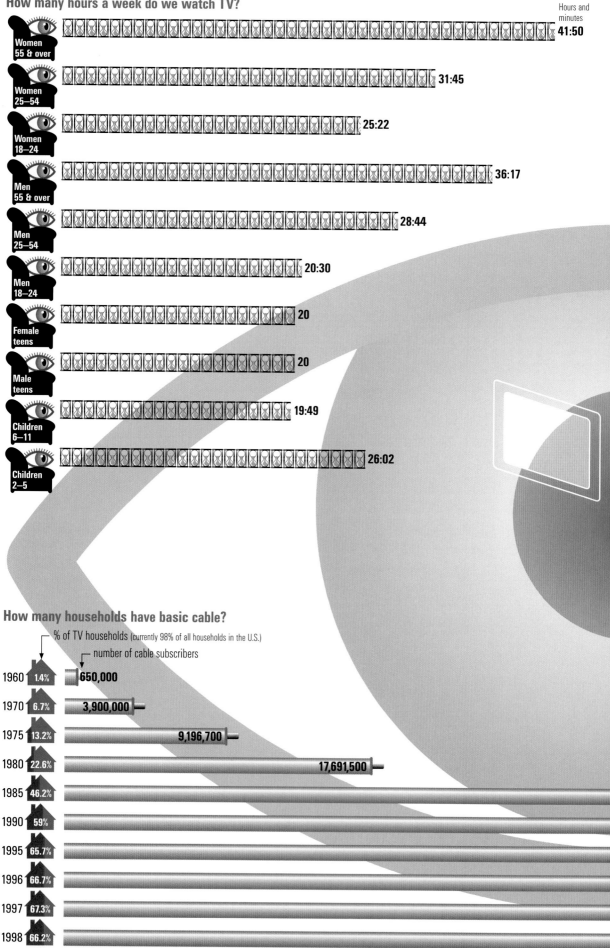

Hours and minutes

Women 55 & over	41:50
Women 25–54	31:45
Women 18–24	25:22
Men 55 & over	36:17
Men 25–54	28:44
Men 18–24	20:30
Female teens	20
Male teens	20
Children 6–11	19:49
Children 2–5	26:02

How many households have basic cable?

% of TV households (currently 98% of all households in the U.S.)

number of cable subscribers

Year	%	Subscribers
1960	1.4%	650,000
1970	6.7%	3,900,000
1975	13.2%	9,196,700
1980	22.6%	17,691,500
1985	46.2%	
1990	59%	
1995	65.7%	
1996	66.7%	
1997	67.3%	
1998	66.2%	

Sources: *Time Almanac*; *World Almanac*; *Wall Street Journal Almanac*; *The New York Times*

Rating points: rating is the percentage of all homes with televisions, whether or not they are in use. One rating point is 1,008,000 households.

Share is the percentage of homes with televisions in use. So if **Friends** has a 17.8 rating and 30 share, that means that 17,942,400 people watched it, and that number was 30% of the viewing audience at the time.

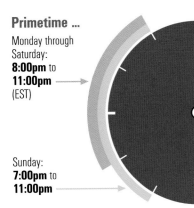

Primetime ...

Monday through Saturday:
8:00pm to **11:00pm** (EST)

Sunday:
7:00pm to **11:00pm**

... and primetime viewers

millions

Mon 96.7
Tue 94.2
Wed 91.1
Thu 96.9
Fri 80.7
Sat 77.1
Sun 88.6

Television

Who's watching TV? How are the networks doing?

?

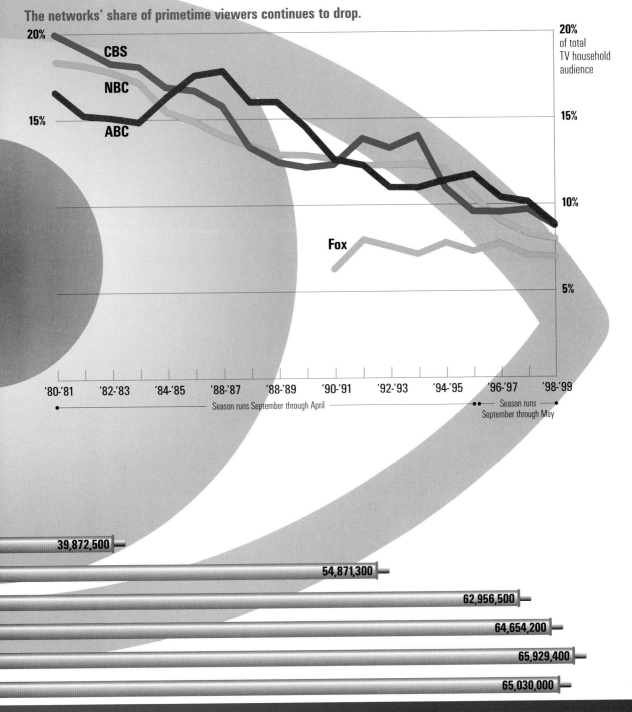

The networks' share of primetime viewers continues to drop.

20%

CBS

NBC

15%

ABC

Fox

20% of total TV household audience

15%

10%

5%

'80-'81   '82-'83   '84-'85   '88-'87   '88-'89   '90-'91   '92-'93   '94-'95   '96-'97   '98-'99

• ———————— Season runs September through April ———————— • • Season runs September through May

39,872,500
54,871,300
62,956,500
64,654,200
65,929,400
65,030,000

Nielsen Media Research Inc. is the largest TV audience measuring company in the U.S. In 1999, VNU, the Dutch publisher of **Billboard** magazine made a deal to buy **Nielsen** for $2.5 billion. TV network executives think that **Nielsen** has consistently under-reported viewers. The networks experimented with a different way of counting viewers, called **Smart** (Systems for Measuring and Reporting Television), and then abandoned it.

In September 1999, **TN Media** reported that 11.8% of TV-watching households were African-American and that four of the six U.S. TV networks (**ABC** 14%, **CBS** 18%, **UPN** 45% and **WB** 23%) over-represent African-Americans in their primetime programming. **Fox** (7%) and **NBC** (8%) were the only two networks that fell below. Source: **Jack Myers, The Myers Report**

While 66% of adults have watched part of a TV infomercial, only 12% of viewers have watched one in its entirety.

UNDERSTANDING TODAY

OUTLOOK:
Data front approaching from Rhode Island

INSIDE:
People overwhelmed by tsunami of information

LATEST

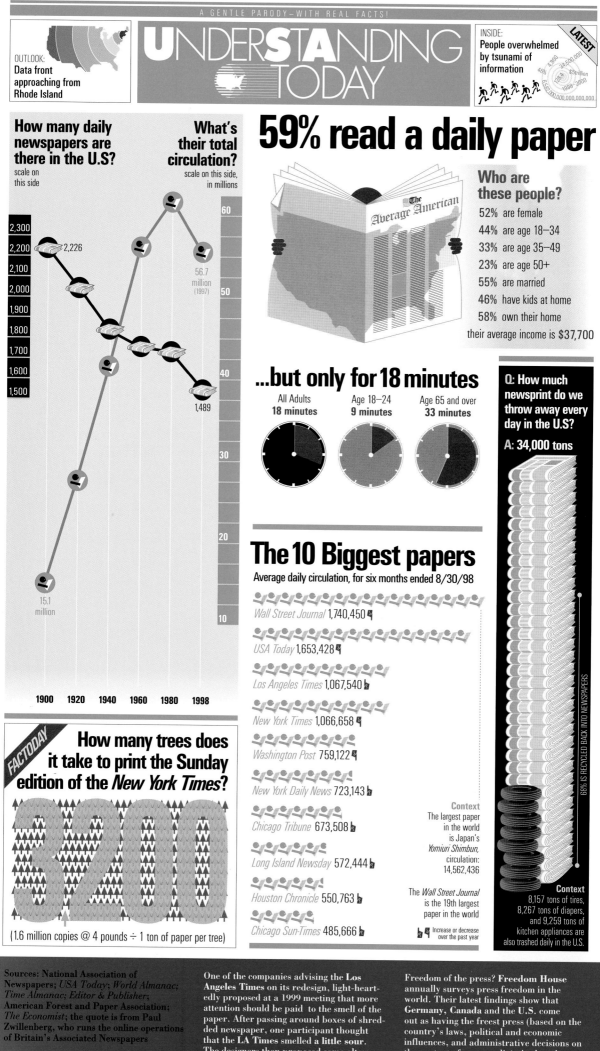

59% read a daily paper

How many daily newspapers are there in the U.S?
scale on this side

What's their total circulation?
scale on this side, in millions

2,300
2,200 — 2,226
2,100
2,000
1,900
1,800
1,700
1,600
1,500

60
50
40
30
20
10

56.7 million (1997)

1,489

15.1 million

1900 1920 1940 1960 1980 1998

Who are these people?

52% are female
44% are age 18–34
33% are age 35–49
23% are age 50+
55% are married
46% have kids at home
58% own their home
their average income is $37,700

...but only for 18 minutes

All Adults
18 minutes

Age 18–24
9 minutes

Age 65 and over
33 minutes

Q: How much newsprint do we throw away every day in the U.S?
A: 34,000 tons

68% IS RECYCLED BACK INTO NEWSPAPERS

The 10 Biggest papers
Average daily circulation, for six months ended 8/30/98

Wall Street Journal **1,740,450**

USA Today **1,653,428**

Los Angeles Times **1,067,540**

New York Times **1,066,658**

Washington Post **759,122**

New York Daily News **723,143**

Chicago Tribune **673,508**

Long Island Newsday **572,444**

Houston Chronicle **550,763**

Chicago Sun-Times **485,666**

Context
The largest paper in the world is Japan's *Yomiuri Shimbun*, circulation: 14,562,436

The *Wall Street Journal* is the 19th largest paper in the world

Increase or decrease over the past year

Context
8,157 tons of tires, 8,267 tons of diapers, and 9,259 tons of kitchen appliances are also trashed daily in the U.S.

FACTODAY
How many trees does it take to print the Sunday edition of the *New York Times*?

3200

(1.6 million copies @ 4 pounds ÷ 1 ton of paper per tree)

Sources: National Association of Newspapers; *USA Today*; *World Almanac; Time Almanac; Editor & Publisher; American Forest and Paper Association; The Economist*; the quote is from Paul Zwillenberg, who runs the online operations of Britain's Associated Newspapers

One of the companies advising the **Los Angeles Times** on its redesign, light-heartedly proposed at a 1999 meeting that more attention should be paid to the smell of the paper. After passing around boxes of shredded newspaper, one participant thought that the **LA Times** smelled **a little sour.** The designers then proposed some alternative scents: laundry detergent, hand lotion, citrus, coffee and doughnuts. The coffee smell and doughnut smell were the winners. (Source: *The New York Times*)

Freedom of the press? **Freedom House** annually surveys press freedom in the world. Their latest findings show that **Germany, Canada** and the **U.S.** come out as having the freest press (based on the country's laws, political and economic influences, and administrative decisions on the content of news media). At the other end of the scale are **China** and **Indonesia.** More than four out of ten people in the world live in countries where the press is not free.

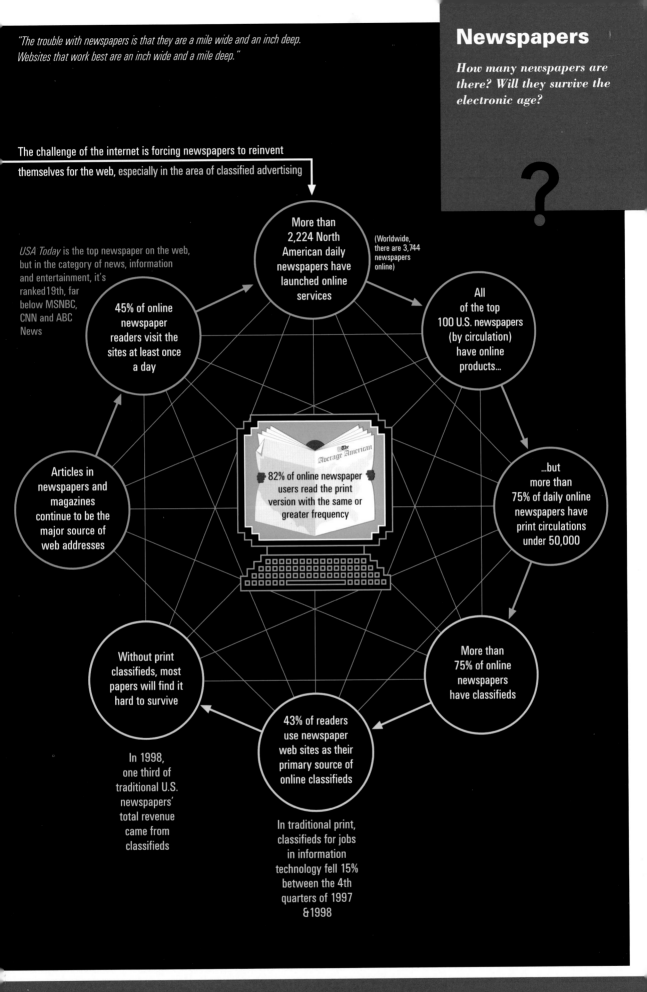

Newspapers

How many newspapers are there? Will they survive the electronic age?

?

"The trouble with newspapers is that they are a mile wide and an inch deep.
Websites that work best are an inch wide and a mile deep."

The challenge of the internet is forcing newspapers to reinvent
themselves for the web, especially in the area of classified advertising

USA Today is the top newspaper on the web,
but in the category of news, information
and entertainment, it's
ranked 19th, far
below MSNBC,
CNN and ABC
News

More than
2,224 North
American daily
newspapers have
launched online
services

(Worldwide,
there are 3,744
newspapers
online)

45% of online
newspaper
readers visit the
sites at least once
a day

All
of the top
100 U.S. newspapers
(by circulation)
have online
products...

The *Average American*

82% of online newspaper
users read the print
version with the same or
greater frequency

Articles in
newspapers and
magazines
continue to be the
major source of
web addresses

...but
more than
75% of daily online
newspapers have
print circulations
under 50,000

Without print
classifieds, most
papers will find it
hard to survive

More than
75% of online
newspapers
have classifieds

43% of readers
use newspaper
web sites as their
primary source of
online classifieds

In 1998,
one third of
traditional U.S.
newspapers'
total revenue
came from
classifieds

In traditional print,
classifieds for jobs
in information
technology fell 15%
between the 4th
quarters of 1997
&1998

The top 50 magazines in 1998, by revenue ...

▨ = total (subscriptions, newstand sales, and advertising)   ▨ = just advertising

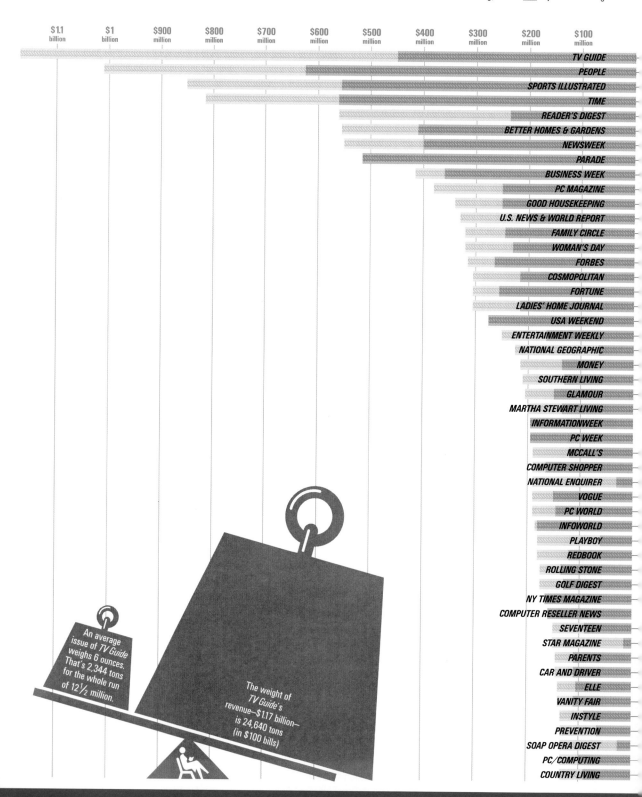

| $1.1 billion | $1 billion | $900 million | $800 million | $700 million | $600 million | $500 million | $400 million | $300 million | $200 million | $100 million |

TV GUIDE
PEOPLE
SPORTS ILLUSTRATED
TIME
READER'S DIGEST
BETTER HOMES & GARDENS
NEWSWEEK
PARADE
BUSINESS WEEK
PC MAGAZINE
GOOD HOUSEKEEPING
U.S. NEWS & WORLD REPORT
FAMILY CIRCLE
WOMAN'S DAY
FORBES
COSMOPOLITAN
FORTUNE
LADIES' HOME JOURNAL
USA WEEKEND
ENTERTAINMENT WEEKLY
NATIONAL GEOGRAPHIC
MONEY
SOUTHERN LIVING
GLAMOUR
MARTHA STEWART LIVING
INFORMATIONWEEK
PC WEEK
MCCALL'S
COMPUTER SHOPPER
NATIONAL ENQUIRER
VOGUE
PC WORLD
INFOWORLD
PLAYBOY
REDBOOK
ROLLING STONE
GOLF DIGEST
NY TIMES MAGAZINE
COMPUTER RESELLER NEWS
SEVENTEEN
STAR MAGAZINE
PARENTS
CAR AND DRIVER
ELLE
VANITY FAIR
INSTYLE
PREVENTION
SOAP OPERA DIGEST
PC/COMPUTING
COUNTRY LIVING

An average issue of *TV Guide* weighs 6 ounces. That's 2,344 tons for the whole run of 12½ million.

The weight of *TV Guide's* revenue—$1.17 billion— is 24,640 tons (in $100 bills)

Sources: *World Almanac; Time Almanac; Advertising Age; The Washington Post*

How many readers are there? Some magazines publish their readership, as opposed to how many copies they sell (the circulation). In the celebrity gossip field, **People** magazine claims 35 million readers from a circulation of 3.7 million. So just over 9 people read each copy of **People** magazine. **Entertainment Weekly** claims 7.7 million readers, from a 1.5 million circulation, meaning that five people read each copy. **US** magazine claims 3.8 million readers, from a circulation of 1 million.

Note: Modern Maturity had a circulation of 20.5 million in 1998, but its total revenue was $112 million making it number 58 in the **Ad Age** ranking.

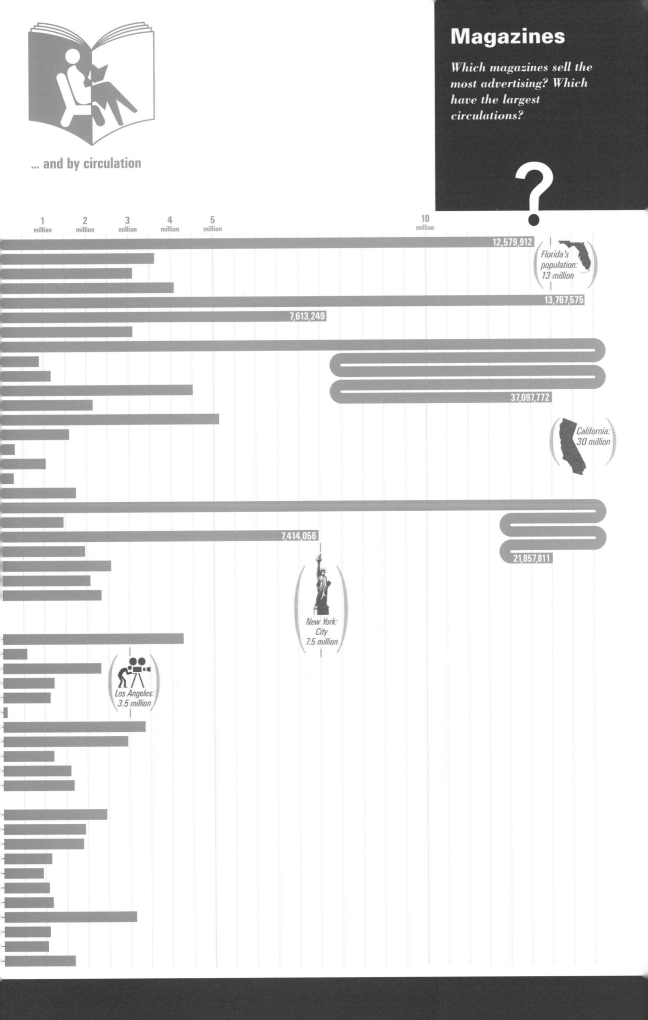

Magazines

Which magazines sell the most advertising? Which have the largest circulations?

?

... and by circulation

1 million | 2 million | 3 million | 4 million | 5 million | 10 million

12,579,912

Florida's population: 13 million

13,767,575

7,613,249

37,097,772

California: 30 million

7,414,056

21,857,811

New York: City 7.5 million

Los Angeles: 3.5 million

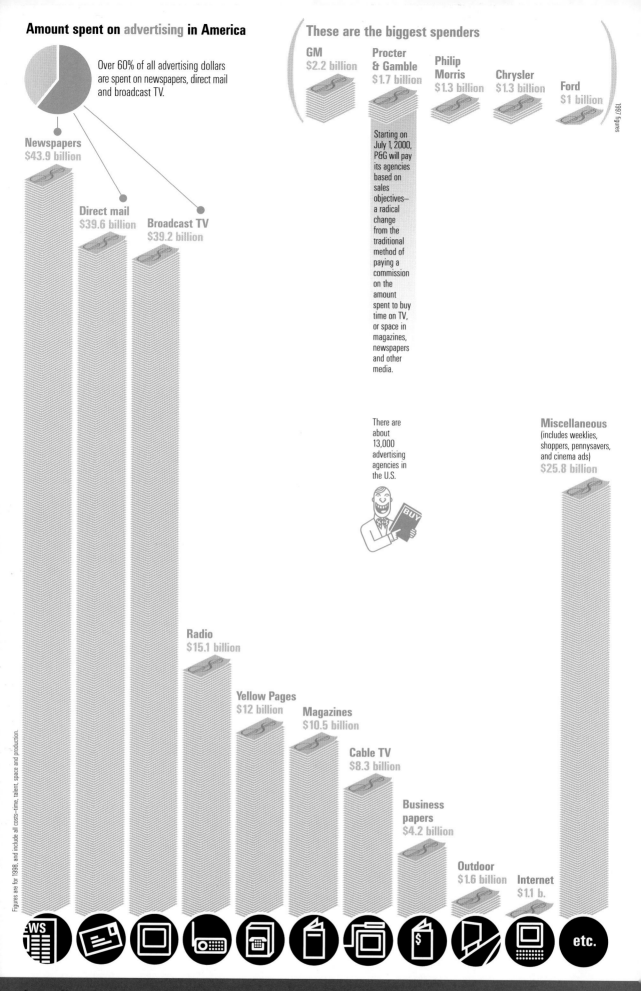

Amount spent on advertising in America

Over 60% of all advertising dollars are spent on newspapers, direct mail and broadcast TV.

Newspapers
$43.9 billion

Direct mail
$39.6 billion

Broadcast TV
$39.2 billion

Radio
$15.1 billion

Yellow Pages
$12 billion

Magazines
$10.5 billion

Cable TV
$8.3 billion

Business papers
$4.2 billion

Outdoor
$1.6 billion

Internet
$1.1 b.

Miscellaneous
(includes weeklies, shoppers, pennysavers, and cinema ads)
$25.8 billion

Figures are for 1998, and include all costs—time, talent, space and production.

These are the biggest spenders

GM
$2.2 billion

Procter & Gamble
$1.7 billion

Philip Morris
$1.3 billion

Chrysler
$1.3 billion

Ford
$1 billion

1997 figures

Starting on July 1, 2000, P&G will pay its agencies based on sales objectives—a radical change from the traditional method of paying a commission on the amount spent to buy time on TV, or space in magazines, newspapers and other media.

There are about 13,000 advertising agencies in the U.S.

BUY

Sources: National Association of Newspapers; McCann-Erickson Inc.; *World Almanac*; *The New York Times*

The number of advertisements/promotions (and minutes) on prime-time network programming in 1998: **ABC** 127 ads (47 minutes); **CBS** 128 ads (49 minutes); **NBC** 141 ads (49 minutes).

Currently, the networks average 15 minutes, 44 seconds of non-program material per hour. **Grant Tinker** remembers that it was 6 minutes to the hour when he was producing the **Mary Tyler Moore Show.**

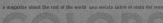

Spreads on the following pages are from these issues of **Colors Magazine.**

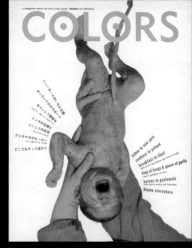

The richest 20 percent of the world's population has 82.7 percent of the world's money.

here's where the
money
lives

The most universal expression of racism isn't violence; it's the systematic denial of economic opportunities to people of color. The poorest 20 percent of the world's population gets only 0.2 percent of the money loaned by commercial banks. Without access to credit, the poor stay poor… and powerless.

On this map, the size of each country is in proportion to its wealth.
Sur cette carte, la taille des pays est proportionnelle à leur richesse.

151–160	**HOW DESIRABLE IS EACH COUNTRY TO LIVE IN?** The U.N. Human Development Index compares nations in
121–150	terms of literacy, life expectancy and income. The higher
91–120	a country's number, the higher the quality of life there.
61–90	**QUEL EST LE PAYS OÙ L'ON A LE PLUS ENVIE DE VIVRE?**
31–60	L'indice de l'ONU sur le Développement Humain compare
1–30	les pays au termes d'analphabétisation, d'espérance de vie et de revenu. La qualité de vie dépend du chiffre obtenu.

CANADA

USA

UK

SPAIN

BRAZIL

USA MONTANT ANNUEL DE LA DETTE EXTERIEURE PAR HABITANT: 2.301US$
Bill Gates, l'homme le plus riche des USA (on y compte 64 milliardaires), est le fondateur de Microsoft, société de software. Agé de 36 ans, il pèse 5.9US$ milliards. La valeur marchande de sa société, créée il y a 17 ans, est supérieure à celle de General Motors. Connu pour ses enfantillages, il organise des soirées à "thème" pour ses employés—comme celui de l'Afrique: et les invités de lancer des flèches, de mettre les noms de pays Africains sur une carte géante et de jouer au "Jungle Jeopardy", un jeu/ questionnaire informatique.

USA EACH U.S. CITIZEN'S ANNUAL SHARE OF THE FOREIGN DEBT: US$2,301
The richest man in the USA (home of 64 billionaires) is Bill Gates, who started the computer software firm Microsoft. Gates, 36, is worth US$5.9 billion and his 17-year-old firm now has a higher market value than General Motors. The billionaire, who's known to have a playful streak, has "theme" parties for his employees. One theme was Africa. Partygoers shot blow darts, tried to fill in the names of African countries on a giant map and played a computer quiz game called "Jungle Jeopardy."

Mexico MONTANT ANNUEL DE LA DETTE EXTERIEURE PAR HABITANT: 1.067US$ Un seul homme, le milliardaire Carlos Slim Helu, possède la majorité des parts de la compagnie de téléphone Mexicaine, Telefonos de Mexico. Il l'a acheté pour 1.7US$ milliards en 1990. L'an dernier, il a réalisé 2.3US$ milliards de profit. Au Mexique il y a actuellement 7 lignes de téléphone pour 100 habitants (61 pour 100 habitants en France). Un million de demandeurs sont sur liste d'attente: un client attend normalement un an avant d'avoir le téléphone.

Mexico EACH MEXICAN'S ANNUAL SHARE OF THE FOREIGN DEBT: US$1,067 One man, billionaire Carlos Slim Helu, owns most of Mexico's telephone company, Telefonos de Mexico. He bought it for US$1.7 billion in 1990. It earned US$2.3 billion in profit last year. In Mexico there are currently seven telephone lines per 100 inhabitants (compared to 61 per 100 in France). A million orders are on a waiting list and a customer typically waits a year to have a phone installed.

Brésil MONTANT ANNUEL DE LA DETTE EXTERIEURE PAR HABITANT: 785US$
C'est au Brésil qu'existe la plus grande disparité entre pauvres et riches. Pour certains, à Rio de Janeiro, la chirurgie esthétique est un 'must'. Des seins parfaits peuvent coûter jusqu'à 20.000US$, des fesses fermes jusqu'à 10.000US$. Cependant, dans les bidonvilles des montagnes autour de Rio, un cinquième des personnes dans les vingt ans passent pour 'nains': ils mesurent 13 cms de moins que la normale du fait de malnutrition. Les pauvres ont un tiers de moins à manger qu' en 1960.

Brazil EACH BRAZILIAN'S ANNUAL SHARE OF THE FOREIGN DEBT: US$785 Brazil has the world's greatest disparity between rich and poor. Among the beautiful people of Rio de Janeiro, plastic surgery is a near necessity. Perfect breasts can cost up to US$20,000 and taut buttocks go for as much as US$10,000. Meanwhile, in the slums that cover the mountains around the city, a fifth of people in their 20s are considered dwarfs; they're five or more inches below normal height due to malnutrition. Poor Brazilians now eat a third less than they did in 1960.

Anguilla Les Caraïbes est le point de jonction de l'économie du Nord et du Sud. Au Cap Juluca, une station balnéaire sur l'île d'Anguilla, le premier prix pour une chambre d'hôtel en pleine saison est de 390US$ par nuit. La femme de ménage gagne, par mois, 33US$ de moins que ce que l'hôtel prend pour une nuit.

Anguilla The Caribbean is where northern and southern economies meet. At Cap Juluca, a resort on the island of Anguilla, the lowest priced room during peak season is US$390 per night. The maid who cleans the room earns US$33 less per month than the resort makes off the room in one night.

World Bank HEADQUARTERS: WASHINGTON, D.C., USA. ANNUAL BUDGET: US$21.5 MILLION. MEMBER NATIONS: 172. The World Bank and the International Monetary Fund (IMF) were started after World War II to finance the reconstruction of Europe and Japan. Later they turned their attention to the development of the Third World. Member nations donate money to the bank and the fund and vote to allocate that money. Voting power is based on the amount donated. The USA controls almost 20 percent of the vote. Japan controls about 8 percent. The bank and IMF have been helping poor nations pay off the debts incurred in the late 1970s and early 1980s, when big international private banks, overflowing with OPEC money, were lending money aggressively and indiscriminately. However, the World Bank lends only to such countries as Bolivia (see page 52), which agree to a drastic economic restructuring.

Banque Mondiale QUARTIERS GENE-RAUX: WASHINGTON D.C., USA. BUDGET ANNUEL: 21.5US$ MILLION. NATIONS MEMBRES: 172 La Banque Mondiale et le FMI, fondés après la Seconde Guerre Mondiale, ont financé la reconstruction de l'Europe et du Japon. Ils s'occupèrent ensuite des pays du Tiers Monde. Les Nations membres donnent de l'argent et décident par vote de l'attribution des fonds. Le nombre de voix est proportionnel à l'argent accordé: les USA contrôlent presque 20 pour cent du vote, le Japon environ 8 pour cent. La Banque et le FMI ont aidé des pays pauvres à rembourser les dettes contractées fins des années 70 et début des années 80, quand les banques privées internationales, croulant sous l'argent de l'OPEP, prêtaient à qui voulait. Cependant la Banque Mondiale n'aide que les pays comme la Bolivie (voir page 52), qui acceptent de se plier à des plans de restructuration draconiens.

Les plus riches 20% de la population mondiale possèdent 82.7% de l'argent du monde.

voici où vit l'argent

□ = US$18.9 BILLION OF THE GROSS WORLD PRODUCT
□ = US$18.9 MILLE MILLIONS US$ DU PRODUIT MONDIAL BRUT

La manifestation de racisme la plus répandue n'est pas la violence, mais la marginalisation économique des gens de couleur. Les plus pauvres 20 pour cent de la population mondiale n'obtiennent que 0.2 pour cent de l'argent prêté par les banques commerciales. Sans facilités de crédit, les pauvres restent pauvres... et sans pouvoir.

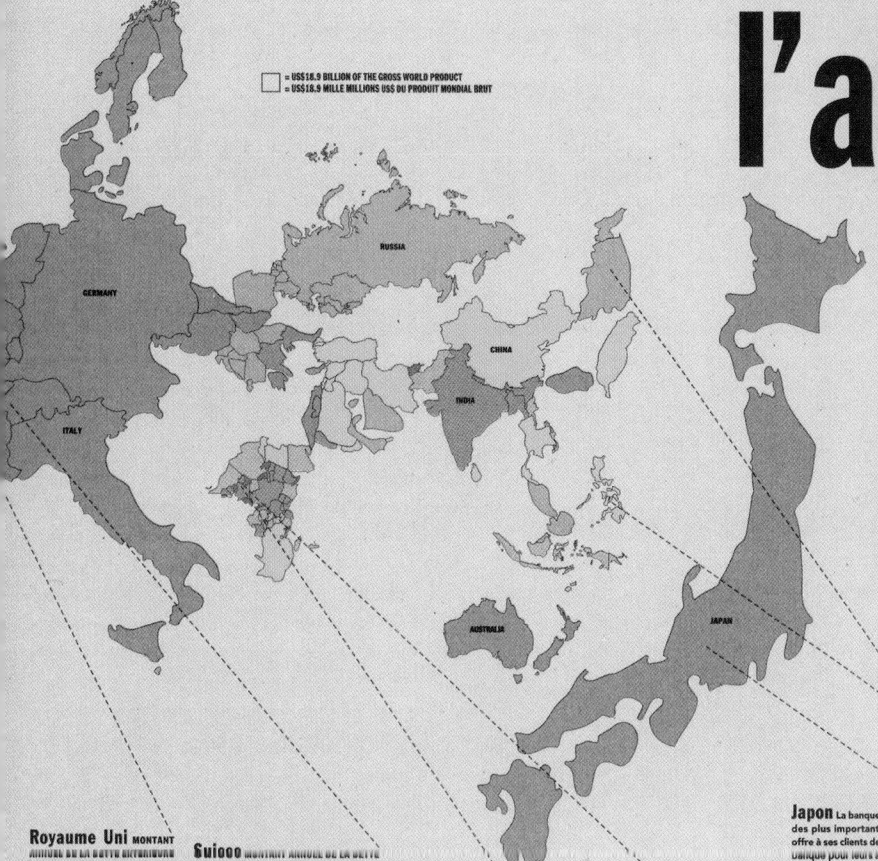

Map labels: RUSSIA, GERMANY, ITALY, CHINA, INDIA, AUSTRALIA, JAPAN

Royaume Uni MONTANT ANNUEL DE LA DETTE EXTÉRIEURE PAR HABITANT: 285US$ La Jaguar XJ220 est la voiture la plus chère du monde: elle coûte environ 705.500 US$. Quelques 1 500 personnes ont passé commande. Au total, 350 voitures vont être fabriquées. On trouve une réplique de la Jaguar de type-D, faite à la main, pour les enfants chez Harrods, à Londres: 36.000US$ seulement.

United Kingdom EACH U.K. CITIZEN'S ANNUAL SHARE OF THE FOREIGN DEBT: US$183 The highest priced production car in the world is the Jaguar XJ220, which lists for approximately US$705,500. Some 1,500 people have "applied" to buy this car. A total of 350 will be made. A hand-built replica of the D-type Jaguar intended for children is available at Harrods department store in London for only US$36,000.

Suisse MONTANT ANNUEL DE LA DETTE EXTÉRIEURE PAR HABITANT: 0US$ Athina Roussel, 7 ans, est la plus jeune milliardaire du monde. Elle a hérité de 1.5US$ milliards à la mort de sa mère, Christina Onassis. A sa majorité, elle aura accès à sa fortune. En attendant, elle vit avec son père, Thierry Roussel, héritier de la firme pharmaceutique, à Lussy-sur-Morges, en Suisse. Sa rente est de 4.25US$ millions par an. Cependant, ce n'est pas une enfant gâtée: à la neige, il faut qu'elle porte ses skis.

Switzerland EACH SWISS CITIZEN'S ANNUAL SHARE OF THE FOREIGN DEBT: US$0 The youngest billionaire in the world is seven-year-old Athina Roussel. Athina inherited US$1.5 billion upon the death of her mother, Christina Onassis, and she'll gain control of it when she turns 18. Meanwhile, she lives with her father, pharmaceuticals heir Thierry Roussel, in Lussy-sur-Morges, Switzerland. Her allowance is about US$4.25 million a year, but she isn't spoiled: on ski trips, she's obliged to carry her own equipment.

Nigeria EACH NIGERIAN'S ANNUAL SHARE OF THE FOREIGN DEBT: US$285 Five freighters full of industrial waste were shipped from Italy (per capita income US$15,120) to Koko, Nigeria (per capita income US$250), where a farmer was paid US$8,750 to store the waste on his land. This was a bargain for the Europeans and a fortune to the farmer. Local children played in the waste and villagers took the storage drums to use as food containers. The waste, however, was toxic and radioactive. It caused chemical burns, premature births, poisoning deaths and other maladies. The farmer died from poisoning.

Nigeria MONTANT ANNUEL DE LA DETTE EXTÉRIEURE PAR HABITANT: 285US$ Cinq cargos remplis de déchets toxiques furent envoyés d'Italie (revenu par habitant: 15.120US$) à Koko, au Nigéria (revenu par habitant: 250US$), où l'on a payé 8.750US$ un fermier pour stocker les déchets sur ses terres. Bonne affaire pour les Européens, pactole pour le fermier. Les villageois se servaient des barils comme garde-manger. Les enfants jouaient dans les déchets, qui, toxiques et radioactifs, provoquaient brûlures chimiques, naissances prématurées, empoisonnements et diverses maladies. Le fermier est mort intoxiqué.

Japon La banque Swana, l'une des plus importante du monde, offre à ses clients des comptes en banque pour leurs animaux, avec un carnet de chèques et une photo d'identité. Chien, Chat ou Lézard (les Japonais donnent généralement des noms génériques à leur animaux) peuvent avoir leur propre compte en banque; utiles pour visites au vétérinaire et frais d'enterrement. Les derniers sacrements pour votre petit chat peuvent coûter 400US$ et une pierre tombale peut aller jusqu'à 2.400US$.

Japan Sanwa Bank, one of the world's largest banks, is offering its clients savings accounts for pets, with a passbook and a photo ID. Dog, Cat or Lizard (Japanese usually assign their pets generic names) can hold accounts in which their masters set aside money for special treats, veterinarian visits or funerals. Last rites for Kitty can run US$400 and a tombstone might cost another US$2,400.

Philippines Une législation vient d'être proposée pour punir la mise à mort des chiens volés: dans les zones urbaines, les animaux errants atterrissent souvent dans le dîner. Cette mesure condamnerait torture, abandon et abattage de chiens et chats volés. Toute infraction entraînerait deux ans de prison et 200US$ d'amende.

Philippines Legislation was introduced to outlaw slaughtering stolen dogs for food. In rural areas, stray pets often wind up on the dinner table. The measure would outlaw torture, neglect and slaughter of stolen dogs and cats. Violators would be subject to two-year jail terms and fines of US$200.

Corée du Sud MONTANT ANNUEL DE LA DETTE EXTÉRIEURE PAR HABITANT: 735US$ Le Daewoo Group, conglomérat Sud Coréen, fabrique des circuits électroniques et des armes. Il développe aussi des hôtels et vend des actions. Ses 120 000 employés génèrent autant d'argent liquide qu'en gagnent les 40 millions d'habitants du Kenya, Somalie, Tchad et sept nations des îles réunis.

South Korea EACH SOUTH KOREAN'S ANNUAL SHARE OF THE FOREIGN DEBT: US$735 A South Korean conglomerate, the Daewoo Group, manufactures electronics and weapons, develops hotels and sells securities. Its 120,000 employees generate as much in annual cash sales as the more than 40 million people of Kenya, Somalia, Chad and seven island nations earn combined.

COLORS ⑤⑤

The poorest 20 percent of the world's population shares 1.4 percent of the world's money.

here's where the
people
live

In this issue of COLORS, we've outlined the physical differences between the earth's peoples. But to be honest, we don't think racism has anything to do with skin, hair or eyes. Those features just provide easy targets. Racism is about money and power.

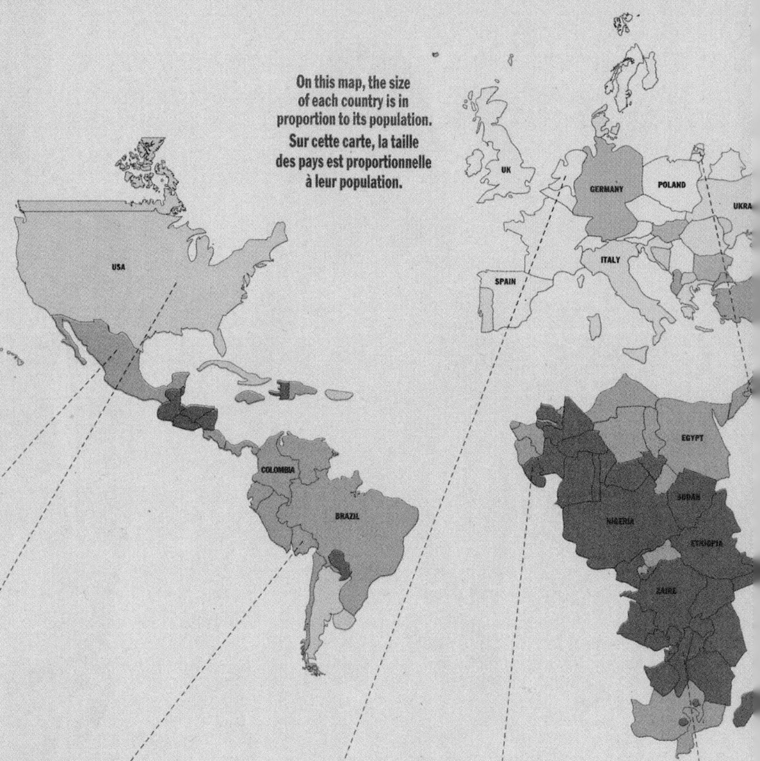

On this map, the size of each country is in proportion to its population.
Sur cette carte, la taille des pays est proportionnelle à leur population.

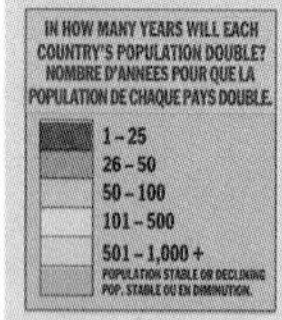

IN HOW MANY YEARS WILL EACH COUNTRY'S POPULATION DOUBLE? NOMBRE D'ANNÉES POUR QUE LA POPULATION DE CHAQUE PAYS DOUBLE.

- 1 ~ 25
- 26 ~ 50
- 50 ~ 100
- 101 ~ 500
- 501 ~ 1,000 +
- POPULATION STABLE OR DECLINING. POP. STABLE OU EN DIMINUTION.

Map labels: USA, COLOMBIA, BRAZIL, UK, GERMANY, POLAND, UKRAINE, ITALY, SPAIN, EGYPT, SUDAN, NIGERIA, ETHIOPIA, ZAIRE

Mexique REVENU ANNUEL PAR HABITANT: 2100US$ Tous les ans, dix millions de tonnes de pulpe de café, déchet toxique, sont jetés dans les rivières à travers le monde. Quant à eux, les Indiens Nahuatl, à Cuetzalan, utilisent cette pulpe comme lit pour champignons comestibles—en remplacement des troncs d'arbre sur lesquels ces fungi poussent généralement. Ces champignons qui diversifient l'alimentation locale, servent aussi à enlever la toxicité de la pulpe, utilisée alors comme engrais et aliment pour animaux. La coopérative Tosepan Titatakiske (Ensemble Nous Gagnerons), aidée par un prêt gouvernemental de 40.000US$, a créée cette entreprise prospère.

Mexico ANNUAL PER CAPITA INCOME: US$2,100 Twenty billion pounds of toxic coffee pulp, the waste generated by coffee-bean processing, is dumped annually into the world's rivers. Nahuatl Indians in Cuetzalan are now raising edible oyster mushrooms using this pulp as a bed—a substitute for the logs on which these fungi usually grow. The mushrooms add variety to the local diet and also detoxify the pulp, transforming it into animal feed or fertilizer. This successful business was started by a cooperative called Tosepan Titataniske ("Together We Will Win") and was backed by the Mexican government, which loaned the mushroom growers US$40,000.

USA REVENU ANNUEL PAR HABITANT: 20.910US$ Le village de Southampton, un terrain avec vue imprenable sur la mer, près de New York— une maison peut y coûter 8 millions US$—appartenait aux Shinnecocks, une nation de Natifs Américains, pêcheurs et baleiniers. Ils croyaient, contrairement aux habitants actuels, que la terre et la mer étaient la propriété de tous. Ils sont concentrés maintenant dans une réserve (320 hectares) à Shinnecock Neck, où ils possèdent des petits parcs à huîtres. Grâce à de scrupuleuses méthodes d'élevage, ils régénèrent les eaux locales ainsi que la santé financière de leur tribu.

USA ANNUAL PER CAPITA INCOME: US$20,910. The village of Southampton, a slice of prime oceanfront real estate near New York City— where a nice house might cost US$8 million—used to belong to the Shinnecocks, a Native American nation of fishermen and whalers. Unlike the current inhabitants of Southampton, the Shinnecocks believed in sharing the land and the sea. They now occupy an 800-acre reservation on Shinnecock Neck, where they have a small oyster hatchery. Through careful breeding they help rejuvenate local waters and the tribe's financial health.

Bolivie REVENU ANNUEL PAR HABITANT: 620US$ Afin d'obéir au règlement pour pays endettés du FMI, la Bolivie a dû dévaluer sa monnaie et suspendre la TVA, entraînant une forte dévaluation. En conséquence, le pays dépend encore plus des produits importés, ce qui implique fermeture d'usines et montée du chômage. Les femmes de la coopérative Eco Laime, près de Cochabamba, tricotent des pulls pour survivre. A 20US$ pièce, ces pulls sont trop chers pour les Boliviens; ils sont exportés. La dette Bolivienne a été contractée dans les années 70 et 80 quand le gouvernement prit en charge le passif des hommes d'affaires (copains d'anciens dictateurs) qui n'avaient pas remboursé leurs emprunts aux banques internationales. Plus de 4.8US$ millions auraient été détournés sur des comptes bancaires personnels.

Bolivia ANNUAL PER CAPITA INCOME: US$620 To comply with International Monetary Fund rules for debtor nations, Bolivia has devalued its currency and suspended import duties, producing massive inflation. It also increased its dependence on imported goods, causing factories to close and unemployment to skyrocket. "If we didn't do this, we'd have nothing to eat," explains one. But even at US$20, the sweaters are too expensive for most Bolivians and must be exported. Bolivia's debt was incurred in the 1970s and '80s. When private businessmen (cronies of former dictators) defaulted on loans from international banks, the Bolivian government assumed the debt. Allegedly, much of the US$4.8 billion wound up in the borrowers' private bank accounts.

Pays-Bas REVENU ANNUEL PAR HABITANT: 15,920US$ Le Max Havelaar Foundation supervise la vente d'environ 6 tonnes de café venant de Haïti, Nicaragua, d'Ouganda, Zaïre ou ailleurs, du moment que soient respectés certains principes: les fermes productrices doivent être de petites unités, gérées en famille, démocratiques; elles doivent être écologiquement correctes, et ne pas avoir la moindre politique de discrimination. En diffusant ce café produit par ces fermes pilotes "dans tous les supermarchés, toutes les épiceries et à tous les coins de rue", la fondation veut promouvoir égalité économique et conscience environnementaliste.

The Netherlands ANNUAL PER CAPITA INCOME: US$15,920 The Max Havelaar Foundation markets 11.7 million pounds of coffee from 300,000 growers in Haiti, Nicaragua, Uganda, Zaire and elsewhere who follow certain progressive guidelines: farms must be small, family run, democratically controlled, ecologically sound and utterly nondiscriminatory. The foundation promotes economic fairness and environmentally sound practices by selling the coffee from model farms at "every supermarket, every grocery store and every street corner."

Sierra Léone REVENU ANNUEL PAR HABITANT: 220US$ Avec une espérance de vie qui est la plus basse du monde (42 ans), le Sierra Léone regorge pourtant d'or, de diamants et de bois. Malheureusement, les terres les plus riches sont aux mains du Libérien Charles Taylor. Devenu multimilliardaire en vendant les richesses du Libéria—caoutchouc, fer, bois—à des Européens rapaces, il a envahi son voisin; le demi-million de Sierra-Léonais, enfermés à l'intérieur des lignes rebelles, subsistent de racines et de choux palmistes.

Sierra Leone ANNUAL PER CAPITA INCOME: US$220 Although it has the world's lowest rate of life expectancy (age 42), Sierra Leone is rich in resources such as gold, diamonds and timber. Unfortunately much of the best land is now controlled by Liberian Charles Taylor and his rebel army. Taylor has become a multimillionaire by selling off Liberia's resources—rubber, iron, timber—to eager European buyers. Now he's invaded Liberia's neighbor, and the half million Sierra Leoneans trapped behind rebel lines are subsisting on roots and palm cabbage.

Botswana REVENU ANNUEL PAR HABITANT: 1600US$ Le Rural Industries Innovation Centre à Kanye, près de Gaborone, capitale du Botswana, fabrique des instruments qui permettent aux ruraux d'avoir un métier. Il évalue, à travers des enquêtes, les besoins de la nation afin de mettre au point des technologies adéquates, ainsi une pompe actionnée par un moulin à vent, qui fournit l'eau pour le bétail et les cultures, ou bien encore un four de boulanger, fait à partir de jantes de roues de camions, soudées ensemble. Sponsorisé par le gouvernement et par des organisations privées, le centre a pour but de résoudre localement des problèmes technologiques.

Botswana ANNUAL PER CAPITA INCOME: US$1,600 Rural Industries Innovation Centre in Kanye, near Botswana's capital of Gaborone, develops tools that rural people can use to earn a living. The center conducts periodic surveys of the nation's needs and develops appropriate technology, such as a windmill-driven pump that provides water for livestock and crops or a bakery oven made from two truck-wheel rims welded together. Funded by the government and private donors, the center is dedicated to devising local solutions to technological problems.

Les plus pauvres des 20% de la population mondiale se partagent 1.4% de l'argent du monde.

□ = 5,321,000 PEOPLE
□ = 5,321,000 PERSONNES

RUSSIA
CHINA
SOUTH KOREA
JAPAN
IRAN
PAKISTAN
INDIA
BANGLADESH
VIETNAM
THAILAND
BORNEO

voici où vivent les gens

Dans ce numéro de COLORS, on a souligné les différences physiques entre les peuples. Mais soyons honnêtes, le racisme n'a rien à voir avec la peau, les cheveux ou les yeux, qui sont des cibles trop faciles. Le racisme, c'est une histoire d'argent et de pouvoir.

Chine REVENU ANNUEL PAR HABITANT: 350US$ Le plus important grand magasin d'Asie va bientôt être construit à Shangaï, par Yaohan, du Japon. Des sociétés comme Procter & Gamble ou Benetton parient sur l'ouverture de la Chine à l'économie de marché. Les fabricants de voiture rêvent du jour où les cyclistes Chinois voudront tous acheter des voitures. En 1950, il y avait 53 millions de voitures dans le monde. En 1989, 555 millions. Il y en aura 830 millions sur la planète, si le milliard 200 000 de Chinois se mettent à en acheter à la cadence des Japonais.

China ANNUAL PER CAPITA INCOME: US$350 Soon Shanghai will boast the largest department store in Asia, built by Yaohan of Japan. Corporations from Procter & Gamble to Benetton are cashing in on China's new openness to capitalism. Auto manufacturers dream of the day when the bicycle-riding Chinese will all buy cars. In 1950 there were 53 million private vehicles in the world. In 1989 there were 555 million. If the 1.2 billion Chinese owned automobiles at a rate comparable to the Japanese, there would be 830 million cars on the world's highways.

Philippines REVENU ANNUEL PAR HABITANT: 710 US$ Sous la dictature de Ferdinand Marcos, les Philippines ont construit ce qui est peut-être l'usine nucléaire la plus coûteuse du monde; plus de 2 billions US$. Elle devait être finie en 1985; elle fut mise au rencart en 1986. Dans les coûts de l'opération, on inclut 80 millionsUS$, que Westinghouse, le principal fournisseur, a prêtés à Marcos et son copain de golf Herminio Disini. Les Philippines paient aujourd'hui des intérêts de 250.000US$ par jour à cause de ce projet. Plus de 36 pour cent du budget annuel va dans le remboursement des dettes, alors que seulement 11 pour cent va à l'éducation, la culture et le sport, 3.5 pour cent à la santé.

Philippines ANNUAL PER CAPITA INCOME: US$710 Under dictator Ferdinand Marcos, the Philippines built what may be the world's most expensive nuclear power plant. Costing more than US$2 billion, the plant was supposedly completed in 1985 and mothballed in 1986. The cost allegedly includes about US$80 million that the plant's main supplier, Westinghouse, handed to Marcos and his golfing buddy Herminio Disini. The Philippines now pays more than US$250,000 a day in interest on this project. More than 36 percent of the nation's annual budget goes to paying off debts while education, culture and sports get a total 11 percent and health gets 3.5 percent.

Australie REVENU ANNUEL PAR HABITANT: US$ 14.360 US$ Les Aborigènes d'Australie n'ont jamais abandonné leurs droits sur leurs propres terres aux colonisateurs Européens, qui commencèrent à débarquer au 18ème siècle. Pas plus qu'ils ne renoncèrent à leur droit à l'auto-détermination. On leur a tout pris par la force. Les adhérents de l'association non-Aborigène Pay the rent ("Payez le loyer") donnent un pour cent de leurs revenus à une société fiduciaire, utilisée par les Kooris de Victoria, libres de tout engagement. Jusqu'à présent, Pay the Rent a recueilli 14.000US$. Une partie sert dans la lutte pour la reconnaissance des droits des Aborigènes sur leurs terres.

Australia ANNUAL PER CAPITA INCOME: US$14,360 Australia's Aboriginal people never gave up their land rights to the European settlers who began arriving in the 18th century. Nor did they willingly give up their right to self-government. Both were taken by force. Members of Pay the Rent, an organization of non-Aboriginal Australians, pledge about one percent of their gross income to a trust fund that is used by the Kooris of Victoria, no strings attached. To date Pay the Rent has raised almost US$14,000, some of which has been used to further awareness of Aboriginal land rights.

Estonie REVENU ANNUEL PAR HABITANT: US$3.800 Les ethnies Russes, qui se sentent rejetées d'Estonie, sont attirées par l'Afrique du Sud, où la minorité blanche cherche toujours à attirer les immigrants Caucasiens. L'avantage financier est évident. En Afrique du Sud, les Blancs se font en moyenne 21.700US$ par an, comparés à 3.800 US$ gagnés en Estonie (un peu plus que les 3.650US$ gagnés par les Noirs en Afrique du Sud).

Estonia ANNUAL PER CAPITA INCOME: US$3,800 Ethnic Russians who no longer feel welcome in Estonia are being lured to South Africa, where the white minority is always trying to attract Caucasian immigrants. The financial advantage is obvious. Whites in South Africa make an average US$21,700 per year compared to US$3,800 annually in Estonia (which is still a little better than the US$3,650 black South Africans make).

Grameen Bank BANGLADESH ANNUAL PER CAPITA INCOME: US$180 In many countries, a very small loan can mean the difference between a life of desperation and one of relative stability. Founded in 1983, Bangladesh's Grameen [Village] Bank hands out loans (typically of US$50), mostly to women because "women see the worst kind of poverty." The loans help people buy basic tools, such as rice hullers and looms. By 1990 the bank had granted US$278 million in small loans; 98 percent have been repaid in full. Grameen now has bicycle bankers who go out looking for landless peasants in need of capital. Banks based on the same principle have started in other parts of Asia, in Africa and even in the USA, where people in poor areas are routinely denied credit.

Grameen Bank REVENU ANNUEL PAR HABITANT: US$180 Dans certains pays, un petit prêt d'argent démarque une vie de relative aisance d'une vie de misère. Fondée en 1983, la Banque Grameen (Bangladesh) prête plutôt (en général 50US$) aux femmes "parce qu'elles endurent la pire des pauvretés". Avec ces crédits, les gens achètent des outils de base, décortiqueuse à riz et métier à tisser. En 1990, la banque a prêté un total de 278 millionsUS$; 98 pour cent ont été remboursés. La banque envoie ses employés en vélos prospecter les paysans sans terre ayant besoin d'un petit capital. Des banques s'inspirant du même principe apparaissent ailleurs en Asie, en Afrique et même aux Etats-Unis, où les gens de certaines régions pauvres se voient régulièrement refuser des crédits.

COLORS 53

A TRILLION DOLLARS!

How much is a trillion? How many?

A trillion is such a staggering amount that it's impossible to comprehend.

Let's put it this way:

If you counted to a trillion out loud, one number per second, it would take you 31,688 years.

And a trillion dollars is . . . a Lot of Money.

Given inflation, currency devaluations and the on-going development of bigger, deadlier, and therefore more expensive weaponry, the international military-industrial complex may soon be getting—and spending—a quadrillion ($1,000,000,000,000,000) or even a quintillion ($1,000,000,000,000,000,000).

Of course, not all the money spent on "defense" is wasted. Nearly 50 million people have been successfully killed in wars since 1945. But in the financially shaky USSR, approximately 20 percent of the gross national product is consumed by nonproductive military spending. In the financially shaky USA, the Pentagon buys spare toilet seats for C-5B cargo planes at $1,868.15 a pop. Financially secure Switzerland still pays $500 a year to every farmer to store mules and horses in case of a military emergency.

Five hundred here, a billion there, and pretty soon you're talking real money.

**military
budgets
by country
in US dollars
国別の軍事費
（ドル）**

— USA
286.8 billion
— USSR
117.48 billion
— Germany
33.7 billion
— UK
33.4 billion
— France
33.03 billion
— Japan
28.12 billion
— Italy
18.98 billion
— Saudi Arabia
13.84 billion
— Iraq
13.3 billion
— South Korea
10.89 billion
— Canada
10.19 billion
— India
9.25 billion
— Iran
8.77 billion
— Taiwan
8.55 billion
— Spain
7.96 billion
— the Netherlands
7.47 billion
— Australia
6.38 billion
— Egypt
6.38 billion
— Israel
6.32 billion
— China
6.13 billion
— Sweden
5.51 billion
— South Africa
3.92 billion
— Greece
3.79 billion
— Switzerland
3.78 billion
— Turkey
3.28 billion
— Czechoslovakia
3.22 billion
— Pakistan
2.89 billion
— Syria
2.49 billion
— Thailand
2.04 billion
— Cuba
1.83 billion

1 兆ドル！

1兆ドルってどれくらい？。ゼロ何個？。

1兆なんて数字　実感がわかないよ。

こうゆうのはどうかな。

1秒に数字を一つ言うとして、1から1兆まで数えると、31,688年かかる。

1兆ドルね・・・・すごい金額だよな。

インフレだの、貨幣価値の目減りだの上に、もっと効果的な兵器を開発するとなると、当然もっとお金がかかるけど、世界の軍事産業にかかる金額ってすぐに千兆ドル（$1,000,000,000,000,000）とか百京ドル（1,000,000,000,000,000,000）とかになるんじゃない。

もちろん〝防衛費〟の全部がムダに使われるわけじゃない。1945年以来、5千万の人が戦争で死んで財政的にガタガタのソ連じゃGNPのだいたい20パーセントが非生産的な軍事費として出てるし、同様のガタピシのアメリカでも、国防省がC-5B形輸送機のトイレシートに国民一人当り、1,868,15ドルをかけている。財政が安定しているスイスは万一の軍事的非常事態にそなえてロバや馬の確保に年間500ドルを農民全員に払っているんだからね。

ここで500あそこで一千万ていうと実感わくでしょ。

this year,
the combined nations
of the world will spend about
a trillion dollars
on their military needs.

$1,0000000,0

今年、世界で大体1兆ドルの

お金が軍事費として

使われるそうだよ。

US $1,000,000,000 = 1,799,400,000,000 Soviet rubles, 1,602,200,000,000 German marks, 546,150,000,000 British pounds, 5,459,800,000,000 French francs, 137,200,000,000,000 Japanese yen, 1,119,500,000,000,000 Italian lire, 3,745,000

But wait a minute...

Imagine one glorious Polynesian afternoon Taufa'ahau Tupou IV, the king of Tonga, is riding his bicycle. A goat wanders across his path, causing His Majesty to fall and hit his head. When he awakens, he's seeing things a little differently. When he looks at Tonga's military budget—$1.5 million, which wouldn't buy him much of a war, really—he decides he'd rather do something nice with it instead. He scraps his army and, with the money he saves, buys rare, collectible Tongan postage stamps (shaped like bananas and coconuts) and sends them to each of the 800,000 residents of neighboring Fiji.

The Fijians are so touched by this gesture that they decide on the spot to spend their entire military budget ($19.7 million) hosting a fish fry for the 17.1 million people of Australia.

Deeply moved, the Aussies promptly commit the $6.4 billion they were about to waste on soldiers and military hardware to purchasing the Falkland Islands from Mother England as a gift to Argentina.

正しいことをする
のに遅すぎるとい
うことはない。

イギリスの諺

でもちょと待ってね

こうしよう。ある天気のいいポリネシアの午後のこと、トンガの王様、タウファアハウ・トゥッポー4世は山羊をよけようとして、乗ってた自転車から落ちて頭を打ってしまう。目覚めた時、王様はやまてはちょっと違った目で見るようになっていた。

トンガの軍事費に（1500万ドル位だから、実際大したことには使えないけれど）目を通した時、王様はそのお金をもっといいことに使おうと決める。それで軍隊を解散して、不要になったお金で、珍しいコレクターが喜ぶ貴重なトンガの切手（バナナやココナッツの形の）を買って各国のフィジーの80万人一人一人に送ることにした。

とても感動した。フィジー人はその場で彼らの軍事費（1970万ドル）を1710万人のオーストラリア人のために魚のフ

Overwhelmed, the Argentinians allocate their $1.1 billion to providing each and every one of the United Kingdom's 57.4 million citizens with an individual tango lesson.

Dizzy with unaccustomed excitement, the British resolve to reward their former colony India for having long provided their only source of flavorful food. The U.K.'s entire $33.4 billion defense budget goes to purchase 32 bottles of Evian a day for each of the 1,576,800 Indian children who would otherwise die this year from drinking impure water.

Grateful India's $9.3 billion can now be better spent shifting a fraction of its colossal movie industry to Pakistan, to establish Sacred Cow Studios. SCS employs thousands and produces a series of hit romantic-comedies ridiculing religious bigotry, the oppression of women and political corruption.

Gleeful, Pakistan's $2.9 billion can be used to pay for a year's worth of monthly fortune-teller consultations so desperately needed by every one of their 16 million Afghani neighbors.

Delighted, Afghanistan decides it can get a bigger bang for its 286.6-million military buck by supplying each of the 10 million Soviet women between the ages of 18 and 22 with a tube of Chanel's "Regal Red" lipstick and a bottle of "Satin Red" nail polish.

Inspired, the leaders of the USSR (where women now have an average of 5.5 abortions) to commit their annual $117.5 billion to research and develop a truly effective and safe contraceptive. Soviet science comes through.

Everyone on Earth is greatly relieved.

Feeling more than usually festive, the Dutch dedicate their $7.5 billion to spreading the gospel of bicycling. They buy 19.5 million 18-speed mountain bikes and safety helmets—one for each inhabitant of Mexico City, where lead from auto exhaust is found in the blood of many children at levels high enough to cause brain damage.

Caught up in the universal spirit of things, the government of the USA reallocates the $700 a minute it spent on military aid to El Salvador in the 1980s, and instead sends a pineapple pizza to each of the 5.3 million Salvadorans. Mexico City residents use their spanking-new bikes to form a 2,300-mile pizza delivery brigade from San Diego to San Salvador.

Sated, El Salvador can now better dispose of its $224 million. It dispatches its (unemployed) death squads to Spain to plant flowers, recobble the streets and deal decisively with the street mimes of Madrid.

Pleased, Spain can devote a portion of its $8 billion to donating hundreds of millions of (full) wineskins to Washington, D.C., and a small herd of Pamplonan bulls to New York City.

The sight of those bulls charging down Wall Street gives such a boost to the morale of the stockbrokers that the market skyrockets. The shock renders the US government temporarily sane, and it decides to spend its money promoting the health and welfare of the people. Newly enlightened (maybe it was the Spanish wine), Congress votes to reallocate the $286.8 billion defense budget to a variety of good works:

$100 billion to AIDS research (50 times the current allotment).

$35.1 billion toward the purchase of 64.8 billion Trojan condoms. (A dozen for every man, woman and child on earth. The kids can use them for balloons.)

$5.4 billion to distribute to each of them the helpful pamphlet "How to Use a Condom."

$27.2 billion to enroll each vitamin C-deprived Eastern European in Harry and David's Fruit of the Month Club (January: crisp mountain apples. February: juicy oranges, etc.).

$285 million (formerly the price of a B-1 bomber) will provide basic immunization against measles, chicken pox and diphtheria for the 575 million children in the world who need it. Two-and-a-half million lives are saved in a year.

$82.9 billion buys a pair of Levi's 501 blue jeans (button fly, shrink to fit, $15.35 wholesale) for every single person on earth.

$35.6 billion goes to UNICEF, which it uses to promote and distribute Oral Rehydration Therapy—a simple mixture of salt and sugar dissolved in water—which prevents 90 percent of deaths from diarrhea, in developing countries the number-one killer of children under age five.

With the money left over, the USA bankrolls a 12-month gig for Jerry Lewis in Paris's Roland Garros Stadium. Jerry gets a million a show—and after a year, even the French get over him.

Brazil pays its bills.

Proud France can never totally disarm. But she does devote a modest portion of her $33 billion military budget to establish charming

Parisian pieds-à-terre for the million Kurdish refugees who have fled Iraq.

Sentimental Iraq waxes nostalgic for the Kurds, and comes to realize the value of ethnic diversity. Its $13.3 billion military budget goes to a campaign to preserve the endangered indigenous cultures of the world, such as the 13 million Central American native peoples of Mexico, Nicaragua, Panama and Costa Rica.

Tiny Ireland borrows against the next 47 years of defense expenditures it will no longer need to make, and buys the house a round. A pint of Guinness for everyone on the planet.

The Germans, who are fond of stout, decide to use their entire $33.7 billion to send 280,833,333 top-of-the-line Braun juicers to Israel. That's 64 juicers per Israeli.

Astonished, Israel does the right thing. The Knesset dedicates its entire $6.3 billion arms budget to hire Palestinians to squeeze fresh orange juice for the Egyptians, the Jordanians, the Syrians, the Lebanese, the Iranians, the Saudis and even...the Iraqis.

The Palestinian people can now afford some real estate, and donate their entire (unknown) defense budget to the purchase of soothing hot towels and slippers for the 3 million travelers who fly international routes on any given day.

Everyone gets a good night's sleep.

—ELISSA SCHAPPELL AND ROBERT SPILLMAN

00,000 (and how to spend it
問題はこれだけの金額
をどう使うかだ。)

Austria	1.61 billion
Kuwait	1.54 billion
Nicaragua	1.42 billion
Brazil	1.41 billion
Portugal	1.25 billion
Argentina	1.1 billion
Philippines	1.05 billion
Sudan	956 million
Mexico	709 million
Poland	700.73 million
Chile	559 million
Ethiopia	471.59 million
Ireland	458.4 million
Jordan	383.22 million
Colombia	374.13 million
Zimbabwe	363 million
Bangladesh	348 million
Burma	334 million
Afghanistan	286.56 million
Nigeria	277 million
Peru	245 million
El Salvador	224 million
Albania	171.2 million
Lebanon	154 million
Mozambique	113 million
Senegal	106 million
Luxembourg	90.44 million
Bolivia	86.8 million
Paraguay	61 million
Zaire	46.56 million
Ghana	42.56 million
Rwanda	36.63 million
Togo	30.01 million
Jamaica	25.06 million
Fiji	19.73 million
C.A.R.	18.67 million
Niger	17.37 million
Belize	9.94 million
Iceland	0
Vietnam	?

ライのピクニックを催すことにした。

これに深く 感動したオーストラリア人はすべての兵隊で軍事兵器を購入、対フォークランド島をイギリスから買って、アルゼンチンに贈ることに決めた

そりゃもう 今度はアルゼンチン人は感激し、11億ドルでイギリス国民5740万のタンゴの無料個人レッスンを受けられるようにした

エキサイト することに慣れてないイギリス人にこれはクラッときて、昔の宗主国インドに援助せずにいたが...に報いようと思ったのだ イギリスの国民負担334億ドルはこの年、汚い水を飲んで死ぬと156万7600人の子供一人一人に毎日32本のエヴィアンとなった

この好意に 感謝してインド人は93億ドルにのぼる巨大な映画産業の一部をパキスタンに移して、「聖なる牛スタジオ」(SCS)を作るのに使おうと思う SCSは何万人という人を雇い、家族問題、女性差別、政治腐敗などをからかうミュージカル・コメディのヒット・シリーズを制作することになる

そして、 今度はパキスタンが29億ドルを隣の1600万下のアフガニスタン人が必要としている毎日の運勢占いの一年分の謝礼として贈ることにした

喜んだ アフガニスタンは、2億8660万ドルを軍事費に使うよりもよっぽど効果があるというので、シャネルの「リーガル・レッド」リップスティックと「サテン・レッド」マニキュアを18才から22才の女性1千万人に使い

これに 到達されたの少の指導者は「ソ連各地では現在平均で5回の中絶を経験があるという、年間1175億ドルを...

本当に効果的な安全な避妊法を研究にあてる そしてソ連の科学は晴れてそれに成功するのだ

これで 全て丸めもひと安心よね

普段より もっとお祭り気分になったオランダ人は自転車の普及に邁進する。1950万台の18段変速マウンテン・バイクとヘルメットを購入し排気ガス中の鉛のために血液中の鉛に発見されるというメキシコ・シティの全住民に贈った

この 世界的助け合いの精神に触発されてアメリカ政府は、1980年代には軍事援助費として毎分700ドルの割合でエル・サルバドルに送っていた援助金を、そこのパイナップル・ピザを送り換えた そこでメキシコ・シティの住民は自慢の新しい自転車で、サン・ディエゴからサン・サルバドルまでの2,300マイルのピザの宅配隊を結成した

エル・サルバドルは、これで2億2400万ドルをもっと有効に使えるので、失業した死の部隊はスペインに派遣され花を植えたり、通りを修繕したり、マドリードの大道やパントマイムを...

さて、スペインの番だけど、スペインは80億ドルをワシントンDCの街角である黒ずくめのワイン袋と、そしてニューヨーク市にはパンプロナの牛を一群献上する

この が ウォール街を走るのをみて、ストック・ブローカーの意欲は上向くので市場は急騰、アメリカ政府はナ一時的に頭がおかしくなって、世界の健康福祉を促進にお金を使う決定（多分スペインのワインのせい）に急に頭が明るくなって議会は2868億ドルの国防費をもっといいことに使うことに賛成する

千億ドル エイズ研究に（今の50倍だ）

351億ドル を648億個のトローヤン・コンドーム購入に（全世界の男・女・子供に1ダースずつ 子供は風船に使えばいいね）

54億ドル は「コンドームの使い方」のパンフレットを配るのに使う

272億ドル はビタミンCの足りない東ヨーロッパの人々のための「フルーツ・ザ・マンス・クラブ」マンスリークラブの会員資料料に（1月はシャーという楽しい山のマウンテン・アップル、2月にはジューシーなオレンジ、なんてかんし）

2億8500万ドル（B-1型爆撃 機の値段だった）は世界の575万の子供のにしゃしん感染、しうがいや の予防接種に使う これで年間、250万人の命を救えるんだ

829億ドル は世界中の一人一人にリーバイス501（ボタンフライボタンで体にあわせて縮む、やつ、卸値は$15.35）を配る

356億ドル はユニセフに送られて、秋の塩砂糖まぜ、水に塩と砂糖をとかす簡単なもので、この一つの方法に使う これが発展途上国の下の子供の最大の死因、下痢による90パーセント、を一掃する

残ったお金で、アメリカはパリのローラン・ガロスタジアムの12ヶ月間ジェリー・ルイス公演の資金を出す ジェリーは一回の公演で100万ドル儲けると、1年を越えて、いくらフランス人だって彼から卒業するだろうね

ブラジルは借金を返す

ブライドの 悪いフランス人は完全に武装解除はできないまでも、330億ドルのほんの一部で、イラクから逃れた百万人ものクルド人難民のために粋なパリ風の住いを作るでしょう

そうすると、 イラクはクルド人が懐かしくなってきているような人達がいる国家の価値もわかるようになるかもしれない、330億ドルの軍事費を世界の滅びつつある文化を守るキャンペーンにつかうため、たとえば、メキシコ、ニカラグア、パナマ、コスタ・リカなどの中米源住民1300万人のためなんかに

この先、47年間の国防費はいま要らなくなったので、小国アイルランドはみんなに酒を奢ることにした 地球上の人間全員にギネスのパイント樽、なんてシャレているこ一わい

スタウト・ビール が好きなドイツ人は、337億ドル全部でイスラエルにブラウン社製の最高級ジューサー280,833,333台贈る 一人のイスラエル人に64台のジューサー

これには イスラエル人もびっくりして正しいことを始めのだろう イスラエル国会ネセトは63億円の兵員弾薬予算で、エジプト人、ジョルダン人、シリア人、レバノン人、イラン人、サウジアラビア人、そしてイラク人のためにもフレッシュ・オレンジ・ジュースを絞るのにパレスチナ人を雇うことにした

パレスチナ人 はこれでいくら不動産を買う余裕が出来て、ワイらいくらの知らないけれど、毎日国際線の飛行機を利用する300万の旅行者に気持ちのいいホット・オシボリとスリッパを提供するに使うことにする

これでみんなゆっくり眠れる

Saudi Arabian riyals, 310,860,000,000 Iraqi dinars, 725,080,000,000,000 South Korean won. Note: One US trillion (1,000,000,000,000) = one UK billion.

7

(hunger) is a relative term. What you eat usually depends on the colo

(hambre) es una palabra relativa. Lo que comes normalmente depende

japan

Average per capita daily consumption: **2918 calories**

22.1 kg
raw sugar
azúcar en bruto

7.7 kg	**7.2 kg**	**43.7 kg**	**5.2 kg**	**45.8 kg**	**69.3 kg**
tomatoes	beef	wheat products	bananas	dairy products	alcoholic beverages
tomates	carne de vaca	productos de trigo	bananas	productos lácteos	bebidas alcohólicas

england

Average per capita daily consumption: **3268 calories**

16.9 kg	**19.0 kg**	**83.5 kg**	**7.1 kg**	**130.2 kg**	**41.1 kg**
tomatoes	beef	wheat products	bananas	dairy products	raw sugar
tomates	carne de vaca	productos de trigo	bananas	productos lácteos	azúcar en bruto

nigeria

Average per capita daily consumption: **1989 calories**

5.2 kg	**2.1 kg**	**2.3 kg**	**14.3 kg**	**1.8 kg**	**3.6 kg**
tomatoes	beef	wheat products	bananas	dairy products	raw sugar
tomates	carne de vaca	productos de trigo	bananas	productos lácteos	azúcar en bruto

"Cabbages should speak." Nigel Yeoman M 36 greengrocer Murrayshire, England

of your skin.

el color de tu piel.

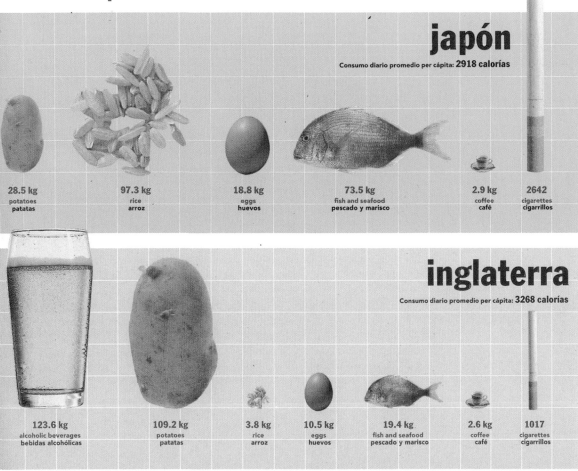

japón

Consumo diario promedio per cápita: **2918 calorías**

28.5 kg	97.3 kg	18.8 kg	73.5 kg	2.9 kg	2642
potatoes	rice	eggs	fish and seafood	coffee	cigarettes
patatas	arroz	huevos	pescado y marisco	café	cigarrillos

inglaterra

Consumo diario promedio per cápita: **3268 calorías**

123.6 kg	109.2 kg	3.8 kg	10.5 kg	19.4 kg	2.6 kg	1017
alcoholic beverages	potatoes	rice	eggs	fish and seafood	coffee	cigarettes
bebidas alcohólicas	patatas	arroz	huevos	pescado y marisco	café	cigarrillos

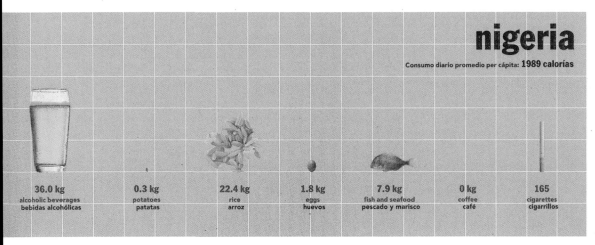

nigeria

Consumo diario promedio per cápita: **1989 calorías**

36.0 kg	0.3 kg	22.4 kg	1.8 kg	7.9 kg	0 kg	165
alcoholic beverages	potatoes	rice	eggs	fish and seafood	coffee	cigarettes
bebidas alcohólicas	patatas	arroz	huevos	pescado y marisco	café	cigarrillos

"'Las coles deberían hablar." Nigel Yeoman V 36 verdulero Murrayshire, Inglaterra

(energy)
(energía)

United States
Estados Unidos

Haiti
Haití

Dominican Republic
República Dominicana

En este mapa, el tamaño de cada país es proporcional al consumo total de energía.
On this map, the size of each country is in proportion to its total consumption of commercial energy.

= 102,854 million tonnes of coal equivalent
= equivalente a 102.854 millones de toneladas de carbón
= 10,285
= 1,029

¿Cuanto está aumentando o disminuyendo el consumo de energía? Estos colores indican el cambio en porcentajes de 1980 a 1990.

< -25%	-25% - 0	0 - +25%	+25% - +50%	+50% - +100%	> +100%

How much is the use of energy increasing or decreasing? These colors indicate the percent change from 1980-1990.

The world would be different if the countries got bigger when they used more energy. Developing countries would fight just to stay on the map, dwarfed by those with the most power. Above, the countries are re-sized according to each state's total energy use. No surprises here; the large industrialized nations have all the power. The colors show the rate of increase (red) or decrease (green) of each nation's energy use. Developing nations show the highest rates, but the total use for most of these countries is so low that they barely show on the map.

Country	Per capita use of commercial energy (kg of coal equivalent)	% increase in energy consumption 1980-1990
WORLD	1932	+19.7
AFRICA	428	+44
Algeria	1482	+49.3
Angola	90	-13.8
Benin	48	+25.1
Burundi	20	+84.7

Cameroon	244	+55.1
Cape Verde	108	-28.6
Central African Republic	35	+75
Chad	18	+3
Congo	372	+512.3
Côte d'Ivoire	189	+19.7
Egypt	736	+84.3
Equatorial Guinea	153	+100
Ethiopia	26	+60
Gabon	715	+2.6
Ghana	101	-8.7
Guinea	85	+6.5
Kenya	111	+17
Liberia	93	-74.5
Libya	4721	+193.8
Madagascar	40	-36
Malawi	35	-12.9
Mali	24	+13.5
Mauritania	578	+300.3
Mauritius	494	+84.5
Morocco	368	+41.5
Mozambique	31	-73.3
Niger	59	+71.3
Nigeria	188	+70.6
Reunion	838	+35.8
St. Helene	143	0

Senegal	141	-15.1
Seychelles	1145	+75.6
Sierra Leone	74	+18
Somalia	52	+103.7
Sudan	64	+6.6
Togo	62	+19.1
Tunisia	831	+61.9
Uganda	24	+29.5
United Rep. of Tanzania	36	+14
Western Sahara	522	+20.8
Zaire	66	+19.8
Zambia	201	-25.2
Zimbabwe	650	+39
NORTH AMERICA	6936	+6.2
Aruba	3917	+36.6
Bahamas	2490	-45.5
Barbados	1659	+34.7
Belize	652	+34.1
Bermuda	4828	+37.9
British Virgin Islands	1769	+91.7
Canada	10255	+8.2
Cayman Islands	4760	+52.6
Costa Rica	587	+37.4
Cuba	1445	+12.2
Dominica	366	+57.9

Dominican Republic	366	-6
El Salvador	247	+35.6
Greenland	4661	-0.8
Grenada	682	+141.7
Guadeloupe	1431	+93.3
Guatemala	188	-12.4
Haiti	51	+3.1
Honduras	170	-3.1
Jamaica	831	-47.5
Martinique	1768	+83.8
Mexico	1753	+32.6
Montserrat	1333	+126.5
Nicaragua	260	+2.8
Panama	612	-9.3
Puerto Rico	3006	+5.1
Trinidad and Tobago	6856	+17.6
United States	9958	+5
U.S. Virgin Islands	11707	-67.4
SOUTH AMERICA	1003	+20.4
Argentina	1825	+20.1
Bolivia	355	+13.2
Brazil	766	+24.6
Chile	1249	+44.5
Colombia	771	+25.6
Ecuador	726	+35.3

"We should be able to kill insects just by looking at them." Shaq Mohammed M 8 street child Bombay, India